Was Hinduism Invented?

Was Hinduism Invented?

Britons, Indians, and the Colonial Construction of Religion

BRIAN K. PENNINGTON

MISSIONARY INFLUENCE OR HOW TO MAKE CONVERTS.

UNIVERSITY PRESS

2005

OXFORD
UNIVERSITY PRESS

Oxford University Press, Inc., publishes works that further
Oxford University's objective of excellence
in research, scholarship, and education.

Oxford   New York
Auckland   Cape Town   Dar es Salaam   Hong Kong   Karachi
Kuala Lumpur   Madrid   Melbourne   Mexico City   Nairobi
New Delhi   Shanghai   Taipei   Toronto

With offices in
Argentina   Austria   Brazil   Chile   Czech Republic   France   Greece
Guatemala   Hungary   Italy   Japan   Poland   Portugal   Singapore
South Korea   Switzerland   Thailand   Turkey   Ukraine   Vietnam

Published by Oxford University Press, Inc.
198 Madison Avenue, New York, New York 10016

www.oup.com

Oxford is a registered trademark of Oxford University Press

Library of Congress Cataloging-in-Publication Data
Pennington, Brian.
    Was Hinduism invented? : Britons, Indians, and the colonial construction of religion /
Brian K. Pennington.
        p.   cm
    Includes bibliographical references.
    ISBN-13 978-0-19-516655-2
    ISBN 0-19-516655-8
    1. Hinduism—India.   2. India—Social life and customs.   3. India—Religious life
and customs.   4. India—Colonial influence.   I. Title.
    BL 1201.P4   2005
    294.5'09'034—dc22   2004054715

Frontispiece: "Missionary Influence or How to Make Converts" (1815). Pitts Theology Library,
Emory University, Atlanta, GA. RG 020 1/2

9 8 7 6 5 4 3

Printed in the United States of America
on acid-free paper

Acknowledgments

Over the years it took to write this book, many people and organizations have provided me direct and material support. I will surely neglect to mention some, but there are still many I wish to thank. An earlier avatār of this work appeared as my doctoral dissertation. The Dean's Office of the Graduate School of Arts and Sciences and the Graduate Division of Religion at Emory University provided research support at the time. Margot Finn read the early drafts with great care and interest. The Center for Research Libraries generously loaned me most of the volumes of the *Asiatick Researches* for an extended period of time. Gillian Evison of the Indian Institute in Oxford helped me locate source materials. Jim Benson of Oxford helped me evaluate the Sanskrit of various missionary translations. As co-director of the dissertation, David Pacini spent many hours on the final draft and, in many intimate conversations, pushed both the concept of the project and its stylistic expression toward greater clarity. Sunanda Sanyal coached me through archaic Bengali passages and was a marvelous conversation partner. Hena Basu helped me locate many important documents and resources in Calcutta.

At various times, Laurie Patton, David Haberman, Bill Meyer, and Joyce Flueckiger have commented on parts of the manuscript. Saurabh Dube read an early draft of the entire manuscript and offered many valuable suggestions. Two anonymous reviewers for Oxford University Press raised some important concerns and focused my thinking in the later stages of writing. Dan Klingensmith has been a willing local conversation partner on all things colonial Indian. I also wish to acknowledge some of the groups to whom I have presented versions of the essays that follow: the Southeastern Commission for the Study of Religion (March 1996); the Conference on South Asia (Madison, Wisconsin, October 1998); the Religion in South Asia section of the American Academy of Religion (San Francisco, November 1997); the Hinduism Group of the American Academy of Religion (Boston, November 1999); a graduate seminar on Religious Transformations in Colonial India at Emory University (October 2001); and the Graduate Division of Religion of Emory University (February 2003).

I am grateful to the Maryville College Faculty Development Committee and its chair, Susan Schneibel, for covering research and manuscript preparation costs. The Ruth Lloyd Kramer Fund provided generous travel support. At a critical stage, Peggy Cowan gave me a quiet cabin to work in. Preston Fields did some careful manuscript editing.

A special word of thanks is due Paul Courtright, at one time my advisor and dissertation director, but always my mentor and friend. I am grateful for the early interest he took in my personal and intellectual well-being, and he remains for me a model of passionate and honest inquiry, warm collegiality, and principled scholarship.

My sons Isaiah and Immanuel have been a steady source of joy and laughter and sure reminders of the truly important things. Isaiah was but a few days old when I began writing and we spent many days of his infancy together on this project: he quietly napping beside me while I wrote. As a newborn himself, Immanuel's birth happily interrupted final manuscript preparations and his cries and ejaculations punctuated my dissertation defense. In all stages of this work, Cindy contributed in so many ways.

A final piece of gratitude goes to the many friends who have fed and housed me, walked with me, and laughed at my arcane obsessions in these years. The couches and dining room tables where writing and conversation took place are as much a part of this book as the miles traveled and dusty shelves perused.

Contents

A Note on Transliteration and Archaisms

Where they have not passed over into common English usage, Indian words have been transliterated according to standard conventions. In the case of some Bengali words, a few minor modifications have been made to reflect actual Bengali pronunciation. The names of most persons are given in unmarked roman characters, but for figures and organizations not well known, the first mention is marked with the proper diacritics.

This work utilizes a number of sources in which spelling, punctuation, and other stylistic matters do not correspond to contemporary conventional American English usage. In most cases, except where the meaning would be obscured or exact reproduction would be highly distracting, the quotations retain original forms to preserve the archaisms and idiosyncracies that might otherwise be lost from the passages.

Was Hinduism Invented?

I

Introduction

The Crystallization of a Concept

Sometime between 1789 and 1832, the British perception of Hindu
religious traditions underwent a seismic shift. Sir William Jones had
complained in 1789 that Hindu mythology confronted the historian
with a virtually impenetrable "cloud of fables," but by 1832 utilitarians and missionaries were rejecting not only Jones's abiding appreciation for the antiquity and beauty of Hindu literature, but also his
sense of the ever-proliferating, unbounded, and ungoverned character of Hindu religious forms. Their many differences notwithstanding, Protestant evangelicals and utilitarians a generation after Jones
were united against the Orientalists he represented in their insistence that, beneath a veil of confusion and contradiction, Hindu
traditions operated with clear, regular, and sinister principles that
demanded disclosure. These attacks inspired Hindus to new efforts
at self-representation. In precolonial periods there had been an ad
hoc character to the manner in which Hindus chose to describe
themselves. When the occasion demanded it, Hindus could portray
themselves as a homogenous people, especially vis-à-vis their Muslim "other," or locate alterity in their own midst. With the development of the modern colonial state, however, the representation of
Hinduism evolved as an act of political and religious significance
previously unprecedented among Indians or those who ruled them.
While the British proposed and debated the unity, character, and
content of Indian religion, Hindus responded with apologetic, correction, and reconstruction of the coherence and nobility of their
traditions. In the shadows and under the auspices of the emerging
colonial state, Hindus and non-Hindus alike etched the contours of

the modern world religion we now routinely call "Hinduism" and its attendant identities.

This book argues that this brief span of years was decisive for the development of modern Hinduism, conceived of as a world religion comparable in scope and character to other major faiths, such as Christianity, Buddhism, and Islam, and imagined today as the defining cultural heritage of the modern nation-state India. The changes I chart are both conceptual and actual. The turn of the nineteenth century witnessed a range of legal, cultural, economic, and social transformations wrought by the encounter between Britons and Indians that had far-reaching implications for not only how each group *thought* about Hindu religious beliefs and practices, but also how (mostly) Indians *practiced* them. Although my approach is thematic rather than chronological, two events bookmark the period of time under consideration. First is the publication of the inaugural volume of the Asiatick Society's *Asiatick Researches* in 1789. Composed by men with close ties to the East India Company and the British government of India, it was the first scholarly publication on South Asia widely available in Britain. Second is the final 1832 decision by the crown in London, in the face of a massive and organized Hindu protest and a forty-year tradition noninterference in the religions of Indians, to uphold Governor-General William Bentinck's abolition of the occasional practice of what the British called *satī*, the immolation of Hindu women on their husbands' funeral pyres. This period of time began with the British public in almost complete ignorance of Indian religious ideas and traditions, but closed with the metropole awash in images, artifacts, and anecdotes brought home from European contact with Hindus. This influx of information sparked a sharp rise in popular interest and brought the weight of British public opinion to bear on the colonial administration. The knowledge the public imbibed was, of course, conditioned—many would say tainted—by the interests and agendas of those assembling and disseminating it. As a result of increasingly lurid coverage of Hinduism, missionaries were introduced into East Indian Company territories in 1813, satī was banned in 1832, and the British management of Hindu temples was withdrawn in 1838.

It would be a severe historical misrepresentation (albeit a faddish one, to be sure) to suggest, as many have, that Hinduism was the invention of the British. Adapting to the colonial milieu, Hindus themselves entered a dialectic space in which they endorsed and promoted the British publication of ancient texts and translations, resisted missionary polemic, and experimented with modifications, alterations, and innovations in Hindu religious forms. "Adapting" perhaps implies more passivity than I intend, for many Hindus possessed considerable power to effect changes in social and religious arrangements under the conditions of the Raj. Colonialism was never a regime of absolute power; indeed, it often found itself ministering to the needs and desires of certain classes of Indians whose support it required. Sumanta Banerjee's *The Parlour and the Streets* is the most significant work to date to examine the ways in which different classes of Indians appropriated, resisted, or took advantage of conditions created under colonialism. Banerjee is most concerned to describe the contrast between elite and plebeian culture under the growth of the Raj. *The Parlour and the Streets* finds a systematic erasure of the folk culture of nineteenth-century Bengal by English and Hindu elite classes and also an atmosphere of vigorous, satirical resistance to those classes in popular religion and folk performance. This folk culture and resistance gradually lost out, Banerjee argues, to Hindu elites of many contrasting political persuasions who nevertheless accepted and normalized more sedate, urbane forms of religious expression. To put it another way, Banerjee's work suggests that the shape of modern Hinduism was the outcome of a contest among Hindus operating in a milieu of severe power differentials and hardly the unique creation of the British either in thought or in act.

One point I am making is familiar enough to historians of the period and theorists of religion: colonial encounter certainly created the circumstances under which Hinduism, in terms of a world religion, comparable to other "great" traditions such as Christianity, Buddhism, and Islam, emerged not only as an idea, a composite portrait of various, sometimes contradictory traditions, but also as an incipient reality. I must stress from the outset, however, that I cannot accept the position that Hinduism was invented in the nineteenth century by Europeans as an administrative or academic convenience that did violence to some vast array of mutually exclusive Indian religious communities and traditions. I critique this argument in chapter 6 in somewhat greater detail, but here it should be noted that I oppose such a position for two reasons. First, the claim that Britain invented Hinduism grants altogether too much power to colonialism; it both mystifies and magnifies colonial means of domination and erases Hindu agency and creativity. Second, the assertion that Hinduism is a concept and reality foreign to India prior to the arrival of the British introduces an almost irreparable disruption in Indian traditions that can only alienate contemporary Indians from their own traditions. I regard the appropriation of the authority to pronounce some version of a tradition an impostor as an illegitimate intervention of academic historiography into the sphere of religion itself, a sphere over which practitioners alone should have custody. Many hundreds of millions of people today identify themselves as Hindu and resonate with the literary and ritual traditions that they associate with the idea of Hinduism. The claim that Hinduism is merely a modern invention is tantamount to a theological statement about the normative constitution of religious identity, hardly the appropriate or customary turf of the historian.

This book holds, then, to the distinction made by Brian K. Smith between the questions it is proper for scholars of religion to address and questions which they must abjure, and it argues, in its closing pages, for an appreciation of that distinction and a greater rapprochement between scholars and practitioners of Hinduism who, after all, have different motives and ends in mind. In a series of articles, Smith has developed the position that the study of religion from within the secular academy may and must make pronouncements about what theologians within a tradition say. This responsibility includes countering false historical claims such as those made today by Hindu nationalists who would purify Indian history of what they deem foreign influences.[1]

But, Smith insists, this act is different from pronouncing what a religious tradition (e.g., Hinduism) *is*, and it is different from declaring what a tradition *should be*. Smith writes that the deconstructionist scholar who denies the correspondence of Hinduism to observed social and historical reality "has in essence . . . declared that he or she knows (normatively) what traditional indigenous authorities do not, [and] that he or she arrogates to him- or herself the exclusive right to speak for Hinduism, albeit negatively." Smith paraphrases the arguments of such deconstructionists in these words: "we know what (the religion formerly known as) Hinduism really is and, contra you Brahmins (and Orientalists, and neo-Hindus, and Hindu nationalists, and anyone else who challenges our authority), it is nothing but a collection of fragmented, disparate, localized, particularistic, and ever-changing mini traditions."[2]

Having pointed out the incongruity and hubris of such claims, Smith, however, seems satisfied to leave the two parties to their separate spheres, blithely talking past one another: historians and social scientists on the one hand, their data on the other. Here I would take one step further. If the canons of religious faith are not those of academic historiography, it is for precisely this reason that, in a global atmosphere electric with religious resentment of secularism, liberalism, modernity, and the West, scholars must operate with transparency and a willingness to engage living human subjects and communities. The idea that scholars and practitioners operate, indeed, should operate, within their neatly partitioned domains, is both naive and dangerous.

I must be emphatic on one point: mine is not a call to tailor history to satisfy practitioners, to couch academic arguments and conclusions in language and categories practitioners might find palatable, or to dilute in any way the analysis of historical and social practices. It is, rather, a plea to recognize that the academic study of religion does not take place in a vacuum. It has, perhaps increasingly so, real effects on the lives of those whom we study and represent, on their sense of identity, and, at the macro level, on relations between global religious communities, cultures, and peoples. Scholars of religion can, by turns, provoke resentment among religious communities, validate cherished histories, or provide fodder for contests internal to a religious traditions. One of this book's major arguments is that Hinduism, as it is now practiced and conceived, is best regarded as the result of continuous historical processes that include but by no means are reducible to interventions by Orientalists, missionaries, and British administrators. I am maintaining, that is, that Hinduism is not simply a historical latecomer smuggled in by Europeans who required her presence. In making the case, this study rests on its own documentary sources, both British and Indian, and on the work of scholars such as Eugene Irschick, David Lorenzen, Hugh Urban, Will Sweetman, and others whom I engage in the book, which together point to the myriad ways that Hindus have historically conceived their own traditions and identities. This work is not, however, an apology for the designs of contemporary Hindu nationalists who are now attempting to rewrite Hindu traditions as the pristine efflorescence of ideas and principles entirely indigenous to the subcontinent and unsullied by foreign interventions or outside influences. It regards, rather, religious traditions as social phenomena always already in flux, subject to exercises of power and resistance to it, reflective of prevailing social, political, and economic conditions, and inclusive of multiple, often antagonistic voices that preserve encounters, conflicts, and subaltern knowledges. In this respect, contemporary Hinduism has no privileged position. It is neither the anomaly among so-called world religions, which alone or in small company emerged fully formed as the tool of foreign interests, nor the unalloyed vessel for the ancient wisdom of Mother India. Religions, all of them, have histories, and histories can be very messy things. On this point—that religions are ordinary and everyday affairs—I am in full agreement with Russell McCutcheon, with whom I later disagree on other matters. Historians do neither history nor practitioners a service by mystifying or denying that the history of any religion is a "history of identities, of their creation and dissolution in a continuous process of reproduction and change."[3] To write the colonial encounter in India, then, is to enter ineluctably into contemporary struggles waged by scholars and Hindus alike to delineate Hindu belief and practice for the postcolonial world, and in no way can it be a purely academic exercise.

Shifting British Attitudes: 1780s–1880s

This book examines a brief but significant moment in the long history of Britain's most immediate and direct connection to India. In order to situate this moment in its fuller context, a sketch of the longer history of this relationship and some indication of the multiple ways in which missionaries and other Britons conceived Indian religions and the ways in which Indians responded seems in order.

Let me begin with the contemporary moment. The single most significant aspect of global Hinduism today may well be the rise of Hindu nationalism and the stunning successes it has experienced in recent years despite the predictions of its many doomsayers. The birth of these political sentiments is often dated to the formation of the Indian National Congress (later, the Congress Party of India) in 1885. The history of Hindu nationalism, a political ideology born of a complex weave of the modern notions of "Hindu" and "nation" reaches back, however, at least a century earlier, surely dating to the first Indian informant's attempt to "spin" a European scholar's representation of Hinduism in favor of some perceived Indian interest. This collaboration marked the first formal meeting of European religious categories (specifically, Christian ones), and nascent Indian national interests. I return to contemporary Hindu nationalism shortly, but here let me note that these twentieth- and twenty-first-century political and religious movements are direct heirs to the history of much earlier interaction between Britons and Indians, and the collective Indian memory of this history continues to sustain religious nationalism in India.

From the chartering of the East India Company in 1600 by Elizabeth I and the establishment of the first British factory at Surat in 1619 until the decisive British victory against the Nawab of Bengal at the Battle of Plassey in 1757, the relationship between Britain and India was largely shaped by the Company's commercial interests. This period witnessed the decline of the Mughal Empire and the competition of various European powers for military and economic footholds in different territories under the Mughals and in the various small kingdoms that dotted the subcontinent. Following the Battle of Plassey, the Company assumed the role of *diwani*, or revenue agent for much of eastern India from the weakening central powers in Delhi, making the British de facto rulers of the region. The next hundred years saw the East India Company emerge full force, through conquest and treaty, as the colonial governors of most of the subcontinent. This period culminated with the bloody Sepoy Mutiny of 1857–58. The brutal manner in which British forces put the rebellion down portended the dawn of the Imperial era proper, with London assuming direct control of Company territories at the close of the rebellion. There now remained little ambiguity in the state of affairs between British rulers and Indian subjects. With the British established as clear overlords through violence and coercion, ruling ideologies that took for granted the superiority of British blood and culture over their Indian counterparts also gained ascendency. Corresponding with the appearance of the modern nation-state in Europe, these attitudes and practices sowed the seeds for assemblage of an organized nationalist movement. Voluntary religious-cum-political associations along with a vernacular press first appeared in the early decades of the nineteenth century, but the establishment of the Indian National Congress in 1885 signaled the shift to a recognizably nationalist ideology. An association of English-educated, elite Indians had begun, quietly at first, to demand a wider role for Indians in the government of their land and peoples.

Wedged between the Battle of Plassey and the appearance of the Indian National Congress was a 130-year period of unprecedented social and economic transformation in which Britain and India publicly imagined several Hinduisms into being. For each party, imagining Hinduism was both a political exercise and an effort to consolidate knowledge about self and other. Prior to the establishment of firm control of extensive territories by colonial powers, travelers and missionaries were the primary sources of information about India for Europeans. Equipped with only a fragmentary knowledge of Indian religion and constrained by European classical and biblical tropes, the traveler's representation of Hindu religious ideas and practices ranged from the fantastic to the monstrous.

Catholic missionaries from the European continent established the first sustained encounter between Christians and Hindus, and their struggles to comprehend and address Hinduism in many respects replicated their own internal theological and institutional crises. Ines G. Županov's study of the clash between Robert de Nobili and Gonçalo Fernandes captures much of the essence of Catholic concerns in the seventeenth century and the ways that Hindus and Hinduism were implicated in European political struggles over class and the power of the church hierarchy.[4] Parties of competing persuasions invoked Hinduism in theological debates about whether Catholic Christianity should accommodate or resist the cultures it encountered, but those debates reinscribed much deeper and more pervasive rifts among theologians and church officials in Europe. Joan-Pau Rubiés takes the slightly longer historical view to establish that Jesuit missionaries in south India were the first Europeans to seriously analyze and elaborate a version of Hinduism, but in a manner that reflected more pressing debates about Christian identity. The Jesuit dispute over accommodation to idolatry issued from deeper anxieties about the nature of the relationship between European culture and Christianity, and hence the missionary movement warned of a fundamental shakeup in Christian self-understanding by finally dissolving the marriage between religion and civilization.[5]

If many of the characteristic features of missionary polemic that are at the center of this book were already in place by the eighteenth century thanks to earlier travelers' accounts,[6] the nineteenth century introduced a new tone of confidence into the politics and discourse that surrounded India and Hinduism. Kate Teltscher observes that with the British accession to the diwani in 1765, the practices and sites for the representation of India fundamentally changed, and with the defeat of Tipu Sultan in the south in 1799, Britain had registered its imperial destiny. Consequently, a more sure-handed and commanding style of representation ushered in the nineteenth century.[7] Many others have seen similar connections between a rising interest in conceptual mastery of Hinduism and a drive for political and military mastery of Hindus. Partha Mitter attributes increasingly polemical representations of Hinduism to a vast increase in the quality and quantity of information about India that could be turned against it.[8] Thomas Trautmann's *Aryans and British India* blames the eclipse of a nearly ubiquitous British Indomania of the late eighteenth and early nineteenth century by a rapidly spreading Indophobia on the rise of a racist science that legitimated the subjugation of Indians.[9] No one would now challenge the claim that imperial ambition both fed and fed off of the practices of representation back home.

By virtue of their close and sustained contact with Hinduism and their eagerness to publish their experiences and discoveries, missionaries were vital sources of information for government administrators and their church sponsors alike. We must exercise extreme caution, however, not to reduce the place of Christianity and missions to supporting actors in a larger epic drama, making them merely a "metonym of a global movement"[10] and subsume, thereby, the place of religious imagery, imagination, and motivation under the articulation of colonial strategy. It would amount to a similar half story to suggest that Hindu reformers or their orthodox opponents were merely vying for social or political position by promoting religious ideas and organizations inspired by their encounter with the British. I return many times to this theme and argue for writing religion into, rather than out of, colonial history. It is clear that religion often functions as a tool of repression and a mask for hegemony; the likes of Voltaire and Marx have made it impossible for us not to see this. But religious aims, disciplines, and doctrines are themselves motivating forces and material factors in the lives of peoples, and they have, moreover, been instrumental in resisting oppression. Taking religion as cause and not just effect, as substance and not just veneer, is essential in any history that does not wish to reinscribe the postmodern marginalization of religious belief and identity onto contexts suffused with them.

There are any number of other ways that one might chart the shifting attitudes that the British displayed toward India and her religions in this period. I select two for special mention because their original insights nearly forty years ago helped set an agenda for studying cultural encounter in colonial India, and additionally because they highlight the limitations of a certain historiographic approach. George D. Bearce's *British Attitudes toward India, 1784–1858* identified three distinct British political interests in competing representations of Hinduism. First, philosophical conservatives like Edmund Burke praised the accomplishments of Indian culture and urged a policy that would allow Indian principals to govern India. Second, humanitarian, religious, and utilitarian voices urged the westernization of India as a means of modernization and advancement. Finally, imperialist sentiment was convinced of European superiority and the benefits of direct British rule over India.[11] Each specific party, Bearce trained us to recognize, had its own stake in the degree to which Hinduism was understood as a positive or negative force in Indian society. David Kopf's path-breaking *British Orientalism and the Bengal Renaissance* spells out the internally contested character of colonialism as Orientalists, Anglicizers, and evangelical missionaries debated their incompatible visions for India and manufactured corresponding images of Hinduism. Invoking European historical experience, he further reconstructs a Bengali reaction to these British disputes as a "renaissance" of Hindu religious vigor.[12] Kopf moved beyond Bearce by recovering Hindu resistances to and appropriations of British attitudes, but he gave significant credit for the renaissance to the influence of British ideas and institutions. These two works both, however, seem now severely constrained by their commitments to the historical view that influences flow along channels, primarily from metropole to colony, and by their failure to perceive how colonialism establishes a whole milieu whose interactions continuously shaped and reshaped the state and social relationships on both sides of the ocean. Such a model inevitably rehearses some of colonialism's own authority claims by demonstrating the many and widespread effects the British Raj had on India but ultimately fails to account for the ways that Britain itself was transformed by the experiences of colonization and empire. Additionally, Kopf and Bearce also regard colonialism as principally the effect of collective attitudes, intentions, and policies, rather than as a largely unconscious, unintended system of often contradictory, contested power arrangements that pervaded the British/Indian encounter at every level.

A third account takes a wider temporal and geographic view. In *India and Europe: An Essay in Understanding* (1988; original German edition 1981), Wilhelm Halbfass produced what is, perhaps, the most balanced and extensively researched study of the intersection of Indian and European thought to date.[13] His main thesis proposed that in the ongoing encounter between East and West, traditional Indian thought has been gradually overwhelmed by the categories and central preoccupations of European thought. In their efforts to affirm a distinctive identity and tradition both to themselves and to others, beginning in the early nineteenth century and increasingly so since then, Indians have resorted to western categories and concepts or reinterpreted Indian concepts in western ways. Halbfass maintained that the European, especially British presence in India "affected the very self-understanding of the [Indian] tradition and turned out to be inescapable even when it was rejected or discarded. For it began to provide the means even for its rejection, and for the Hindu self-affirmation against it."[14]

Few today would contest the claim that the globe continues to be radically impacted by western ideas and values, although many might take issue with the notion that traditional Indian thought has been vanquished.[15] Since his study was first published, however, several developments, some academic and some political, suggest ways we might now rethink Halbfass's findings. First, his model for power dynamics seems somewhat limited in the wake of subaltern and postcolonial studies. Halbfass portrayed a coherent western tradition of thought and dominance that, by virtue of both force and inherent persuasion (in its obvious mastery of science and technology, for example), overcomes or insinuates itself in all indigenous discourses. Such a characterization now calls for greater nuance and attention to the multiple ways Indians have contested westernization. When Halbfass gave attention to Indian resistance, he found it only weakening and compromised in its adjustments to the limits of dialogue with Europeans. Moreover, Halbfass confined himself to discourses of the most learned kind. In his concern for philosophy, he left out some fascinating and instructive modes of encounter at the popular level. Even when treating religious thinkers and texts, for example, Halbfass neglected religion itself as an important site of encounter.[16] Religious practice and religious experience, both elite and popular, might have shed light on Indian and European discourses in encounter, but they do not appear in his work.

As a third point on which I believe Halbfass's project now begs some revision, I would propose this: any suggestion that "real" or "traditional" Indian thought has not survived must today be rethought or recast so that it speaks from and to a more contemporary geopolitical reality. We have certainly come to see that the purely historical question of continuity vs. rupture in the evolution of Hindu thought is quite complex, but in addition, the climate in which the historian of India now writes is much changed since the original publication of *India and Europe*. The manufacture of a longing for an imagined "true" and "ancient" indigenous Indian tradition, one many Indians believe was suppressed under colonial and secular Indian states, today contributes to the production of sometimes violent agitations for a Hindu India restored to its former glory and supremacy. In this context, both Indian and western scholars have been attacked for derisive attitudes toward Hinduism and for interpretations of historical data that run contrary to histories imagined by Hindus of many stripes. Chapter 6 speaks more fully to this situation, but certainly the careful scholar who cared above all about mutual understanding would address this contemporary discussion and clarify the manner in which his or her conclusions are to be taken. To narrate history in order to appease potential enemies of academic freedom would be to abrogate one's fundamental responsibility as a historian, but to write as if oblivious to the way history is now received and mobilized for or against political causes would itself be folly, an indication of the dangerous attitude that scholarship is above and outside public life.

In addition to the depth of his scholarship, what endures most in Halbfass's work is his scrupulosity, well before postcolonialism and subaltern studies made it necessary, in granting full agency and subjectivity to the Indian and European authors he treated. In no sense did he render Indians unsuspecting agents of their own domination, and his work is rich with the sense of living traditions in contact. Even given its focus on philosophical thought, *India and Europe* is a book about full human beings, a work motivated by and suffused with the highest scholarly standards and a genuine belief in the possibility of mutual understanding, a faith one encounters less and less these days. Had Halbfass survived to engage our own critical moment of East/West encounter, his careful and sensitive scholarship would certainly have aided us in discovering ways for India and the West to forge a new set of mutual understandings in a relationship that has continued to shift and grow over half a millennium.

"A Mess of Encounters"

The postmodern turn has sensitized historians to the need constantly to undermine their own tendencies to reification and essentialization of their operative concepts. An accounting of plurality and difference—in social identities, historical trends, the authorization of power, and elsewhere—has become the normative mode of historiographic writing. The particular, the local, and the subaltern have animated much recent historical analysis in an attempt to uncover previously obscured knowledges and experiences and to undermine dominant discourses. There are countervailing trends, of course, including the work of those who would now return to macro narrative and comparison informed by the power-knowledge critiques of the late twentieth century, confident that a second naivete is possible.[17] I have tried in many respects to keep my own narrative of the events I wish to present unburdened by jargon and theory. For this reason, and for the fact that I have chosen a narrow range of primary sources to make a larger point, it may be important to clarify a few matters about the concepts and terminology I employ, and especially the manner in which this study regards such contested, frequently essentialized categories as "western," "colonialism," "Hindu," and "religion."

In the closing line of his important book on religion and modernity, Peter van der Veer employs the phrase "a mess of encounters" to suggest a complex web of attractions and resistances at every level of society on both sides of the cultural and geographic divide between Britain and India.[18] Individuals and groups of different interests and persuasions confronted one another in circumstances that varied widely at any given moment and over time. Van der Veer and others make it abundantly clear that colonialism was, moreover, an experience that unfolded not only in the colony, but also in the metropole. Encounter quietly became a constitutive element of nineteenth-century British life and state as the public became increasingly familiar with the religious and material culture of India.[19] Colonialism, even colonialism involving a defined site such as India, operated not as a single force, but as a set of polyphonic discourses and polyvalent centers of authority situated in diverse settings. Furthermore, it was not a relationship whereby one power unambiguously dominated another. Without understating the violence and dehumanizing subordination on which it was predicated or the vast differential in wealth and power that it produced, it must be acknowledged that colonialism did not only impact India. It enveloped and transformed society and social relations at all levels in both Britain and India. The plurality of encounters and relationships made possible by the British colonization of India demands careful scrutiny of discrete sites of encounter in order to illuminate the very messiness of colonialism, the diffusion of its influences along different avenues and in multiform settings. This study examines a discrete set of influential sources, including missionary tracts, the Orientalist journal *Asiatick Researches*, and the Bengali newspaper *Samācār Candrikā* in order to highlight the ways in which colonialism and religion shaped and reflected one another in the context of expanding British rule.

There are, indeed, risks and shortcomings to any such approach. As I presented some of the material in this book to faculty and graduate students at Emory University, Laurie L. Patton made the persuasive case that in a genuinely postcolonial, post-essentializing study of religion and culture, every analytic text would undermine itself by suggesting its own limits. In keeping with this sentiment, with which I concur, I would currently say that a wider lens might well show features I do not highlight in greater relief. In giving voice to the particular, I no doubt overlook starker trends. More troubling to me personally, however, are the limits of my own language training and the paucity of turn-of-the-nineteenth-century sources that might testify more broadly to Hindu reactions, resistances, and accommodations to colonial interventions. The scarcity of such sources and my own inability to read many of them leave that element of this book's argument particularly underdeveloped. A fuller complement of Hindu voices is especially necessary for us to fathom the complexity of the Hindu encounter with Britain. A more nuanced appreciation of variety and difference would, in turn, allow us to draw more carefully considered general conclusions about colonialism.

Even more carelessly evoked than "colonialism" is another monolith, once figured as savior, now more often as demon, that is featured in so many historical and historiographic discourses: the "West." If we have become more sensitive to the need to nuance and qualify our invocations of the East, of gender, identity, culture, and so forth, historians, it seems, are only recently awakening to the facile and clumsy way we often invoke the West with the implicit assumption that it communicates a set of concrete ideas and experiences. The bifurcation of East and West continues to inform the work of even the finest historians of intercultural encounter, and I fear that I, too, may be culpable in this respect. Many scholars seem seduced by the notion that the West is possessed of some overarching, unifying history and teleology. These scholars assume what Edward Said only somewhat more carefully argues about British, French, and American imperialism, namely that they together possesses "a unique coherence."[20] My own informal glance at the indices of some of the most highly regarded postcolonial histories of India strongly suggests that some of the very same scholars who would decry any essentialism of the East or any segment of it take considerably less care when invoking the West as a category. This book's contribution toward disentangling the many threads woven into our concept of the West involves clarifying the distinctiveness of particular administrative and Christian discourses initially emanating from Britain and indicating the shifts internal to each as they grappled with India and Hinduism. Even as specific and tightly circumscribed a group as Anglican Britons could be sharply at odds with one another about the nature and aims of their tradition. At this point, we can only offer conjecture about the multivocality of the colonizing West when there is much work yet to be done, for example, studying the elite and popular French, Dutch, German, and Portuguese reactions to the peoples they colonized. The "West," in short, can only come to mean something again once we plumb its complexities and puzzle anew about what might constitute its coherence.

Difference for difference's sake, however, is no scholarly virtue. Advancing our understanding of colonial encounter involves more than an ever-narrower focus on an expanding array of subgroups. It lies, additionally, in our ability to train our analytical gaze to different depths and to define the character of that particular depth we claim to be investigating. Meaningful, precise, and instructive statements of both wide and narrow sweep can indeed be made about social, cultural, or ideological matters so long as the claims are theoretically and empirically grounded. The distinction between a sloppy and an incisive invocation of some macro entity lies in the author's full articulation of a prior level of appreciation for the dissonances, internal tensions, and multivocalities inherent in any global regime such as "colonialism" or the "West." I maintain that there are constructive appropriations of these categories, but constructiveness is determined by a self-conscious, carefully informed usage, and perhaps one tinged with a little irony.

In the concluding chapter, I address the concepts "Hinduism" and "religion" in light of the intervening analysis of early nineteenth-century discourses on the subjects. I argue there what I am also suggesting here about the concepts "colonialism" and the "West," namely that the need to continually undercut their tendencies to reification and dehistoricization does not, however, altogether nullify their value as heuristic devices for gaining some purchase on the events in question. Simply put, I cannot travel the road to complete discontinuity and acquiesce in the fragmentation of history and human experience to which the most radical postmodern critique of totalizing discourses must lead. I take it, rather, to be the scholar's duty not only to contextualize and historicize her data, but also to generalize and theorize, tasks which the fetishisms of difference and experience cannot execute. I may well want it both ways, but neither the notion that cultures and histories have nothing to say to one another nor the easy correlation of diverse histories and experiences seems to me a responsible posture for a historian. The work that follows attempts to hold these two things in tension—to accept that there are parallels, overlaps, and mutual reflections in human historical experience and to remain aware that we must constantly scrutinize the very categories with which we establish and characterize these commonalities. To take only one representative of the kind of concern for radical difference that I wish to avoid, I find S. N. Balagangadhara's rejection of the category "religion" as an apt cross-cultural comparative device problematic. Indeed, there are myriad ways in which Hindu and Christian traditions differ in the character and content of their normative models, but I refuse to accept that religion is now so ossified and monothetic a concept that it cannot accommodate a careful elaboration of these significant differences. I would argue, to the contrary, that "religion" is increasingly flexible and polyvalent, both in academic and popular parlance. In fact, even the most probing critics of the category "religion," such as McCutcheon and Richard King, appear to be unable to proceed without it. In what follows, this book readily, but I hope, carefully and self-consciously, engages and invokes these contested categories.

Religion and the Colonial Everyday

Since the publication of Said's *Orientalism* in 1979, religion has taken a back seat in much historiography in favor of some type of discourse analysis that regards forms of religious expression as reducible to other factors. I do not address Said's work in any detail in this book because so many others, including some of those on whose work I rely, have undertaken careful and thoughtful reflection on the import of his vast influence. His death just as this book was going to press will surely occasion new appraisals of his life, his activism, and his scholarship. To select some whom I believe have provided especially trenchant critiques I would mention Trautmann and Halbfass, both of whom find Said's sweeping condemnation of Orientalism undernuanced and overly polemical.[21] The trend toward writing religion out of history has acquired its force from several different directions. Marxist thought, of course, has always regarded religion as both inauthentic consciousness and compensatory comfort in which the oppressed seek some expression of their condition. Said himself said little about religion except as it represents or is represented by rival religious systems. In his work, religion always appeared refracted through someone else's gaze, their justification or pretext for the exercise of power. Indebted to Foucault's own identification of the intimate connections among power, knowledge, and representation, Said gave impetus and cover to some postcolonial historiographers to treat religion as a mask for political and social ends.

In much of the early work of the Subaltern Studies Collective, religion is virtually absent except, perhaps, as a site for colonial intervention. One important exception is the work of Partha Chatterjee who, in the first volume of Subaltern Studies reminds historians that, to subaltern classes, "religion . . . provides an ontology, an epistemology as well as a practical code of ethics, including political ethics. When this community acts politically, the symbolic meaning of particular acts—their signification—must be found in religious terms."[22] His awareness of the irreducibility of religious consciousness as stimulus to human activity and source of cosmological and social concepts, stands in contrast to Ranajit Guha's famous manifesto in the same volume that proposes the goals and aims of subaltern studies without once mentioning religion, and this in a call for a new history of colonial India, an arena in which British and Indian religiosity could hardly be more significant.[23] Chatterjee, however, seems to recognize the viability of religion as an analytical category only with respect to oppressed classes. And while Marxism and postcolonialism have been erasing the distinctiveness of religion as motive for political action and framework for understanding political action, some trends in the study of religion itself, especially the kind of social scientific work done by scholars such as Russell McCutcheon and Donald Wiebe, have also contributed to the idea that religion is epiphenomenal to society at large and therefore functions neither as cause nor motive for social behaviors.

Among postcolonial historians, however, forms of religious expression have in recent years received increasingly serious attention. Saurabh Dube, for instance, has written a sensitive and compelling account of the Satnamis of Central India, members of a low-caste religious movement that appeared in the early nineteenth century.[24] While Dube places religious practices and discourses squarely in the economy of symbols and gestures that reflect the negotiation of social power, he regards religion and its reform in nineteenth-century India as lived belief and practice whose internal significations and codes are meaningful and causative. Dube displays these ethnographic sensitivities with respect to both the Satnamis themselves and the Christian evangelical missionaries who took an interest in them. In taking this path, he was preceded by John and Jean Comaroff, who first demonstrated the manner in which ethnography of religion could serve as a useful tool to the historian of colonialism. Also worthy of mention here is the work of David Hardiman who, critical of secular-minded historians who see religion as only primitive, false consciousness, has sought to portray the religiosity of ādivāsīs as stimulus to subaltern resistance rather than ideological superstructure imposed from above as a tool of repression.[25]

In his study of the Kartābhajās of colonial Bengal, Hugh B. Urban has also produced a work that treats religious devotion as an expression of resistance to oppression by Indian elites and the colonial state. Urban, indeed, is not afraid to invoke "spirituality," a category widely regarded as too diaphanous to be of any use. Instead, he finds it relatively true to the experiences and expressions of religious peoples. Less radical but more pervasive than overtly revolutionary religious movements, everyday spirituality functioned as a critique and figured in the rejection of hegemony often overlooked by historians such as those of the Subaltern Studies Collective whom, he says, have restricted their analysis to open and violent revolt.[26] Countering Marxist reduction of religion, Urban observes that just as religion can often express relationships belonging to another level of human interaction such as the economic, so religious devotees can employ signs from these other realms "to express profoundly religious concerns and spiritual ideals."[27] His attempt to foreground religious expression reveals what the antithetical intent to strip it of any distinctive or causative features obscures: that religion can supply the context and motivation for transformation of social relations and the strategic appropriation of dominant signs and models.

The book that follows addresses a series of encounters between British Christians and Hindus of the subcontinent around the turn of the nineteenth century. Many before me have pursued similar projects, and very fine work continues to emerge on this site of interreligious, intercultural, power-laden, colonial contact, but I have undertaken this study with my eye toward religious ideologies, concepts, and practices. The colonial historiography of the British in India must do justice to the place of religion—Hindu and Christian—in that encounter. With respect to Christianity, it must neither deny its power by rendering religious thought and motivation a thin, disingenuous veneer to colonial ambition, nor overlook the role that Christianities in Britain played in colonial arrogance and violence. The course and shape of the British experience of India at the turn of the century partook, especially at the popular level, of uniquely religious emotions and drives. With respect to Hinduism, historiography must discover Hinduism's manifold transformations in the early modern period to be genuinely Hindu and not mere mimesis of British ways. Theorizing that fails to engage religious discourses and religious subjectivities on their own terms unconsciously and perhaps unwillingly further effects the marginalization of religious communities and subordinates not only their cognitive claims but also their communal and individual identities to the demands of the secular nation-state. I have attempted, as an antidote, to interject something of what Gerald Larson has called in his *India's Agony over Religion* a "religious studies perspective." In attempting to supplement the work of those who espouse modernization, subaltern, or world-systems theorizing, Larson has described such an approach as a "perspective that focuses on the high salience of religious experience, not simply in terms of its manifestation in historical, social, economic and political contexts, but also in terms of its substantive content, that is, its basic intellectual and spiritual claims."[28] I take Larson to be urging historians and social theorists not to write religion out of the equation, but to recognize its critical role in contemporary and historical movements.

My pursuit of such an approach has compelled me to engage especially three sets of ideas. The first is the history of religions as the tradition of academic theorizing that most readily accepts and employs the concepts internal to religious traditions. Second is the post-Foucault, post-Said practice of theorizing colonial encounter and its aftermath that many call "postcolonial." It is this set of approaches that I find most helpful in demystifying the power relations that religious discourses often aim to obscure. In many ways, then, this book can be read as an attempt to balance and hold in tension two approaches that may well be regarded as antithetical. To make history of religions and postcolonial theory mutually corrective of the other is not to call theory into question, but to underscore the ultimately fragmentary and partial account that any set of theories can offer messy human histories. To establish an over-arching framework that might allow an account of this meeting between Christian Britain and the Hindu subcontinent has also required that I address a third set of ongoing discussions among scholars. This third set of conversations has interrogated the very categories that have nursed the precritical acceptance of the idea that such social identity markers as "Hindu" and "Christian" are species of the genus "religion." Whether "Hindu" and "Hinduism" are valid categories and whether "religion" is an apt unit of cross-cultural comparison are questions that have generated animated, sometimes heated debate. This controversy, which has largely unfolded over the decade that this book was researched and written, has provided me with an ongoing prod to think carefully and strategically about my own use of such ideas.

Even though I reject the fetishizing of difference, I find in postmodern-ism's call to underscore particularity an important recognition that apparent wholes such as colonialism, Christianity, Hinduism, and so forth, are profoundly ambiguous, internally contested, and multivalent entities. It seems to me that no responsible history of intercultural encounter can now play fast and loose with such ideas and must endeavor to contextualize deeply the sites of encounter it chooses to explore. The challenge to the historian for theorizing such global movements as colonialism is to maintain an appreciation for the specificity of local contexts while speaking directly and intelligibly about larger trends.

I have approached this challenge by focusing on certain pieces of periodical and tractarian literature that reflect contested discourses and shifts in their assumptions and strategies. I examine most closely the religious newspapers *Samācār Candrikā* and the Church Missionary Society's *Missionary Papers* as well as the early academic journal *Asiatick Researches*. These particular works are well suited to bearing the burden of the larger claims I will make about colonial Hindu-Christian encounter and how religion permeated colonialism's every tissue. By virtue of their circulation, prominence, influence, or historical precedence, they each point to significant sites of Britain's engagement with India and offer a glimpse into some facet of colonial encounter. Studying specific publications possesses some distinct advantages over other kinds of archival research. The missionary movement, colonial ambition, and Hindu resistance to both, each distinct, competing, but interlocking ideological programs, were not only broadly conceived and centralized movements. They were also locally variable, on-the-ground efforts guided by overarching aims and principles but fully reactive to specific contexts and their fluid characters. Public opinion was both a target and tool of these movements, which aimed to harness popular outrage or enthusiasm while also shaping them. Tractarian and periodical literature is immediately formed by and formative of distinct public opinions. I examine specific publications in order to preserve the character of a particular editor's engagement with a well-defined audience in the context of specific social, political, and religious events. It is the everydayness of the interactions among Hindus and Christians, whether face-to-face or via an image, anecdote, artifact, or other medium, that I wish to retain in my analysis. Encounter took place on Calcutta verandahs and in London parlors, in Sunday school classrooms in Manchester and in mission schools in Assam, and in village economies on both continents. Observing the implicit, and sometimes explicit, exchanges that authors and editors conducted with their audiences allows us to detect not only their artless and natural evolution, but also the historically contingent character of the emergence of modern religious forms such as Hinduism and evangelical Christianity.

Chapter 2 examines the genesis of missionary strategies derived by upper-class evangelicals in the heart of the metropole. Situated at the center of colonial power, such men as William Wilberforce and Charles Grant conceived of a comprehensive evangelization of Britain and India alike that would employ the benighted pagan and vulgar factory laborer as reflections of one another. Such an approach clearly illustrates how modern forms of colonial encounter took place not along avenues of diffusion between metropole and colony but under an umbrella of power relations and signs shared by those in Britain and India who would be mutually transformed by the experience. Missionary bodies such as the Anglican but evangelical Church Missionary Society viewed the working classes of Britain as sources of income and energy but also as targets of the very proselytization they were preparing for India. The British church's own struggle to address and accommodate the working poor whom industrialization and high-church polity had marginalized accounts for much of the style and scope of its missionary societies.

Chapter 3 examines the ways that missionaries processed their concrete experiences of contact with Hinduism and discerned, as a result, a conceptual and ritual core to an array of Hindu communities and deities. The execution of the strategies examined in chapter 2 was subject to the exigencies of first-hand contact on the ground in India. The evangelical Protestant missionary encountering lived Hindu tradition for the first time salved his disorientation and confusion with the ointment of his own theological categories. A strain of Christian iconoclasm then being nurtured by rampant anti-Catholic polemic in Britain fashioned a system of Hindu theology and ritual for British audiences that focused squarely on image worship and cast Hindu ritual as an infantile version of the idolatry condemned in the Christian Old and New Testaments. Idol worship and an imputed attendant logic offered the working-class audiences of British missionary newspapers a systematized, coherent, pan-Indian Hinduism.

Alongside the development of missionary discourses about Hinduism, Orientalists in the employ of the East India Company derived their own sets of idioms and tropes to represent Hindu traditions, but these were no less religious in their motive or concerns. The publication history of the journal of the Asiatic Society, the *Asiatick Researches*, spans the entire period of time this book covers, and it shows in bold relief some of the shifts in colonial strategies and discourses that occurred in this period of time. Founded by William Jones as an advertisement for the beauty and antiquity of Indian civilizations, the *Asiatick Researches* displayed from its beginning a close alliance with the designs of the colonial state. As the evolving state discarded Orientalist policies that sought rapprochement with and accommodation of Indian traditions, the journal itself came to reflect a colder conquest of the minds and territories of Indian subjects. Chapter 4 argues that a conceptual systematization of Hinduism parallel to that seen among evangelical missionaries is evident in this journal, but that what distinguishes the Orientalist imagination is an enchantment with the natural world of India, whose profuse and lush flora and fauna functioned as tropes for religion in India as well. An initial fascination with the apparently self-multiplying, polymorphic pantheon and mythology of Hindu India reflected a similar scientific wonder among the Society's naturalists. Just as that wonder would give way to a quest for mastery, so the officials of the colonial state who authored the articles published in the *Researches* demonstrated their own growing sense of intellectual command and moral superiority over what they came increasingly to identify as Hinduism.

While advancing print technologies were helping to shift the meaning and weight of public opinion in Britain, they would also contribute to a transformation in the consciousness of Hindu identity in the colony. Vernacular newspapers written by Indians (as opposed to those written by missionaries) with explicitly religious themes and aims began to appear early in the third decade of the nineteenth century. Virtually all of these newspapers are now lost, and only fragments survive in translation in contemporaneous English newspapers. Among the very earliest newspapers to survive in any substantial run of issues is the biweekly Bengali paper *Samācār Candrikā*, published by Bhabān-īcaraṇ Bandyopādhyāya and associated with the anti-reformist organization the Dharma Sabhā. First formed to protest the government's proposed ban on satī, the Dharma Sabha took to the presses in an effort to galvanize broad Hindu support among disparate castes and classes. In so doing, it proffered a version of a homogenous Hinduism with a centralized authority similar to that emerging among reforming organizations such as the Brahmo Samaj but with an explicitly traditionalist, brahmanical agenda. Chapter 5 examines a one-year run of this paper to sketch the contours of an elite Bengali Hindu response to missionaries and Orientalists.

The final chapter makes the case for the retention of certain received categories and approaches in the study of Hindu traditions in response to several recent critiques that argue that terms such as "Hinduism" and "religion" cannot find meaningful analogues in Indian traditions and that scholars ought therefore to dispense with them. In varying ways, this is the upshot of important work by S. N. Balagangadhara, Russell McCutcheon, Richard King, and Timothy Fitzgerald in recent years. While I accept much of their own opposition to the reification and mystification of these ideas and applaud their efforts to achieve wider recognition of the political and social elements of religious belief, practice, and identity, I am troubled by some of the implications of a full-scale retreat from interreligious dialogue and comparative history of religious traditions that their work can either demand or imply. In some instances utterly dismissive of religious faith, practice, or identity, this deconstruction of widely accepted categories is not without significant political ramifications. In an atmosphere of global religious upheaval and transformation, it can promise only to exacerbate the clash of identities and communities with one another and with the secular academy. To put it simply, Europe, North America, and India are today all in need of new models for structuring the relationship of religion and the nation state. The simultaneous estrangement of religious communities from public life and nationalization of religious identity speak to the tensions inherent in the loyalties demanded by religious faith and citizenship. Some trends in the academy today seem to offer not solutions to this impasse, but rather encouragement to further talking at cross-purposes.

2

The Other Without and the Other Within

It was no coincidence that Britain awoke to the condition of its laboring classes at the same moment that it imagined the imperiled state of the pagan soul. The two events are intimately related, even inseparable, elements of the near-global transformation of religion in the nineteenth century that would produce both evangelical Christianity and modern Hinduism. The late years of the eighteenth century saw the emergence of a multitude of charitable bodies devoted to the material and spiritual benefit of the illiterate and unprivileged of both British and foreign extraction. The antislavery movement, the evangelical awakening, the proliferation of missionary societies, the spread of Sunday schools, and the large-scale distribution of popular religious tracts are all evidence of a growing cultural concern. Sparked in large measure by aristocratic compassion and ingenuity, these movements nonetheless drew their strength and stamina from broadly based popular enthusiasm for the causes they espoused. A concerned sector of Britain's elite successfully generated and then harnessed mass interest to assemble a collection of sophisticated organizations dedicated to the general improvement of the unlettered, the unwashed, and the unchurched. Central to this push for cultural reform was a form of populist, proselytizing Christianity known as "evangelical." Alongside evangelical Christianity emerged the concept of a unitary Indian religion later known as Hinduism. I am concerned in this chapter especially to describe certain transformations in Anglican Christianity as products of Britain's "discovery" and manipulation of religions in lands it occupied. The so-called invention of Hinduism, a closely related development, will be the subject of subsequent chapters.

The evangelization of non-Christian foreigners was to benefit civilization at large: it would elevate the poor and the powerless in Britain, it would rescue pagan souls falling into damnation overseas, and it would protect the interests of their common rulers as well. At home, a religious awakening was to stem the tide of French radicalism; abroad, it would assist the consolidation of British influence. Whether cynical patrons of an oppressive status quo or bold champions of liberal reform, the men and women who battled parliamentary and ecclesiastical resistance to missionary ambitions were the forebears of much that we take to be modern: the end to forced servitude, universal education, the popular press, economic globalization, and religious nationalism.

As background to these social and religious programs, the construction of religion in early nineteenth-century Britain involved a number of closely related phenomena: the development of an academic discipline to identify and describe certain facets of human behavior, the first descriptions of such traditions as Hinduism and Buddhism as discrete, self-contained religions, and the development of new identities, practices, and concerns among Christians in Britain. The construction of religion, however, was more than an imaginative exercise involving category formation and descriptive discourses. It also involved the manufacture of actual religious ideas and practices for Christians and non-Christians alike. New religious ideas and practices appeared across the globe in places touched by British colonialism, and they conformed to the categories and descriptive habits of the emerging study of religion.

At the turn of the nineteenth century, the reforming gaze of leading Anglican evangelicals fixed on two figures: the British laborer and the benighted pagan–ideal types this age itself constructed in popular and bourgeois literature and in the public performances of sermon and political speech. Although very far from a united body of opinion and belief, evangelical Christianities in early nineteenth-century Britain displayed a set of common and widely recognized concerns that saw these two groups as bound together in their mutual spiritual impoverishment. The industrial revolution, which shattered traditional village life in many areas, created the material conditions for the appearance of the laborer. It drew members of a rural culture into a hostile urban environment, stripping them of their accustomed relations and religion, while its factories often stripped them of their health. Anxiety over rapid economic change and its impact on what many referred to as the "lower orders" inspired the production of the figure of the impoverished and exploited laborer in need of legislative protection and Christian compassion. The benighted pagan was a different sort of creation, equally the concern of popular literature and public ritual speech, but less constrained in its outlines by the concrete experience of British authors and readers. At the turn of the nineteenth century, Christian authors made little effort to distinguish non-European peoples, seeing a rather uniform and uniformly debased paganism across the globe. Early literature recommending Christian missions offered up a "primitivist pastiche," a "careless composite of non-European colors and customs" for public consumption.[1] In many cases, the tribes and rites that came to fascinate nineteenth-century

Britain were playing out their own histories for centuries before there was a European presence to report them. In one sense, the encroachment of the knowing colonial subject only "discovered" what was already there to be found. In another, however, the image of the savage heathen was a product of certain forms of knowledge, political relations, and religious prejudices particularly modern in character.

The parallel between the poor of Britain and the heathen of the colonies was a thoroughly commonplace trope of the nineteenth century. One London observer of the poor echoed a common belief when he remarked that "the notions of morality among these people agree strangely . . . with those of many savage tribes."[2] Susan Thorne has recently concluded, "It seems almost impossible for evangelicals to describe, and arguably even to think about, the labouring poor . . . without comparing them in some way to the empire's heathen races."[3] In both habit and habitation, bourgeois and missionary literature presented these two groups (as yet internally undifferentiated), as two sides of the same miserable coin.[4] Both stood in need of the civilizing influence of Christian evangelism, and both would require a missionary journey beyond the protective embrace of British civilization into uncharted wilderness.[5] The tropical jungles of Africa, India, and the Pacific Islands, and the bleak industrial jungles of London and Liverpool seemed to cry out for Christian intervention. By mid-century, Henry Mayhew (*London Labour and the London Poor*, 1861), John Hollingshead (*Ragged London*, 1861), and Charles Dickens (*Bleak House*, 1853) would decry the savagery in Britain's cities and conclude that "the primitive and the pauper were one in spirit, one in spiritlessness."[6]

Consequently, similar means for their improvement and reform were adopted. Professions of faith in the Christian god alone were not enough: to the missionary mind, a wholesale reformation in lifestyle, attitude, and comport would be necessary to effect the transformation from heathen savagery to Christian civility. John and Jean Comaroff enumerate the common strategies that civilizing Christian mission pursued in regard to both populations:

> (1) to create the conditions for—and an attitude of—"cleanliness,"
> thereby achieving a world in which all matter, beings, and bodies
> were in their proper place; (2) to reform sexuality by encouraging le-
> gal, Christian marriage and the creation of nuclear households, thus
> putting an end to "drunken indulgence" in "child-breeding"; (3) to
> spread the ideal of private property, beginning with the family home;
> and (4) to reconstruct gender relations and the social division of la-
> bor.[7]

These processes are all evident among the working-class subjects this chapter treats. What I am especially interested to examine here, however, is the manner in which this same campaign played one group against the other, taking the image of the primitive as the very means by which to achieve its civilizing goals for the British pauper.

Metropoles and Colonials

British experiences in and of distant lands were not isolated from events at home, but part and parcel of developing domestic concerns and practices. As Bernard Cohn has observed, "metropole and colony have to be seen in a unitary field of analysis."[8] Antoinette Burton is among those who have taken pains to point out that the myth of "Britain's insularity" from its colonial possessions has been "one of the most enduring fictions" of the colonial and imperial chapters of British history[9] and that British domestic life "sponsored a variety of possibilities for colonial encounters of the most casual and the most spectacular kind."[10] By the 1830s, Britain was awash with images, goods, and books from places abroad, and the average Briton must have had regular exposure to the colonies through commerce and popular discourse. So thoroughly was Britain saturated with colonial images that the *London Quarterly Review* would observe at mid-century that "many a small tradesman or rustic know more of African or Polynesian life than London journalists."[11] Colonialism, together with its consequences for religious practices and identities, "was and is not just a phenomenon 'out there' but a fundamental and constitutive part of English culture and national identity at home."[12] Despite the average five months' travel time that separated Britain from India and the relatively small number of people making the passage in either direction, colony and metropole, center and periphery collaborated in the construction of religious identities and practices for the subjects who inhabited them. As John and Jean Comaroff have put it, "colonialism was as much about making the center as it was about making the periphery. The colony was not a mere extension of the modern world. It was part of what made that world modern in the first place."[13] It contributed, among other things, to the distinction of religion from other spheres of human activity and to the development of discrete, mutually exclusive religious identities.[14] Colonialism was not a process located only among those peoples who became subjects of foreign rulers. Rather, colonialism drew into its orbit colonizers and colonized alike, and its most effective masquerade was its pretense to affect only those subjected to foreign domination.

I am suggesting, therefore, that Cohn's plea for a "unified field of analysis" and other calls to draw attention to the dual fields of colonial influences do not go far enough in undermining the bifurcation that haunts postcolonial studies. It is critical to keep in mind that "colonialism . . . was less a process that began in the European metropole and expanded outward than it was a moment when new encounters with the world facilitated the formation of categories of metropole and colony in the first place."[15] One is easily seduced by colonial- and imperial-era discourses that strike such bold contrasts between European and native, resulting in historiography that replicates self/other constructions. The challenge we face is to write colonial history with a heightened sense for the pervasiveness of colonizing practices and concepts, which constituted identities that crossed racial, ethnic, and class boundaries. Such boundaries themselves are products of colonial ideology, part of what the Comaroffs imply are a core identifying feature of modernity. Implicated in colonial policy and practice were not just the representations of native others, but also the articulation of race, class, and gender in Britain itself. The development of racial ideologies emerged from "representations of savagery, licentiousness, and basic truths about human nature that joined early visions of the 'others' of empire with the 'others' within Europe itself."[16] Just as the English middle classes maintained an "intense" attachment to colonial expansion, "for the very good reasons that middle class identity had been made dependent on it,"[17] the character and identity attributed to working and lower classes paralleled those of Britain's colonized subjects.[18] Likewise, British notions of Indian masculinity corresponded to power differentials between the two communities and nationalist ideals for British marriage and motherhood imbibed, reflected, and nurtured colonial ideologies.[19]

The impact of colonialism, therefore, is not to be measured solely or even primarily by an assessment of its manifestations and effects beyond Europe. To undertake such an enterprise masks the means by which social relations among the colonizers were altered not simply as a secondary effect of colonization, but as its very spirit; the two are of a piece. For these reasons, the almost feverish concern of many Christian groups to create and circulate an intricately sketched image of the heathen must be understood in the context of the formation of and education in multiple British identities. The production of this image and its dissemination throughout Great Britain display the means by which identities were created for individuals and, in many cases, contested by them. I turn now to describe one of those processes and show how propertied but evangelical elements among the Anglican Church employed the idea of colony to instill the British laboring classes with a sense of their own religious identity.

A Missionary Age

The drive in Protestant Britain to improve the intellectual, spiritual, and material conditions of those outside the salutary influence of English education began with the founding of the Society for Promoting Christian Knowledge (SPCK) in 1698. A growing desire to share with the rest of the world the knowledge and wealth that blessed English culture characterized at least the next century and a half. The charity school movement of the 1730s and the Sunday school and antislavery campaigns of the later eighteenth century flowered into the missionary movement around the turn of the nineteenth century. This trend began in an effort to educate those British subjects who remained rough and ignorant, exiled in foreign plantations far from the refining influence of English civilization. At the time, many Christians and social reformers were already offering a hand as well to the dark interior of Britain, seeking to improve the coarse lives of the factory worker, the coal miner, and the street peddler. As this concern for the working poor and the destitute extended to foreigners under British influence, the missionary movement was born.

The SPCK had limited itself to the distribution of Bibles, New Testaments, Common Prayer Books and religious tracts to the poor, intending simply to assist other organizations by providing them literature. By so circumscribing its activities, it had hoped to avoid any doctrinal or denominational controversy that might impede its chief goal—expanded literacy in fundamental Christian teachings. In the colonies, it had a mandate only to establish libraries on British plantations, but not to provide instructors or ministers. Its founder, Thomas Bray, realized the need for such persons and petitioned the King in 1701 to charter a sister organization to send missionaries to British colonies. Like the SPCK, the Society for the Propagation of the Gospel in Foreign Parts (SPG) wished to provide spiritual instruction to other British people and initially addressed only the Crown's agents in the Americas: soldiers, planters, and so forth. In his charter, King William III worried that in so distant and wild a place as America, his "loving subjects" would "be abandoned to Atheism and Infidelity," without the maintenance of orthodox ministers of the gospel.[20] The preacher of the SPG's first annual sermon in 1702 was clear about the organization's priorities: "The design is, in the first place, to settle the State of Religion as well as may be among *our own* people there . . . and then to proceed to the best Methods [we] can towards the *Conversion* of the *Natives.*"[21] Soon, however, in opposition to the wishes of the group's founders, members of the SPG felt that the conversion of the heathen ought to assume greater significance,[22] and this theme came to dominate many of the anniversary sermons of the eighteenth century.[23] Until the formation of the Church Missionary Society (CMS) a century later, the SPCK and the SPG represented the Anglican Church's only organized efforts for actively spreading the Christian faith. A CMS historian noted that these groups were "at the lowest point of energy and efficiency"[24] by the end of the eighteenth century, when they were awakened by competition from Anglicans and Dissenters alike. With the expansion of British power and influence, many sensed a need to augment the efforts of these bodies and to promote the spread of the gospel among the foreign subjects of the British Crown more zealously.

In the two decades spanning the turn of the nineteenth century, three major bodies devoted expressly to training and commissioning missionaries were formed, along with two national societies designed to provide them direct aid. In addition, many smaller societies were born, and the SPG and SPCK experienced new vigor. This awakening began in 1792, when William Carey helped found the Baptist Missionary Society and in the next year became its first missionary. His plea for Christian attention to the state of the non-Christian soul was among the first calls in English to the promote the *general* salvation of pagans.[25] Certainly it has become the most famous. He urged the evangelization of not just those non-Christians under direct British control, as the SPG and the East India Company's evangelical Chairman of the Court of Directors Charles Grant had, but of all he saw in peril of damnation.[26] Christian responsibility extended not merely to those who labored on the British-owned plantation, but to the whole globe. In contrast to the reasoned arguments of the SPG sermons, the tone of Carey's *An Enquiry into the Obligation of Chris-*

tians to Use Means for the Conversion of the Heathen was urgent, fueled by the energetic populist piety that is often credited with the rapid spread of Methodism and evangelical religion generally. Carey's legendary struggles and successes in India inspired two other infant societies. In 1795, a group of Christians from several different denominations together founded the London Missionary Society (LMS), which later developed into a strictly Congregational body as other denominational societies appeared.[27]

At the same time, a group of evangelical clergy and laity in the Anglican Church were meeting to discuss issues that concerned the state of established religion in Great Britain. Their meetings culminated in the formation of the Church Missionary Society (1799), one of the most important and successful British missionary bodies for most of the next two centuries. Within a few years, the Methodist and Scottish churches followed suit.[28] In addition, several existing or new organizations took up the task of aiding these societies through the collection of money and the publication of literature for their use. The Religious Tract Society (RTS, 1799) and the SPCK were enlisted to print Bibles, New Testaments, and tracts for distribution abroad.[29] The British and Foreign Bible Society (BFBS, 1804), whose first president was John Shore, Lord Teignmouth, a former governor-general of India, assumed responsibility for distributing translations of the Bible worldwide. Deliberately multi-denominational, the sole mission of the BFBS was "the circulation of the Scriptures, and of the Scriptures only, without note or comment."[30]

This sudden proliferation of organized concern for the propagation of Christianity marked the commencement of the "Age of Missions." Within a few years, Christian Britain had become passionately interested in the eternal condition of countless souls who had heard of neither Christ nor the power of his religion to lift them out of the misery that plagued them in this life and would, barring their conversion, pursue them beyond the grave. These societies displayed interest in both the foreign pagan and the domestic pauper. Institutionalized missions followed upon the earlier evangelical revivals of the eighteenth century and marked, as Susan Thorne has pointed out, the emergence of the sense that paganism and sin were properties of people spatially and socially removed from the missionary. Whereas George Whitefield and John Wesley saw sin potentially lurking in the heart of every individual, the sudden appearance of numerous missionary organizations relied upon the identification of discrete communities of heathenism both within and outside of Britain:

> The institutionalization of the missionary impulse—the formation of organizations and the appointment of functionaries explicitly devoted to missions—depended upon there being identifiable boundaries between the missionary and his target population. For missionary work to be institutionalized, its proponents had to have a priori knowledge of where to recruit as well as where to station their missionaries. Missionary institutions depended, in other words, on sinners and the saved living in geographically separate worlds, whose connection missionaries could be sent out to effect.[31]

Both home missions and foreign missionaries imagined themselves to be penetrating a darker world, and similar ideas about sin and strategies for attacking it prevailed in both contexts.

The RTS, BFBS, and SPCK did much of their work among the laborers and illiterate in the British Isles and provided material support through funds and literature to overseas missions. A spirit of cooperation and common purpose animated these groups, and many of the same people sat on the governing committees of these different organizations. William Wilberforce, Charles Grant, Henry Thorton, John Shore, and others occupied the governing chairs of groups who worked to spread the gospel both at home and abroad.[32] In their minds, the tasks were identical, requiring many of the same efforts and resources: persuasive preaching, accessible literature, available churches, and abundant clergy. With proper organization and sufficient means, they hoped that the gospel would march across the globe, sweeping untold multitudes into its ranks.

Molding British Christians:
Evangelicals and the Laboring Classes

There is no small irony in the fact that Hinduism would play a major role in reversing the decline of British Christianity. By the eighteenth century, institutionalized, Protestant Christianity in Britain had retreated in large measure from engagement with working classes and the poor.[33] The disempowered stayed home on Sundays in great numbers, while churches and chapels filled with those more well-to-do. Attendance at traditional worship had become a middle- and upper-class practice.[34] In so far as religious life requires a certain amount of leisure, this fact about church attendance seems related to the long hours that factories demanded of laborers. Evangelicals were instrumental in the passage of Sabbath laws and in then promoting church and Sunday school attendance among the working classes during the leisure hours they had thus acquired.[35]

This is not to say that the "lower orders" did not exhibit their own forms of religiosity. Much scholarship has focused on the religious beliefs and practices that animated working-class life and has urged us to discard the once-prevailing view that much of laboring England was unconcerned with worship, prayer, or preaching.[36] If some scholars have been blind to the religious life of these classes, they are in good company. Eighteenth-century clergy and upper-class laity mourned the unchurched status they attributed to the poor. Even if Christianity attracted the working poor in the late eighteenth and early nineteenth centuries to fields, temporary chapels, street corners, and private homes to hear the bible read and preached, many clergy at that time lamented the decline of religion among Britain's marginalized.[37] Regardless of the actual state of religious life among the working poor, the general perception among most observers was that Anglican Christianity was irrelevant in the mills and factories.

The anxiety of these observers may have reflected the condition of their own churches. One historian of the period remarks that "in the educated classes the prevailing style of religion tended to become rational, moralistic and cautious; the emotional temperature was low, and the level of commitment required was fairly low too."[38] In the early nineteenth century, Christian leaders and their critics anguished over the absence of poorer folk in the churches and the denominations' failure to attend to their spiritual condition. Most church folk attributed the situation to the church's dereliction of its duty rather than to a disinterest among the poor. Churches castigated themselves and each other for failing to make worship attractive to the less fortunate and for intimidating them with expectations of a certain style of dress and demeanor. One mid-nineteenth-century commentator denounced "the almost total want of sympathy manifested by ministers of religion of every denomination with the privations, wants, and wastes of the working classes."[39] In 1789, the Bishop of Chester learned that many in his diocese did not go to church "for want of decent clothing."[40] A London costermonger confirmed this fear fifty years later when he confessed to Henry Mayhew that the working poor of the city, seeing only well-dressed folk exiting churches on Sunday, "somehow mix up being religious with being respectable," and thus they excused themselves from their religious duty.[41] Mayhew himself wrung his hands: "I am anxious to make others feel, as I do myself, that *we* are the culpable parties in these matters."[42]

The roots of the problem were not just social but also theological. On the one hand, churches served as enclaves for the respectable merely because the formality of worship, dress, and manner alienated those unfamiliar with such practices (see figure 2.1). Consequently, denominations moved to make to make worship more informal and lively, and services were often held outside the churches and chapels in halls and lecture rooms.[43] On the other hand, the doctrine and practice of some denominations discouraged them from proselytizing among the poor. Many dissenting Calvinist bodies, believing church membership to reflect divine election, had little theological motive for evangelization. If God's grace were irresistible, those who were destined to salvation sat already gathered in the visible church. A "stultifying" Calvinist orthodoxy in mid-eighteenth-century dissent believed that active evangelism interfered with divine providence and obscured God's grace.[44] Only competition with an increasingly organized system of Methodist itinerant preaching and a rising evangelical temper began to break the hold that self-sufficient isolationism had held over independent, dissenting bodies.[45]

At the turn of the nineteenth century, many of these Christians in Britain expressed an anxious concern to draw the lower classes into active church membership, a project which would require more than simply dragging factory workers through the door on a Sunday. Evangelical sentiment found the general destitution of laborers to extend not to their spiritual condition alone, but also to their manners, their pastimes, their dress, and their education. Mere attendance at worship would never transform these classes; what was needed was a wholesale reformation of their character. The task of turning thousands of Britain's dirty poor into confessing Anglican Christians would require more

FIGURE 2.1. The Polite Preacher (1796), illustrating the deadened state of
Anglican preaching and the need for an evangelical revival with broad
appeal to the working class. Pitts Theology Library, Emory University,
Atlanta, Ga. RG 020 4/1

than a transformation from within. The evangelization of the poor, therefore,
soon took up both the questions of external demeanor and internal disposition.
More than attendance at worship or confession of faith, the Christianization
of the working classes came to demand an expression of this new identity and
newly acquired knowledge in fresh habits.

The formation of Sunday schools was one means by which denominational
leaders could mold and fashion the previously unchurched into persons they
saw more recognizably "Christian."[46] A belief that salvation was partly an educational issue fed the drive to spread these schools throughout Britain. With-

out a knowledge of the promises delivered in the scriptures, no soul could reach its eternal destiny. In order to give the multitudes access to the scriptural texts, some clergy began to establish schools where illiterate laborers could learn to read on Sunday before or after the worship services. Most of these schools aimed not to provide a general education that would benefit the laborers professionally, but to teach reading alone, for only this skill was necessary to know the gospels.[47]

Preeminently embodying the national concern to reform the manners of lower society through education and evangelization was renowned crusader Hannah More (see figure 2.2). After founding a boarding school for girls with her four sisters in Bristol, More spent most of her adult life producing mor-

FIGURE 2.2. Hannah More (1809), pamphleteer for good manners and Christian virtue among Britain's working poor. Pitts Theology Library, Emory University, Atlanta, Ga. RG 020 3/4

alistic literature targeted at youths, the working classes, and the privileged of the British nation. Her titles formed a significant part of the RTS catalog of cheap tracts, and she was "the first British woman ever to make a fortune with her pen."[48] More was a primary force in the spread of charity schools for the education of the poor. Motivated by a sincere concern for the disadvantaged and an abhorrence of all things radical, her approach to literacy was both theological and practical. She was concerned not only to snatch imperiled souls from the devil's jaws, but also to improve the material lot of her students through a refinement of their habits.[49] Reading the scriptures provided an acquaintance with the religion of salvation as well as a code of social conduct that befitted those who professed such a religion.[50] Membership in the body of Christ was to manifest itself in external demeanor. Just as foreign missionaries were beginning the catechumenate by stripping the native convert of his immodest dress in favor of more dignified western attire,[51] so More busied herself with tuning the bodies of Christian laborers to the requirements of their new faith.[52]

Susan Thorne has regarded evangelism in the early nineteenth century as a means of social control deployed both in Britain and abroad that displayed "a distinctively middle-class alternative to gentry modes of authority."[53] Among dissenters especially, she claims that missionary philanthropy represented a manner of tutoring the disempowered that implicitly protested against upper-class neglect of the "lower orders" at home and against colonial policies that seized native lands and peoples without reparation. She writes, "the politics of missions in their founding phase were implicitly, if not explicitly oppositional, conveying as they did a critique of the political establishment's claims to moral authority."[54] Thorne's class argument does not altogether hold up with regard to Anglican missions and evangelism, which were widely spearheaded by the wealthy and powerful. More herself was sponsored by William Wilberforce, and, as we have seen, the major philanthropic and missionary bodies of the Established Church were initially products of gentry money and ideas.

Furthermore, More addressed herself to all of England, rich and poor. She wanted the rich to abandon their dissolute lives and the poor to learn virtue. Often criticized for her apparent conservatism, More's energetic political activity seemed rather to hearken for social change and religious reformation.[55] Her chief goal, perhaps, was to instill habits of economy in the poor. She promoted frugality as a virtue that would issue forth in material blessing and spiritual maturity. The daily practice of small virtues was a beginning point for the formation of a disciplined Christian character. She preached honesty to the working poor, imploring them to treat customers and employers fairly in the petty transactions that constituted their livelihood. More described the devastating effects of gin and gambling to them, pastimes that robbed the wage earner and vendor of their meager incomes and reduced them to a scavenging existence. In one ballad she composed, an honest coachman boasts about his family:

Though poor, we are honest and very content,
We pay as we go, for meat, drink, and for rent;
To work all the week I am able and willing,
I never get drunk and I waste not a shilling.[56]

Reflecting the new ideas of evangelical and missionary philanthropy that promoted teaching the poor new habits of thrift rather than direct relief, More's description of the material poverty of laborers did not suggest their victimization by a system of economic exchange, but their lack of piety and virtue.

To the poor, More preached that satisfaction with one's lot and discipline with one's earnings were the first steps to a richer Christian life. She aimed less at raising the laborer above her station than at deepening her awareness of the religious character of that station and its ordained place in the divine economy. Although active in the abolition movement, More sometimes seemed to recommend an attitude of deference toward one's superiors even to the enslaved.[57] She taught further that temperance in all matters would manifest itself in outward appearances, both in carriage and in dress.[58] An education in cultured dress and manners would then initiate laborers into a society fundamentally religious in nature whose members included representatives from all economic stations. Participation in this society would necessarily include attendance at public worship, the site at which the various classes could ritually display their underlying identity through the unifying practices of prayer, song, and common dress.[59]

More's story of "Betty Brown, the St. Giles Orange Girl" described this very transformation from vicious resident of the dark alleys to mannered member of an Anglican congregation. An orphan who had survived on the streets by her wits, Betty thought she had found a friend in a moneylender, Mrs. Sponge, who had lent her five shillings to buy produce to sell and then collected a sixpence for its use every evening. Betty naively believed Mrs. Sponge to be her savior and gladly paid her usurious rates. As Sponge required, Betty boarded at her house, taking an expensive room with six other lodgers and drinking the gin Sponge urged her to buy. One day, a Christian woman buying Betty's oranges was struck by her honest face and civil manners. Striking up conversation, she heard the details of Betty's employment and recognized Mrs. Sponge's exploitation. The lady urged Betty neither to drink gin nor eat Sponge's food but to save her own five shillings to pay back the crooked landlady. This, she explained to the girl, would earn her that extra sixpence each day. Although the woman would willingly have given Betty the money herself, she refrained, for she maintained that more good came from instilling habits of economy than outright charity. When Betty had succeeded in saving her sum, Mrs. Sponge tossed her out in a fury. The other woman then set Betty up in her own trade and gave her a new gown and a hat, "on the easy condition that she should go to church." There, Betty heard for the first time that she was a sinner, and she vowed improvement and honesty. The streetwise peddler then promised to be an example to those in her trade and to serve God all week long as well as on Sundays. Although still an orange girl, she was fundamentally transformed and belonged to a new community. Thus, Betty "by industry and piety, rose in the world."[60]

By spreading Sunday schools and reforming the manners of both the poor and the rich, More hoped to instill a unifying Christian character in all classes of Britons. Betty Brown and others like her showed how all classes could live in harmony without threat to existing social hierarchies if joined by religious devotion and ruled by the dictates of their common faith. More held firmly that Christianity was a practical religion that ought to seep into every corner of an individual's life and to infuse the whole person with her religious identity. Christianity was "a transforming as well as a penetrating principle," which affected every deed and thought. Its action was uniform as well, working the same effects on people of every station: "Christianity enjoins the same temper, the same spirit, the same dispositions, on all its real professors."[61] A newly found national religion would produce a new national character, a society of Christians from all manner of living allied by a common profession of faith and exhibiting a common dress and demeanor. By their sheer numbers, the transformation of the lower orders was essential to the success of this project, for just as Betty Brown demonstrated the progress one might achieve through the cultivation of small virtues, so the "lower people" were "numerically, if not individually important." Their participation in a national religious culture was necessary, for "the peace of the individual mind and of the nation is materially affected by the discipline in which these inferior orders are maintained."[62]

One very significant factor motivating upper-class concern for the religious education of laborers was an intense fear of Jacobinism. With the French Revolution raging just across the channel, established interests were just as concerned to prevent an uprising as to save souls or to make workers more socially presentable. Limited education could serve this purpose admirably by providing the poor a stake in the dominant culture against which they might otherwise revolt.[63] Literacy campaigns gave students not only a particular skill, but also a sense that their identity was somehow tied up with the interests of the ruling classes.[64] Instilling in them the religion, manners, and speech shared by the ruling elite could bridge the alienation they might otherwise feel. Not only would proper Christians recognize their spiritual kinship with their co-religionists, they would as well be less inclined to resent their material lot and more inclined to accept their station.[65] Remarked one evangelical in an open letter to Parliament, "the true Christian . . . will never listen to French politics, or to French philosophy."[66] In a dialogue addressed to "all the mechanics, journeymen and labourers in Great Britain," More tried to convince workers of the folly of revolution, urging the working person that the shortest route to social reform was to "mend thyself."[67]

Smiling Hypocrisy?

No one has suffered more abuse on this account than More's patron and friend, William Wilberforce, Member of Parliament from 1780 to 1825 (see figure 2.3). His evangelical zeal on behalf of foreign and domestic "heathen" wished to extend to them not only the Bible but also the upright life that Christian piety and humility would bring. Having experienced conversion on a tour of the continent when he was twenty-six, Wilberforce spent the remainder of his life applying his considerable social and political standing to the reform of English society in both its private and public manners. Wilberforce is best remembered for his tireless fight to abolish the British slave trade. Its final defeat in 1807

FIGURE 2.3. William Wilberforce (1809), Parliament's moral and evangelical crusader. Pitts Theology Library, Emory University, Atlanta, Ga. RG 020 3/3

was considered in many ways his own personal victory. He pushed as well for the expansion of literacy and even battled on principle for the emancipation of Roman Catholics, whom he personally considered little better than the heathen.[68]

Despite his liberal crusades and early radical leanings, Wilberforce became frank in his expressions of hatred for revolutionary politics, and he eagerly supported many of Pitt's repressive measures. In 1815, he voted for the Corn Laws, which maintained high grain prices despite impassioned protests by the poor, and in 1819, voiced approval of the Peterloo Massacre, in which the Liverpool magistrate killed eleven people and wounded four hundred in a crowd gathered to hear speeches demanding the reform of Parliament. Perhaps his most notorious act was the ruin he heaped on an impoverished London family with no radical leanings who had printed Thomas Paine's *Age of Reason* solely to turn a small profit. It would seem that Wilberforce's concern for the poor did not extend to the direct amelioration of their condition. Like many of his generation, he accepted their lot as inevitable or even foreordained and found any attempts to realign the social order that placed them there seditiously evil.

Wilberforce was concerned foremost with the public morality of his nation and believed Britain's establishment on Christian principles ought to dictate both the morality of its people and the character of its foreign policy. He hoped to amend the public amusements and private conduct of his fellow subjects at home. In practice, he was considerably more concerned with the vicious living of the lower classes than with the debauched customs of those more well to do; more occupied with attacking the carnal sins plaguing Britain than the spiritual malaise emptying the churches. Gin, bear baiting, and gambling drew his fire. While his chief literary work urged "Christians in the higher and middle classes"[69] to set an example to the lower classes by practicing a Christianity that was more than nominal, his tactics with respect to the two groups suggest a noteworthy lack of empathy with the poor. He sought among the well to do to "make goodness fashionable"[70] and steered away from "desperate measures" by which he might "injure rather than serve the Cause."[71] On the other hand, he mercilessly prosecuted defenseless perpetrators of petty immoralities such as Sabbath-breaking and the publication of lewd materials. He deliberately targeted minor crimes, arguing that "the most effectual way of preventing the greater crimes is publishing the smaller, and endeavouring to repress that general spirit of licentiousness which is the parent of every species of vice."[72]

Wilberforce planned the launch of his public campaign carefully. In 1787, the man who professed his divine vocation to be "the reformation of [my country's] manners"[73] managed to prod George III into issuing a "Proclamation against Vice and Immorality" that squarely criticized the dissolute habits of the lower orders. Described by the CMS as his "devout but afflicted" majesty,[74] a reference to George's very public bouts of insanity, the king vowed prosecution of all those engaging in "excessive drinking, blasphemy, profane swearing and cursing, lewdness, profanation of the Lord's Day," those producing "loose and licentious prints, books and publications," and any involved with public gambling and unlicensed places of entertainment.[75] Appearing then to jump on the royal bandwagon, Wilberforce formed the Proclamation Society (replaced by the Society for the Suppression of Vice in 1802), which sought to stamp out the vicious practices that degraded the British working poor.[76] At the same time as it attacked dueling and the lottery, the Proclamation Society preached the sanctity of the Sabbath and the duty to employ the leisure time it provided in the service of God.[77] The Proclamation Society was no impotent collection of moralistic gadflies, but an arm of the monarch that prosecuted primarily the poor for immoralities that disturbed "the King's peace, Crown and dignity."[78] Its preoccupation with working-class vice inspired Sydney Smith's satire recommending that the group "should denominate themselves a Society for suppressing the vices of persons whose income does not exceed £500 *per annum.*"[79]

Wilberforce is a complicated historical figure, for he presented two distinct faces: liberal crusader, passionately battling slavery and poverty, and repressive killjoy, bent on legislating public morality. We shall see the same ambiguity in his perception of the Hindu. Indeed, it is difficult for the twentieth-century critic to evaluate his career. Was he "stamped with the marks of [his] times" but forgivable because his legacy was "of supreme significance to the world"[80] or a "smiling hypocrite who not only bound the poor man with the chains of discriminatory laws but tried to make him grateful for them as well"?[81]

Assessing the motives and evaluating the character of the long-deceased are always delicate matters.[82] We can make some sense of Wilberforce's apparent hypocrisy when we see that it emerged from a profound conflict between his passion for aiding the disadvantaged and his abhorrence of values and habits that deviated from gentle Christian society. He found this privileged class to possess the moral constitution and refined manners that would provide Britain a national character model. Industry, frugality, and respect for national institutions and political traditions were, to his way of thinking, both social and religious duties. He imagined that external conformity would produce and reflect an internal acquiescence to social and political norms. Wilberforce's campaigns on behalf of the laboring poor of Britain involved efforts to cultivate a national religious identity that demanded not just assent to certain doctrines and submission to particular authorities, but the adoption of distinctive dress and manners. Like More, his evangelical zeal focused not just on the transformation of the laborers' hearts or the consent of their understanding, but also on the conformity of their bodies. A Christian nation would reflect its faith in the attitude of its visible form. As did foreign missionaries abroad, these Christian crusaders in Britain often took the imposition of "modest dress" to be a first step the in the evangelical and pedagogical process, a brand of social control John and Jean Comaroff have called "civilizing colonialism." The missionary effort at home took not only literacy as its task, but the education of the body as well.[83] The possession of religious truth, these teachers believed, would manifest itself in one's external manner.[84] Failure to conform to expected norms of appearance, behavior, and even speech would evince a merely superficial conformity to the revealed ways of Christianity. Were the transformation complete and the religious identity fully internalized, one's habits and one's carriage would naturally and easily follow.

I do not wish to puzzle here about the apparent hypocrisy or divided loyalties of those upper-class evangelicals who preached forbearance and love on the one hand and ferociously castigated the heathen—domestic and foreign—on the other. What I am after, however, is more along the lines of a non-polemical examination of the process Gerald Larson has termed "religionization," which he describes as "the manner in which 'religion' and the 'religious dimension' develops and changes over time."[85] Such an approach recognizes the important contributions of other theorizing, but attempts to point out what many other approaches miss, namely, "the high salience of religious experience, not simply in terms of its manifestation in historical, social, economic and political contexts, but also in terms of its substantive content, that is, its basic intellectual and spiritual claims."[86] In the current deconstructionist and postcolonial milieu, it is easy to overlook the coherence and integrity of the religious convictions of evangelical missionaries, whether or not they were complicit in the colonization of minds and bodies. What is at stake, I believe, is whether we are willing to grant elites what some postcolonial historians have begun to accept with respect to subaltern classes, namely, that religious cosmologies, ontologies, and epistemologies are themselves causal agents in historical transformations, and that reducing them to oppressive superstructures obscures rather than clarifies their role in human history.

When it comes to the question of how scholars judge those who claim to speak legitimately or authoritatively for a tradition, Brian K. Smith has recently made a similar point more bluntly: "This query," he writes, "seems to me to be one that we in our guise as secular scholars of religion have no right to address."[87] He appears to recommend that the academic study of religion avoid entanglement with issues arising from within religious traditions. In this case, I take his advice to mean that it is not our place to declare whether William Wilberforce's actions were in conflict with his convictions, whether, that is, he was a hypocrite. Although I may not hold to Smith's restrictive understanding of public scholarship, I am concerned to highlight those religious dimensions of missionary experience often overlooked or dismissed in postcolonial historiography, experience which, I agree with Smith, it is not the scholar's place to second guess. If social reformers like Wilberforce had investments in a particular set of social arrangements at home that blinded them to the possibility of a more equitable distribution of the wealth that was largely concentrated in their hands, it is essential also to recognize that this particular set of social arrangements possessed a sacred significance for them. Rightly maintained, an abhorrence of their coercion would also recognize that the vision that inspired them was more than a convenient justification for their privilege. It drew its power also from the belief in a sacred cosmos so ordained. I will urge equal caution with respect to British representation of the Hindu. Here it will be sufficient to remark that to take the religious claims and worldviews of historical subjects seriously need not mean we naively forget that religious maxims may be easily manipulated to serve vested interests. We can, however, remain truer to the experience of social reformers and missionaries if we avoid the opposite error of reducing Christian discourse about cultural and religious otherness to political terms alone. If this discourse appears at the confluence of power and knowledge, we must remember that the categorical structure of the knowledge that the social reformers and missionaries deployed reproduced cosmological schemes that they were unable or unwilling to critique. A more "enlightened" view may cite their base motives and strategies, but to miss the passion aroused by an imagined cosmic economy that channeled countless individual souls to regions of eternal torment, and to miss the significance of such practices as the regulation of language, dress, and sexual conduct for evangelical understanding of individual fates, is to examine the actions of Christian subjects solely by factors other than those that framed their most deeply felt convictions and motivations. The task all along for Wilberforce and others we shall meet was to transform the British quarters of the globe and establish in and among them a community that, in its exhibition of a public morality, reflected Christian intuition about the end and meaning of the universal order. Formed according to that morality, its members would possess a common identity despite their distribution across various economic classes and ethnic lines—a cosmic principle made manifest. Faced at home with a populace threatening revolt and alienated from the ruling class by virtue of religion and material culture, social reform and missionary evangelism promoted the adoption of a religious identity that both underscored a common national character and reflected a divine ordering in which that nation played a critical role.

Too Established, Too Churched: The Church Missionary Society and the Hierarchy

The character of the identity that Wilberforce and his associates wished to instill in the laboring class took shape from their particular denominational standing. However global their aspirations, these men remained committed to an Anglican ideal.[88] Much of the impetus for this campaign came from an informal association of moderate Anglican Evangelicals in the London suburb of Clapham. Members of the "Clapham Sect" shared an elevated social standing, connections with the ruling forces of government, and a concern to bring the Christian gospel to all people in Britain and abroad.[89] This group sought ways of directing public policy along channels that would extend the reach of Christian institutions and ideas. Among their numbers were members of Parliament; prominent clergy, and government officials, including men with strong connections to India, like the chairman of the Court of Directors of the East India Company, Charles Grant, and a former governor-general of India, John Shore, later Lord Teignmouth. Although various forms of Dissent helped stoke evangelical embers nationally, these men remained firmly committed to the Established Church.[90] They shared very many beliefs with their fellow evangelicals in other denominations, a fact that permitted unprecedented cooperation among these various bodies and mission societies,[91] but their allegiance to the Anglican Church lent their crusade a particularly national character. Their ambitions to evangelize the colonies and incite widespread religious reform at home relied on more than the Holy Spirit: where possible, they invoked legislative and royal muscle. They fought, for example, for parliamentary funds to build hundreds of new national churches in areas without them.[92] The same strategy is evident in their missionary aspirations. Whereas Dissenters like William Carey emphasized the duty of all Christians to assist in the dismantling of heathenism by prayer and alms, those in the Clapham Sect were more likely to recommend legislative action at home and abroad and to underscore the responsibility of British ruling authorities to effect change.

A comparison of the evangelical careers of Grant and Carey is instructive. A powerful administrator in the East India Company, Grant was responsible for laying much of the groundwork for the spread of missions in India. He secured the appointment of such evangelically minded chaplains for the British residents of India as David Corrie, Henry Martyn, and Claudius Buchanan. In 1787, he started his own short-lived private mission in Goamalti, India, near Malda. Five years later he produced a closely argued pamphlet that urged the British civil and ecclesiastical powers to begin organized construction and staffing of missions in India in order to lift its peoples out of the misery to which their religion had condemned them. Carey had titled his famous plea "An Enquiry into the Obligation of Christians to Use Means for the Conversion of the Heathen," and Grant's piece, written in the same year (1792) and proposing the same end—the evangelization of the "heathen"—was called "Observations on the State of Society among the Asiatic Subjects of Great Britain."[93] Carey looked forward to the moment when the East India Company Charter might permit committed and spiritually motivated individuals into the subcontinent, wheras Grant pressed for "measures which might be adopted by Great Britain for the improvement in the condition of Asiatic Subjects."[94] The Baptist preacher stressed the power of spiritual commitment, the Anglican administrator the power of the government and the established church.

The campaign for a reinvigorated, unified, and evangelical national church can be seen against the backdrop of the invention of Great Britain as a nation and of British patriotism as the cement that held together people otherwise separated by class, language, dress, history, and gender. Linda Colley has described the development of this sense of national identity and values as a product of numerous foreign wars, and above all, of religious sentiment. A "common investment in Protestantism" helped Scots, Welsh, English, and a few Irish of all classes and both genders to discover some binding identity over against France, the "haunting embodiment of the Catholic Other" and Great Britain's perennial enemy.[95] Britishness became a important preoccupation of the people, and for the Clapham Sect and others, this Britishness necessarily implied an association with the national church, however much they desired the transformation of that institution.

So while they relied on the power of their government and its church, these Anglican Christians often had a difficult relationship with them. In its early years, and during the entire period covered by this study, the relationship of the CMS to the established church was troubled for various reasons, political, ecclesiastical, and theological. The greatest obstacle to broad Anglican acceptance of the CMS was its association with the evangelical revival then underway in Britain. This revival's courting of the poor, its emotionalism, and its pandenominational character all met both official and popular opposition. Much of the Society's public statements and its construction of Hinduism must be viewed in the light of its campaign to achieve legitimacy in the eyes of the church hierarchy. This issue was a matter not just of attaining institutional recognition, but also of bringing the evangelical revival to bear on the institutional life of the church. At stake was the maintenance of a particular set of traditions over against the sweeping clerical and ritual reforms that Anglican evangelicals desired.

The CMS emerged out of weekly discussions held by the Clapham Sect beginning in 1783 to probe possibilities for institutional and spiritual reform in the established church. On 18 March 1799, John Venn had posed the question: "What methods can we use more effectually to promote the knowledge of the Gospel among the Heathen?"[96] The group landed on a threefold solution: they resolved to establish a body that would emulate the organizational structure of the primitive church, to choose missionaries whose sole motivations were spiritual, not "worldly," and to begin on a small scale like the first Christians. Above all, this body was to be established on "the Church-principle, but not the high Church-principle."[97] All wealthy, committed Anglicans, the founders of the CMS sought to distance themselves from the more formal features of the institutional life of the church.[98] They were searching for ways in which they might effect some alteration in organization and administration of the body and in the primary theological commitments of clergy and laity alike.

Out of this meeting, the "Missionary Society for Africa and the East" was officially formed on 12 April 1799. When it began to call itself the "Church Missionary Society" in 1812, certain members of the hierarchy heaped scorn and wrath upon the infant body for presuming to represent the national church. From the beginning, its founders intended the CMS to be a voluntary society of men and women who were also members of the established Church of England. Its aim was to find Anglican clergy willing to serve abroad as missionaries and at the same time to lobby for the support of the institutional hierarchy. At no time did its organizers claim to represent the church per se, but only to be concerned members who found its active participation in evangelization of indigenous peoples of the British colonies to be a direct scriptural injunction.[99] Their goal was precisely to pressure the Anglican church to devise institutional means for enacting Jesus' Great Commission to "go into all the world and preach the gospel to the whole creation" (Mark 16:15).

It was the CMS's overt evangelical stance and its open cooperation with Dissenting churches that raised the suspicion of the Anglican hierarchy. Given its willingness to cross denominational borders, many members of the clergy wondered what exactly was "churched" about the Church Missionary Society. In 1817, a vigorous public debate broke out in Bath over this very question and marked a crisis point in the CMS's national campaign. In the end, the rash action of one archdeacon and the sectarian spirit displayed by Anglican opponents of the CMS gained for the young body an important moral victory.

The controversy stemmed directly from the CMS's linkage of the British working classes with the conquered heathen subjects of the British colonies. In order to sink firm roots and stir up popular support, the governors of the CMS had worked out a strategy that relied on auxiliary societies, founded at the local level, that would permit lay participation in the evangelization of the heathen. It hoped this national network would build a broad base of financial aid to missions and help awaken popular interest in bringing Christianity to those peoples under British rule. By offering all members of the church a role in this effort, the CMS was able to build a strong organization out of the occasional exercise of interest on the part of those who attended these local meetings or concerned themselves with the heathen as a sort of hobby.[100] To spark interest, the CMS capitalized on the popularity of the public meeting or lecture, which many in nineteenth-century English society attended as a regular evening pastime. In general, these meetings promised the middle and working classes informative entertainment, often tinged with controversy and public spectacle.[101] The CMS would normally form a local organization by first advertising such a public meeting, chaired by a local nobleman or gentleman sympathetic to the Society's goals.[102] A recognized name ensured the CMS good attendance and a respectful reception, and its reputation as an evangelical body and the lurid nature of its presentation of the heathen kindled a voyeuristic hope for scandal.[103]

In Bath, such a meeting, chaired by the Lord Bishop of Gloucester, was called for the first of December 1817. The bishop was one of the vice-patrons of the CMS, but he had no jurisdiction in the area of Bath and Bristol, whose presiding bishop had very politely turned down the initial invitation to chair the meeting.[104] When two local clergy affiliated with the CMS received a similarly polite refusal from the archdeacon, Rev. Josiah Thomas, they invited the bishop of Gloucester.

When the day arrived and the secretary of the local organization rose to introduce the purpose and aims of the meeting, Archdeacon Thomas stood and asserted his authority over the meeting as the highest ranking cleric of the district. He then proceeded to denounce the character of the CMS and its supposed usurpation of Anglican ecclesiastical authority. His primary objections were three: first, that the Society for the Propagation of the Bible in Foreign Parts had already been established in the church to achieve the same ends as the CMS, which was therefore encroaching on the jurisdiction of an arm of the church. He protested, second, that the CMS's solicitation of pennies from widows, servants, and schoolboys was unworthy of a society associated with the Church of England. Finally, he attacked the CMS on the grounds that its sympathy with a "new sect" in the church, calling itself "serious Christians" or "Evangelical Ministers" tended toward the subversion of church authority by appealing to theological claims made by evangelicals in other denominations and by openly cooperating with these other denominations in promoting missionary expansion. He insisted, to the befuddlement of his audience, that

Anglican affiliation with dissenters would promote religious feud in Britain. Following his furious protest, Thomas stormed out of the hall, refusing to hear any reply to his objections. The crowd, which had endured his tirade on the threat that he would call in the magistrate and have the meeting forcibly disbanded, apparently carried on with the scheduled presentation.[105]

What infuriated Thomas most was the evangelical inspiration that drove the CMS. Contemporary accounts characterized his arguments about church authority and religious strife as patently absurd, his tone as shrill, and his behavior as altogether unbecoming of one in his office. Although he insisted that he held proselytism among the heathen to be a central and holy Christian duty, and he praised the SPG for its role in that effort,[106] Thomas nonetheless found fault with the CMS, whose aims were precisely the same.

Following his disruption of the meeting, Thomas published his address and immediately spawned a small industry in counterprotests. Among the more memorable was the satirical *Second Protest Against the CMS*, which appeared shortly after Thomas's. Invoking popular British ideas about Hinduism, the author ironically attacked the CMS

> as having a decided tendency to annihilate the very politic and saga-
> cious practice of burning those widows whose tears for their hus-
> bands are not sufficient to extinguish the flames; and of devoutly
> roasting children for the humane gratification of their gods; of mer-
> cifully choking a troublesome relation in the mud of the Ganges; of
> dutifully dissecting and swallowing piece-meal a diseased parent; of
> drowning vociferous or deformed babies.[107]

These charges, referring to actual or imagined Indian practices, indicate the centrality of India in the missionary strategy to incite public outrage and mobilize public support. Other members of the CMS and unaffiliated laypeople responded in print more seriously, lauding the society for promoting biblical Christianity abroad and for supplementing, rather than usurping, the work of the SPG.[108] One respondent chided Thomas for finding the collection of insignificant sums to be degrading, pointing to Jesus' acceptance of the widow's mite.[109] Another demonstrated Thomas had no authority on civil or ecclesiastical grounds to disrupt or disband the meeting.[110] While the CMS annual report for 1818–19 noted the "opposition" that it had faced that year, the controversy turned out to be a tremendous public relations boon for the Society.[111] The report expressed its thanks for the "great increase of interest and feeling in its behalf."[112] Josiah Pratt "rejoiced" in the conflict, which swelled the CMS coffers and generated both a five-thousand pound grant from the SPG and SPCK to the new bishop in Calcutta for local missions and a royal edict commanding congregational collections on behalf of missions to India.[113]

The aim, then, of those supporters of foreign missions who so infuriated some leaders of the clergy was more than the spiritual and moral improvement of distant peoples conquered by their armies. What they asked of the church was not just the delivery of missionaries and scriptures overseas, but also an entire shift in the national orientation to established religion. They hoped to inspire the church to be more actively concerned with the diffusion and animation of the Christian faith both abroad and at home; one invested, that is, in the transformation not only of heathen souls but also of British religious life. Concerned with the defection of poorer Britons to those Dissenting bodies more actively involved in domestic evangelization, one clergyman, speaking on behalf of a National Society for the Education of the Poor in the Principles of the Established Church, saw eternal and temporal benefits to broadening Anglicanism's appeal, hoping that the promotion of a "national doctrine and discipline" among the poor would "be the best means for preparing them for the Kingdom of Heaven," and for making them "more fit for their stations in the world."[114] The CMS was discovering that a campaign against an imagined heathen religion could serve that purpose admirably.

Domestically, the Church Missionary Society believed it was promoting the interests of the church and the nation, even if certain of its leaders were blind to those interests. By publicizing its work to eradicate paganism among all classes and engaging volunteers in its efforts, it hoped both to gain new adherents and to bind existing members more closely to the church. In its eighteenth annual report, the governing committee identified itself as "members of the Established Church . . . ardently longing for the increase of her real strength and glory"; it congratulated itself for "awakening the zeal of Churchmen to the Cause of Missions" and thereby "attaching to her, more strongly than ever, the affections of her members."[115] In promoting the salvation of the world in this way, these evangelical leaders of the Society felt assured they were combating the "mournful deadness" that had plagued eighteenth-century British Christianity.[116] Evangelization was also a matter of honor to these Anglicans. Other denominations had already formed missionary societies and sent missionaries abroad. Their tales of struggle and occasional success were then reaching British reading audiences. The CMS was unwilling to let the church hierarchy sit by and allow Dissenters to claim credit for bringing the gospel to foreign lands that lay squarely within the political and ecclesiastical reach of the British government. The CMS saw that Dissenting missionary bodies and their "reflections on heathenism were deployed in ways that undermined the Anglican establishment's moral credibility."[117] Commercial and military agents of the Crown were already established in so many foreign places that it seemed a dereliction of Christian duty not to extend the material and spiritual benefits of Britain to the heathen as well.[118] Already famous in Britain, William Carey began work for the Baptist Missionary Society in 1793, but missionaries were outlawed in British India at that time, and he actually had to avoid British territory in India in order to preach. When other Christian bodies were extending a hand to the naked and the damned, and even the Roman Catholic Church could claim "the glory of the zeal for the propagation of the Gospel among the Heathen," the CMS saw the need for some far-reaching transformation in the Church of England. The pressing issue for these evangelicals was how to "redeem the character of our Church from the opprobrium of neglect."[119] Images of the pagan, both descriptive and visual, would provide strong encouragement to that redemption.

The Church Missionary Society and Public Performance

In its efforts to enliven the British church from within, while simultaneously casting abroad for souls, the CMS pursued several avenues for generating public interest both in its own activities and in the condition of the "pagans" who populated British colonies. As many of its early members were clergy, sermons were one vehicle by which the CMS spread word about the society. Advertised in advance, and preached often before large audiences, sermons extolling the need for missions frequently found their way into print as a tracts, which were in turn circulated on a much wider scale.[120] These addresses cited a variety of reasons for supporting the CMS, a successful strategy for procuring charitable donations Donna Andrew describes as a "multimotive" approach.[121] The same structure and phrasing regularly recur in different sermons, indicating that the society may have provided source materials and outlines to local clergy.

A quite typical example of this genre was Rev. Josiah Allport's *Sermon Preached at Coleford on July 18, 1813, in Aid of the Church Missionary Society*. He began his oration by invoking the bifurcation of the human race: millions of "idolaters" and "Mahomedans," "lying in wickedness," "dead in sin," and "ready to perish," labored under ignorance and darkness abroad, in "countries containing seven or eight hundred millions of people." The eschatological and geographical estrangement of Britons and Indians, however, was only part of the story. Allport noted that many of these unredeemed souls were "fellow-subjects" of the congregation, living in lands under the political or military control of Great Britain who could therefore lead them into a global Christian community. This was the central paradox of the missionary cosmology: absolute Other partook in common human history and nature. Underscoring the loyalty of the audience and the foreigner to the same monarch, he emphasized their common temporal destiny and held out hope for their common eternal destiny as well. He asked for donations for the CMS, pleading with the people to redeem "the honour of your country, so intimately connected with these wretches, and deriving abundant wealth from them."[122] Among them were numbers passing into death every day, unaware of the promises of Christ. The highlight of his address, however, was the detailed description of rites characterized as absurd and cruel, taken from recent missionary intelligence.[123] India figured prominently in this regard, with Rajput infanticide and human sacrifice at Jagannath's temple illustrating his point.[124] Finally, he offered a firm reminder of Jesus' command to make disciples of all nations and of the responsibility of the Anglican Church to seek the salvation of all souls. He recalled to the congregation the blessings their nation brought them, blessings made possible only because at some earlier date, missionaries had come to the British islands from other nations, and he admonished those present to pass on this mercy and bring "deliverance to the captives who have not yet heard of the life and immortality brought to light by the Gospel."[125]

Public meetings and special services such as this one helped the society establish local affiliates through which it could maintain interest and to which

it could delegate the responsibility for collecting funds. CMS committee members often traveled to towns and villages to arrange and address such meetings.
In a single calendar year (1820–21), Edward Bickersteth, then Assistant Secretary to the Committee, later infamous among many Anglicans for his sudden
conversion to an apocalyptic theology and virulent anti-Catholicism,[126] attended
fifty-three public gatherings from Edinburgh to the Channel Islands and Corn-
wall to officiate at anniversary and founding celebrations. His grueling pace,
although tremendously profitable to the Society's ends, was achieved, a report
noted, only at "no little sacrifice of domestic comfort."[127]

The extensive delegation of responsibility and authority to local auxiliary
societies and even to individuals was responsible for much of the early success
of the CMS. Content to provide the inspiration and the tools, the Committee
trusted in the spiritual motivation and energy of its local affiliates, allowing
them to pursue their interest in the conversion of foreign souls independent
of London's direct oversight.[128] This institutional structure represents an early
example of a voluntarism within an ecclesiastical body for the formation of a
moral community with specific social goals—an advance toward the alleviation
of poverty that the eighteenth century had addressed almost exclusively
through philanthropy.[129] This hands-off approach enacted Pratt's dictum that
the Society abide by "the church principle, but not the high church principle."
Its refusal to centralize its organization too tightly gave rein to its affiliates to
adjust their aspirations and activity to local circumstances. By tapping the enthusiasm of volunteers, the CMS attempted to maximize a feeling of identification with and participation in its efforts. Once established, these local aux-
iliaries were free to collect funds, conduct meetings, solicit membership, and
distribute information about the CMS and its projects within the bylaws of the
parent society. Typically, the Committee was unconcerned with the particular
form or membership of those local groups who used its name, provided they
"call[ed] forth the zeal of well-disposed Persons," sought individuals to volun-
teer as missionaries, distributed information, aided in the further establishment of branch associations, and procured collections.[130]

The *Missionary Papers'* Construction of Paganism

The single most important factor in the early success of the CMS was its
publication and distribution of literature featuring missionaries and their direct
confrontation with paganism. The CMS displayed a noteworthy resourceful-
ness and perspicacity in its use of the press at home. In general, it steered wide
from the controversialist tactics that drove so much of the nineteenth-century
press. It was uninterested in generating support by promoting domestic strife.
Where necessary, the Society defended itself against the occasional attack, but
the tone of these responses was generally restrained and respectful. It seems
no one affiliated with the CMS took issue in print with the tactics or theology
of any other Protestant missionary body. If it avoided domestic controversy,
however, the CMS did, nonetheless, find the sensationalist press useful to its

purposes in one respect. In 1816, it began publishing a now largely lost news-letter, known in its internal documents as the *Quarterly Papers* but published under the title *Missionary Papers for the Use of Weekly and Monthly Contributors to the Church Missionary Society.*[131] In these papers, the CMS found ways to attract hundreds of thousands of readers to its cause and to engage them in the evangelization of the "heathen." Its lurid picture of heathen life and the pious battle that its missionaries waged began to draw a wide readership and to attract many small contributions for the amelioration of the spiritual and material conditions the paper detailed.

The Society provided the paper free to those who donated a penny a week or more. Distribution and collection took place through local affiliates. Inde-pendent collectors who had taken the task upon themselves to solicit funds for missions funneled these monies to the Society in London. In return, the So-ciety supplied them with copies of the *Missionary Papers* to distribute to con-tributors. The *Missionary Papers* urged readers to assume the responsibility of asking money from employers, schoolmates, friends, and relatives. Just as those who gave a penny a week were rewarded with the *Missionary Papers*, so those who could collect a shilling per week from others received full member-ship in the Society, a privilege which would cost any other individual a guinea annually, and a subscription to the *Missionary Register*, a detailed newsletter describing the activity of all British missionary groups. By this means, the task of collecting funds was passed down through various networks of local organ-izations and independent concerned parties, and at the same time, the papers generated further interest in the plight of the heathen and inspired others to take up the work of collecting money. This democratic and populist approach to charity differed from the more hierarchical measures of the Church of En-gland in two ways that mark the rise of "self-help" over "relief" as a model for charity in the late eighteenth century. First, it appealed for contributions from those usually considered potential recipients of charity. Second, it worked at a grassroots level rather than through established charitable bodies.[132]

The layout of the paper remained consistent and familiar from quarter to quarter and reflected recent dramatic rises in the stamp tax on newspapers, which impacted the layout and publication schedule of papers across the coun-try. In order to halt the spread of radicalism, Parliament had enacted increas-ingly burdensome laws in 1797, 1815, and 1819 that effectively priced news-papers out of the reach of the poor. Single-sheet newspapers and those that published less than once every twenty-six days escaped most taxation. These laws had the effect of increasing the appetite for cheap reading material among the poor.[133] Aiming at the very audience targeted by Parliament, the *Missionary Papers* consisted of a single sheet, folded to make a four-page pamphlet. Its cover bore a wood-cut engraving below the masthead that provided the subject matter for that particular issue and served to educate the reader in some aspect of religion and society in the territories the CMS coveted as mission fields. In general, the illustration depicted an act invariably presented as some dark pa-gan rite, or—when there was good news to report—Christian schools and churches on the edge of the jungle or the smiling face of some native convert in a waistcoat. Its captivating illustrations and the accounts that accompanied them aimed either to shock the readers into action or to excite them with the imminent triumph of Christianity in the colonies.

An explanation accompanied the engraving, describing the rite pictured and attempting some indigenous rationale to shed light on the logic of the practice in question. The style was simple. Short, clear sentences peppered with rhetorical questions addressed the reader directly in a conversational tone. The rhetoric alternated between pity and ridicule. The heathen were, on the one hand, objects of compassion and prayer, but on the other, targets of derision and mockery. The authors rebuked the heathen for their alliance with Satan, their worship of "the God of this world," and their perversion of reason and devotion, but the writers also anguished at their poverty of spirit, their lack of education, and their ignorance of the gospel. Below the crude figures of some Hindu images, one author asked incredulously, "What? Are these monstrous and ridiculous figures the gods of the Heathen?" but then urged the reader to remember "these millions of your poor fellow-subjects" in evening prayers.[134]

The paper also brought its readers accounts of life in the missionary field that detailed the harsh physical conditions these "soldiers for Christ" endured and the apparent spiritual darkness they confronted. Readers were thrilled with stories of narrow escape from jungle serpents and travel by dog sled across hundreds of miles of frozen landscape.[135] Even more gripping were likely the pained accounts depicting missionaries witnessing the cruelties of pagan superstition firsthand, helpless, without the readers' financial assistance, to offer Christian alternatives. On these matters, *The Papers* frequently quoted William Ward, a Baptist missionary with William Carey at Serampore. His rendering of a festival in honor of the Hindu goddess Kali was filled with gory details of devotees piercing their bodies and tongues with metal rods and dancing indecently through the city.[136] The papers portrayed missionary life through the details of exotic encounter that would call forth the readers' desire to spread British religion and civilization.

After the engraving and its description, each issue also presented portraits of individual Christians working at home for the improvement of foreign souls. It often told the tale of a poor British soul, a widow or perhaps a schoolchild who made some concrete sacrifice to collect her penny for the redemption of pagans abroad. Many were said to go without a candle for one night or to sacrifice their scant pocket money. One pastor said of the poorest woman in his parish, "though tea was her only beverage, and often her only meal, she has, for some months, deprived herself of sugar, in order to contribute her penny, which she does with great regularity every week."[137] Finally, each issue closed with an exhortation to work on behalf of the evangelization of the heathen in whatever means possible—by contributing or collecting money, distributing information, forming local associations, or simply through prayer.

In devising this paper, the Committee "displayed a high degree of audience consciousness,"[138] and they had projected concrete goals for the publication of the paper. Indeed, when Rev. Thomas had castigated the infant Bath society for stooping to collect pennies from widows and schoolchildren, he had flung a barb close to its heart. The brash tone and juvenile style of the journal aimed directly at an unsophisticated audience, as did its appeals for the tiny amounts, which would build a powerful missionary empire. In its description of its collection strategy, the Society openly confessed that its quarterly papers were to "consist of a few pages of striking Facts and Anecdotes; with Addresses and Exhortations, adapted to the level of the Labouring Classes and the Young."[139] Their audience were to be those who had traditionally stood on the margins of Anglican church life. The method of diffusing collections along a pyramidal structure enabled them to reach a large number of people whom weekly sermons might not have found.

Paganism and Pedagogy

It is possible to conclude a cynical motive here, as Rev. Thomas himself had: the CMS shamelessly exploited a naive audience as an untapped financial resource. Although the contributions may have been small, the large numbers that its system of collection tapped would yield a sizeable sum. But one might see in its solicitation among the poorer classes not simply entrepreneurial calculation, but a larger strategy fully consistent with an evangelical desire to broaden the appeal and reach of the church. The CMS saw the pennies that its readers contributed not as mere fractions of the pounds to which they would amount, but as a means through which otherwise ignored Anglican subjects could assume an active role in the life of the church. This literature openly promoted evangelization of non-Christians abroad, but its covert aim was a parallel Christianization of British subjects excluded from church life. The Committee observed that

> this system of engaging, according to their power, the Labouring Orders and the Young in this work of charity, has a direct and important influence on the real strength and honour of that Church of which we are Members. Facts are multiplying daily, which demonstrate the growing attachment of those persons to the Church, whose minds are interested in the great objects of the Society, and who are themselves associated in its charitable labours.[140]

The Society openly acknowledged its readership and its hopes for them. A headline proclaiming the "Charity of Labouring People and Children" confessed that some thought it wrong to take money from poor workers, but the Society was sure that those "who truly love their Lord and the souls of the Heathen, will never withhold their offerings when they can spare."[141] The CMS regarded these two particular groups—"the Labouring Orders and the Young"—as requiring a spiritual pedagogy that would acquaint them with the general principles of evangelical religion and apply them to their own condition. One minister wrote that the campaign to aid the missionaries in his parish had sparked a "revival of religious feelings" among confessed Christians, but more remarkably, that the stories of the conversion of some heathen "had led many to inquire into the state of their own hearts, and earnestly to seek their own salvation."[142]

One further effect of such publication and organizational practices was the laborer's clearer sense of his identification with Britain and its national character, and his difference from the pagan Other. In direct addresses, this newspaper called on the worker to serve his nation by taking up the cause of the unconverted heathen. It invoked an implicit spiritual and cultural hierarchy that exalted the British laborer over an undifferentiated, composite Pagan Other. Underscoring the non-European's troubling religion and geography, the CMS identified for the laborer an underclass that elevated his own status. Often the epitome of the dissolute and downtrodden in other nineteenth-century literature, alongside the Hindu, the domestic poor in missionary literature experienced an upward displacement and redemption. Having now been made a partner to Britain's civilizing mission and the Anglican Church's evangelization of the colonies, the laborer became a more stable force in British society and more firmly invested in what the government and church took to be national aims.[143] This literature competed directly with the illegal, unstamped radical papers intended for the same laborer and urging rebellion, and it served, therefore, to combat the spread of discontent and revolution, especially after the Peterloo Massacre of 1819.[144]

The various sections of the *Missionary Papers* worked together to create a unified impression of the state of the heathen, the duty of the British Christian, and the place of these previously disenfranchised Anglicans in the church. The paper promoted a national religious awakening by illustrating the evil and folly of human religious innovations in the absence of Christian revelation. Its characterizations of foreign religious practices not only conveyed information recently uncovered by missionaries abroad, but they also provided the CMS a forum for describing the nature of Christian piety for the uninitiated. Simple juxtaposition made the point effectively: Where Hindus were carnal and cruel, Christians were spiritual and compassionate; where they practiced avarice and deceit, Christians showed generosity and honesty; where they were irrational and undisciplined, Christians were scientific and composed. Hindus (quickly the exemplary heathen), for example, let crowds of poor pilgrims die along the roads and outside the temples, and they casually threw coins on the bodies of those who had sacrificed themselves to the gods. Claudius Buchanan described two children crouched at the dead body of their mother, surrounded by dogs, jackals, and indifferent pilgrims. Asked about their home, they replied they had no home except with their mother. "Oh," he mourned, "there is no pity . . . no mercy, no tenderness of heart, in Moloch's kingdom."[145] This demonic Biblical imagery portrayed the Hindu as the quintessential pagan Other, allied with the arch-idolaters of Old Testament Canaan. The image of the pagan served not just as the symbol for a body of British knowledge of the other, but also as a device for the transmission of a certain brand of Christian identity that would stand in contrast to this imputed pagan character and to the character laborers were then held to exhibit. In disclosing the savage condition to the working poor, the papers could establish a context for conveying the religious lessons that were germane to both and for promoting the institutional and theological transformation of Anglicanism.

The heathen served, however, not just as a negative example, for no one feared that British laborers and children were moved to commit human sacrifice (or become Hindus), but also as a vehicle for introducing elementary theological concepts to novice Christians. In the second issue, for example, an Indian "Fakeer" appeared seated on a leopard-skin cloth, holding his arms permanently crossed above his head until his limbs had become withered and useless in order to accumulate merit with his gods in heaven. To those who mistakenly believed that these men practiced these austerities in order to cleanse themselves of sin, the paper insisted that "very few of these deluded men have any idea of their being sinners" but do these things simply to gratify their pride. Only a few have an inkling that they might be polluted by sin, and these rejoice to hear the gospel and the words "the blood of Jesus Christ cleanseth from all sin."[146] Through this illustration of a Hindu practice, the authors gently commended to their readers central tenets of evangelical Christianity: the necessity of their own conviction of their sinfulness and their acceptance of the all-sufficient sacrifice made by Christ on their behalf.

Similarly, the keeping of the Sabbath was an important issue for many evangelical preachers of the early nineteenth century. Slack attendance at worship, a general disregard for the service among those who did attend, and a belief that most laborers spent this holy day in sloth, drink, or gaming became the subjects of public discussion.[147] In the third issue of the *Missionary Papers,* its authors drove home the necessity of honoring the seventh day through an account of the first Sabbath kept in New Zealand by a chief eager to have the missionaries introduce their new religion to the islanders.[148] Having built a pulpit and makeshift pews the day before, the chief assembled his people for Sunday services: "a very solemn silence prevailed—the sight was truly impressive." The members of the congregation were mystified by the new teachings, but eager to penetrate their meaning. The author praised their demeanor and discipline. The message, no doubt, was not lost on the laborers who read of this back in Britain.[149]

Alongside these quiet lessons about Christian piety ran more overt representations and pleas. Each issue shared the story of some charitable person in Britain who had furthered the cause of missions through his or her small witness or contribution. The subjects of these stories invariably reflected the target reading audience. Widows, laborers, and most poignantly, school children displayed their faith in the Anglican Church and their concern to extend its dominion over the poor and ignorant heathen. These tales conveyed simple lessons about piety by presenting models of Christian conduct clad in the everyday life and speech of the readers. Some issues specifically addressed "Christian Fathers," "Mothers," "Children," or "Servants." In its second year, for example, the *Missionary Papers* printed a letter from a maidservant who had collected eleven pounds for a fund to build a ship to carry missionaries to and from their destinations. She identified with the church's missionary representatives, who, like her, were far from home serving others. The editors praised her devotion and urged other servants, in the words of Jesus, "Go thou, and do likewise."[150] This kind of encouragement offered to the working poor not only provided them the means by which to enact their faith, it also promoted the same ideas about thrift and personal financial responsibility celebrated by Hannah More.

Many Sunday school classes used the *Missionary Papers* as a classroom text. The affecting portraits of heathen—especially Hindu—life won many children to the missionary cause. One supporter asked for a number of copies for her Sunday school class, writing that the children "are very eager to obtain them; and never fail, on the receipt of them, to bring their Pennies and Twopennies with great alacrity."[151] Other issues featured children, one describing "An Idolater Converted by means of a Little Girl." The child of a missionary in Bombay had been walking with her native servant when they passed a Hindu temple. As he stepped aside and bowed to the deity placed at the door, the girl chided him, "Sammy . . . your God no can see—no can hear—no can walk— your God stone!" When told that her god made and saw everything, Sammy learned from her the Lord's Prayer, the Creed, and some hymns. Her father, the missionary, was surprised and edified to see Sammy come into family worship one morning, remove his turban, and join the family in the Lord's Prayer, after which he became a "consistent Christian."[152] The obvious moral of these stories was that no contribution was too small, and no person too insignificant to advance the kingdom of God. In addition, these tales modeled a Christian witness for the readers. The subjects of the stories were recognizably like the readers themselves, performing religious duties that they themselves could undertake.

A final consistent feature of the papers was a call to prayer on behalf of the heathen. Frequently, this plea formed the closing lines for the quarter. It asked prayers for the heathen, for the safety of missionaries, for the success of their labors, and for an increase in volunteers to bring the gospel abroad. This act, undertaken by all concerned Christians, would provide connective tissue to the fragmented body of Christ. Whether rich or poor, British and foreign Christians could unite in prayer and speak with one tongue, all drawing together in a single purpose. Indulging its habit of quoting liberally from scripture, the *Missionary Papers* professed that in prayer, all Christians would "stand fast in one spirit, with one mind, striving together for the faith of the Gospel."[153] Prayer was the one resource common to all Christians; the "one way in which all, however poor, may most effectually support and comfort the Missionaries, and assist them."[154] Occasionally, the papers printed prayers and litanies on their back page for the use of readers so that all might unite and speak the same words.[155] Each individual's participation was neither symbolic nor token, but, like her penny, an important and meaningful contribution that, together with those of others like her, would offer a significant aid to the ongoing mission that Christ had left them long ago. The eschatological vision proposed by these acts—a single Christian community, united worldwide by prayer and common purpose—represented a desire to transform the model of a bounded Anglican community presupposed in previous decades by the SPG and others.

The *Missionary Papers*, it should be clear, were interested in far more than emptying their few pennies from the pockets of the working poor. Their mission embraced, moreover, others beside the benighted savage in some distant jungle. The quarterly papers were informed by a specific pedagogy in the broadest sense of the term. They sought to convey information about the world and about human nature at the same time as they tried to inform, train, and mold a particular kind of Christian subjectivity for their readers. These interests ran alongside the more openly avowed wish to bring the gospel to all the corners of the globe. The CMS campaign to collect small amounts from a large number of working people and children, and to provide them in turn with accounts of the Society, of religions abroad, and of basic Christian conduct and responsibility, reflected a strategy to extend the church in two directions at once. The Society took seriously the Great Commission of the New Testament to make a church of all the nations, for it did not ignore the unchurched within British borders. Nor did it aim only to remind them of their loyalties and duties. The CMS provided concrete measures by which those who sought a fuller communion with the church could vote with their feet. In contributing money, praying, attending meetings or distributing literature, laborers and schoolchildren molded themselves along the lines of the character they were to assume. They *became* Christian by *being* Christian. The identity they thus assumed was real and tangible, a fact easily confirmed to themselves or to others by the activity they undertook and the manner they bore. The CMS helped extend and transform the body of Christ by showing people in Britain and elsewhere how to carry themselves as members of that body.

Pence and Pounds

The success and impact of the *Missionary Papers* may be judged from the Society's records of its publications and income.[156] Surviving circulation and income figures are incomplete, but they present a sufficiently consistent picture of the Society's growth and the importance of the small contributions encouraged by the papers. In its second year of publishing the *Missionary Papers* (1817), the Society printed 176,814 copies, or somewhere over forty-four thousand issues each quarter. In two years, that figure had nearly doubled. In the fifth year, the number of printed issues had grown to 515,000, nearly tripling the paper's initial circulation. For a time, the Society stopped publishing these figures, and the next time we find them, eleven years later in 1831, the number had leveled off to 444,000, where it remained for the next year before climbing back to over a half million by 1837. To provide a comparison with other newspaper circulation of 1834–36, Wiener reports that "only a handful of the more successful working-class journals achieved weekly sales in excess of ten thousand," and that readership for all such newspapers in London "varied from one hundred thousand to two hundred thousand."[157]

The official records of the CMS never separately recorded the income generated by the *Missionary Papers*, but one can, on the basis of surviving records, hazard a guess. In the very unlikely event that every printed copy had in fact generated thirteen pence, the paper would have reaped nine thousand pounds in 1817, a year when its total income was twenty-three thousand pounds, and twenty-eight thousand pounds in 1821, a year for which the income of the society is not available. More likely, many issues were given gratis or wasted. Still, the program must have been tremendously successful, for the society continued to increase circulation and declare the same purposes for the paper. Even making a very generous allowance for waste and even for the possibility that many copies were freely distributed, it still seems quite reasonable to assume that the small contributions that the papers elicited may well have generated several thousand pounds in 1817, their second year of publication. The financial importance of the paper to the CMS is also indicated by the society's rapid growth in income. In 1812, four years before the *Missionary Papers* began publication, annual subscriptions to the CMS did not even amount to one thousand pounds.[158] Even if these estimates are very rough, they at least demonstrate that the *Missionary Papers* featured prominently in a public relations and fund-raising strategy that helped the Society to blossom in the late teens and twenties.

When we compare the *Missionary Papers'* circulation figures with those of Sunday school literature, whose audiences would have been similar and in many cases have overlapped, we find again that the *Missionary Papers* were a tremendous publishing success. They easily rival all other juvenile missionary magazines of the later century, a genre in which the *Missionary Papers* were a previously unacknowledged pioneer.[159] Laquer reports that Carus-Wilson's three Sunday school papers together sold fifty thousand copies per month. The Sunday School Union published a tract each month in editions of twelve thousand to fourteen thousand. Only the Religious Tract Society posted an annual average better than the *Missionary Papers*, selling twenty-five million to thirty million tracts in about forty years.[160]

Whatever their place in the British public's imagination, these papers and the missionary society that produced them help illustrate that in the context of British colonialism, in metropole and colony alike, the construction of religion took place on many levels. It was a task that utilized scientific and philosophical advances of the day and the data yielded by the colonization of Asian, African, Pacific, and American subjects to isolate and characterize religion as a discrete human phenomenon. Constructing religion was not, however, simply an intellectual exercise involving the manipulation and categorization of data. As we see here, it entailed widespread changes in the beliefs and practices of Britons and their colonized subjects alike. What the *Missionary Papers* represented as the religious life of India took its particular shape by virtue of an underlying domestic project that colored its every aspect. Although the publication aimed ostensibly at communicating "Facts and Anecdotes" about the heathen and, on the basis of these horrifying impressions, at collecting funds for his or her conversion, it assisted readers in the formation and internalization of their Anglican identity. At the same time as the *Papers* sketched an image of the heathen, it was molding real living and breathing members of the church. The two constructions are aspects of the very same process; one needs to be seen in the context of the other. These constructions, one imaginative and one manipulative, moreover, were deeply implicated in the production of new Hindu discourses and practices as well as in the articulation and development of "religion" as a category of human behavior. But these are events I shall take up in later chapters. At this point, I turn to the emergence of Hinduism as a primary occupation of missionary literature and the missionary's systematization of Hindu religion.

3

"Scarcely Less Bloody
than Lascivious"

The early nineteenth-century missionary preacher confronted Hindus in many places: in the bazaar, the mela, the schoolroom, outside temples, and on the roadside.[1] To hear contemporaneous popular Christian literature tell it, however, the chief adversary of the evangelical missionary was not the implacable Hindu devotee, or even the brahman priest who kept him in spiritual and physical servitude, but the material object of Hindu devotion itself. Animated by the alluring and deceptive powers of Satan, it was the idol that was blamed for commanding Hindu fascination and worship and thwarting the missionary's crusade for the sweeping religious transformation of India. Popular literature extolling the missionary's confrontation with Hinduism conjured as his nemesis what Sanskrit and some vernaculars call *vigraha* (figure) or *mūrti* (embodiment)—the physical object of Hindu worship, various in the forms and names of the different gods and goddesses it assumed, but one in its capacity to subvert human reason and natural piety. This epic formula pitting the missionary against the Hindu idol quickly assumed a preeminent place in popular Christian literature, feeding the British appetite for outrageous stories from the colonies. Antipodal to the piety promoted by the missionary spinning it, this tale of brazen, archetypal idolatry contributed to India's overshadowing all other colonies in the British popular imagination. In the manifestation of the strongly nationalist religious subjectivity described in the previous chapter, the evangelical missionary's confrontation with the Hindu idol encoded so many other contrasts critical to the crystallization of a British sense of national self: reason vs. irrationality, Christian vs. pagan, mind vs. body, freed vs. enslaved, and so forth.

In this chapter, I sketch early British missionary exegesis of image worship and treat this set of representations as one of the single most significant cognitive acts in the construction of Hinduism, a religion consistent, or consistent enough, in dogma and rite to warrant its identification as a coherent, pan-Indian entity. None of the authors treated in this chapter ever used the term "Hinduism." The word, it seems, did not appear in the English language until the early nineteenth century, although recently some scholars have revised the once accepted 1829 date and the common wisdom that the word was of British origin. The first use of the term now appears to have been in an 1816 comment by Hindu reformer Rammohan Roy.[2] Indeed, one primary fault these early missionary critics found with Hindu deities, beliefs, and rites was their tendency to a self-multiplication that at first defied a systematic ordering. They were initially bewildered by the array of "Hindoo" practices that confronted them with a swarm of devotees, gods, and a confounding multitude of practices and doctrines. Nevertheless, missionary critics quite soon announced the discovery of a common logic that motivated these practices. The idea of Hinduism, now common in the West and South Asia alike, was in no small regard an outcome of popular missionary representations that presented Hinduism as a mechanistic system with a sound, if perverse, logic. Missionaries' systematization of the diverse practices they encountered had far-reaching ramifications for British understandings of Hinduism.

To interrogate the missionary contrivance of a systematic Hinduism, this chapter elaborates something like what Richard H. Davis has characterized as a particular "dispensation" for perceiving and comprehending Hindu images. I am aiming, following Davis, not to treat missionary apprehension of Hindu images as a corollary to an interpretive strategy for generating popular support for their cause, although we must certainly consider strategic factors in what was, after all, a carefully strategized campaign. The theological outlook of evangelical Christianity of early nineteenth-century Britain conditioned its foreign missionaries more deeply, engendering in them a whole "outlook on the cosmos, on divinity, on human life and its possibilities, and on the role of images in a world so constituted."[3] The missionary's comprehension of Hindu images and their worship partook, as any other viewer's would, of "historically grounded and socially shared understandings of the systems . . . by which things are ordered and administered," and this shared cognitive map "set the epistemic frame within which the world [came] to be known and acted upon."[4] In examining missionaries and the Hindu worshipers they encountered, it would be useful, therefore, to look beyond matters of theology and past their strategies for promoting or contesting religious regimes and appreciate that missionary and Hindu alike had previously inherited "very different ontological and moral premises"[5] about the status of the material world and the role of images in it. Lest we be tempted to assume that missionaries got it wrong, and a Hindu dispensational understanding of their religious images was more authentic, let me make it clear that, in my view, the missionary dispensation itself calls out for the kind of serious scrutiny commonly turned on nonwestern traditions in order to shed light on colonial ideology, interreligious encounter, and the creation of modern forms of religious practice and identity.[6] I would point out, moreover, what Peter van der Veer has so deftly made clear, and as I elaborate in chapter 4, that the formations and shifts underway in British Christianity in the nineteenth century are mirrored, complemented, and mutually constituted by those in Hindu India. Together Britain and India, Hindus and Christians engaged in the devising of something that the later nineteenth century would take for granted: a coherent, cohesive, pan-Indian Hinduism.

Manifestation vs. Idol

Richard Davis offers an excellent and concise treatment of different Hindu theologies of the image, and I will only offer the briefest summary of the main ideas behind the practice here, as little more is necessary to comprehend the missionary's misapprehension of image worship.[7] The general theological idea that framed popular Hindu veneration of images turned on the distinction between the divine absolute without qualities (*nirguṇa brahman*) and that which takes on perceptible qualities (*sāguṇa brahman*) as an act of gracious condescension toward humankind. Its assumption of qualities makes the divine presence available for human veneration in the forms of discrete divine personalities. Specific images both represent the attributes of these individual gods and house their divine presence. Images, therefore, serve pedagogical functions by directing the worshiper's attention to specific divine qualities, and they allow direct (or mediated—the point is disputed among Hindus) contact between devotee and deity. Some images are fashioned as iconic representations of gods and goddesses, including the well-known multi-armed figures who represent Hindu ideas about the specific powers, qualities, and domains of discrete deities. Others may offer an aniconic representation not intended as an anthropomorphic likeness (sacred stones and the Shiva lingam are common examples), but embodying the divine presence nonetheless.[8] The temple and devotional Hinduism that missionaries so ferociously castigated apprehended the images of its worship as both the bounded presence of a specific divine personage—Shiva, Kali, and the like—and as visual aids transparent to more distant cosmic presences and ultimately to their undifferentiated common source and identity. When the rationalist Hindu reformer Rammohan Roy campaigned for a monotheistic Hinduism stripped of image worship, Mṛtyuñjaya Vidyālaṅkāra, a pandit to several British officials and missionaries and Roy's opponent, put the matter this way:

> If you revere *paramātmā* [the supreme spirit], then, as it says in the shastras, you should give homage to mūrtis as its various images. ... There is no point in denying the *devatātmā* [the spirits of the distinguishable gods embodied in mūrtis], because these are the very substance of *paramātmā*. ... It is like a forest full of trees: if you be-

lieve in the forest, how come you do not believe in the trees? If you say that we believe in paramātmā but not in the devatātmā, this is like saying there is speech but no tongue.[9]

Baffled and offended by Roy's modernist piety, Mrtyuñjaya argued for an immediate relation linking a single cosmic force, its multiple manifestations in discrete Hindu deities, and the images that housed them.

Evangelical missionaries, on the other hand, viewed Hindu images through a complex series of cultural and religious lenses that refracted them in an increasingly negative fashion. At the root of this dispensation was the Hebraic command, common to the three monotheisms rooted in Abrahamic traditions, that human beings not fabricate and worship images as representations divine things. Many Protestant traditions, moreover, had adopted a set of attitudes displayed in Pauline texts and further magnified by the more radical reforming movements of the sixteenth century that regarded the religious images of Roman paganism and Roman Catholicism as wicked worship of the "flesh" in defiance of the purely spiritual nature of the godhead.

As Moshe Halbertal and Avishai Margalit point out in *Idolatry*, a rich study of Jewish traditions regarding non-Jewish religions, the Hebrew Bible's objections to idolatry can have different concerns at their root. "Idolatry" describes not a single offense, but a collection of forbidden practices gathered under a single concept. The category idolatry could refer to any human infidelity to a god who demanded an exclusive relationship with his devotees, and so biblical authors such as Hosea often employed the metaphor of adultery when describing the Hebrews' idolatrous worship of other gods. Sometimes biblical authors forbade any physical representation of God in order to protect God's honor and difference. It was the hubris of representing the absolute Other, not the worship of foreign or material deities they regarded as especially blasphemous.[10] Biblical concerns, Halbertal and Margalit demonstrate, were intramural, directed largely at monotheists who might mistakenly, rather than wickedly, attribute to God characteristics drawn from humans' temporal and spatial experience. In the Middle Ages, Jewish philosopher Maimonides further developed the idea that idolatry was primarily conceptual error. He exposed the unintentional idolatry of those ostensible monotheists who violated God's absolute unity by means of anthropomorphic verbal imagery when, for example, they conceived of God as a complex being predicated by such qualities as "merciful" or "just."[11]

Whereas the Hebrew Bible opposed idolatry on the basis of several quite distinct principles, evangelical literature about pagans, and particularly Hindus, in the early nineteenth century was not so nuanced. It was idolatry in its most fundamental sense, one easily understood by their working-class audience, of which missionary newspapers and pamphlets accused Hindus: the veneration of physical images as the very godhead. The authors and editors of popular anti-Hindu literature did not couch their critique in terms of the practice of representation, nor did they address verbal representations of the deity, but honed in, rather, on the adoration of material forms. They did not seem to consider, moreover, that the second commandment (in the Protestant enumeration of the decalogue) might in fact prohibit two things, plastic representations of creation and the veneration of them: "you shall not make for yourself a graven image, or any likeness of anything that is in heaven above, or that is on the earth beneath, or that is in the water under the earth; you shall not bow down to them or serve them" (Deut. 5:8). Evangelical opposition to Hindu graven images took its cue from the second clause alone.

It was the New Testament, however, especially Pauline thought about the nature and effects of image worship found in Romans 1:18–32, that primarily informed the missionary's understanding of Hindu practice.[12] In the NRSV translation of the passage, Paul locates the source of idolatry in human failure to grasp creation as merely transparent to divine truths:

> Ever since the creation of the world his eternal power and divine nature, invisible though they are, have been understood and seen through the things he has made. So they [pagan idolaters] are without excuse; for though they knew God, they did not honor him as God or give thanks to him, but they became futile in their thinking, and their senseless minds were darkened. Claiming to be wise, they became fools; and they exchanged the glory of the immortal God for images resembling a mortal human being or birds or four-footed animals or reptiles (20–23).

That was not the end of the matter, however, for Paul further elaborated on the moral effects of image worship, which included various sexual tendencies and violent impulses:

> Therefore God gave them up in the lusts of their hearts to impurity, to the degrading of their bodies among themselves, because they exchanged the truth about God for a lie and worshiped and served the creature rather than the Creator. . . . Their women exchanged natural intercourse for unnatural and . . . men committed shameless acts with men. . . . They were filled with every kind of wickedness, evil, covetousness, malice. . . . [and were] full of envy, murder, strife, deceit, [and] craftiness (24–29).

Paul understood the initial sin of image worship to ensnare the devotee in an escalating cycle of greater and greater sin. The worship of images is foolish because it denies the testimony of nature and reason to a transcendent deity and wicked because it withholds the praise due the creator for creation of those subordinate things now worshiped. Morally, the effect is devastating. Having cast their lot with the things of this world, idolaters now cannot escape it and are compelled, rather, to satisfy their own carnal nature through unbridled sexuality and violence.

We would be misled, however, if we took the missionary's self-understanding at face value. It must be noted that missionaries, contrary to their rhetoric, were "no less preoccupied with material enterprise or with things corporeal" than those they uniformly painted with the brush of idolatry.[13] The ill health and physical suffering of many Indians were often on their mind, as were the dress, dining habits, and sexual mores of converts and potential converts. The matter goes beyond missionary ministering to and discipline of Indian bodies. Their theologies and conversion strategies were also deeply implicated in particular understandings of the human body and its relation to the divine. Observing that missionaries implicitly held that divine things would come to Indians especially through the sermon but also through song and scripture, John and Jean Comaroff conclude that missionaries privileged the register of the ear over that of the eye; that the whole practice of proselytization was predicated on the assumption that "speech acts [alone] had the capacity to conjure up the presence of God."[14] I suspect, could we press them today on the matter, that the organs these missionaries themselves would identify as essential to the apprehension of divine truths would be the brain and the heart, the former for its capacity to reason clearly about sacred matters and the latter as seat of the emotional realization of one's sin and need for redemption. The evangelical movement in Britain read its sacred texts' admonitions about image worship in light of broader cultural trends, combining rational thought and religious sentiment, enlightenment and Romanticism, a scientific temper and a liberal, crusading spirit, all of which affected its analysis of Hindu religious practice.[15]

The combination of these religious and philosophical predispositions resulted in a hierarchical dualism represented in the following table:

+	−
Christian	Hindu
mind	matter
spirit	flesh
sacred text	idol
congregational prayer and sermon	image worship and bloody sacrifice
moral religion	priestly religion

British Antecedents

At this point it might be well to examine more closely how prior trends in British religion might have contributed to a representation of Hinduism that was both characteristically evangelical and characteristically British. I have earlier alluded to the apparent fact that, despite their presence in many other places around the globe, missionary bodies in Britain rapidly fixed on Hinduism in their literature as the preeminent instance of contemporary paganism and as the chief opponent to the global spread of Christianity. A preliminary answer as to the reason for this rapid rise to prominence seems to be already in place: the ways in which evangelical Christianity and popular Hinduism perceived images were diametrically opposed; the two faiths were natural and

logical enemies, at least insofar as an already embattled and dualistically inclined missionary theology was concerned.

It seems critical to me to preserve the specificity of missionary experience
and representation, not so that we obscure complicity of mission and empire,
but so that we perceive more keenly the complexity of the encounter between
Europe and India. Even if, therefore, I must take issue with the anti-missionary
bias that seems to inform Antony Copley's work on conversion and mission
in India, I think he raises a critical problem when he demands that historians
take note of the specificity of missionary experience and ideology. In this regard, it bears noting that the British reaction to Hindu image worship, para-
doxically fascinated and horrified, cannot be separated from longer-standing
British Protestant anxieties. The missionary's fierce rejection of popular Hinduism is fully consistent with other developments and traits in some British
Christianities and represents a specific religious reaction. A brief look at the
ambivalent British appropriation of the island nation's own pagan past and its
virulent Protestant anti-Catholicism all shed light on the missionary polemic
about idolatry, which might otherwise resemble either simple Christian chauvinism or an unambiguous indication of colonial arrogance and might.

Recovery and Rejection of the Druids

The hundred years following 1750, which brought England through Romanticism and into the Oxford Movement's reassessment of Anglican theology and
discipline, also ushered its people through a reappraisal of their own pagan
ancestral heritage.[16] Mid-eighteenth-century thinkers came to regard Druid beliefs and practices, whose vestiges could readily be found in stone ruins and
folk culture, as part of contemporaneous England's own past, rather than the
depraved religion of the barbaric heathen whom the Romans and their own
Saxon ancestors had exterminated. Britain came to view paganism not as alien
religious practice, but as the sometimes noble heritage of Britain itself.

At the dawn of the Industrial Revolution, antiquarian research into the
manners and customs of the ancient Druid inhabitants of Britain helped nurture a British appreciation of its own past and provided some sense of unity
and continuity to a culture facing the lasting social and economic change that
modernity would entail. As Sam Smiles notes, the discussion provided "pro-
vincial pride and cultural distinction of considerable importance in a world
where the pressures of industrialization were uprooting communities, engendering social mobility and upsetting the settled values vested in the old aristocratic and agricultural orders."[17] The integration of the Scots and the colonization of Catholic Ireland show Britain involved in similar campaigns to
identify and consolidate honorable strains of paganism in British history that
could be assimilated to a sense of an ancient British national tradition.[18] Proto-
anthropological discourse about Celts and Druids fortified an emerging British
national identity.

Eighteenth-century British examination of the Druids displays a characteristic Romantic nostalgia for a lost past pieced together from fragmentary

ruins and legends. Druid paganism inspired not a moral revulsion, but a wist-
ful longing. British appreciation for its pagan history echoes Orientalist construction of a romantic Hindu past distinguished by keen religious insight and
an intuition for natural revelation. Romantic notions about a shared human
history ordered the history of non-Christian peoples, often subsuming them
into biblical narrative, and so some Christian antiquarians declared their common heritage with the Druid religion. Earlier works about Britain's Druid past
like Anglican clergyman William Stukeley's *Stonehenge: A Temple Restor'd to
the British Druids* (1740) and his *Abury: A Temple of the British Druids* (1743)
located the roots of Druid religion in patriarchal Israel.[19] In spite of widely
accepted evidence that they practiced human sacrifice, the Druids became
known for their wisdom and learning. Henry Rowlands's *Mona Antiqua Restaurata* (1723), even though it acknowledged the Druids' worship of idols, spoke
of "their innate Faculties, deeply impress'd with the Sense of a Deity." Rowland
described their "peculiar mode of worship" but nevertheless presented Druids
as a society where an "antient famous Sect of Philosophers, Politicians, and
Divines" pronounced "the Power and Perfections of the Immortal Gods."[20]
Blake and other Romantic authors persisted in this vein into the nineteenth
century.[21] And while, as Smiles notes, this legend of a noble people did not go
unchallenged by reminders of their bloodthirst, such accounts in the eighteenth century were largely academic and had little impact on the popular
impression.[22]

It was only after the first decade of the nineteenth century, at the same
moment when evangelical optimism climaxed and reports of ritual brutality in
India began to circulate widely, that the Druids came to be described in terms
of the same cruelty and barbarity as Hindus in India. Often, like Indians,
Druids were constructed as a race of bifurcated consciousness, in whom deep
wisdom coexisted with inhuman brutality.[23] Blake himself displayed this divided impression. He praised their wisdom, but also produced a number of
prints that showed Druids carving up their victims.[24] Paintings and plates depicting the Christian conversion of the Druids became popular, as did altar
scenes demonstrating their cruelty. The *Missionary Papers* itself took up the
Druids in 1829, displaying a Cornish altar and describing the dark rites that
surrounded it. Cruelty and "promiscuous adultery" constituted the "degraded
barbarity of Britain!"[25]

It seems, then, that stinging Christian repudiation of Indian religious practice emerged at the same time as Britain rejected its own heritage of idolatry
and human sacrifice. Sometime around 1810, historians and commentators
turned against idolaters, past and present, European or non-European, as Romantic celebration of the past gave way to a progressivist framework for human
history that disregarded archaic insights and accomplishments and pursued
the general improvement of humankind, especially through the diffusion of
European social norms and Christian religion. Once-noble savages subsisting
on natural reason, Druids metamorphosed in the popular imagination into
barbaric heathen who practiced gruesome cruelty until the progress of rational
and revealed religion stamped them out. Emerging at almost precisely the same

moment and following a similar evolutionary course, the portraits of Druids and Hindus display striking similarities. We see them, moreover, enlisted in the same campaign to clarify and fortify a nationalist religious subjectivity that would assert its character through a repudiation of all idolatrous and diabolic religion.

Catholic Emancipation and Anti-Catholicism

Missionary condemnation of Hinduism also echoed nineteenth-century British anti-Catholicism. Although anti-Catholicism in England was as old as the Reformation, in its most organized form, anti-Catholicism was a mid-nineteenth-century phenomenon,[26] and despite frequent harangues against their Catholic counterparts in India, Protestant missionaries showed little hostility to Roman Catholics as a body. They welcomed the piety of those who took the gospel (rather than the pontiff) as their guide and even expressed hope that sincerely pious Catholic efforts at evangelization might succeed.[27] Nevertheless, in India, Protestant missionaries complained loudly about the deceptions of their Catholic counterparts and about their easy accommodation to paganism for the sake of making converts. Early nineteenth-century exchanges between the two groups of missionaries reinforced a mutual suspicion of one another inherited from their domestic rivalry, and the lines of attack by Protestant missionaries on both Hindu and Catholic ritual are virtually identical, often deliberately conflated.

Protestant anti-Catholicism commands our attention in two respects: its role in the political arena and its place in popular discourse. Both were becoming more prominent in the early and middle nineteenth century.[28] The issue of Catholics' place in English society became a burning political issue in the 1820s, although the attacks only developed their most vicious tones after Catholic Emancipation, when George IV gave his reluctant assent to the Catholic Relief Act on 13 April 1829.[29] This act did away with tests and oaths required of members of Parliament since the Glorious Revolution of 1688. These requirements had included a repudiation of the Catholic doctrine of eucharistic transubstantiation, often at the heart of Protestant charges of Roman Catholic idolatry. Various governments and opposition groups had battled for emancipation since the turn of the century, and some had met with success in the House of Commons, only to be consistently foiled by the firm resistance of the House of Lords and Kings George III and George IV. Woven into Parliamentary and popular discourse about the position of Catholics in Britain were English attitudes toward the Irish, concerns about the foundation of the British state, and the religious character of the nation.[30] Gauri Viswanathan is surely right to see emancipation as the point of emergence of the modern nation state in Britain, founded on the privatization of religion, but she gives no attention to the popular backlash it produced.[31] As D. G. Paz's *Popular Anti-Catholicism in Mid-Victorian England* has well illustrated, anti-Catholicism was epidemic in Victorian Britain, having many sources and appearing in many distinct forms. Debates in Parliament seldom stooped to air ancient prejudices—although

Henry Drummond once warned the Commons that all convents were "either prisons or brothels"[32]—but they ran parallel to a sometimes-vicious popular anti-Catholicism that assaulted the superstition, priestly tyranny, and idolatry endemic to Roman Catholic piety.[33] Bishop Lloyd of Oxford saw it as the dominant issue of the day, remarking to Member of Parliament Robert Peel that the Catholic question was "mixed up with everything we eat or drink or say or think."[34]

Thus, while Parliamentary debate proceeded along lines that addressed ecclesiastical and legal issues, a more sinister attack developed in popular pamphlets. Organizations whose sole aim was the retention of Catholic disabilities appeared in response to an increasingly organized Catholic defense.[35] A tractarian offensive against Catholicism, couched in categories drawn straight from the Reformation, was launched to check a militant campaign for emancipation. Catholics, these pamphlets warned, gave their ultimate allegiance to the Pope, and political power in their hands would surely undermine British sovereignty. Priests withheld the gospel from the laity and thereby perpetuated their spiritual slavery. The clergy interposed itself in the relationship between God and the individual and refused to nurture the individual Christian conscience. A description from a hundred years earlier, published in the popular newspaper *Weekly Observator*, aptly summarizes the stereotypes that had been aired by every generation since Reformation, which found new life in the struggle for legal emancipation and its backlash:

> A Papist is an Idolater, who worships Images, Pictures, Stocks and
> Stones, the Works of Mens Hands; calls upon the Virgin Mary,
> Saints and Angels to pray for them; adores Reliques . . . He . . . pre-
> fers Traditions before the Holy Scriptures; thinks good Works alone
> merit Heaven; eats his God by the cunning Trick of Transubstantia-
> tion . . . and swears the Pope is infallible.[36]

Through most of the nineteenth century, these and other stock characterizations of Catholics circulated freely in the press and in meeting halls.[37]

Increased Protestant experience of non-Christian practice at their missionary stations soon linked Catholics to the savage heathen abroad in their alleged mutual affront to the principles of purely spiritual worship. The collusion of Roman and Indian idolatry was a persistent theme in relations between Protestant and Catholic missionaries in South India.[38] Roman idolatry was seen as an ally of Hindu belief and worship, banding with it to bar pure gospel Christianity from taking root among the Indian people. James Hough charged that Jesuits made Hindu converts only "to exchange the idols of their own superstition for the images of Rome . . . [and to] substitute the crucifix . . . for the lingum."[39] To European Protestants, processions by Indian Catholics were indistinguishable from those conducted by their Hindu counterparts, displaying all the pomp, chaos, and superstition of the most offensive Hindu parades. By conferring the name "Christian" on those who continued to practice such manifest idolatry, Roman Catholic missionaries, especially the Jesuits, it was said, were preventing any real spiritual awakening in India and frustrating Protestant efforts at real religious transformation. John Poynder, a shareholder in the East India Company and an astonishingly prolific pamphleteer and propagandist, campaigned against Catholic and Hindu idolatry and the British government's abetment of both with inflammatory pamphlets bearing titles such as *Human Sacrifices in India*.[40] His earliest publications included another work against idolatry, *Popery the Religion of Heathenism* in 1818.[41] "Every false or corrupt religion is a sanguinary and persecuting religion," he declared,[42] and cited two of the clearest contemporary offenders: Roman Catholicism and Hinduism.

There can be no doubt about the strong connections between the construction of Hindu idolatry and British anti-Catholicism. Evangelical constructions of Hindu idolatry, however, did not merely graft Protestant prejudices onto Hindu targets. For one thing, the most vocal critics of Hinduism spoke directly from their own experiences in India. Furthermore, virulent and widespread anti-Catholicism was not at its most vicious until after the 1820s, a decade or two after the most sensational stories about Hindus began to circulate among missionary-minded church people. Anti-Catholicism at home, moreover, was closely linked to political anxieties, and its rhetoric tended to target not ritual and theological issues, but questions of state security and the treachery of Roman Catholics.[43] Nevertheless, anti-Catholic discourse dated back three hundred years and had shown periods of particular vehemence. The Gordon Riots of 1780, in which mobs demanding repeal of the relatively mild Catholic Relief Act of 1778 attacked Catholic targets in London, would have been an item of personal memory for many British evangels.[44] It seems quite clear that Protestant objections to popular Hinduism partook of a history of opposition to Roman Catholic ritual, belief, and polity. The coexistence of similar lines of attack on Roman, Druid, and Hindu religious practices suggest a pervasive Protestant Christian rationalism that was suspicious of the ritual use of images and any other institutional religious forms not governed by individual reason. Alone, however, these resources seem insufficient to the project of constructing Hinduism. The decisive contribution was the concrete experience of missionaries in the field who met Hindu idols and priests face-to-face and whose reports of these confrontations would prove a galvanizing force for constructing and guiding Christian discourse about Hinduism.

Abbé Dubois and Catholic Counterrepresentations

The specificity and potentially limited purchase of British Protestant evangelical constructions of Hinduism are readily evident when we examine the thought of other Christians interested in India before the second quarter of the nineteenth century. A look at the work of the most famous Catholic missionary of the time, a French priest, Abbé J. A. Dubois, reveals that others with deep Christian antipathy to Hindu religious culture might be inclined to perceive relations between Hindus and Christians differently when their objections were unconnected to British nationalism. Dubois engaged in a frank exchange on the character and prospects of Christian missions with English Protestant missionaries in the 1820s in which he strongly protested evangelical representations of Hinduism.[45] He did this on the basis of extensive knowledge of India, having labored for thirty-one years in South India before returning to France in 1823, discouraged at the unlikelihood of Indians ever embracing Christianity in any significant numbers. He had earlier composed a manuscript, *Hindu Manners, Customs, and Ceremonies*, describing Hindu social and religious life, which had been translated into English and published in London in 1816 by the East India Company.[46] It served as an important source of knowledge about Hinduism for many years. There is considerable evidence now that Dubois plagiarized most of this work,[47] but for my purposes, it is enough to say he was accepted as the author of the piece at the time and built his reputation on it.

Although he claimed to find it tedious, Dubois had dressed, eaten, and lived according to the rules and customs of the Hindus among whom he worked in order to gain their confidence. Like his contemporary, William Ward, he denounced Hindu idolatry and superstition, contrasting "the wickedness and incongruities of polytheism and idolatry" with the "beauties and perfections of Christianity."[48] He lavishly praised the spread of British dominion, which he witnessed during his tenure in India, as the best means of freeing Indians from the tyranny of indigenous rulers and brahmans.[49] He spoke very little of the Catholic Church, preferring instead to refer to "Christianity," and he steered away from most partisan declarations. Acknowledging that some Roman Catholic missionaries had accommodated themselves too far to Hindu custom and adopted an "additional superstructure of outward shew, unknown in Europe, which in many instances does not differ much from that prevailing among the Gentiles," he confessed that some Catholic missionary tactics were "far from proving a subject of edification to many a good and sincere Roman Catholic."[50] Dubois, it is clear, was interested not in the nominal conversions other Catholics might have achieved, but in a full-scale spiritual and devotional reformation among Hindus.

However much Dubois' own goals may have been in line with later Protestant missionaries, and however unlike other Catholic clergy in India he may have been, he soon ran afoul of evangelical chaplains and missionaries in India who also sought the Christianization of the subcontinent. When he returned to France in 1823, Dubois immediately published some of his correspondence under the title *Letters on the State of Christianity in India; In which the Conversion of the Hindoos is Considered Impracticable*. This work argued that Hindus would never commit to Christianity on a large scale and that many missionaries were wasting their efforts and resources in trying. Not only did he try to counter the optimism then infecting Protestant missionary bodies, he also attacked their most cherished strategy: the translation of Scripture into native tongues.[51] Dubois spoke from his long experience among Indians and warned that mere translation of the sacred texts would further prejudice the people against Christianity, which they already held in great contempt.[52] He warned that on every page of the Bible were "things deeply wounding to their feelings and prejudices." In general, the frequency of blood sacrifices in the Old Testament made the Christian God look to brahmans like one of the inferior Hindu deities who delighted in such distasteful offerings.[53] The use or mention of wine was offensive,[54] and Dubois reported that Hindus often turned away upon hearing that Christ was the son of a carpenter and preached to fisherman, facts that associated his god with two of the lowest castes in the area in which he lived.

Dubois also mocked William Carey's Serampore mission outside Calcutta for believing that it had the competence to translate the Scriptures into fifteen Asian languages. Such a project, he thought, would occupy all the educated people in Europe for a half-century if properly executed. Poorly translated vernacular versions of the Scriptures then circulating in India met with scorn, derision, and plain confusion, and their errors were magnified in a culture that executed its public performances and literature in an elegant, high style.[55]

Dubois thought the time for the conversion of Indians had passed and that the morally repugnant manners of most Europeans and the unadorned character of Protestant worship would only further alienate the Indian people from Christianity. Echoing even the most vehement Protestant denunciation of Catholic abuses in India, Dubois strongly criticized full-scale Catholic accommodation to the vice and idolatry of Hindu worship in order to gain merely nominal converts as "shameful," but he averred that Hindus were a sensual people easily attracted to the show of Catholic worship.[56] He found an even greater obstacle to evangelization in the fierce attitude of many Protestant preachers to whom Hindoos were "nothing but barbarians, without a spark of virtue."[57] In an appendix titled "Vindication of the Hindoos, both Males and Females," he attacked the work of Serampore missionary Ward, mourning that "a peaceful and submissive people have been made the target of malevolence."[58] He criticized Protestants for spending hundreds of thousands of pounds to blanket the subcontinent with Bibles when Hindus needed food and clothing far more urgently.[59] He defended the character of the Hindu people, angrily refuting Protestant insinuation about Hindus's lack of honesty and civility as simple lies aimed at attracting public attention and money. He rebuked Ward for declaring on his famous visit to Liverpool that Hindu women were virtual slaves, without a touch of chastity or maternal instinct.[60]

Dubois met with two sharp Protestant responses that charged him, in spite of his efforts to distance himself and other good Catholic Christians from the abuses of the church, with the worst of Roman papists and idolaters. A Mr. Henry Townley attributed Dubois' failures as a missionary to God's rejection of his accommodation to Hindu custom. Townsend accused the priest of "advocating the perpetuity of real and substantial idolatry."[61] The abler response came from James Hough, chaplain of the East India Company in Madras and later renowned for his important *History of Christianity in India*. The gospels provided, he argued, a truth that no human person had the authority to amend. If Hindus were sensual people, they were no different from the rest of the human race. It was the duty of Christian ministers, moreover, to help overthrow these inclinations. Indeed, the primacy of the spiritual over the sensual was the central Christian insight, Hough maintained, and any religion that taught otherwise was pagan at its core. Catholic missionaries in India had done nothing more than swap the idols Hindus worshiped while leaving their hearts unconverted.[62] Hough chided Dubois for not answering the Protestant charge that Catholicism was a corruption of Christianity; this, he insisted, was the central issue in their debate.[63] Missionaries ought not to be concerned that their Scriptures offending heathen sensibilities, for this had happened innumerable times in the diffusion of Judaism and Christianity—the very intent of the gospel was to humble human pride.[64]

Whether or not Dubois wrote *Hindu Manners, Customs, and Ceremonies,* his later letters and the fact that he took credit for composing it show us a number of things. First, evangelical accusations notwithstanding, there were a range of accommodative strategies at work among Catholic missionaries, from a wholesale compromise of defining Christian practices that both Dubois and his evangelical detractors strongly opposed, to a reasoned and moderate accommodation of the kind perhaps advanced by Robert de Nobili, to the simple recognition that popular Hinduism and Catholic Christianity had many things in common—their appeals, for example, to a variety of sensory registers—that could be emphasized and exploited. Second, their mutual objections to full-scale accommodation were no basis for rapprochement between Catholic missionaries and evangelicals. Finally, therefore, the distinctiveness of the evangelical construction of Hinduism had more than casual connections to British national identity.

The Missionary Experience: Death, Conversion, and Class

If the debate between Protestant and Catholic missionaries suggests that there were primarily ideological concerns at work in the evangelical construction of Hinduism, it may be well to reflect on the role of the firsthand experience of missionaries, especially in order to take seriously the subjectivity of those concerned and to avoid rendering them blind agents of impersonal forces. A missionary dispensation for understanding Hindu image worship apprehended the idol, perhaps ambiguously, as both foolish and wicked. If occasionally they could laughingly mock Hindu idols, missionaries' real fears of actual demonic presences in India exacerbated their anxiety over their own well-being and safety in a socially, physically, and politically hostile setting.

We could do no better in this respect than to revisit the trials associated with William Carey and the founding of the Serampore mission, the first modern British mission in India, established in Dutch territory under the authority of the Baptist Missionary Society twelve miles upriver from the colonial city of Calcutta and across the river from the army outpost of Barrackpore. Carey's own first years in India proved a severe spiritual and physical trial. He toiled in indigo fields in the jungles outside Calcutta, struggling to found a viable mission and support the sizeable family he had brought with him: his four children, a sister-in-law, and his first wife, who had fallen into insanity upon her arrival in the land that she had dreaded from a distance. In the meantime, by prior arrangement with Carey, a journalist named William Ward completed his theological studies in England and gathered the equipment he would need to start Carey's missionary press in India. He landed at Calcutta along with three other colleagues in October 1799. Within three weeks of their arrival one of their party would be dead of fever, and only a few months later another would fall, leaving Carey, Ward, and Joshua Marshman, three giants in the history of Christian missions, to establish the most influential missionary settlement in Indian history.

As this early attrition rate for the BMS indicates, the missionary vocation was an exceedingly perilous undertaking, and the personal danger to which each man and woman deliberately subjected themselves became legendary. Home publications of missionary societies made much of the exotic risks that their soldiers for Christ faced, and although some of this rhetoric no doubt served the societies' domestic needs for legitimation and income, there was no small element of truth to these dramatic portraits. Missionary reports resounded with the imagery of death, a daily fact that missionaries faced, both as a risk to themselves, and as a force always present to them in the ravages of poverty and sickness among the peoples to whom they ministered. The difference in climate between England and India could scarcely have been more marked, and disease was a threat that awaited the arrival of every shipload of Europeans. Anxiety over death and the demonic forces that missionaries would identify as its source permeates their accounts of their journeys and their work. Constant reminders about the constitutional threats that Europeans faced in India and the ruinous social and religious practices that shadowed their potential converts tinged even the most celebratory accounts of missionary successes.

The eerie first baptism that the Baptist mission performed attests to the dark mood that could attend these missionary labors. Although presumably a cause for joyous celebration, Carey's baptism of a native named Krishnapal (see figure 3.1), an accomplishment he secured only after having worked in Bengal for eight years, was darkened by the outcries of furious brahmans who hoped to intimidate the young man and the delirious rantings of two Europeans overcome by the event.

The first of these deranged witnesses was John Thomas, who had joined the missionary cause when he met the crusading Charles Grant in Calcutta in 1786. A surgeon in the service of the East India Company, Thomas labored for three years at Grant's failed mission in Goamalti. The doctor's volatile personality and bad debts forced Grant to disassociate himself from him, but on a trip to England, Thomas heard of the BMS's efforts to send a mission team to India. Carey accepted the offer of his services, and, after undertaking numerous devices to avoid Thomas's creditors, they set out together for Calcutta in 1793. While Carey learned Bengali, Thomas worked to retire his debts, and by the time Ward and Marshman arrived with their doomed colleagues, most of the New Testament lay translated into a barely intelligible vernacular, giving them all hope that they would find converts soon. But it was still two years before the mission could perform its first baptism. When Thomas had successfully

FIGURE 3.1. Krishna Pal, William Carey's first convert, from G. W. Hervey, *The Story of Baptist Missions in Foreign Lands, from the Time of Carey to the Present Date* (St. Louis, Mo.: Chauncy R. Burns, 1885), 16.

extracted a public pledge from one Indian man to commit himself to Christ, only to have him disappear during a farewell visit to his family, he suffered "a great depression of spirits" so severe that his colleagues feared for his sanity.[65] Soon after, however, he set the broken arm of a native named Krishnapal and shared with him the gospel message. Years of labor bore fruit at last. Krishnapal renounced his caste at the end of 1800 by dining publicly with the mission-aries. Following his latest disappointment, Thomas became so "frantic with joy" at this event that his excitement propelled him into complete lunacy, and his ecstatic outbursts became so violent that his missionary brethren were forced to shackle him.[66] Carey's wife, who had stubbornly resisted going to India and who had mocked her husband's missionary aspirations from the first, had also lost her reason in this land that had taken one of her children and for which she had no love.[67] She herself had been in restraints for five years, another victim to India's apparent inhospitality to those who would challenge its gods.

Thus it was that on the 28th of December, in the closing moments of the eighteenth century, the first convert for India's most famous missionary was baptized in the following eerie scene. Carey escorted Krishnapal and his own eldest son Felix to the river for the rite, at a spot still marked by a simple cross memorializing the event (see figure 3.2), hemmed in by crowds of Europeans and Indians, many utterly hostile to his intentions. Some Europeans wept at the spectacle, a missionary account declared, while Indians cursed the missionaries and Krishnapal. Carey went forward with the sacrament, immersing the two young men, and, as he administered the rite, an early Serampore history recalls, "Mr. Thomas, who was confined to his couch, made the air resound with his blasphemous ravings; and Mrs. Carey, shut up in her own

FIGURE 3.2. The site of Krishna Pal's baptism as it appears today. Photograph by the author.

room on the opposite side of the path, poured forth the most painful shrieks."[68] Although a triumph for the mission and a moment of personal satisfaction for Carey, it unfolded nevertheless, in an atmosphere rent with what he and his colleagues could only have interpreted as the fury of Satan. Casualties to the cause, these two demented souls personified the opposition the missionaries faced and the cost at which their victories were won.

In missionaries' reports to their supervising societies and in the popular literature celebrating the missionary's confrontation with the idol, we can also read the articulation and negotiation of class identities and social hierarchies. In the early nineteenth century, British foreign missionaries came largely from "a notably narrow band of the social spectrum,"[69] made up mainly of working classes and artisans. The societies for whom they labored, however, had coalesced as the sites of patrician patronage and middle-class political agency.[70] No small part of the tension, suspicion, and even acrimony that characterized relations between missionaries and their sponsors is attributable to class conflicts. In the field, missionaries could turn the tables on their converts. In a bid to elevate his own status, the missionary tended to exercise a patronizing authoritarianism over those Indians who joined the community rather than employ them as equals.[71] In metropole and colony, we find the missionary lodged uncomfortably in "the interstices of a class structure undergoing reconstruction."[72] The missionary was thoroughly invested in the possibility of his own upward mobility despite the pointed attempts of middle-class and patrician patrons of missionary societies to fix his subordinate place. Carey the cobbler and Ward the printer offer two clear instances of men transforming themselves in the mission field, traversing the social distance from artisan classes to the world of scholars and powerful shapers of colonial policy. In the missionary's own reports of his daily combat against a Hinduism thoroughly devoted to the worship of demonic images, we may see his own attempt at self-legitimation and his desire for affirmation from his social betters. Their sponsoring societies, however, could defy the missionary's aims and wishes by appropriating his narrative for their own social purposes. Abridged and sensationalized for a working-class audience, the missionary's experience was cast in a disciplinary tone that communicated to such an audience that *even* the likes of them could be a vehicle for another's salvation.[73] William Ward's journal testifies to his own painful awareness of his social inferiority to other Englishmen in India. When he and Carey were summoned to an irate Governor-General Minto for chastisement regarding preaching and writing that were inciting Indians to anger, Ward, unsure himself of etiquette and protocol, fretted more that Carey would shuffle before Minto and shove his hat under his left armpit.[74]

My point in this section, following the work of historians like the Comaroffs, Thorne, and Van der Veer, is that the missionary dispensation for comprehending idol worship must be viewed in terms wider than simple ideology, be it evangelical or colonial. The missionary's outlook reflected a religious worldview conditioned, as all things religious, by complex social, economic, political, and personal factors. Some might more readily recall the polemical tone and decidedly "bigoted ideology" that could characterize British Protestant missionary discourse.[75] I am no apologist for bigotry or narrow sectarianism, but a full accounting of missionary productions demands that we also recall the great self-sacrifice the missionary undertook, the unmistakable peril he faced in his devotion to a cause, and his anxious concern to secure a tenuous social location with respect to both British and Indian societies. The centrality of death and demonic spirits in the popular literature of missionary societies were more than hyperbole for extolling missionary courage and emptying Christian pockets. Missionary reports from India also reflected the experience of foreigners in a land whose native inhabitants and British rulers often resented their presence. Their accounts of Hinduism were forged in physically, politically, and spiritually hostile surroundings. Plagued with anxieties and fears about their own health, regularly reminded of colleagues who had lost their lives or reason, uncertain of their own social location, and preaching to crowds whose reactions ranged from indifference to amusement to hostility, missionaries found expression for their darker misgivings in their production of what is surely part of their speckled legacy: a fabricated Hinduism crazed by blood-lust and devoted to the service of devils.

Ethnography in Infancy: William Ward and the "Hindoos"

It was in these circumstances that William Ward of Serampore (see figure 3.3) published his massive, four-volume *Account of the Writings, Religion, and Manners of the Hindoos* between 1807 and 1811. He followed it in 1815 with a much abridged but still imposing pair of volumes titled *A View of the History, Literature and Mythology of the Hindoos.*[76] The first version is little-known today and rather mild in its attitude toward Hinduism, reflecting a period of intense scrutiny of the Serampore mission by colonial officials who had threatened to close down the press in retaliation for a Persian pamphlet that abused the prophet Muhammad and provoked a furious Muslim outcry.[77] Even among Ward's contemporaries, only this two-volume second edition, with its long, venomous preface, was widely distributed. As an observer in the field of actual Hindu life and culture, Ward's work was given much credibility in his time, particularly by Christians and utilitarians to whom Ward provided a welcome antidote to the public impression circulating in Britain at the time that Hinduism was a poetic and refined religion. This British Indomania, as Trautmann calls it, had been stoked especially by translations such as Sir William Jones's *Śakuntalā* and Charles Wilkins's *Bhagavad Gītā*, but which would, in no small measure because of Ward, give way to an Indophobia allied with greater imperial pretensions.[78] When Ward suddenly died of cholera in Serampore in 1823 at the age of fifty-four, he had already contributed more than virtually any other person in Britain to the construction and diffusion of knowledge about India and its religious character.[79] Dubois had singled his work out for criticism

FIGURE 3.3. Rev. William Ward, from G. W. Hervey, *The Story of Baptist Missions in Foreign Lands, from the Time of Carey to the Present Date* (St. Louis, Mo.: Chauncy R. Burns, 1885), 53.

because Ward's picture of Hindu life had exercised great influence among not only Christian audiences but also politicians and bureaucrats determining Indian policy.

Ward had spent his youth as a printer and editor in Derby and Staffordshire, laboring at times on behalf of semi-radical causes, an undertaking for which he was twice tried unsuccessfully by the Crown. Raised by a pious Methodist widow, Ward experienced conversion at the age of twenty-six, gave up journalism, and joined the Baptists, dedicating himself to the education of the poor while retaining his passion for social and economic justice. Ward's gentle nature and deeply compassionate spirit are manifestly evident throughout his Indian journal, which recounts his aversion to meat eating, his sympathy for poor Indians, and his delight in living among them.[80] A chance meeting with William Carey, who was rallying support in 1793 for the mission to India he was about to found, awakened Ward to his vocation in the dissemination of religious knowledge and civil society among Indians. His transformation from

critic of British culture and society to an agent of its transmission abroad
appears to resemble the kind of "conversion to conformity" that is characteristic
of former artisans and apprentices of the period.[81] Ward would later achieve
celebrity in England and America when he would become the first missionary
from the East to return to England in 1819. He conducted an extended speaking
tour, campaigning in both countries on behalf of the missionary movement.

Ward's study of Hindu culture represents his attempt to present a factual
survey of the Hindu culture and history to which he had a deeply ambivalent
relationship. A member of William Jones's Asiatic Society, he authored an
unpublished paper on the Sikhs and once proposed a museum to house Indian
religious artifacts for scholars who would come to study them.[82] Nevertheless,
Hindoos shows him in obvious contempt for much of contemporaneous Hindu
practice. Although his bias is clear, and the evangelical commentary that runs
alongside his reports of Hindu rites sometimes threatens to overwhelm the
narrative, there remains beneath a balanced and thorough description of religious practices for which Ward never developed any real appreciation. Although it seems too much to call *View of the Hindoos* "unrivaled as a repository
of detailed information," Ward's comprehensive survey at least aimed to convince readers of the folly and vice of Hinduism by a clear and accurate rendering of its beliefs and practices.[83] A generation later in a footnote to his
edition of Mill's *History of British India*, Sanskritist Horace Hayman Wilson
offered this assessment: "Mr. Ward . . . is neither an experienced nor an ad-
mirable witness. . . . Although an intelligent man, he was not a man of comprehensive views, and his views were necessarily still more narrowed by his
feelings as a missionary; his testimony, therefore, although not without value,
must be received with considerable distrust, and admitted only with constant
qualification and correction."[84] The major flaws in the final product come primarily not from factual errors, but from a selective highlighting of certain
sensational events, his uncritical reliance on hearsay, and his generalizations
about Hindu ritual on the basis of his observations of local Bengali practices.[85]

The work is historically significant for three main reasons. First, as a very
early attempt to survey the religious beliefs and practices of Indians, it both
assumes and projects an underlying unity to disparate sects and traditions,
unambiguously suggesting that superficial diversity notwithstanding, the religion of India might be conceived as Hinduism. Second, it provides very detailed accounts of the religious practices and domestic life among contemporaneous Bengalis of various classes, most of which were thoroughly ignored
by Orientalist scholars of the day.

Finally, and most important, *Hindoos* shows Ward to be among the first
Europeans to adopt an ethnographic stance. He turned from linguistic and
textual studies to something closer to an anthropological model that concerns
itself not with the textual past but the cultural present, a model not widespread
until Bronislaw Malinowski came to champion it in the twentieth century.[86]
Ward observed and analyzed people engaged in religious performance, and to
a degree, he was able to overcome the bias in favor of texts that mars contemporaneous Orientalist accounts. Ward attempted to paint the actual deeds, con-

victions, and moods of those Bengali Hindus he studied aside from the ide-
alized versions of religious practice available in Sanskrit texts. For this last
reason, Ward is one of Europe's earliest and best proto-ethnographers. Although there can be no doubt his evangelical biases deeply colored his representations of Hinduism, one might consider also how his commitment to the
condition of the souls of real, individual actors enabled, rather than impeded,
his observational abilities. I would suggest that his own religious convictions
encouraged Ward to take the experiences and beliefs of marginalized Hindus—
especially lower castes and women—more seriously than contemporaneous
Orientalists had.

Indeed, evangelical assumptions about the unity and perfectibility of all
humankind starkly distinguish this proto-ethnographic stance from the racist
anthropology of the later nineteenth century, which was based on scientific
models assuming unbridgeable racial difference rather than the common heritage and destiny of humankind.[87] What characterized evangelical proto-
ethnography, however, was not only the texture but the luridness of its detail.
These features are characteristic of early nineteenth-century missionary reports
about Hinduism and stem from a habit of perception less pronounced in other
Christian traditions. Evangelical theology inclined the missionary to consider
individual experience seriously and to observe closely the changing material
and emotional fortunes of those he or she hoped eventually to convert. Missionaries' published journals, their reports to supervising missionary boards,
and their letters to denominational newspapers spoke of village life, popular
ceremony, and the deprivation of the impoverished. Missionaries carefully followed the lives of individuals out of both genuine biblical compassion and an
eagerness for converts. Hence *Hindoos*' double-edged character: richly detailed,
brimming with compassion for the poor and ignorant, but unrelentingly hostile toward the priests and moral influence of Hindu culture.

Ward's first volume endeavored to treat the history, manners, and literature
of the Hindus, and his second their religion. This division, of course, proved
awkward and led Ward into some confusion and repetition. The impression
he leaves is nevertheless clear and uniform. The work hinged on a distinction
between the discoveries of ancient Hindu philosophers, which Ward presented
as a type of reasoned monotheism, and the many deviations from this rationalism, which marked the rest of Hindu history and culture. In this regard,
Ward remained within the explanatory framework that shaped Orientalist representations of India. Ward had, however, only faint praise for the ancient
philosophers, and he attacked the Hinduism of the masses as wicked folly, a
fraud perpetuated by self-interested brahmans on an ignorant and deluded
populace. *View of the Hindoos* repeated the by-then familiar claim that Hinduism had undergone a serious degradation since its original insights and a
decline from a nobler age—an Orientalist construction of Indian history based
on the classical/medieval periodization of Europe. Also like the Orientalists of
Calcutta, Ward privileged a historical mode of knowing: *View of the Hindoos* is
replete with complaints about the admixture of fable and "true" history in the
Puranas and other narratives of the past. He admitted the extreme antiquity

of the culture and its literary traditions, but found the latter entirely unreliable, as "the Hindoos have never had a wise and honest historian."[88]

Ward did not dismiss texts out of hand, often finding them useful for explicating the religious sentiments and rationale of the people. Relying on the findings of Sanskrit scholar Henry Colebrooke, Ward conducted very long discussions of the Vedic texts, the six Hindu schools of philosophy (the *darśanas*), and the whole known corpus of other Hindu literature. He argued, however, that the essence of religion lay not in texts but in actual practice, and, on that basis, he declared that the reports of an elegant, refined, and philosophical Hinduism displayed willful blindness to its real, observable effects in society. It was the living Hinduism that counted, that which animated the lives of the common people, not the abstract philosophy of texts unconnected to the daily rhythms of Hindu life.

Ward attacked the ruinous and oppressive effects of Hindu social ordering. He assigned caste supreme influence in determining the debased moral and religious character of the country, pouncing on "its flagrant injustice, its shocking inhumanity, and its fatal impolicy in paralizing the genius and industry of the country."[89] For Ward, popular Hinduism as Indians actually practiced it was the invention of brahmans, and caste the means whereby they turned this false religion to their material advantage. Antony Copley has argued that missionaries never pointed to caste as a fundamental evil in Indian society until their failure to convert masses of Indians was evident and they sought a scapegoat,[90] but Ward, already shaped by the radical politics of Europe, regarded caste from the first as manifest oppression. The system bore the clear marks of men who "designed to deify themselves."[91]

His trenchant criticism of Hindu social structure also targeted the general ill treatment that Hindu women received. He attacked the practice of child marriage, which often left a bride widowed and thus unmarriageable before she had ever lived with her husband and forced many women to turn to prostitution. The general end of Hindu marriage he found to be female servitude.[92] With even more vehemence, Ward denounced Indian refusal to educate women as "barbarous." The ramifications of this neglect extended not just to the women themselves, who were thus denied the possibility of becoming full intellectual companions of their husbands, but also to the Indian people at large. Unlike European mothers, who made a significant impact on their culture through the institution of motherhood, Indian mothers were incapable of "forming the minds of their children, and of giving them that instruction which lays the foundation of future excellence."[93] (We should recall here that Abbé Dubois would completely reject Ward's characterization of Hindu women and their condition as an insult to generally honest and devout women.)[94]

Ward proved himself a keen observer of daily Bengali life. He carefully and patiently recorded speech in bazaars and homes, cataloging Bengali idiom with almost obsessive dedication, and recording such examples of common conversation as marital quarrels and neighborly gossip.[95] He concluded that Indian speech tended toward extremes of exaggeration, with "a mixture of flattery, and fulsome panegyric" in Indians' personal address to one another.[96]

In this context and elsewhere, he invoked the image of the effeminate Bengali, prone to flattery, deceit, and laziness.[97] This hyperbole, he decided, was merely a matter of effete custom: "it pleases without deceiving any body."[98]

Satī was for Ward an important indication of Hinduism's inherent cruelty toward women. He demonstrated its sanction in various sacred writings and provided numerous eyewitness accounts of the rite, including his own. He and Carey calculated that within a thirty-mile radius of Calcutta, over four hundred widows had been burnt in 1803 alone. He accorded it a unique place in history and culture, assuring the reader that "nothing equal to it exists in the whole work of human cruelty."[99] He readily cited other means by which Hinduism gave sanction and encouragement to violence. Religious suicide was common, he claimed: resourceful idolaters had even devised a mechanism for cutting off their own heads.[100] Infanticide, he said, was entirely accepted. Mothers tossed their babies to the alligators off Saugor Island, where the Ganges flows into the ocean in fulfillment of vows they made when praying for children (figure 3.4). Others exposed their sick infants in trees in order to expiate evil spirits, but ants and birds left only tiny skeletons suspended in the baskets. Rajputs killed newborn girls rather than suffer the expense of marrying them.[101]

Ward's second volume, devoted entirely to the subject of religion in India, reads at times as an anthology of sacred texts, at others as a diary of personal experience, and at still others as an evangelical exegesis of pagan idolatry. Ward appears mystified by the very category of religion, unclear whether to treat it as a distinct cultural phenomenon or not. His two volumes propose a clear separation between literary heritage and social history on the one hand and religion on the other, and yet, as we have seen, he was unable to treat either literature or society without foregrounding their religious underpinnings. He divorced doctrine from religious act in order to show that Hinduism in practice mocked its own highest ideals, but he implicated religious teachings in the many shortcomings he identified in Indian society. Because Ward was primarily interested to condemn the immorality of Hindu culture, he was determined both to separate popular religious practice from esoteric text and to charge Hindu religion itself with social ills.

Ward leveled the blame for all the evils of Hinduism on its polytheistic idolatry; ultimately, it was their conception of deity that cultivated Hindus' moral depravity. The theme soon became a linchpin in missionary constructions of Hinduism. Christians displayed moral superiority because they worshiped one God "in spirit and in truth, but in the Hindoo system, we have innumerable gods, all of them subject to discordant passions."[102] The basic fault of the "Hindoo system" was that it had "no one principle" on which the mind might rest, no "anchor to the soul, both sure and steadfast,"[103] no "one operative principle" for moral instruction.[104] It was the Hindu commitment to many gods, and thus to innumerable, conflicting moral demands, that had blinded Indians to the efficacy of a single moral principle that might govern the whole of their ritual and social lives. Devotion to an abundance of gods had fragmented their moral sense, dragged it in different directions, and com-

FIGURE 3.4. Sacrifice of a baby at Saugor Island, a favorite missionary illustration of the violence inherent in Hinduism, from G. W. Hervey, *The Story of Baptist Missions in Foreign Lands, from the Time of Carey to the Present Date* (St. Louis, Mo.: Chauncy R. Burns, 1885), 101.

pelled contradictory and self-serving behavior. The ends of various religious acts were disconnected from one another because they aimed to please discrete gods. These observations led Ward to conclude that Hindu religion was utterly void of moral theology: "as there is nothing of pure morality in the Hindoo writings, so in the ceremonies of this people nothing like the rational and pure devotion of a Christian worshiper is to be found."[105] For the most part, he saw only empty ritual, performed carelessly, without the hope or intention that it might "mend the heart."[106] It showed no inclination to instill moral principles or to stir the soul to higher thoughts. At its best, Hindu ritual was empty and pointless; at its worst, positively destructive of natural conscience, blunting all human feeling. He was adamant that "there is not a vestige of real morality in the whole of the Hindoo system; but . . . it adds an overwhelming force to the evil influences to which men are exposed, and raises into a horrid flame all the impure and diabolical passions which rage in the human heart."[107] He built to this conclusion by surveying quickly, in rapid-fire form, the collection of sins characteristic of Hindu social customs: marital infidelity, ingratitude, flattery, chronic deceitfulness, cruelty, murder, covetousness, gambling, and ostentation. The concluding pages of his chapter on religious ceremony delivered blow after blow to the Hindu character. "Hindoos have sunk to the utmost depths of human depravity," and their religion "has never made a single votary more useful, more moral, or more happy."[108] In contrast, he testified that "the Christian Religion . . . has turned millions upon millions from vice to virtue . . . [and] banished misery from all its sincere recipients."[109] He argued that the doctrine of perpetual reincarnation had a pernicious effect on Hindu morality, for it allowed people to treat all their sins as the effects of previous births and hence they would seldom "charge their consciences with guilt for committing them."[110] He found that the belief in or hope for an eventual "absorption" influenced the practice of idolatry very little, for the concept was too abstract and the prospect too distant to motivate moral behavior. The popular practice of idolatry, he thought, had little interest in the matter of the soul's liberation.

Ward returned repeatedly to deeds of violence and acts of eroticism as fundamental to the practice of Hinduism. Neither aberrations nor anomalies, satī, infanticide, and human sacrifice were central practices dictated by the Hindu faith. Ward charted 10,500 annual deaths directly attributable to the idolatrous practices of Hinduism. Satī and deaths on pilgrimage accounted for nine thousand; religious suicide, infanticide, and death hastened on the banks of the Ganges he estimated at five hundred each.[111] He similarly attacked the "filth" of Hindu ritual, especially its songs and dances, and made frequent allusions to even more shocking licentious practices he would not disclose. Linga worship ("the last state of degradation to which human nature can be driven"),[112] was an easy target, but its symbolic overtones and mythical justifications Ward avoided, calling them "too gross, even when refined as much as possible, to meet the public eye."[113] He cast these erotic practices in sinister tones, as if they embroiled the devotees in the darkest passions. A frequent target of missionary venom, the temple to Jagannātha at Puri served to illustrate both the brutality and obscenity of popular Hinduism.[114]

His closing remarks to the second volume drew the conclusion to which he had been building all along. Hindu idolatry worshiped the divine energy, which it found to subsist in many different forms and objects. Hindus all professed a belief in one god, but a god so distant from human experience that they could not know or address it: "neither the object of worship, of hope, nor of fear," the Hindu divine being was impotent as a moral force.[115] In an "indwelling scheme," divine energy was diffused among creation, and rather than the one god itself, Hindus worshiped those beings in whom this energy was most concentrated: their idol gods and the brahman priests.[116]

This image of Hinduism, carefully developed over two large volumes, describing a polytheistic system whose idolatrous practices located divine presence in physical images and creatures and thereby nurtured sexual immorality and physical violence, came to have a very significant influence on the ways the Britain conceptualized Hinduism in the nineteenth century. Ward had a very clear and direct impact upon Christian discourses, particularly those broadly thought of as "evangelical." For many years to come, even up until the mutiny of 1857, passages and images from *View of the Hindoos* appeared in Christian literature in the English-speaking world. Ward also provided James Hough an important source for his *History of Christianity in India*, an authoritative and generally reliable chronicle still much in use today. Episodes and passages from the *Hindoos* feature prominently in Hough's sections on the period of the British presence in the subcontinent. Ward's influence went much further, however, extending also to utilitarian circles with whom evangelical Christianity had an ambivalent relationship. James Mill's very influential and controversial *History of India* (1817) drew liberally from Ward. This book, highly critical of Indian civilization and manners as a whole, often caustically dismissive in its tone, helped justify a British drive for a fuller and more complete colonization of India. Hence, although the substance and tone of Ward's work were challenged early on, even by the colonial administration and Christians such as Abbè Dubois, it became a centerpiece in the British construction of Hinduism and in the political and economic domination of the subcontinent.

Claudius Buchanan and the Anglican Conquest of India

There could have been few characters in British Calcutta more brash and zealous in the first decade of the nineteenth century than the Reverend Claudius Buchanan, evangelical chaplain to the British army and vice-provost of Fort William College. There could have been, moreover, few who had as much influence on the ways British Christians imagined Hindus.[117] Together with Ward, Buchanan did more to shape the early- to mid-nineteenth-century British reception of Hinduism than any other explicitly Christian writer of the era. Whereas Ward, however, staked his credibility on quiet observation and studious diligence at composing a detailed portrait of daily Hindu practice and its moral outcome, Buchanan made his point by the sheer magnitude of his moral outrage. Deliberately provocative, he offered no subtle analysis, but succeeded in giving evangelical Christians a say in determining parliamentary policy toward India by virtue of his sweeping and indignant attacks on Hindu idolatry and its moral effects. Many evangelicals expressed gratitude for precisely this frankness. Charles Grant once described Buchanan's style as employing "a good deal of truth, ability, indiscretion and offensive language."[118] Marduke Thompson of the CMS in Madras was similarly equivocal, writing to Josiah Pratt in London that "some people wish to discredit [his] account of India . . . [but] England as well as India should acknowledge the debt she owes to Dr. Buchanan."[119]

Although born into a pious family in Scotland, Buchanan did not embrace the Christian religion until his mid-twenties. Having fallen in love with a young girl of a higher station, he left Scotland at the age of twenty-one, intending to make his fortune on the continent so that he might return and marry her. After concocting an acceptable fiction for his parents, he traveled from his village on foot, playing the violin to earn his food and lodging along the way, and often suffering considerable want. When he finally arrived in London, he had abandoned his plans to go to the continent and took up employment with various solicitors, all the while assuring his parents that he was in the service of some gentleman as tutor to his children.

A series of encounters led to his acquaintance with the Reverend John Newton, a prominent London evangelical who comforted and encouraged the young Buchanan who was by then beginning to feel the aimlessness of his spirit and his career. Under Newton's influence, Buchanan made the sudden and unexpected decision to enter the ministry. His conversion and his awareness of his vocation were simultaneous: "after fervent prayer," he recalled, "I endeavoured to commit myself and my services into the hands of Him who alone is able to direct me."[120]

Buchanan's training for the ministry was made possible when Newton recommended him to Henry Thornton of the Clapham Sect, who then became his patron and sent him to Cambridge. During his stay there, Buchanan met Charles Grant, recently returned from India, who, together with Thornton and Newton, encouraged his inclination to pursue an army chaplaincy abroad. The idea took shape slowly, but in his last year, Buchanan showed some interest in the diffusion of Christianity, citing approvingly the hope of Sir Isaac Newton that infidel armies might ravage the pagan world, in order that Britain could "strew with Bibles the vacant land."[121] Grant appointed him to a chaplaincy in the East India Company only six months following his ordination to the diaconate, and he received his priest's orders soon after so that he might go abroad. Buchanan arrived in Calcutta on 10 March 1797, two days before he turned thirty-one. For nearly three years he served the military there, deeply unhappy with the isolation he suffered at the outpost of Barrackpore and with the general absence of religion among the English in India. His passion for the evangelization of the "heathen" of India awakened only gradually; his biographer did not discover any mention of Hindus or their religion in his papers until two full years of his residence in India had passed. Buchanan's first recorded reference to Hinduism charged that it induced in Indians an "imbecility of body, and imbecility of mind," and he declared that under the influence of the Hindu religion their moral powers had been for ages in "a profound stupor." Buchanan was convinced that their state was so depraved that "many ages must . . . elapse before the conversion of India is accomplished."[122] He further painted for his correspondent an essentialized Hinduism that fed on violence and obscenity:

You know the character of the Hindoo superstition. It is lascivious and bloody. I know no epithet that embraces so much of it as either of these two. Of the first I shall say nothing: I shall not pollute the page with a description of their caprine orgies in the interior of their temples, nor the emblems engraved on the exterior. Their scenes of blood are not less revolting to the human mind. Human sacrifice is not quite abolished; the burning of women is common; I have witnessed it more than once.[123]

Shortly after penning these sentiments, Buchanan married and received an appointment to the third chaplaincy under the Calcutta presidency. His isolation had ended and he soon became a prominent figure in English society there. Early in 1800, he was appointed vice-provost to the new College of Fort William, which Governor-General Lord (Richard) Wellesley, inspired by Orientalist appreciation of the classical heritage of India, had established for the instruction of young men seeking to enter the Company's service.[124] Although staffed with some men of impeccable evangelical credentials, with Buchanan, its president David Brown, and Sanskrit professor William Carey all assuming prominent posts, the College was controversial among evangelicals at home. Charles Grant, William Wilberforce, and others suspected that the college's training of East India Company servants would encourage their accommodation to Indian beliefs, practices, and values, rather than reinforce their sense of cultural difference and superiority.[125] Others, who saw in it only the opportunity for idleness, debt, and foppery among young, incoming servants, derided it.[126] In 1806, the East India Company would set up an alternate college at Haileybury in England, largely at the instigation of Grant and other evangelicals, in order to better control the content and character of instruction its servants were receiving.[127]

Although associated with a college that many believed to be steeped in the Orientalist appreciation for Indian civilization and religion, Buchanan's elevated position in an institution so closely connected to the governor-general provided him a prominent platform from which to launch his attack on Hindu idolatry. Although Wellesley demanded that the college promote effective governance of India through an acquaintance with its languages and traditions, probably to appease the evangelical Grant, he had enlisted Buchanan to draw up the actual rules and curriculum. Buchanan balanced Wellesley's Orientalist agenda with a rigorous program in western classics and Christian theology. A liberal and classical education, he hoped, would allow Company servants to evaluate the culture and religion of both India and its British rulers, measure them against one another, and draw what he believed were the obvious conclusions about the relative merits of their governing ideologies. From his academic post in Calcutta, Buchanan was also able to establish prizes at several British universities for the top essays on the compatibility of colonization and evangelization. Cambridge, for example, awarded a sum in Buchanan's name to the essayist who most eloquently addressed "the best means of civilizing the subjects of the British empire in India, and of diffusing the light of the Christian religion throughout the eastern world."[128]

In 1805, Buchanan had published in England what one historian calls "the first influential evangelical tract on India."[129] In this work, Buchanan argued for an expansion of the Anglican Church into India and the establishment of an Indian episcopacy to oversee Anglican clergy and the spread of Anglican Christianity in India. Its full title is cumbersome, but illustrative of Buchanan's general argument: *A Memoir of the Expediency of an Ecclesiastical Establishment for British India, Both as the Means of Perpetuating the Christian Religion Among Our Own Countrymen; And as a Foundation for the Ultimate Civilization of the Natives.* He claimed that the recent defeat of the Mysore and Mahratta kingdoms by British armies left India looking "submissively for British civilization."[130] He hoped to transform the religious landscape in India, "where there is no visible church, and where the superstitions of the natives are constantly visible, [and where] all respect for Christian institutions wears away."[131] With the 1813 renewal of the East India Company's charter, the same renewal that paved the way for missionaries to work in India, Buchanan would see his efforts bear fruit, and in 1814 Thomas Middleton was installed as the first bishop of Calcutta.

Buchanan followed that work with *Christian Researches in Asia*, a report on the state of religion at large in India based on his tour of the subcontinent in 1806. He surveyed a number of religious institutions, both Hindu and Christian, in preparation for the more pervasive Anglican establishment he had begun promoting. He tried to identify Christian resources already present, the state of specific Christian communities, and the sites of the most heinous pagan crimes so that new clerics might be dispatched to those places. *Christian Researches* demonstrated the horror of idolatry and the beneficial effects of Christianity by contrasting two Indian settings—the Jagannātha temple complex in Puri and the Indian Christian community in Tanjore. Buchanan's descriptions of Jagannātha quickly became famous, and various Christian authors have repeated them many times in other literature (see figure 3.5). To reach Puri, he traveled a route crowded with pilgrims, and when he was still two weeks outside the city, he observed, "We know that we are approaching Juggernaut ... by the human bones which we have seen for some days strewed by the way."[132] Colonies of vultures and jackals seemed to live exclusively on the human flesh of dead pilgrims who covered the road "before and behind us as far as the eye can reach."[133] In a particularly grisly note, he described the cooperation of the vultures and the dogs in disposing of the bodies: the vultures consumed the intestines while the dogs tore the tougher flesh with their teeth.[134] Recalling the indifference pilgrims showed to two children clinging to their dying mother, he mourned, "O, there is no pity at Juggernaut! no mercy, no tenderness of heart in Moloch's kingdom."[135] Though horrified at these scenes of degraded humanity, Buchanan was to express uncontained outrage at the image of Jagannātha itself. Employing a biblical paradigm, he referred to the idol as "the Moloch of the present age" by virtue of the human sacrifices it commanded. He claimed to have witnessed two people, a man and a woman, place themselves under the wheels of the huge cart to be crushed to death in self-sacrifice to the god. Other devotees threw coins on the bodies "in appro-

PROCESSION OF JUGGERNAUT, AT THE GRAND HINDOO FESTIVAL OF THE RUTT JATTRA.

FIGURE 3.5. Carnival atmosphere as a devotee sacrifices himself to "Juggernaut" during the deity's annual procession, from the Church Missionary Society *Missionary Papers*, Midsummer 1817.

bation of the deed," but within a short time the bodies were taken aside and devoured by scavengers so that nothing remained but bones.

Reiterating the formula he had proposed in his first recorded mention of Hindu practice, he linked this cruelty to the erotic dancing and singing staged around the temple for Jagannātha's amusement. After a brief survey of these performances, Buchanan was willing to assert that "the characteristics of Moloch's worship are obscenity and blood." So shocked and overwhelmed was he at these sexually explicit scenes that he confessed he himself "felt a consciousness of doing wrong in witnessing [them]."[136]

Buchanan assured his readers that the outrageous excesses of Hindu worship as he described it accurately reflected the moral life of most Hindus as well. These were not the benign and mild people many travelers had suggested. Recounting his initial reaction to the rites at Jagannātha, he wrote:

> This, I thought, is the worship of the Brahmins of Hindostan, and their worship in its sublimest degree! What then shall we think of their private manners, and their moral principles? For it is equally true of India as of Europe; if you would know the state of the people, look at the state of the temple.[137]

By contrast, Buchanan was delighted by his visit to Tanjore. The attentive native congregations, the civility of the raja, and the graves of Indian Christians cheered him with the prospects for the moral and religious reform of India. He marveled at the people's "becoming dress, humane affections, and rational discourse," and he exulted, "I see here no skulls, no self-torture, no self-murder, no dogs and vultures tearing human flesh!"[138] Like Ward, Buchanan resorted to simple juxtaposition to demonstrate the superiority of rational Christian life to a morally repugnant Hindu culture. Christianity and Hinduism were inverse reflections of one another, but Christianity had demonstrated its effects and its civilizing power to overcome all the crimes and superstitions that tormented India.

Two of Buchanan's other encounters on his tour are worthy of notice, for they underscore his passionate antipathy toward religious practice he saw transfixed by flesh and matter. He investigated the state of native Syrian Christian communities along the southwestern coast of India who traced their lineage to a legendary first-century visit by Jesus' own apostle, Thomas.[139] When the Portuguese had attempted to force their submission to papal authority in the sixteenth century, many "Malabar Syrians" had fled from the coast into the hills, and the English had heard only rumors of them since their arrival.[140] Buchanan set out to discover if they still existed and in what state their religion had survived. He found the people and the churches to exude an "air of fallen greatness," which the Christians told him reflected their suppression by the Inquisition at Goa. They had preserved the ancient Syriac liturgy and some copies of the Syriac scriptures, one of which the bishop presented to Buchanan, who then deposited it in the University Library at Cambridge, where it still lies. The simplicity and purity of Malabar Christian doctrine impressed Buchanan. He entertained the hope that this ancient gem, preserved amid Hindu, Muslim, and Roman persecution, might unite with the Church of England, for its people possessed "the two chief requisites for junction with any pure church; namely, they profess the doctrines of the Bible, and reject the supremacy of the Pope."[141] Still, he thought elements of Syrian Christian practice in need of reform, including the Eucharist, clerical celibacy, and worship practices reminiscent of Roman Catholicism. On his return to England, Buchanan proposed to the Church Missionary Society that it take up the cause of the Syrian churches. The CMS eagerly pursued the project, hoping to reform the Syrian doctrine and worship so the ancient church could shine as a beacon of native Christian piety in a pagan land.[142] Buchanan expressed hope that an alliance between this church and the Established Church of England would help stem "the immense power of the Romish Church in India,"[143] but the working union that was established in 1816 unraveled within twenty years, primarily because Buchanan "gravely underestimated the differences which in fact existed between the Church of England and the Thomas Christians."[144] Initially the Syrian Christians welcomed the CMS, who helped build a seminary, a college, and a grammar school. CMS missionaries counseled the bishop and his clergy, helped to translate the scriptures into Malayalam, and gradually worked toward a full-scale reformation of the church. It slowly became evident to the Syrians, however, that the real desires of the CMS were Anglicization of Syrian churches and their subordination to Anglican polity. At the same time, it became evident to the missionaries that the Malabar churches had more than a nominal or historical link to the Patriarch of Antioch and all the "superstitious" tendencies of his communion. They were shocked to witness the extreme submission the native Christians showed the Patriarch when he visited to angrily protest British interference with the church. The association between the two bodies was dissolved soon thereafter.

Buchanan likewise visited the sizable Roman Catholic populations in the south. Although he had expected to find them in an unsatisfactory condition, he "certainly did not expect to see Christianity in the degraded state in which he found it." He charged that the priests, "better acquainted with the Veda of Brahma than with the Gospel of Christ," superintended a paganized Christianity. He was shocked to find a cart of Jagannātha employed in ostensibly Catholic processions headed by a Roman priest using a Syriac bible. Resorting to his favorite biblical trope, he wryly remarked, "Thus, by the intervention of the Papal power, are the ceremonies of Moloch consecrated in a manner by the sacred Syriac language."[145] The real design of his visit to these areas, however, was to ascertain whether rumors of a continued Inquisition in Goa were true, and to what extent it might be affecting British subjects. The resulting account of Catholicism in India included not only clerical abuse, empty ritual, moral laxity, and papal tyranny, but even a hint of human sacrifice.

Buchanan arrived in the city of New Goa in January of 1808 and, without revealing his intentions, accepted an invitation from a priest, Josephus a Doloribus, later revealed as the second member of the Inquisitional Tribunal, to stay in his apartments on the understanding that Buchanan was surveying the libraries in Goa. Buchanan spent a few days in urbane Latin conversation with the priest, who treated him very cordially and engaged him in friendly theological debate. In this polite atmosphere, Buchanan casually broached the subject of the ongoing Inquisition, showing Doloribus a copy of French traveler Charles Dellon's *Relation de l'inquisition de Goa* (1687), a firsthand account of his own imprisonment there. The Inquisitor was anxious to know whether such damning tales of Catholicism in Goa were well-known in Europe, and, as the popularity of Inquisitional literature was undiminished in the nineteenth century, Buchanan confirmed his fears.[146] Buchanan then pushed the priest further to know whether prisoners still suffered such tortures and how many might be kept in the dungeons beneath them. The priest balked at answering these increasingly pointed questions, declaring the conditions and punishments of the prisoners "sacrum et secretum."

At this point, Buchanan's tactics changed. Previously, he had attempted to ingratiate himself with the priest, expressing common interests and giving no indication that he knew of or objected to the Inquisition. He later told David Brown, Company chaplain and his superior at Fort William College, "I disguised my purpose for the first three days . . . so that, on the fourth day, I attacked him directly on the present state of the Inquisition."[147] Now, he threatened to publish his suspicions and call attention to the establishment at Old Goa if he were not shown the buildings where the interrogations and punishments took place. The priest agreed to meet Buchanan the next morning, and then gave him a cursory tour of the establishment. Here he saw the Great Hall where prisoners had gathered to march through the streets in the annual public parade of heretics known as the *Auto da Fè* that culminated with the reading of sentences and the execution of punishments that might include burning at the stake. With human sacrifice already on his mind, Buchanan demanded to see the dungeons so that he might be assured they did not hold British subjects. The priest refused and abruptly ushered Buchanan out of the compound.

Reflecting on the experience, Buchanan recalled the Roman Empire's conquest of the Carthaginians, which forced them to stop sacrificing their children: "the English nation ought to imitate this example, and endeavour to induce her allies to abolish the human sacrifices of the Inquisition." He then made the more pertinent comparison, directly charging the Portuguese Catholics with the religious violence he imputed to Hindus, arguing that "this case is not unlike that of the Immolation of Females."[148] In a letter to David Brown, he declared that he was "not less indignant at the Inquisition of Goa, than I had been with the temple of Juggernaut."[149] He challenged his readers to protest both instances of idolatrous cruelty: "while we remain silent and unmoved spectators of the flames of the Widow's Pile, there is no hope that we shall be justly affected by the reported horrors of the Inquisition."[150]

The corpus of Buchanan's writing reveals that his chief object was not the extermination of Hinduism, but the conquest of the idolatrous religious culture that infected both Hinduism and Christianity in India. His crusade for a rational, evangelical, and imperial Anglican establishment there was part of his iconoclastic and anti-clerical campaign against the idols and priests that held India in their grip. As Joanne Punzo Waghorne has suggested in her study of British and Indian ritual interaction in South India, there was no small irony in Buchanan's proposed substitution of one hierarchical religious establishment inextricably wed to external ritual for the Hindu and Christian regimes he criticized. In Buchanan's dispensational grasp of Indian idolatry, Hindus, Syrian Christians, and Roman Catholics labored under an enslavement to idols and the priestcraft that administered, mediated, and embodied their power. Anglican external forms, on the other hand, he saw as expressions of higher rational and spiritual perceptions and emotions. Whereas a pure Christian faith of mind and heart alone might simply express its rational religion through concepts and through the metonymy of ritual gesture, idolatry was transparent to no greater truth or insight.

This distinction between favored religious externals that communicate or point toward higher things and those that refer only to themselves is precisely at the heart of many constructions of religious alterity that invoke notions of idolatry to exclude and subordinate others. If, as Richard King proposes, this very species of alterization emerges as a "perennial occurrence" in religious attitudes toward others,[151] I must part from Waghorne and those missionary detractors who see not just irony but also a certain disingenuousness or bad faith on the part of proselytizing missionaries. A more acceptable stance for the historian or ethnographer, and one that certainly informs Waghorne's *The Raja's Magic Clothes* as a whole, is to clarify and theorize religion's categorization and situation of body and matter in a cosmic frame that transcends them; to scrutinize the unconscious and unself-reflective deployment of attitudes, habits of perception, and classificatory schema that constitute any religious culture's dispensation for apprehending and ordering divine and human reality. Religious ideologies the world over are pervaded by self-contradiction and xenophobia. Scholars are not bound to forgive religious practitioners—especially those bolstered by colonial might and resources—their bigotry and arrogance, but to comprehend them in terms of the complex political, social, religious, and personal interactions that give rise to their common human shortcomings.

The Idol and the Essence of Hinduism

Ward and Buchanan were to have lasting impact on the British perception of Hindus. Ward made one journey back to Britain after he first settled in India, and even continued on to the United States to raise money and publicize the Serampore mission, but his early death from cholera on his return to India cut short his battle with idolatry. Buchanan, on the other hand, landed in Britain in 1808 with "no thoughts of ever returning to India again,"[152] and he spent the remaining seven years of his life lobbying for a more forceful Christian presence in India. His effort was rewarded in 1813 when the office of the Bishop of Calcutta was created by the same renewed East India Company charter that permitted missionaries in Company territory, and again in 1833 when the bishoprics of Madras and Bombay were established. He enjoyed a wide reputation among church people, and many mourned his passing in extravagant terms. Shocked by the news, the secretary of the CMS, Josiah Pratt, informed his missionaries in South India, "that great man of God, Dr. Buchanan, is dead!"[153]

The prominent place of the missionaries' simplistic image of a systematic Hindu piety in British social and political discourse and its rapid migration beyond the confined circle of evangelical Protestants is readily evident. William Wilberforce can provide us an entry-point into the process. One evening in 1813 during parliamentary debates on the East India Company charter, this champion of the British abolition of slavery and patron of evangelical causes showed himself something of a comparativist. Having distilled some common features out of heterogeneous Indian religious practices, he offered Parliament his conclusions and then proceeded to a vigorous indictment of Hindu ritual. He assured his fellow legislators that

> to all who have made it their business to study the nature of idolatrous worship in general, I scarcely need remark, that in its superstitious rites, there has commonly been found to be a natural alliance between obscenity and cruelty; and of the Hindoo superstitions it may truly be affirmed, that they are scarcely less bloody than lascivious.[154]

In succinct fashion, Wilberforce iterated precisely the formula we have seen the CMS, Ward, and Buchanan developing, which situated Hindu religious practices squarely within the discourse of idol, violence, and sexual excess. This analysis of the ritual use of images came to dominate public discourse about religion in India, and not only among evangelicals. Its ubiquity confirms Peter van der Veer's observation that the separation of religion from state in nineteenth-century Britain accompanied a remarkable enhancement of religion's ability to shape the public sphere.[155] In pamphlet wars, sermons, public meetings, and political speeches, one finds a British public constituted out of discourse about Hindu religious practices. Lurid in nature, this material invited children, the working poor, and the middle classes to join the elites in debate over Britain's relationship to idolatry. Their common scrutiny of the colonial government's policies concerning temple maintenance and patronage, satī, and missionaries helped forge a common national identity in which Hindu and Christian religion were deeply implicated.[156]

The contribution of evangelical constructions of Hinduism to just such a public bears one further look. Because Ward and Buchanan were among the very few sources of firsthand information on Hinduism widely available in Britain, and because their reports were circulated among parliamentarians and proletarians alike, their work sparked intense national interest in Hinduism that surpassed the attention given other British colonies. The CMS, for example, might have dispatched its first missionaries to Africa in 1804 and to the southwest Pacific in 1809, but it sent no missionaries to India from England until after the East India Company's renewed 1813 charter allowed it, the first arriving in 1816.[157] Nonetheless, although the CMS's *Missionary Papers* briefly pined over the "mental darkness" and the "wild and erratic habits" displayed by the other pagans it had come to know,[158] it was India that quickly commanded its attention.[159] While only one issue of the first year depicted Indian rites, every issue of the second year (1817) and fully twenty-eight, or nearly three-quarters, of the first ten years' issues featured Hindu subjects on its cover as exemplary of the heathen condition. Employing a "racial gothic" discourse that organized data related to unfamiliar cultures by developing a set of "striking metaphoric images to filter and give meaning to a flood of experience and information," the editors of the *Missionary Papers* pared away Ward's often careful research, leaving only his sensational tales.[160] Similarly, they fashioned Buchanan's anecdotes into a simple, coherent message for its reading audience. Over the course of its publication, this journal purveyed a consistent portrait of Hinduism, which cited image worship as the root of its moral depravity and the height of its offense against divine law. As we have seen in the previous chapter, the iteration of these religious and cultural dynamics had more to do with the anxieties about British ecclesiastical subjectivity than the "facts" of pagan practice abroad.

One issue cited the "Folly and Impurity," which the cult at Jagannātha perpetuated (see figure 3.6). The source of these offenses was the worship of the three wooden figures whom devotees claimed were "Juggernaut," his brother "Boloram" [Balarāma] and sister "Shubudra [Subhadrā]." The cover art

CHRISTIAN FRIENDS—

You may well ask, "What strange figure is this?"—We will tell you. Perhaps you have heard of an Idol worshipped by millions of your own fellow-subjects in India, called JUGGERNAUT. The poor people make different figures of this Idol. This is one of them. But you see him dressed up here. The Brahmins, or Priests, have put what they think fine clothes upon him.

We will now shew you another form of him before he is clothed, and the forms of his supposed Brother and Sister.

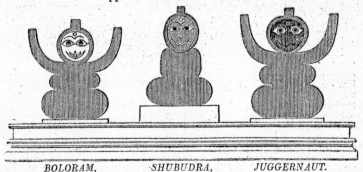

BOLORAM,	*SHUBUDRA,*	*JUGGERNAUT.*
Brother of Juggernaut.	Sister of Juggernaut.	

"What! are these monstrous and ridiculous figures the gods of the Heathen?"—Indeed they are. Boloram is supposed to be the brother of Juggernaut, and Shubudra to be their sister.

FIGURE 3.6. "Juggernaut" exposed, from the Church Missionary Society *Missionary Papers*, Lady Day, 1817.

of this issue featured two contrasting images. At the top of the page posed a resplendent image of Jagannātha adorned for temple worship. He greeted the reader with wide eyes and a slightly demonic grin. The folds of his skirt fell in different directions suggesting movement from below the waist: a darkly seductive pagan dance. The author was quick, however, to strip Jagannātha of his dazzling attire, for these were only the external ornaments that deceived the Hindu's eye and invited his veneration. Below this engraving sat the three figures from the temple, naked. Without their garb they were only crude wooden images, having but a hint of human form. The author exulted in his exposure of Hindu foolishness at its root: "What?" he asked, incredulous. "Are these monstrous and ridiculous figures the gods of the Heathen?"[161]

Later issues presented other objects of Hindu worship in similar tones of scorn and disbelief. Missionaries told stories of British children in India ridiculing servants for their worship of stone idols.[162] Engravings of Ganesha and Shiva appeared on the cover to show in what figures these "benighted" idolaters placed their faith rather than resting on the moral authority of a unitary, absolute God.[163] Another issue displayed casts of the "three principal deities of the Hindoos," Brahma, Vishnu, and Shiva. Describing their various attributes and emblems, the paper mourned that millions "put their trust in these lying vanities, the folly and sin of which any child, educated in a Sunday School in England, could tell them." Such delusion, it declared, was responsible for the ruin of "the souls of innumerable multitudes."[164]

In a show of intellectual and moral mastery, the papers claimed to expose the core of Hindu devotion, its very genius. Stripped of all its show and pomp, the complex and intractable mess of Hindu rite sheepishly confessed its prosaic and pitiable brute veneration of matter, attended, however, with all the consequent sins Paul had enumerated in his epistle to the Romans. Hindus did not merely employ images as aids to meditation, nor did they believe them simply to house concentrations of divine energy; they revered them as gods themselves. This was idolatry in its most basic and primitive form: the worship of material forms as if they were unconditioned divinity. Here lay the root of Hindu crimes. Indians' investment in the sacred nature of their material representations of the god had arrested their perception of purely spiritual realities and communicated false notions about the status of god and human, nature and divinity, spirit and matter. The extreme moral depravity that Hinduism embodied grew out of its attachment to the idol—an attachment that hindered any perception of the spiritual nature of the true God. Because Hindus acknowledged the truth only of limited, finite objects rather than a timeless, spiritual truth, they could conceive of no general moral principle, but obey only the ever-multiplying, disconnected demands of discrete, embodied deities. Idolatry and polytheism went hand in hand because matter appeared in ever-multiplying forms. Unlike spirit, which was rational in nature and therefore unitary, ordered, and abstract, matter displayed no one ultimate form or reason. Each idol was a law unto itself—a bounded universe, both physically and morally. Each deity commanded separate devotion. Addressing individual stone figures, Hindus derived no one single moral outlook. The papers spelled out the outcome of these errors in great, sensationalist detail.[165] Following Paul, they argued that idolatry *necessarily* led to sacrificial brutality and ritual eroticism as well.

Manifold instances of Hindu cruelty were adduced and condemned in great detail: human sacrifice (see figure 3.7), hook swinging, self-mutilation, infanticide, and exposure of the ill. Evangelical representation of satī, however, especially commands our attention, as it will surface as a pivotal point of contest between missionaries and Hindu apologists in chapter five.[166] As the debate in England over the regulation of widow immolation heated up (which finally resulted in Governor-General Bentinck abolishing it in 1829), evangelicals and missionaries were eager to collect and publish eyewitness accounts of the practice. The most comprehensive and famous of these were James Peggs' collected pamphlets published as *India's Cries to British Humanity Relative to the Suttee, Infanticide, British Connection with Idolatry, Ghaut Murders, and Slavery in India.*[167] The *Missionary Papers* devoted three separate issues to female immolation over two years and made very frequent reference to it in other discussions. One theme that emerged again and again was the manner in which idolatry was able to blunt or obliterate the "natural" feelings that were supposed generally to subsist among family relations. Mothers willingly tossed their children to the alligators at Saugor Island in fulfillment of vows, and sons lit the pyre that would consume their living mother along with the corpse of their father. As Teltscher notes, accounts of the satī were deeply ambivalent, emphasizing

HUMAN SACRIFICE TO THE GODDESS JUGUDDHATREE.

FIGURE 3.7. A rendition of an alleged human sacrifice, from the Church Missionary Society *Missionary Papers*, Christmas 1817.

her status as victim of priestly cruelty and her own complicity in the demonic act.[168] A second theme was the responsibility of Britain to act on behalf of these women and the children they would leave as orphans. The missionary argument hinged on the assertion that the victims were British subjects and due all the respect and protection accorded to British subjects at home: "Yes, it is in *British* India, where these agonizing shrieks are heard—where the blood of these Widows flows into a torrent—and where these cries of miserable Orphans are heard."[169]

Regarding satī, missionaries sounded a third theme. Although certain native sketches published in England showed a scene of solemnity and piety, as did one featured engraving for issue XXVI, the actual rite, the CMS claimed, was attended with terrifying shrieks and shouting.[170] The woman often did not ascend the pile calmly, but had to be held down with bamboo poles as she writhed in the flames. The noise of the crowd was said to be "particularly vehement" when Europeans were nearby in order to cover the cries of the dying victim. For most Hindus, the rite did not express or celebrate connubial devotion, but offered its audience a spectacle in gratuitous violence. A British magistrate complained that satī was "not regarded as a religious act, but as a choice entertainment!"[171] Parliamentary papers endeavored to show that deceit, artifice, and force induced the widows to self-sacrifice. Hindus found loopholes where their shastras forbade satī. These assertions of conspiracies rendered the practice in terms of the western metaphors of crime and punishment, rather than in terms derived from religious or theological discourses.[172]

If missionary and popular literature reveled in the detail of widow immolation, it treated its other moral product of idolatry, ritual eroticism, rather differently. Journalistic standards of the time prevented most authors from actually reproducing or describing the obscene practices their missionaries reported. These standards and their own sense of Christian modesty did not stop the authors, however, from suggesting at every appropriate juncture that the same enslavement to the idol that inspired human sacrifice moved Hindus to commit foul and indecent acts. Tales like these played on that "alliance of religion and sex that most disturbs and titillates."[173] The veil of outraged silence that missionary rhetoric cast over certain aspects of Indian worship could only have augmented the power of an eroticized Hinduism to excite the imaginations of a Christian readership. This silence was an effective rhetorical means for suggesting that Hindus had sunk to the depths of depravity in their invention of ritual offenses, a favorite device to communicate disdain and dismiss the rites in question.[174] Authors regularly assured readers that both "indecent and cruel rites are practised in the idolatrous worship of these supposed deities," but then protected them from exposure to such indecency, explaining that "of the impure rites, we shall give no account: it would shock and defile your minds to read the description of them."[175] The substance of these suggestions was not merely that Hindu myth described lecherous deities or that temple art portrayed indecent acts, but that the worshipers themselves engaged in illicit sexual union as part of the unbridled chaos that constituted temple ceremony. Ward described some temple practices as "worship and adultery . . . performed in the same hour!"[176]

In his *Imagining India*, Ronald Inden has characterized these very habits in western representation of Hindu religious beliefs and practices as "essentialist" discourse. Inden defines essentialism as "the idea that humans and human institutions, for example, the 'individual' and the 'nation-state,' are governed by determinate natures that inhere in them in the same way that they are supposed to inhere in the entities of the natural world."[177] He reflects the postcolonial, post-Orientalist objection to a history of western treatments of India that convey a monolithic and archaic culture unable or unwilling to escape its ancient but repressive traditions. I hardly need elaborate further on the manifest essentialism of the missionary's fixation on image worship and the manner in which it packaged the diabolical East. My suggestion here, however, is more fundamental, and it has to do with the limited purchase of this critique of western representational practices. Although Inden has forcefully argued that "Euro-American Selves and Indian Others . . . have dialectically constituted one another"[178] and thus given some account of the impact of colonialism on British society and identities, the linear character of such a model allows us only to appreciate the power of the colonizing forces. It does not recognize indigenous resistances or even the agency and subjectivity of the colonizer. The image of distinct sites of vastly unequal powers linked tenuously by avenues of exchange suggests a rather simple and mechanistic process, and one, moreover, fully directed and dominated by western interests. Inden's work gives us very few means for understanding how and in what ways India specifically or colonialism more generally has helped shape the West. The mutual constitution of East and West has not been merely dialectical if, by "dialectics" we mean, as Inden seems to, a set of mental exercises in concept and identity formation. The process was also material and experiential, governed by conditions that informed the entire colonial world. Artifacts, commercial goods, images, and human subjects with various intentions and ideas circulated throughout the emergent colonial milieu, a milieu defined and characterized by national and individual transformations resulting from global, militarized, intercultural contact. The more enduring contribution of the post-Orientalist, postcolonial critique, to my mind, and one that Inden's work made possible, has been the recognition that colony and metropole belong on the same historiographic map, a map with multiple centers and margins related to one another via twisting, circuitous paths. The very condition for colonial knowledge is the mutual demarcation of identity and subjectivity of both colonizer and colonized. But a dialogic model for understanding the construction of that knowledge, with its poles and avenues of influence, can no longer hold. Something more like what van der Veer characterizes as a "shared colonial imaginaire" was gradually taking shape over time and conditioning India and Britain to think of each other and themselves as actors in the same drama.[179] Colonialism was as much an experience unfolding for British subjects and a determinative factor in British society and religion as it was a conspicuous feature of corresponding Indian realities. The creation of a public arena, for example, constituted out of the enunciation of religion as a distinct class of human activity and the construction of distinct religions: these developments reflect the modifications that both western and colonized knowledges sustained under conditions of colonial contact. The religious categories and social practices of both British Christians and Indian Hindus were transfigured by a colonial modernity. I am not at all implying that there are no significant differences in the Indian or British experience of colonialism, or, worse yet, that a people may as well be colonized as colonizer. I am arguing, however, that any historiography that begins by positing these two peoples mutually representing, influencing, or reacting to one another will fail to apprehend that colonialism overtook, enveloped, and transformed them both.

It is widely recognized now that western essentializing discourses represent more than the colonization of knowledge, for, as my first chapter showed, much more was afoot than the imposition of western categories and models on Indian religious regimes. Western essentialism also signals the repercussions of colonialism for the colonizers, a knowledge permeated by the very Other it is constructed to fear and exclude. Inden maintains that Hindus have been "the object of thoughts and acts with which . . . [the West] has constituted *itself.*"[180] While giving due acknowledgment to the vast power differentials on some registers, I would modify that formulation to deny the West's unchecked ability to be a creature of its own making. It is critical that we also recognize the substantial influence that Hinduism and the experience of encountering Hinduism have had in the evolution and self-understanding of western Christianity. A later chapter will examine Hindus' own experiences of religious and social change simultaneous and parallel to those of evangelical Christianity. Here I have been concerned to show the face of essentialism. Missionary elaboration of the Hindu idol, at first glance an unremarkable exercise of religious bigotry emboldened by colonial violence, under closer scrutiny displays the complex transformations that personal biographies, national histories, political alliances, and class identities of Britons themselves sustained under colonialism.

4

Polymorphic Nature, Polytheistic Culture, and the Orientalist Imaginaire

Two generations after Sir William Jones had died in Calcutta, a fiery Scottish missionary named Alexander Duff poured scorn on the Romantic wonder that Jones had once confessed overcame him as his ship first approached India. Of his state of mind upon first catching sight of the coast of Bengal, Jones had written these now-famous words:

> It gave me inexpressible pleasure to find myself in the midst of so noble an amphitheatre, almost encircled by the vast regions of Asia, which has ever been esteemed the nurse of sciences, the inventress of delightful and useful arts, the scene of glorious actions, fertile in the productions of human genius, abounding in natural wonders, and infinitely diversified in the forms of religion and government, in the laws, manners, customs, and languages, as well as in the features and complexions of men.[1]

Duff contrasted Jones's immediate rapture with India to the way he imagined one possessed of "Christian zeal and love" would first regard the land. Sailing up the coast, such a traveler would catch sight of a landmark familiar to mariners, the temple of "Lord Juggernath." Any fantasies about India's classical past would quickly prove ignorant and naive, Duff surmised, as this Christian reflected on the actual moral effects of Hindu practice and called to mind Hinduism's "infatuated victims of hellish superstitions" and the "carnage that ensues in the name of [their] sacred offering."[2]

The contrast between Jones's and Duff's remarks appropriately conveys the wide gulf that separated two groups of Britons on the question of India. Duff was to carry on in this vein for the rest of his life, continuing the battle engaged by Grant, Buchanan, Ward, and others of an earlier generation. By 1830, evangelicals were emboldened by alliances struck with utilitarians and Anglicists and by the enhanced currency of the perspective that Hindu beliefs and practices were the chief obstacles to a variety of Britain's aims for India, including Christianization, modernization, and the rationalization of society and government. Appalled by more than votaries of idolatry and their crafty priests, these detractors of Hinduism also opposed the image of a benign, or even sublime, religion in Hindustan, an image for which they held Jones largely responsible as the leading light of late eighteenth- and early nineteenth-century Orientalists in Calcutta, the capital of British India.

Jones and Duff epitomize two sides in the British debate over the character of Hinduism and the moral obligation of the colonizer to its practitioners which Thomas Trautmann, in *Aryans and British India*, labels British "Indomania" and "Indophobia." The rapid spread of an evangelizing and Anglicizing phobia after the third decade of the nineteenth century should not, however, obscure the fact that at the heart of the Calcutta Orientalists' apparent passion for some Hindu ideas lay an even stronger commitment to a Christian moral universe and the expansion of the colonial state. "Indomania" is therefore a slightly misleading term, for its exponents fell in love with India on the basis of their ability to write her into a biblical narrative that provided a mythological genealogy for Hindu beliefs and practices. The Indomania inspired and led by Jones, characteristic especially of the earlier nineteenth century and associated with the production of knowledge from the capital of British India, regarded Hindu traditions as corrupted branches of a primeval monotheism. These branches had grown out of primitive humanity's fragmentation following the diffusion of Noah's descendants after the flood and the diffusion of languages following God's destruction of the Tower of Babel, events narrated in the Hebrew book of Genesis.[3] They were, therefore, distant but definite kin to Judeo-Christian monotheism. Christian expressions of Indophobia, however, identified Hinduism with other, more demonic biblical paradigms for paganism, especially the ancient idolatry of the Canaanites and the classical idolatry of Paul's pagan opponents in Greece and Rome. It is undeniably true, moreover, that the Asiatick Society, the flagship Orientalist body, sought and promoted new colonizing strategies. Its deliberations and published papers were suffused with a sense of stewardship over contemporaneous India based on the Society's recovery of a golden Indian past and its rejection of contemporaneous India's popular religious rites and beliefs.

The political naivete exhibited by such fine historians as Garland Cannon and David Kopf, who argue that William Jones established a model for disinterested comparative scholarship, is surely on the wane. There is little life left in the strident claim that Edward Said's groundbreaking polemic on Orientalism amounts to no more than "intellectual mischief."[4] The unmasking of Orientalism proceeds apace, as does the demonstration that the Orientalist's allegedly disinterested comparativism was anything but deeply invested in colonial ideologies. The critique of the Orientalist production of knowledge is not at all, as Richard King helpfully reminds us, "an analysis of the intentions of individual scholars but rather concerns the involvement of the Orientalist enterprise in a wider colonial dynamic."[5] One now commonly finds scholars both crediting William Jones with Indology's founding insights and approaches and charging that "whatever his intentions, however manifold his talents, in mastering Indian traditions, Jones cleared the way for a tradition of mastery."[6]

None of what I am claiming so far is terribly novel. What is insufficiently appreciated until now, however, is the manner in which early colonial Orientalism, especially that generated in the colonial capital, identified a teeming cultural and natural overproduction that it proposed as the very genius of India herself, the very source and character of the alterity Europeans experienced in the encounter with India, and a fundamental feature of Hindu text, practice, and doctrine. Ronald Inden has accustomed us to the idea that modern western commentary has readily compared Hinduism to the tangled jungles of India, an organic metaphor that showed Hinduism to be "uncentred . . . unstable . . . and lacking in uniformity."[7] When he quotes Sir Charles Eliot (1862–1931) to the effect that Hinduism "smacks of the soil and nothing like it can be found outside of India,"[8] however, he is unpacking no mere metaphor. I argue that there is a stronger identification at work between soil and religion in the Orientalist imaginaire, but also, from the other direction, that Inden's condemnation of the "externally imported world-ordering rationality" offered by European colonizing powers to tame the jungle fails to account for the unconscious desire and manifest wonder that inspired and animated the very Orientalist discourses that also further subjected India to western power.[9]

This rest of this chapter examines the Asiatick Society's *Asiatick Researches*,[10] published continuously but irregularly from 1789 to 1839. The Society halted publication as the Calcutta Orientalist's foundational tenet of universal human kinship and its corollary that Britons and Hindus were not-so-distant cousins came under increasingly hostile attack by Utilitarians, Anglicizing administrators, and evangelical missionaries aiming at the subversion and eradication, rather than the recovery and celebration, of Indian religious traditions. The significance of this text for understanding the colonial construction of Hinduism is multifaceted. First, the *Asiatick Researches* documents what it eventually fell victim to: a negative shift in British attitudes toward the religion of India. Established as an elaborate public statement of Jones's conviction that the peoples of the world shared an ancient heritage described by the biblical narratives of the Deluge and the Tower of Babel,[11] over the half-century of its existence, the journal gradually came to reflect and ultimately to succumb to more rigorous scientific method and more rigorous colonial policies of exploitation. Second, the *Asiatick Researches* in its early years is something of the *ur*-text of British Orientalism. I use "Orientalism" both in Said's sense of a tradition of western accumulation and deployment of knowledges that abetted the domination of colonized peoples, and in its older sense, to refer to a production of texts and images inspired by a romantic wonder for the East. It is as a result of Britain's quest for more blunt and effective means of accomplishing the former end that the expression of appreciative discovery came into question. Third and most significant, however "fleeting" and "unstable" its monopoly,[12] this journal published the most widely read accounts of Indian religious history, rite, and text of its era. Its authors and the officers of the Society who produced the *Asiatick Researches* were and remain the most respected authorities of the late eighteenth and early nineteenth centuries. In 1833, the *Asiatic Journal* offered this evaluation: "until within a very few years past, since continental scholars were attracted to the study of Sanskrit, the *Asiatic Researches* comprehended the sum of our knowledge of the classical literature of India; the European inquirer into that literature began and ended his investigation with this work."[13] Simply put, there could be no single more influential text for coming to terms with the development of Hinduism as a modern concept.

At twenty volumes of roughly five hundred pages each, the *Researches* provided Europe with a wide-ranging study of Asia, and India in particular. Its treatment of Hinduism is itself variable. We can, however, identify two periods of nearly equal length in this fifty-year span that offer generally cohesive and distinct analyses of Hinduism based on their response to the cultural and natural excesses they attributed to India generally and to its religious expression in particular. From the dawn of the *Researches* in 1789 until 1810 and the publication of volume eleven, an attitude of appreciative discovery tinged with an ambivalence about the pagan character of Hindu ideas predominated. A pronounced shift is evident after that point, indicating the colonial state's expansion, bureaucratization, and militarization.

Colonial Interests and Colonial Knowledges

William Jones (figure 4.1) sailed for India in 1783, already an established linguist and Orientalist, known especially for a Persian grammar and for French and English translations of a Persian history of Nadir Shah, an eighteenth-century conqueror of North India.[14] A member of Samuel Johnson's exclusive Soho club and well-known in elite English society, Jones arrived in India with a reputation for a political radicalism that may, in fact, have delayed his appointment to India, for it seems he could muster more indignation at European rather than Oriental tyranny.[15] In his early works composed in Britain, he was concerned to show that despotism was not characteristic of Oriental rulers alone, but common to human nature and society.[16] Already he was indulging in his intuition that there was an essential unity of the human spirit across time and space that was to become his central methodological concern. Jones came to India with a well-developed appreciation of Asian languages and with a desire to demonstrate their historical importance and their ancient contributions to western science and literature.[17]

Soon after taking up his appointed seat on the Indian Supreme Court, he convened a meeting of powerful officers and government officials in Calcutta to consider the formation of a scholarly group dedicated to the study of Asia's languages, cultures, religions, geography, and natural resources. His scope was

FIGURE 4.1. Sir William Jones, from *Asiatick Researches, or, Transactions of the Society Instituted in Bengal for Inquiring into the History and Antiquities, the Arts, Sciences, and Literature of Asia,* vol. 1 (London: Printed by J. Swan and Co. for J. Sewell . . . [et al.], 1801), frontispiece. Special Collections and Archives, Robert W. Woodruff Library, Emory University. DS1 .A843 1801 v.1.

ambitious. He proposed to those at the first gathering of the newly constituted body that their aim ought to consist in unlocking the secrets of Asia by directing their inquiries to "Man and Nature; whatever is performed by the one, or produced by the other."[18] After meeting with great irregularity for four years, the Society began to publish selections from the papers read at its meetings under the title *Asiatick Researches.*[19] The first edition, dated 1788, actually appeared early in 1789. The Board of Control at home was ambivalent about the value of such a project, but at Governor-General Cornwallis's urging, the East India Company Press agreed to print the journal on the condition that each member of the Society subscribe at Rs. 20 per copy.[20] For the next fifty years, single volumes appeared sporadically until the Asiatick Society halted publication in 1839, having lost the enthusiasm for new discoveries that had sustained the society's publication and having developed new, more specialized vehicles to convey its increasingly pragmatic interests. When it first emerged, the *Researches* generated intense interest, belying Jones's initial expectations that it would sell poorly.[21] Its initial price and the level of education and leisure it assumed made it at first available only to a small elite in Calcutta and Britain, but reprints of the *Researches* were snapped up quickly. Demand was such that pirated editions very soon appeared, including a bound copy of the first two volumes in 1798. Until 1830, new editions of reprints appeared nearly every year.[22] The tremendous popularity and diffusion of the *Asiatick Researches* validated and enhanced the Calcutta Orientalists' claim to be the definitive source for comprehending the scope and character of Hinduism for their British and wider European audience.

If the journal at first appeared destined for the parlors of those with some measure of education and leisure, its authors were, on the other hand, men engaged in the daily business of establishing and administering Britain's most lucrative colonies. These were not professional scholars, but full-time soldiers and administrators who presented the information they acquired in the exercise of their duties or in the spare hours they could devote to more esoteric studies unrelated to their daily tasks. Jones himself sat on the Supreme Court. He had hoped to complete a compendium of the Sanskrit legal code, but in addition to his judicial interests, he studied botany, Sanskrit musical theory, and Hindu astrology and literature, helping to shape the modern practice of comparative mythology. He apologized in the introduction to the first volume for what he feared would be the inferior quality of the journal by confessing that it had been composed by people devoted to other professions. He explained,

> A mere man of letters, retired from the world, and allotting his whole time to philosophical or literary pursuits, is a character unknown among Europeans in India, where every individual is a man of business in the civil or military state, and constantly occupied either in the affairs of government, in the administration of justice, in some department of revenue or commerce, or in one of the liberal professions. Very few hours, therefore, in the day or night, can be reserved for any study, that has no immediate connection with business, even by those who are most habituated to mental application.[23]

Such a frank confession ought to be a sufficient rejoinder to those who would see in Jones a disinterested and objective scholar untainted by colonial ideology. The men who helped found Indology and the modern study of religion were not "retired from the world," but actively, even eagerly, engaged in directing and managing the affairs of the East India Company. Just as missionary discourse had its clear loyalties and aims, so even these authors, intending to pursue more disinterested scholarship, determined and implemented policy for rulers with enormous military and financial stakes in the way India and Hinduism were perceived.

Physical India: Flora and Fauna

If the standard missionary tropes for rendering India were the demonic and the irrational, the early Asiatick Society perceived the anomalous and the marvelous. Confronting India's alterity demanded similar tasks of intellectual mastery of the missionary and the Orientalist—to discover the principles of a system that lay beneath the curiosities and horrors—but the Orientalists of early the Asiatick Society interrogated the natural Indian world with vigor equal to that they displayed in investigating the social and religious facets of India. One of the Asiatick Society's enduring interests was the profusion of curious natural products on the subcontinent and the discovery of their uses. As I argue below, this quest to describe and classify the Indian natural world proceeded along the same lines that its collective analysis of Hinduism did. For nearly thirty years, the soldiers and bureaucrats who were the authors and editors of this rather sporadic periodical presented India as a land of lush excess whose fantastic cultural and natural productions demanded identification, analysis, and classification. In eighteenth-century natural history an Enlightenment posture of domination over nature and an unease at a new mastery was giving way to pure delight, and among the British colonizers of India we find something of this same attitude in the Asiatick Society's naturalists.[24] In this respect, their passions hearkened back to an earlier generation. Their apparent nostalgia defied an emerging disdain among European intellectuals for the wonder and wonders that had inspired earlier scientific investigation.[25] Often the *Researches* authors suggested potential scientific or medical uses to which particular plants or animals might contribute, but, nearly as often, its authors remarked on the manifest inutility of their findings and marveled only at the rich natural variety of this intriguing new land. In an era preceding the scientific degree and the professionalization of science, the men who contributed such articles to the *Asiatick Researches* exhibited "wonder as a philosophical emotion."[26] They were what Nathan Reingold has called "cultivators," those who contributed great energy and assistance to the development of science, but were not, like "practitioners," employed in careers that used their scientific training or remunerated it.[27] In contrast to the cold and technical reports of a later generation, it is precisely their enthusiasm, the love for a study present in the root sense of "amateur," and the absence of any differentiation between natural science and other sources of delight that characterized the contributions of these naturalists to the early years of the *Asiatick Researches*.[28] For the professional soldiers and bureaucrats who submitted such work to the journal, science had not, as their contemporary Friedrich Schiller suggested, "stolen nature's soul."[29] Science had, instead, uncovered it.

The inaugural volume of the *Researches* presented the first of many articles to extol the botanical wealth of unexplored Asia and to investigate the "marvelous therapeutics" promised by newly discovered Asian plant species.[30] Here, as elsewhere, the journal noted how potential riches remained unexploited and even unrecognized by natives who employed no systematic means for manufacturing useful materials from the land's raw products beyond what their immediate needs required. In "A Description of the Mahwah Tree," army Lieutenant Charles Hamilton enthusiastically reported that *Bassia Butyracea* had the potential for manufacturing a number of products but remained unexploited by Indians.[31] Its unusual flowers, which resembled berries, could be dried and eaten or fermented for liquor. Its edible fruit was similar to the walnut, and in addition it produced a rich oil good for cooking or burning as lamp fuel. Its gum, he thought, was also possibly useful, and its wood was strong enough to be used in ship-building. Hamilton marveled that all this came from a tree that grew in drought conditions and could therefore turn barren soil to profit for farmers, landlords, and the government. He lamented that a "torpid apathy" kept Indians from exercising any ingenuity for the creation of wealth from these obviously rich sources.[32]

Other articles were more suggestive in their implications about the untapped wealth of Asia. One author claimed that on Sumatra, an island the *Researches* identified as Hindu, natives' method for extracting gold from ore consisted of merely smashing the rocks and carving out a few small pieces to trade for their modest needs. They made no effort to trace a vein or to separate the metal more carefully. He was certain that great wealth lay in store for those who could mine the island more systematically.[33]

It would be misleading to suggest, however, that the *Asiatick Researches* regarded India only in terms of its cash value to Britain. Its unextracted potential wealth was just one mark of India's profuse generativity that was the characteristic feature of this Romantic Orientalist imaginaire. The bizarre and the curious were another happy consequence and the subject of numerous authors' enthusiasm for strange plant and animal species produced by the subcontinent. Jones himself introduced this theme with a surprisingly personal account of a loris, or slow-paced lemur, he kept as a pet (see figure 4.2). Offering his report as a memorial to its brief life, he described the lemur as "my little favorite, who engaged my affection, while he lived." The nocturnal creature spent the dark hours hunting grasshoppers or dangling upside down from the top of his cage. Jones described the tender relationship he maintained with the sluggish but affectionate beast and expressed great sadness at his death. In the same volume, Jones translated an Arabic description of the Indian grosbeak, which easily learned circuslike tricks, and Matthew Leslie introduced the Pangolin of Bahar, who challenged English presuppositions about the firm boundaries between species, for it seemed "to constitute the first step from quadruped to reptile."[34] When an autopsy found no trace of food in its alimentary canal, Adam Burt suggested that this bizarre animal subsisted on earth alone, just as plants did.[35]

This was no mere amateurish delight at work. From the beginning, the *Researches* had treated these wonders as classificatory challenges it would pursue only on the basis of careful observation and comparison. Within a few years, it developed a standard format that emphasized plant structure and detailed scientific description for reporting botanical specimens.[36] Even while these articles demonstrated a stringent scientific method in their practices of

FIGURE 4.2. William Jones's pet lemur, his "little favorite," whom he presented in *Asiatick Researches*, vol. 4, 1795. From *The Works of Sir William Jones; with the Life of the Author by Lord Teignmouth* (London: J. Stockdale and J. Walker, 1807).

observation and reporting, they contributed nevertheless to the generation of lore about India as a land of profusion and wonderment by demonstrating the limitations of European botanical and zoological categories in the context of lush Indian generativity. The challenge to mesh accepted European classifica- tory schemes with Indian specimens underscored the impression that India was a land where normative categories, even those believed to be woven into the fabric of creation, did not fit. Only rarely, and usually dismissively, did the naturalists of the Asiatic Society consult native classification of specimens. Conflating the dominion of knowledge with economic and political dominion, the *Asiatick Researches* assumed the colonizing power to classify plant and animal species according to European, Linnean categories.[37] It discovered, when the categories did not entirely fit, not the monsters that earlier Europeans identified, but the marvels of India's polymorphic generativity.[38]

There was, however, a second, subordinate, and darker theme in the *Researches*' discussion of nature. Although many of these reports described benign creations, the journal also displayed awe and respect for the danger that the powerful and deadly beasts of the subcontinent could pose. One doctor supplied the grim tales of the many cobra-bite victims he had treated and his success in isolating an effective medicine.[39] A detailed "Account of the Method of Catching Wild Elephants at Tipura" described the animals' shrewd intelligence and the deadly violence they displayed when finally trapped.[40] Common flies, readers learned, ejected blistering fluids on the skin of any who touched them.[41]

Portraying the natural Indian world as both deadly and marvelous, the *Researches* pursued a descriptive strategy in perfect congruity with its representation of Indian religion. To put it another way, the Calcutta Orientalists of the early *Asiatick Researches* conjured Hinduism as an ancient pagan tradition animated by the same profuse generativity that spawned the marvelous and terrible species of its mountains and jungles. Evangelical missionaries constructed Hinduism as a system of rite and myth organized around image worship, but these Orientalists imagined Hinduism as less a strictly logical (if demonic) system than a fructuous principle whose multiform narratives, ideas, images, and practices might delight the intellect or shock the conscience. Jones and others who wrote for the *Researches* readily voiced indignation and contempt for popular Hinduism as the unfortunate by-product of a religious culture invested in excess—the unpolished, half-conceived expressions that a climate of prolific religiosity would naturally generate but which higher reflection would reject as superstitious piety. Ali Ibrahim Khan, chief magistrate at Benaras under Governor-General Warren Hastings, described a Hindu fire torture used as a test of innocence in legal disputes. Jones's successor to the Society presidency, evangelical Governor-General John Shore, later a prominent member of the Clapham Sect, reported on the cruel violence brahmans inflicted in similar circumstances.[42] The last article of the fifth volume defied Jones's wish that the *Researches* not print mere translations in order to present Sanskrit meditations on the intricate and gruesome operations involved in the conduct of correct human sacrifice.[43] These were the more disturbing manufactures of the very fertile religious and cultural climate elsewhere celebrated by the journal.

One of the reasons the *Asiatick Researches* folded in the 1830s was the increase in tension between discourses about Asia rooted in the sciences on the one hand and in the study of culture, religion, and society on the other. As the aims and concerns of the two distinct disciplinary idioms diverged, expressing them through a single journal became less and less viable. The Orientalist's fully integrated and harmonious India, in which the same laws of profusion and excess generated culture as well as nature, lost its hold on the colonizing imagination, partly for the political reason that such wonderment posed a moral challenge to the evangelical and Anglicist derision for Indian culture, and partly for the academic reason that science and ethnology were differentiating from one another as epistemologies and becoming increasingly specialized in their categories and vocabularies. In addition, conscious rhetorical flourish, ornamentation, and metaphor were passing out of fashion in scientific writing.[44] As knowledge about the physical sciences increased and more nuanced and comprehensive understandings of Asian religions were produced, the two subjects could not co-exist in a single explanatory frame, nor could the fantasy of fertile generativity and infinitely malleable species survive the professionalization of science. In 1828, the Physical Committee, a subgroup of the Asiatick Society established to consider scientific papers submitted for publication, gained a measure of independence from the larger society, electing its own officers and printing its proceedings and articles separately.[45] This event marked a significant turn in the British habits of representing India, for at this point, human culture and its physical setting became constructions of distinctive discourses produced and overseen by separate disciplinary authors who gathered, classified, and articulated knowledge in incompatible ways. The land and people of India no longer figured as the products of the same drives toward multiplication, excess, and overproduction. Natural science shed romantic tropes and discarded the wonder and marvel of early Orientalism as Britain simultaneously augmented its territorial acquisitions. The newly professionalized ranks of a more fully rationalized discipline then rendered the flora and fauna of India familiar and more predictable through the application of its emerging classificatory conventions.

Defying Hinduism: The Other Religions of India

Among the significant contributions of the early years of the *Asiatick Researches* to European knowledge of India was its identification and delineation of India's religious pluralism. At the founding of the Asiatick Society, the colonial administration identified only two religious groups in India, Hindus (spelled consistently with the "u" in this publication—a relatively uncommon usage at the time) and Muslims (usually called Mohamedans), although many officials recognized that the practices and beliefs of Hindus varied widely by caste and region. Charles Wilkins's publication of "Seeks and their College" in 1788 announced the discovery of a third distinct community. For quite some time, Buddhists were considered a subgroup of Hindus, in part because Hindus often included Buddha in the list of Vishnu's avatars. William Jones initially considered them Hindu reformers, but already by 1801, M. Joinville was referring to "Boudhism" when weighing whether it preceded brahmanical religion.[46] Jains did not receive full notice by the Society until the ninth volume of 1807 in two very important articles by Colin MacKenzie and H. T. Colebrooke.

The delineation of other religious groups and traditions played a significant role in the construction of Hinduism in the *Researches*, first because it

contributed to a developing understanding of South Asian religion and a vocabulary for treating it, and second and more significantly because the journal
fashioned Hinduism in contrast to these other religions. The alterization of
Hinduism involved not only establishing a hierarchy of difference between
rulers and ruled, but also constructing histories and communities of indigenous religious protest against the pervasive influence of Hindu ideas and institutions. The *Asiatick Researches*, especially in its early period, before it had
access to many significant texts and reliable native interpreters, offered a description of religious traditions in South Asia wherein each acquired traits in
contradistinction to others. Each assumed, in other words, a place particular
to itself on a conceptual map of the religious landscape of India on the basis
of an unspoken assumption that the traditions in question must resemble
bounded and mutually exclusive entities. Hence, an insight into any particular
religion seemed to enhance the Society's understanding of neighboring faiths.
Under the rubric of bounded, unitary, and competing communities, alterity
and resistance emerged as identifying and fundamental features of Indian
religious diversity. The Orientalist's very idea of religion, partially his own
invention, was established on the idea of communal conflict. The Society regarded Hinduism as the ancient religious substratum of India, the default
religious identity Indians assumed in the absence of other options. Also an
ingredient in what evangelical discourse served up as Hinduism, this fabrication of an oppressive religious tradition backed by the weight of antiquity and
coextensive with the traditional culture of India had the immediate and long-
lasting effect of erasing Hindu subjectivity in western representations. Hinduism appeared irrational while Islam, Buddhism, and Sikhism attracted converts by virtue of their urbane culture or persuasive appeal. These faiths
appeared more rational, systematic, textual, and moral in nature than the Hinduism they opposed. This inherently agonistic, two-dimensional diagram of
the religious of South Asia, conceived on the basis of the European experience
of reform and sect proliferation, identified brahmans with the medieval tyranny
of the Roman Church and drew boundaries between protesting traditions,
imagining South Asian religion as a landscape, with groups and individuals
residing in unambiguous, specific, and well-defined conceptual territories.

   The first discovery of a new branch of Indian religion appeared in the
initial volume of *Asiatick Researches*, when Charles Wilkins presented to the
Society a "sect of people who are distinguished from the worshipers of Brahm
and the followers of Mahommed by the appellation *Seek*."[47] Wilkins's report
was brief and episodic and left Britain little in the way of useful information
about Sikh history, belief, or ritual until the publication of Sir John Malcolm's
more thorough "Sketch of the Sikhs" in 1810.[48] It was precisely the impres-
sionistic nature of Wilkins's account that suggested the Sikh tradition as a foil
to the marvelous and fantastic store of Hindu belief indicated in Jones's and
Francis Wilford's contemporaneous reports on Hindu texts. Cast in an admir-
ing tone, Wilkins's article described a temple in which men treated certain
books with a kind of religious reverence. The scholarly setting and unsuper-
stitious piety of the place impressed him, especially as it inspired a recognition

of the unity, the omnipresence, and the omnipotence of the deity. Sikh veneration of a sacred text Wilkins did not identify (presumably the Guru Granth
Sahib) indicated a rational religion of the book. Wilkins emphasized a number
of other contrasts with Hindu belief. He described the founding Sikh teacher
Guru Nanak as a Hindu apostate whose central concern was moral virtue.
Nanak taught, Wilkins reported, that God filled all space and pervaded all matter, rewarded good and punished evil.[49] A tolerant people, the "Seeks" practiced
no exclusivity based on tribe or race, and they were happy to admit new members, offering even to make Wilkins himself one of them through a simple
initiation ceremony that bound the initiate not to ritual but to creed and doctrine with a pledge to abide by the tenets of the faith and to study its scriptures
under a guru.[50] Wilkins found in the Sikhs ethical and scriptural concerns that
echoed Christianity more than Hinduism. This tantalizing image of a rational,
reformist sect stood in bold contrast to the Society's representations of Hinduism, with its countless frustrating, and often contradictory texts and its arrogant exclusion of westerners.

In the early years of the Asiatick Society, the identification of Buddhism
also figured in the journal's construction of Hinduism. The *Asiatick Researches*
initially showed only a dim awareness that the invocation of the Buddha might
signal a religious tradition fully distinct from Hinduism. Indeed, as it developed, this publication did much to establish the character and internal variety
of Buddhist theology, texts, and communities. The case for the separate identity
of Hinduism and Buddhism and their respective internal cohesion came to
rest not only on the basis of their mutual polemical characterizations of each
other, but on the consensus that Hinduism had fostered a ritualistic, priest-
ridden, amoral religious culture in repudiation of which other religious communities constituted themselves. Although the antiquity, variety, and internal
contradictions of Hindu communities and practices obstructed a neat classification of Hinduism, the *Asiatick Researches* was able to establish a prototypical
Hinduism by delineating other separable and contrasting religious traditions
of South Asia and rendering Hindus as their Others.[51]

The first mention of Buddha came in the first volume from William Jones
himself and testifies already to the concern to isolate and characterize Hinduism along familiar European ideas about sectarian religious identity. Charles
Wilkins had translated a Sanskrit inscription from a copper plate found near
Monghyr that included the name "Soogot," whom Wilkins in a footnote called
an atheist.[52] In a set of remarks appended to Wilkins's report, Jones identified
Soogot as Buddha, whom he knew also as "Sugata" (a common title for the
Buddha, referring to his passage beyond the cycle of rebirth). Jones was eager
to explain that the charge of atheism came from brahmans, who were not
reliable reporters, as it was their system that the Buddha opposed in the first
place. The Buddha was no atheist, but a reformer of priestly religion, and,
Jones remarked, "every reformer must expect to be calumniated."[53]

In the same issue, Lieutenant Samuel Turner reported in detail his 1783–
84 visit to the infant Tishu Lama of Tibet on behalf of Governor-General Warren Hastings. The lama's guardians, who usually kept the child in strict iso-

lation, granted Turner two audiences with him on the basis of the East India
Company's friendship with Tibet. The boy's parents stood near his seat and
conversed with Turner in the presence of the eighteen-month-old child, revealing that the boy had spent the night in anxious anticipation of the visit
from the English gentlemen. In this audience, however, Turner observed that
the lama showed no childish emotion and regarded the English party with a
dignified, serious, and silent air.[54] Ten months later, Turner relayed a colorful
ambassador's report that described the fantastic procession that brought the
boy priest from the monastery to the palace for his official investiture.[55] Although noting an element of unhealthy priestly authority wielded by this young
child, Turner nonetheless paid tribute to the young lama and his religion. The
boy's dignified demeanor, the respect he showed Turner's delegation, and the
general composure with which he carried out his office offered a picture of
Tibet and Buddhism as peaceful, well-ordered, and decorous entities. He included some token criticism of Buddhism's ostentation and priestcraft, but
Turner indulged in none of the diatribe against vanity, folly, and cruelty so
common among observers for the *Researches* investigating contemporaneous
popular Hinduism. Turner offered no indication that he sensed doctrinal or
ritual differences between Hindus and Buddhists, but distinguished them
rather on the basis of disparate moral effect that each seemed to possess.

In the early years of the *Researches*, investigators paid very little attention
to Islam as a religious way of life. Until the seventh volume of 1801, there is
no mention of characteristic religious elements of Islam. Its creed, its ritual,
and its sacred scripture are entirely absent until that issue, when H. T. Colebrooke discussed "Particular Tenets of Certain Muhammedan Sects." He
treated only sufis and other nonorthodox groups, and so even here it was only
by way of noting deviations from a supposed norm that the *Researches* found
occasion to mention the beliefs and practices of orthodox Islam.[56] Pilgrimage,
prayer, or charity found no place in their accounts, nor did practices that may
have been peculiar to South Asian Islam. In an index to the *Researches* published in 1835, the entry for "Hindu" contained eighty references; Islam received only three mentions—one for "Mohammed," one for "Muselmans," and
one for "Musulmans."[57] Muslims made appearances in the *Researches'* construction of a colonial discourse about religion only in terms of their own role
as conquerors and colonizers of India, and their identity and character as religious subjects were excised and erased. This surprising elision stands in
sharp contrast to the discourse that evolved in the journal's attention to Hindus, whose deities, myths, rituals, texts, and moral character the *Researches*
subjected to intense scrutiny for all the years it remained in publication. The
absence is more surprising still given its unflagging efforts to locate and catalog
the religious communities of South Asia. Authors found no reason to interrogate the religion of the Mughals and Arabs, whereas they puzzled endlessly
about that of the Hindus. Even Jones's proposals for studying the histories of
Asian peoples intentionally avoided mention of Islam. His "Fourth Anniversary Discourse on Arabia" refused to discuss the culture and religion of the
region after the seventh century when Islam arrived, and his "Sixth Anniver-

sary Discourse on Persia" treated Sufi poetry and philosophy only briefly and only as they were related to other Hindu and Zoroastrian practices.

Muslims appeared in the *Researches* almost exclusively as rulers of various large kingdoms and as historians who had chronicled dynasties and events that had shaped Asian history. The Orientalists valued Muslim experience for what it could teach them as the most recent foreign rulers of India. Frequently, the *Asiatick Researches'* authors relied on the work of Muslim scholars in order to provide comprehensive histories of their own.[58] On the whole, Bernard Cohn's argument that the British were working to give India what it could not produce itself—a history—applies especially to Hindu India.[59] The history of Muslims in India, they discovered, had already been written. Muslims were portrayed as eminently more rational and credible historians who exercised far more discerning historical judgment than Hindus.[60] In an abridged translation of Mavlavi Khairuddin's history of the Afghans, an article by the late Henry Van-sittart, former governor of Bengal, offered some observations on the ideology and methodology of history that show an impressive degree of foresight into issues that would occupy historiography in the next century.[61] In the essay, he credits the Muslim historian with providing western scholars a valuable resource for assembling a comprehensive history of the region. He argued that such accounts were at points fantastic and unreliable, but that they still offered important insights to the historian, for these fantastic accounts were themselves pieces of history—the history of a people's consciousness of itself. Referring to the translation he was presenting to the society, he remarked

> Although it opens with a very wild description of the origins of that tribe, and contains a narrative, which can by no means be offered upon the whole as a serious and probable history, yet I conceive, that the knowledge of what a nation suppose themselves to be, may be interesting to a society like this, as well as of what they really are: indeed the commencement of almost every history is fabulous; and the most enlightened nations, after they have arrived at that degree of civilization and importance, which have enabled and induced them to commemorate their actions, have always found a vacancy at their outset, which invention, or at best presumption, must supply.[62]

Not only were the Afghan's own delusions of historical grandeur significant to the colonial western historian, but also they revealed in themselves a certain historical consciousness and intellectual achievement on the part of the chroniclers. The very same features of Hindu historiography, however, marked for the authors of the *Researches* the utter failure of that people to come to any historical self-consciousness and demonstrated that Hindu culture itself fostered illusion and deceit.

On the whole, the *Researches* presented the Persian culture with which it associated Islam as elegant and refined. The rulers who were part of this culture could be cruel and intolerant, but they were among the important authors of the artistic and literary legacy of the human race. William Jones also praised Arab culture in spite of its link to a fierce imperial ideology: "if courtesy and urbanity, a love of poetry and eloquence, and the practice of exalted virtues be a juster measure of perfect society, we have certain proof, that the people of Arabia . . . were eminently civilized for many ages before their conquest of Persia."[63] By virtue of their success as rulers of India, Muslims also found their way into the *Researches* as the builders of fabulous palaces and monuments. James T. Blunt, for example, brought the Qutb Minar to the public's attention in 1795, when he described the unfinished work of "Cuttub Shaw" (i.e., Qutb ud Din Aybak, d. 1210), whose rule over the kingdom of Delhi gave him the means to erect such an imposing structure.[64] The Asiatick Society valued Muslim histories not because they clarified religious beliefs and practices or legal norms, but because they both spoke to political successes and failures in governing India and provided the kind of lasting testimony to the character of their rule for which Britain longed. The *Researches* described mosques, monuments and palaces of the Islamic rulers not as expressions of religious impulses, but as products of the patronage that successful rulers of India would exercise as the responsibility of the governing class.

Back-to-back articles in the same fourth volume describe great architectural feats of Hindus and Muslims and spell out a telling contrast quite starkly. When astronomer J. Goldingham argued—correctly, as it would turn out—that the spectacular rock-cut temples at Elephanta were largely Hindu achievements, he set himself up for certain ridicule.[65] Although he produced compelling evidence based on correspondences between the sculpted figures and Hindu mythology, in a skeptical introduction, John Carnac, an army officer who had earned a reputation for success on Indian battlefields, cut the ground from beneath Goldingham. Carnac denied that "so feeble and effeminate a race" as the Hindus could have executed this "great labour."[66] Following this piece, prolific Orientalist author W. Francklin offered "An Account of the Present State of Delhi" that described "spacious gardens" and "many splendid palaces."[67] He devoted no attention to the religious character of the many buildings he mentioned, describing only, for example, the architectural features of the Jama Masjid.[68]

In addition to these major religious groups, the *Researches* presented accounts of small, isolated societies whose religions it reported as separate, distinct systems. The recognition of smaller groups excluded from a larger Indian culture represented the first steps toward the classification of certain native Indian peoples as "tribal," or *ādivāsī* (original inhabitants). This identification found permanent, official recognition in the constitution of independent India, which employed the appellation to refer to those isolated peoples whose culture and language appear distinct from other, larger groups of Indians.[69] Although it claimed these groups were isolated and unique societies, the *Researches* derived a common set of idioms and rubrics for describing their cultures. Rather than underscoring differences among such insular and widely separated peoples, the authors of the *Researches* generated parallels and correspondences based on Romantic notions of primitive humanity to construct a set of shared traits for distinguishing tribal peoples from others on the subcontinent like Hindus, Muslims, and Buddhists. The authors of these pieces consistently dipped into the same well of images to describe an unevolved, often idyllic natural state of human society. These peoples generally practiced simple relig- ions, if any, lived hand-to-mouth directly off of the land, dressed in skins or grass, and, on the whole, presented a friendly demeanor to strangers, untrained by culture to hate, fear, or otherwise shun them. Typical of the nineteenth- century British habit of viewing other civilizations in terms of labor and polit- ical economy, these images harkened back also to earlier eighteenth-century French and Scottish ideas about the simple virtues of primitive society.[70] Pro- jecting utopian fantasies onto the land itself, observers frequently remarked that tribal lands were blessed with an uncommon abundance. The idyllic scene recalled Rousseau and his noble savages, rather than invoking the historical framework of moral degeneration of the primitive common in British ethnol- ogy after the spread of evangelicalism.[71]

G. Hamilton's "A Short Description of Carnicobar," the northeasternmost of the Nicobar islands, is typical of this genre. He communicated to the Society that the island produced whatever the natives required: abundant fruit, fertile soil, plentiful wildlife. The natives were ugly but friendly, and quite willing to eat with Europeans. A great deal of their time they spent feasting and dancing, unconcerned with laying things up for the future. They paid little attention to diet, eating the one food that was easily available to them in large quantities: pork. They led a gay, childlike existence, full of play but little industry, and their cultural life was extremely simple, marked by two central qualities: "their entire neglect of compliment and ceremony" and their strong aversion to dis- honesty of any sort. Lacking sophisticated social norms, they lived in perfect equality with one another, having no notion even of theft, since a person could enter any house and take exactly what he liked or needed.[72] Other contributors echoed Hamilton's impressions that tribal peoples exhibited a kind of childish joviality and a desire for harmony. Relations among individuals were emo- tional: these natives were quick to anger and quick to embrace when their anger was spent. Their use of alcohol was juvenile as well: they consumed it in large quantities, knowing no moderation, and their drunkenness exagger- ated their infantilism all the more. Under the influence, they might occasion- ally fight, but only to "drub one another most heartily, till no longer able to endure the conflict, [then] they mutually put a stop to the combat and all get drunk again."[73] Some tribal societies also seemed to display a simplistic aware- ness of fundamental Christian truths, a simple moral code, and a greater regard for the truth than Hindus or Muslims.[74] Many of these images stand in con- tradistinction to the complicated notions of Hindu culture that evolved in the journal. Hindus produced a vast body of complex ritual, myth, and philosophy; they followed a diet strictly regulated by caste law and calendar; they refused English company at their meals, held themselves aloof, and often were de- scribed as pernicious and deceitful.

Alongside these gregarious tribal natives, the *Researches* sometimes de- scribed simple and natural societies given to darker primitive instincts. The "Inhabitants of the Garrow Hills," for instance, indiscriminately butchered the women, children and elderly of enemy tribes; they beheaded prisoners with a perverse glee, shoving food into the mouths of the decapitated skulls to mock the victims.[75] Observers, nevertheless, portrayed even cruel and bloodthirsty tribal people as bound by a primitive set of uncomplicated social relations. Just as their gentler counterparts addressed strangers with an innocent eagerness, so these people greeted them with overt, unmotivated hostility. Commonly, this sort of tribal brutality was attributed to factors outside their society, thus preserving the notion that in their pure native state, these peoples displayed a natural morality that colonial government could nurture and develop.[76] There was no complex set of ideas about nation, class, or religion at work in these cultures, just a simple hatred of foreigners, which, one Company servant reported, a rational, benevolent government could easily cure by demonstrating its good intentions.[77]

A Hindu Land

Having set the context for analyzing the journal's construction of Hinduism by examining its treatment of non-Hindu subjects and thus providing an impression of its more general interests and aims, I now turn to the ways the *Asiatick Researches* fashioned and introduced a system of Hindu beliefs and practices to a large British audience. In a publication spanning a half-century, no single or unified portrait of Hinduism emerges. What becomes clear, however, is that these scholars worked within a certain set of idioms that produced specific themes and images about Hindus and their religion. Even when they were arguing among themselves, these soldiers, judges, and bureaucrats conversed with accepted metaphors and rhetorical usages that helped to convey and perpetuate general impressions about Hindus and their land. Whereas in earlier chapters I have considered specific ideological agendas and their means of diffusion, we find in the *Researches* not a univocal message about Hinduism, but the efflorescence of an Orientalist imaginaire, a vocabulary and imagery for Indian religion that inscribed the never-fulfilled colonial ambition of complete dominion over Indian territory onto the landscape such that religion and land mutually implied one another, and the question of military and economic conquest was thus folded into Orientalist ethnology of India. Put another way, the Calcutta Orientalists of the first decades of the nineteenth century manufactured as the chief object of colonial desire, a land and culture that cohered in a principal of generativity. India's polytheistic religion and polymorphic ecology mirrored one another. The very allurements of India were simultaneously its dangers, and both together invited conquest. Insofar as Hinduism was a fabrication of the Orientalist imagination, it expressed more general anxieties and desires aroused by the British Protestant encounter with India.

For the fifty years or so that the *Asiatick Researches* remained in publication, Hindu religious phenomena—texts, rituals, temples, social institutions—remained the journal's primary focus. In its first five volumes, spanning 1789–98, of 124 separate articles, 48 dealt directly with Hindu subjects, and 11 or so others addressed issues in which Hindu belief or practice played a major role.[78] These numbers, moreover, do not reveal the fact that even in the significant number of botanical and astronomical contributions that were not exegeses of Hindu texts but original scientific studies by Europeans, certain themes about the subcontinent were present that were associated with the perception of India as a fundamentally and essentially Hindu land. Here it is clear Inden's Hinduism-as-jungle is not simply a western metaphor for the religion. The British Orientalist imagined Indian society, politics, history, religion, and nature all to be products of the same forces of luxurious self-multiplication that pervaded the subcontinent.

So while the journal's initial attention to other religions was spotty and episodic, it attempted a more exhaustive treatment of Hinduism because spotty and episodic knowledge of Hindu traditions spelled incomplete and unstable command over Hindu communities and Indian territory. These early Orientalists fully identified India with Hinduism such that knowledge and command of one necessitated knowledge and command of the other. Themes that were present in studies of Indian flora and fauna, such as their tendency to profuse self-multiplication, turn up again in studies of Hindu texts and practices. Jones himself sounded this identification in his 1796 "Third Anniversary Discourse," which proposed his overview of Asian history by examining the sub-histories of its five nations.[79] Before this infant society, the president defined India as "that whole extent of country, in which the primitive religion and languages of the Hindus prevail."[80] He was only reflecting an older ambiguity borne by the term "Hindu," which, from at least the eighth-century Arab invasion of the subcontinent, could signify land, religion, or both.[81] Jones spoke as if by virtue of the antiquity of the Hindu tradition, its essence had somehow seeped into the soil itself, and he identified India with the presence and practice of these ancient traditions. The religion of India was more than a collection of myths and rituals, more than a human tradition of belief and act, it signified a deep intimacy between culture and territory, the mark of India's alterity that animated Orientalist fantasies of both mastery and immersion. Whatever other religious traditions might make their homes there, the Orientalist held India to be essentially and fundamentally Hindu, but "Hindu" here signaled, rather than the religion of rational subjects, the process of overproduction and excess that both terrified and seduced the architects of British India.

William Jones's Ambivalence: Sublime Simplicity and Depraved Excess

In their early years, the Asiatick Society and its *Asiatick Researches* were largely the product of the vast energy of the Society's founder, Sir William Jones. The character of the society, as well as the style and subject matter of the journal bore the imprint of his personality and interests for the duration of the *Researches*. He set the collegial tone of the pieces and the expectation of conversational exchange between authors, so that the *Researches* developed as a medium for ongoing discussions about issues, translations, and discoveries. Jones's aims were suitably catholic for this sort of dialogue. He praised the infinite diversity of Asia's "religion and government . . . laws, manners, customs, and languages . . . as well as [the] features and complexions" of its people and recognized that inquiries into this array of topics would require the disinterested contributions of many.[82] He proclaimed, therefore, the object of the Society's inquiries to be the augmentation of the West's understanding of "Man and Nature" by examining their Oriental manifestations.[83]

Just as Jones's use of such abstract reifications as "man" and "nature" might suggest, his own contributions to the *Researches* had as their underlying, and often explicit, theme the unity of human history and character, a method, recognized by Cohn that enabled its practitioners to "classify, bound, and control variety and difference."[84] In response to the manifest diversity he had already invoked, Jones argued for a family of nations and outlined a shared human history located in a distant biblical age from whose legacy various peoples of the world had deviated, some more and some less, in the intervening years.[85] It was precisely these deviations, due to causes in both human nature and culture, that provided the scholar with his methodological problem: how to trace the course of history through unreliable documentary evidence to reconstruct the shared history of the human race.

His contemporaries as well as modern scholars have praised Jones for inaugurating modern Indology by demonstrating a genuine appreciation of Hindu thought and literature. Convinced that the land Britain was conquering was "the nurse of sciences, the inventress of delightful and useful arts, the scene of glorious actions, fertile in the productions of human genius [and] abounding in natural wonders," his eager curiosity infected much of Britain by the turn of the nineteenth century. Today, he is remembered among some as "the first scholar to have looked at the east without a Western bias" and as one who changed the shape of European studies of the Orient by forming "enduring relationships with members of the Bengali intelligentsia."[86]

There can be no doubt that Jones truly loved India and Asian learning and that it was through him that eastern literature began to have a real impact on Britain. It must be said, however, that Jones was able to sell some of his fellow Britons on the great value of Indian culture by drawing a sharp distinction between the ancient, elegant, and monistic philosophy of the learned classes in India on the one hand and the priestly excesses that contributed to a corruption of all that was otherwise worthy of scholarly attention on the other. This Orientalist construction of Hinduism's glorious past and precipitous decline took firm root among British rulers and some Indian reformers, permitting official regulation of what evangelicals considered an illicit and immoral popular Hinduism.[87] In Trautmann's British "Indomania" of the early nineteenth century, there are already all the signs of an ascendent Indophobia. Historiography, philosophy, literature, and religion had shone as great human achievements at various distant periods of India's past, but Jones despised the idolatrous tendencies that had turned Śaṅkara's vedānta into gross paganism and disfigured other cultural accomplishments.

Jones's first historical contribution to the *Researches*, his famous essay, "On the Gods of Greece, Italy, and India," expressed his ambivalence about Indian religion, demonstrating both its relationship to the Europe's classical ancestors and its tendency to ornament every insight and thus lose it in the resulting clutter.[88] He laid out a series of correspondences between the names and characteristics of Roman, Greek, and Hebrew deities. These similarities led him to "infer a general union or affinity between the most distinguished inhabitants of the primitive world, a family of nations descended from Noah."[89] This unity, however, had suffered at the hands of superstitious forces that conspired to fragment human community and to distance human consciousness from its history and heritage. Initially practicing the rational, historically self-conscious religion of the biblical patriarchs that venerated a single, rational deity, humankind lost contact with the memory of its ancestral faith after the great deluge that marked the point of its original dispersal.[90] This idea about human descent Trautmann aptly names a "Mosaic ethnology," a reference to the "tree of nations" described in biblical books attributed to Moses that portrays a segmentary descent structure that "ramifies endlessly."[91] Such a discourse of origins and deviations, an understanding of history that reduces it to a "process of division, expansion, and individuation," masquerades as a deciphering of classical Hindu, and Hebrew myth but quietly, as Bruce Lincoln has demonstrated, enters a "recursive spiral," and spins a new myth with the previously inherited images and storylines.[92] Although A. J. Arberry was clearly right in rescuing Jones from Sir John Shore's "pathetically anxious" attempt to manipulate the memory of Jones and fashion him an ardent evangelical,[93] at the very least, William Jones indulged in the very style of narrative construction for which he faulted Hindu historians: uncritically augmenting, nurturing, and elaborating a body of mythical history.

He imagined that a gradual physical and spiritual migration from humanity's origination point resulted in deviations from an earlier, "rational adoration of the only true God."[94] Jones cited three causes for these deviations: 1) the abandonment of historical truth in favor of myth and fable; 2) the abandonment of rational apprehension of the physical world in favor of adoration of heavenly bodies; and 3) the misuse or misunderstanding of poetic and symbolic language as literal. The first was a kind of euhemerism: "the mad apotheosis of truly great men, or of little men falsely called great, has been the origin of gross idolatrous errors in every part of the pagan world." The second demonstrated a similar disregard for the testimony of reason. The third represents a forerunner to Friedrich Max Müller's "solar mythology" thesis wherein Jones faulted the "magick of poetry," whose allegories and metaphors uncritical readers tended to convert into personalities and individual fanciful spirits, thus creating countless deities.[95] Jones's general presumption, then, was of a human society and culture created initially as rational and monotheistic as the biblical texts indicated. He attributed all later elaborations on or deviations from this initial rational, monotheistic state to a segmentation of Noah's descendants after the flood into the nations of the world and the scattering of linguistic groups after the fall of the Tower of Babel. In succeeding generations, different linguistic and ethnic groups gradually altered or forgot their monotheistic heritage preserved in the Bible and to a lesser degree in other ancient literature such as the Vedas.[96]

Jones's three causes for the mutation of divine revelation into myth had one important characteristic in common. They each demonstrated a multiplication of meaning, an indulgence in excess. For Jones, rational representation operated with perfect transparency, exhibiting an unmistakable, unique, one-to-one correspondence between sign and object. Historical figures and events, objects in nature, and even abstract moral and metaphysical concepts were real things that the proper use and interpretation of language would render concretely and accurately. Jones was no realist or nominalist. He was not critical of poetry or allegory per se. Indeed, he was an accomplished poet himself.[97] He held fast throughout his career, however, to the notion that history, religion, and literature in their highest forms were rational pursuits, that their aim was rational expression, and that their subjects were concrete, rationally discernible realities. When religious acts of reading or writing failed to strive for or apprehend such objective realities in a rational spirit, they led the way to paganism, idolatry, and foolish scientific and historical claims.

In his later work, Jones continued to develop his theory that Hindus shared a religious and historical heritage with Greeks, Romans, and Hebrews, and that their records of this heritage and all their learning had been corrupted by centuries of fabrication and accretion to the historical record. "Every branch of knowledge in this country has been embellished by poetical fables," he complained.[98] He wrote of a pure monotheism, once practiced in ancient Persia, that brahmanical theology had corrupted with its priestly apparatus and superfluous deities.[99] He had already discovered that Sanskrit bore resemblances close enough to Latin and Greek to posit an earlier mother tongue of all three.[100] Treating India's mythology as a living relic of Europe's own ancestral heritage, he found similarities between Hindu and Hebrew lore, suggesting both peoples were heirs to Noah, but that the Hindu chronology of the deluge and succeeding human history were so confused and exaggerated that it had mythologized the story almost beyond recognition.[101]

For Jones, it was not only in recording history but also in passing down scientific discoveries that Hindus could not be trusted to leave the materials unaugmented with myth, fable, and needless speculation. Reading scientific documents for their useful information was no less tedious than plodding through mythologized history. The superfluity of the Indian mind was general:

> [G]eography, astronomy, and chronology have, in this part of Asia,
> shared the fate of authentick history, and, like that, have been so
> masked and bedecked in the fantastick robes of mythology and meta-
> phor, that the real system of Indian philosophers and mathemati-
> cians can scarce be distinguished.[102]

Puzzling out astronomical calculations or discerning the principles of Indian music meant entering a textual maze of confusing detail, mythological aside, and an overabundance of names and technical terms.[103] Much of the error of the Hindu mind stemmed from its mythologizing epistemology, which did not distinguish religious ideas from empirical reality. Jones believed that for Hindus "all knowledge, divine and human, is traced to its source in the Vedas."[104] Religion and reason were hopelessly enmeshed because Hindus saw their sacred texts as the repository of all that was true, and so myth and science developed not independently of one another, but fully interlaced, as expressions of the same underlying religious beliefs. All Indian cultural phenomena were at base religious phenomena. Scientists and historians had seen no need to distinguish the empirically verifiable from the mythological. In fact, they multiplied texts' mythological references and digressions.

Other critics have noted themes related to the rise of Romanticism in Europe in Jones's analysis of Asia.[105] He clearly foresaw Romanticism's distinction between Reason as the faculty of clarity and analysis and Imagination as the intellectual ability to combine disparate impressions to create poetry and figurative speech. The first he attributed to the European mind, the latter to the Asiatics.[106] Hindus were gifted poets, but to the detriment of their science. Their propensity to augmentation, elaboration, and mythological digression also prevented them from plotting anything like the clear, linear narratives that characterized European historical and scientific writing. The impulses that drove Hindus to fashion deities and rites endlessly were the same impulses that inspired them to tinker with scientific and historical texts, inserting commentary and mythological aside with each textual revision and recension. Just as Jones found that the land of India itself wildly multiplied fantastic forms, so its native chroniclers could not produce a simple and clear textual presentation. Multiplicity and ornamentation were basic characteristics of Hindu thought, symptomatic of its habitual indulgence in luxury, elaborate ritual, and fantastic cosmology.

Orientalism vs. Ornamentalism

Jones was only echoing familiar British complaints. In evangelical polemic against Hinduism, a common motif mocked Hindus for venerating images so encumbered with offerings of silk, jewels, and flowers as to be all but invisible to their worshipers. Hindu ritual favored lavish show and embellishment to the extent that the ostensible focus of temple worship was no longer clearly discernable. The authors of the *Asiatick Researches* followed Jones's lead and more forcefully conveyed an image of Hindu scientific and historical knowledge as a collection of legitimate discoveries and insights that gradually, over time, had become lost in the numerous overlays of myth and fabrication that generations of expositors had heaped upon it. Just as the very soil and climate of India bubbled forth in exotic and fantastic creatures, so the Indian mind itself endlessly produced competing versions of historical and scientific findings. Unlike Europeans, Indian scholars, it was said, did not build upon one another's work and progress, staircase-like, to higher and higher insight, but manufactured new accounts, one on top of the other and inserted their own, often contradictory, arguments into one another's texts without noting the fact.

The Calcutta Orientalists who produced the *Researches* complained of texts that resembled so much else that they found in Hindu culture, often invoking a kernel-and-husk or pearl-and-oyster image. Overly ornamented with myth, speculation, meditation, lengthy genealogies, and praises to gods and kings, these texts required the Orientalist to sift through various layers of accretions, tossing aside the useless and superfluous detail to find the nugget of genuine historical or scientific truth. Like the Hindu idol buried under layers of silk and jeweled offerings, the authentic, factual, or original discoveries of Hindu thought could not be discerned at a glance.

The very first volume of the *Researches* had sounded this theme. William Jones, setting forth his grand project to sketch the outlines of Asian history by considering the histories of the five Oriental races, complained that Hindu chronicles were wrapped in a "cloud of fables."[107] But he had only sounded a theme; much more was to come. As Ranajit Guha has noted, British access to India's past could only come by way of constructing a diachronic narrative, a mode of rendering the past alien to accustomed Indian ways of representing it.[108] The Orientalist frustration with traditional Indian historical narrative and the intention to supplant it could not have been more obvious. Reporting on the ruins at Mahabalipuram, William Chambers described "stupendous" monuments, intricately carved with countless heavenly scenes, and tried to locate some historical record that might account for their construction. He found none but what he regarded as ridiculously unreliable brahmanical tales about the place. He thought these records priestly fabrications to disguise the truth behind their "wretched superstitions," but took heart in the possibility that hidden in these stories might be "some imperfect record of great events." The great obstacle to discerning a diachronic, linear Hindu history was that India's only historians were poets, and "whatever they relate . . . is wrapped up in this burlesque garb, set off, by way of ornament, with circumstances hugely incredible and absurd."[109] Chambers's visual idiom of ornamentation sat comfortably with emergent British notions that Hindu culture and Indian lands were prone to exuberant overproduction.

Other authors made the same sorts of remarks about Hindu science. On the whole, the authors of the scientific articles in the *Researches* were genuinely impressed with the accomplishments made in mathematics and astronomy by Hindu scholars. Reuben Burrow, a career mathematician who had taken an appointment to India in order to make the money necessary to allow him to pursue his research unfettered, learned Sanskrit and struggled through Indian mathematical treatises. He praised Hindu discoveries, including a method for calculating the moon's parallaxes that was more accurate than the general rule recommended in European nautical circles and a rule for doing permutations not found in the West.[110] He also argued that Hindus had described certain principles of algebra earlier than Europeans.[111] John Playfair, a professor of Mathematics at Edinburgh, was so intrigued by Hindu accomplishments in his field that he wrote to the Society with a list of issues he thought worthy of pursuing in Hindu texts.[112] As with Hindu history, however, the truly useful accomplishments of scholars lay buried in texts densely filled with speculation, myth, and debate. Samuel Davis alerted the Society that underneath its mythic garb, Hindu astronomy could boast of real achievement, but discovering it required much tedious reading. Alongside computations of the moon's eclipses, he found speculation about fantastic Hindu divisions of time into kalpas and yugas. In order to find genuine scientific reasoning, one had to learn to discern the layers of the text and separate out the priestly foolishness from the learned discourse. The same text might account for a lunar eclipse with both brahmanical descriptions of Rahu devouring the moon and detailed astronomical calculations of times and motions. India's true scientists were up against the priestly guardians of Hindu mythical traditions, and whereas some bolder souls attacked unscientific opinions outright, most rational scientists could present their findings only by cautiously integrating their discoveries with the tales of the brahmans.[113]

Francis Wilford's Gnostic Scholasticism

One form that this push to penetrate the layers of needless ornamentation and extract the prized gems of Oriental knowledge took was the comparative method exemplified by Francis Wilford, in which he painstakingly correlated Hindu, Greek, Egyptian, Hebrew, and Latin sources to argue that ancient Indian sages had possessed stores of esoteric knowledge that latter-day idolatrous superstition had perverted and obscured. Wilford's obsession with finding parallels in various mythologies and his gnostic quest for a lost, ancient wisdom was by no means unique or original. He followed a set of inquiries pursued by William Jones and Jacob Bryant (1715–1801) before him to reconstruct the ancient unity of the human race and its wisdom through philological means.[114] It was Wilford's dogged insistence on the validity of conclusions he drew on the scantiest and most fanciful of linguistic evidence and his stubborn refusal to allow embarrassment and scandal stemming from poor personal and historical judgment that set him apart. It might be tempting dismiss Wilford's work as misguided and unfounded scholarship of no contemporary significance. O. P. Kejariwal in particular has tried to isolate Wilford's work from that of the other contributors to the early volumes of the *Researches*. He admits only, for example, that Jones "fell prey" to Wilford's theories and fails fully to acknowledge that Jones accepted them for publication and endorsed Wilford's approach on the whole.[115] Even Thomas Trautmann, who recognizes that Wilford's work represented widespread ideas, allows William Jones to distance himself from Wilford's wilder claims and tarnished reputation.[116] Wilford's research, however, if not each and every of his conclusions, was clearly seductive to Jones, the Asiatic Society, and its readership. He composed nine separate essays, some in multiple parts, totaling almost a thousand pages—very nearly 10 percent of the entire bulk of the collected *Asiatick Researches*, the very journal praised as its influence waned for once having "comprehended the sum of our knowledge of the classical literature of India." Further, Jones himself publicly endorsed many of Wilford's findings, declaring in print that he had abandoned his initial mistrust of Wilford's scholarship when he examined the sources himself. Jones told the readers of the *Researches*, "I am happy in bearing testimony to his perfect good faith and general accuracy," but, he also warned, "we must ever attend to the distinction between evidence and conjecture."[117] The issue here is not at all one of variable linguistic rigor and insight, for William Jones utilized the same comparative linguistic method as Wilford and embraced his etymologies, but of the pervasiveness of the ideas of the unity and antiquity of human wisdom, the communion of ancient sages, and the desecration of these hallowed inheritances by superstitious and polytheistic inclinations.

Wilford's first contribution to the *Researches* was an attempt to identify an Indian city named "Tagara" in ancient Greek texts with modern-day Deogir.[118] Here he freely admitted he was not competent in Hindu antiquities or languages,[119] a shortcoming that was to lead to his great embarrassment. In "On Egypt and Other Countries Adjacent to the Cali River, or Nile of Ethiopia," Wilford attempted to demonstrate that much of Hindu mythology consisted of Indian recollections of contact with the wisdom of the pharaohs' Egypt. As many linguists of the day, he relied heavily on superficial resemblances among different foreign words and fashioned many erroneous etymologies to account for his speculations. He expressed bold confidence in the method of correlating names and words on the basis of phonological similarity:

> So striking, in my apprehension, is the similarity between several
> Hindu legends and numerous passages in Greek authors concern-
> ing the Nile, and the countries on its borders, that, in order to
> evince their identity, or at least their affinity, little more is requisite
> than barely to exhibit a comparative view of them. . . . (T)here is
> abundant reason to believe that the Hindus have preserved the reli-
> gious fables of Egypt, though we cannot yet positively say by what
> means the Brahmens acquired a knowledge of them.[120]

Among the conclusions this method produced were the claims that the pyramids of Egypt were brahman temples to the Hindu goddess Padma Devi and that the Nile found frequent mention in Sanskrit texts as the Nila, or blue river.[121] In a later piece, Wilford, taking a cue from Jones, tried to identify the biblical Noah with Satyavrata, the mythical seventh Manu of the *Bhāgavata Purāṇa* who survived the flood that began the current age.[122] He also argued that the brother of Krishna, Balarāma, since he was progeny of Vishnu, was by that fact "Harikula," or "of the family of Vishnu," and by derivation, "Hericula, Heri-culas, and Hercules."[123]

By correlating various figures from different literary traditions, Wilford aimed to demonstrate the impossibility of contemporary Hindu claims about the life spans and accomplishments of their heroes, and thus utterly to destroy "their monstrous system, which I have rejected as absolutely repugnant to the course of nature and human reason."[124] He relied wholly and implicitly on the Orientalist historiographical dichotomy that held ancient Hindus to be wise and pious people who reflected and developed the same timeless wisdom conveyed in the cultures of other great civilizations, but found contemporary Hinduism to be tainted by brahmanical pride, cultural chauvinism, and the inflation of the importance of historical and mythological Hindu characters.

Wilford's passion for his message eventually overran his attention to detail. In "The Sacred Isles of the West," a six hundred–page essay endeavoring to show that the British Isles were revered in ancient Sanskrit texts, Wilford confessed publicly that he had been duped and that many of his arguments had no textual basis whatsoever. The brahman pandits he had commissioned to survey Hindu literature for him had fabricated evidence in order to please Wilford and continue in his employ. They went as far as to actually compose documents with the names and places Wilford hoped to find mentioned to give credence to his ideas about the ancient communion among races. Almost unbelievably, he forged boldly ahead, constructing more virtually baseless theories about the ancient intercourse of sages. His stubborn pursuit of linguistic evidence that would undermine India's overburdened historical narratives and render her merely a "museum of Europe's past"[125] continued without further qualification in the very article in which he revealed his error and his assistants' deception. Kejariwal's assessment of his notions about ancient Indian reverence for Britain is lavishly generous, calling them the "solitary statement of a theory."[126] Dismissed within a generation, and soon utterly forgotten, Wilford remains, nevertheless, a major character in the British construction of Hinduism for the legitimacy his turgid academic prose lent to the image of a tradition groaning under the weight of its priests' theological and literary excesses.

Colebrooke's Ritual Turn

With the participation of H. T. Colebrooke in the Asiatick Society beginning in 1794, the *Asiatick Researches* took up a new interest in the ritual practices of Hindus. The brief hegemony of the Calcutta Orientalist over British discourse about Hinduism was here clearly beginning to wane as the qualified Indomania of a relative handful of scholars and administrators was drowning in a torrent of popular disgust and lurid fascination with idolatrous Hindu rite. While Jones was at the helm of the publication, its emphasis remained squarely on texts, literature, and artifacts, especially as means for ascertaining Hindu belief and Indian history. After Jones's death in 1794, the Society continued to function under the leadership of evangelical Governor-General Sir John Shore, who himself contributed only a single essay to the journal, a piece with a noticeable anti-brahmanical cast that decried the violence and oppression the lower orders suffered under priestly "superstitions."[127] The Society then languished in inactivity under two disinterested presidents until Colebrooke injected it with new life as its leader in 1806.[128] In the meantime, he had already contributed eight articles to the journal, some of great historical importance. He brought with him new methods for enumerating and evaluating Hindu phenomena that more fully explicated institutional and regional variations in Hinduism.[129] Colebrooke was interested not just in what the texts themselves offered in the way of cosmology, history, or science, but also in what they suggested about Hindus as ritual actors and embodiers of a religious identity. Colebrooke was no ethnographer, even in the primitive manner of William Ward or William Carey. He confined his analysis to Sanskrit texts rather than observing and reporting on ritual or social action. His essays, however, introduced into the *Researches* the intuition that a religious tradition was more than the sum of ideas expressed in elite texts, and the Asiatick Society moved away from confirming and correlating the names of countless deities and kings and toward the study of Hindu actors and action.

Colebrooke's first article, "On the Duties of a Faithful Hindu Widow," published in the fourth volume of 1795, drew attention to the textual sanctions for the practice of satī, then beginning to attract wide attention in the British public.[130] We see again here the agenda of the Asiatick Society driven by the interests of the East India Company. Religious practices were quickly becoming policy issues for the Company under pressure from political leaders and evangelicals. Ritual had become the problematic feature of Indian religion, in the same way that literature and history were timely for a previous generation of Company officials seeking to construct institutions of law and government in line with Indian social arrangements and religious doctrines.[131] Colebrooke determined that, although endorsed in certain sources, satī had always been exceedingly rare and had, over the years, acquired a number of ritual components not found in his oldest sources. He examined a range of texts to judge the Hindu claim of the practice's antiquity and therefore its legitimacy in the eyes of contemporaneous Hindu authorities. Without clear textual mandate, preferably from the oldest and therefore most authoritative texts, a practice was subject to regulation or abolition by British rulers who could thus circumvent their pledge to noninterference in the religion of their colonial subjects. This equation of antiquity with authority provided a means for the colonial government to control the variety that they actually encountered.[132] Colebrooke opened the way for Britons to define, circumscribe, and thereby regulate Hinduism on the assumption that ancient Sanskrit authors provided legitimate testimony but contemporaneous native testimony could reflect a corrupted tradition. In later articles, Colebrooke continued to craft an officially sanctioned body of Hindu practice not by taking recourse to contemporary Hindu authorities but, in fact, by disregarding any such interpretation and cutting straight to classical textual testimony.[133]

Resident and superintendent of Benaras, later governor of Bengal, John Duncan demonstrated what the transition to a properly ethnographic approach could accomplish in his 1798 "Account of Two Fakeers," about two men he had come to know in Benaras.[134] Engravings of each man exoticized the asceticism the article aimed to demystify, but Duncan gave each subject considerable space to shape his own narrative and he reproduced their own words at length. The first, named Prān Pūrī, was pictured with his arms over his head where the renunciant had held them until they had withered and became immobile. He spoke of being a former respected emissary between Governor-General Hastings and the government of Tibet. He had retired from the world to seek release in Benaras, where Duncan found him in this ascetic posture. The second "fakeer," Paramsvatantra ("supreme self-possession"), would appear years later in the Church Missionary Society's *Missionary Papers*, his voice silenced and his experience mocked as an illustration of popular Hinduism's folly and superstition.[135] Duncan displayed him on a bed of spikes, apparently undisturbed by pain or discomfort (see figure 4.3). By way of explanation, Paramsvatantra recounted his quest for a divinized status which the gods would award him as payment for this self-torture. He had demanded that a Raja who had interrupted his meditations construct this bed of spikes for him or suffer a holy man's curse. The piece stands out from the rest of the *Asiatick Researches* for the unedited and unvarnished testimony to their religious motivations and aims the subjects were permitted.

Whereas Jones and the founding members of the Asiatick Society had found Hindu literary production itself idolatrous in its preference for ornamentation over clear, transparent disclosure of verifiable historical or scientific fact, under Colebrooke, the *Researches*, in its second generation, castigated Hindus for the augmentation of textual authority with superfluous ritual act. The relationship between ritual text and ritual action assumed a high profile in the journal's research agenda. This program demanded both textual translation and exegesis on the one hand and ethnographic thoroughness on the other. The grasp of Hindu ritual thus achieved would disclose the absence of a correspondence between text and act, and thereby arm the colonial government to attack Hindu practices whose condemnation by Britons and reforming Hindus alike was threatening to destabilize its rule. Satī, hook-swinging, infanticide, and a host of brahmanical inventions were cast out of an official colonial Hinduism by British scholars and administrators who assumed the rights to define its boundaries. Multiplication, excess, and ornamentation, the imagined perpetual antagonists to the delineation of clear and distinct Hindu ideas, continued to dog Orientalist enthusiasm for the subject. In the early years of the *Researches*, the clarity and precision Britain sought would be merely academic, a means of making sense out of a mass of data by scholars and administrators residing at the geographic center of political and military power in British India. By 1830, however, with vast tracts of India in the possession of the East India Company now seeking to govern a large and diverse population, order and discipline came to be administrative and military tasks—a labor to which a transformed Asiatic Society would contribute.

The *Asiatick Researches*, 1810–1836

In the second half of its life, as British domination of the subcontinent became both more sure and more anxious, the *Researches* began to occupy itself with

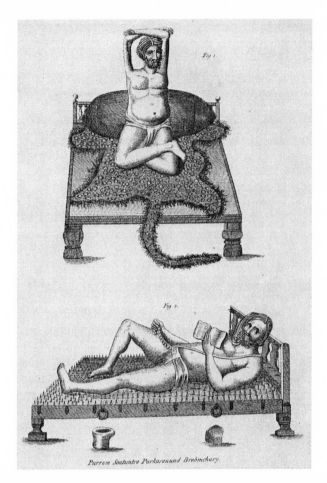

FIGURE 4.3. A Hindu ascetic profiled in *Asiatick Researches*, vol. 5 (1798), from William Jones, *Supplemental Volumes to the Works of Sir William Jones: Containing the Whole of the Asiatick Researches hitherto Published Excepting Those Papers Already Inserted in His Works* (London: Printed for G. G. and J. Robinson . . . and R. H. Evans . . . : T. Davison, 1801), plate facing page 834. Special Collections and Archives, Robert W. Woodruff Library, Emory University. AC7 .J65 supp. V.2.

the more mundane bits of knowledge it deemed necessary for effective and complete hegemony. Increasingly, it published geographical studies, censuses, and regional reports. When it dealt with religion, it showed a growing interest in the daily religious life of ordinary people over general beliefs or ancient literature. Popular ritual, distinct sects, and vernacular languages appeared as topics of discussion. Three factors seem especially to have accompanied or contributed to this shift to statistical and ethnological thinking: the presence of Horace Hayman Wilson's more comprehensive methodology for studying religion, the colonial state's drive to complete Britain's geographical knowledge of its possessions, and the differentiation of separate discourses for scientific and ethnological inquiries.

Horace Hayman Wilson's Living Hinduism

Horace Hayman Wilson's work did not appear in the *Researches* until volume fifteen of 1825, when he introduced a translation of "An Essay on the Hindu History of Cashmir," which he declared "the only Sanskrit composition yet discovered, to which the title of History, can with any propriety be applied."[136] To the remaining six volumes he contributed nine pieces, including the two-part "Sketch of the Religious Sects of the Hindus," his most significant contribution to the journal.[137] Wilson brought to the *Researches* an appreciation for religious subjectivity and for the complex social and historical nexus situating religion absent from earlier concern for Hindu history and literature. He never abandoned the most ancient religious texts or his belief in their ultimate authority to judge matters Hindu, but he worked to complement this ancient witness with portraits of contemporary living Hinduisms, whether he believed they could claim textual sanction or not. His "Sketch" explicitly countered the notion of a unified faith and offered an encyclopedic catalog of various Hindu subgroups whose identity and character he had gleaned from modern texts, both popular and scholarly. Significantly, however, he augmented this information with oral reports from Indians he interviewed in Bengal who aided him by "filling up or correcting . . . the errors or omissions" of his textual sources.[138] His reliance on the firsthand, subjective interpretations of contemporary informants marked a new turn in British studies of Hinduism. This rather late recognition of the importance of native informants for more than translation assistance distinguished nineteenth-century British ethnology from its counterpart on the continent, whose exponents like DuPerron, Sonnerat, and the Abbé Dubois had long regarded the witness of religious subjects as critical, not just subsidiary, religious data. Although he continued to hold firmly to the idea of a sharp distinction between "pure" (i.e., textual) Hinduism and what he called its "popular" forms, Wilson shook British ethnology from its textual stupor and awakened it to the institutional, communal, and ritual life of religious groups.

Where earlier formulations stressed Hinduism's likeness to the landscape of India itself—tangled, messy, irrational, profusely self-multiplying—Wilson's firm command of his material and his clarity in exposition showed the religion of India to be intricately developed and differentiated. With Wilson, the scholarly British encounter with Hinduism no longer reads like a colonizer's initial overwhelmed and anxious assumption of power or like a Romantic fantasy superimposed on dimly comprehended data. If Jones's enthusiasm and industry brought Hinduism into the imagination of the educated British public, and Colebrooke's facility with Sanskrit cracked its most ancient texts, Wilson's awareness of a living tradition and its historical antecedents established the modern study of religion in Britain at the same time that it announced the colonial state's determination to monitor, and thus potentially to intervene in, the expression of religious and communal identity. Subsequent British ethnology would view popular Indian religion not just as something that "had to be normalized and located in a discourse that would make India into . . . a living museum of ancient practices from which earlier stages of universal world history could be recovered," but as an organic component of Indian social relations, an attitude that rendered Hindu ritual subject to administrative surveillance and scrutiny.[139]

His entry on the Liṅgāyat sect reveals Wilson's careful analysis but also the potential bureaucratic ends a more comprehensive and complex rubric for religion could serve. Worshipers of Shiva in the form of the linga, this South Indian sect was potentially fodder for less-rigorous scholars of India drawn to report on lurid matters. Wilson's erudition, however, clarified the nature of the symbol and refuted popular British notions about its graphic representation of a human organ that aroused erotic emotions in devotees. He exhaustively referenced Puranic sources for the worship, described devotees' appearance, and tried to document the group's geographical dispersion.[140]

Wilson moved easily in the *Researches* from such ethnological inquiries to the study of ancient inscriptions, coins, and literature. In his analyses, he did not, as did Jones and Wilford, choose freely from different texts to sketch the tradition with broad strokes, neither did he practice the sort of comparative method Cohn describes as the effort to "construct a history of the relationship between India and the West [and] to classify and locate their civilizations on an evaluative scale of progress and decay."[141] He communicated clearly, nevertheless, the sense that Hindu history was complex and the religion varied widely from period to period, region to region, class to class. He aimed to highlight distinctions within the tradition and to promote awareness of its diversity. To be sure, Wilson continued to maintain the sharp distinction he inherited between popular and philosophical versions of Hinduism and to hold to an essentialist framework for religion. He showed a disdain for popular forms, which he considered generally so many bastardizations of purer doctrine, the consequence of a universal "Spirit of Polytheism" that infected many religions.[142] Speculative religious thought and popular religious practice both invited his scholarly energy, the former on its own merits, but the latter only as the variegated and labyrinthine creations of the same pagan or polytheistic instincts that all races possessed and that reforming government must confront.

Physical India: Geography and Landscape

As the British in India began to contemplate new tasks and responsibilities commensurate with the expansion of their territory and power, the *Asiatick Researches* began to consider the land of India in a new light. While flora and fauna continued to interest some contributors and readers, other naturalists pondered the further geographical reaches of the subcontinent. In time, not the natural processes and products of the land, but its vast, distant mountains and its winding rivers quickened the British imagination.

As early as the sixth and seventh volumes (1799 and 1801), articles appeared charting the particular journeys of travelers through little-known areas of India.[143] With the eleventh volume of 1810, however, a distinct genre of travel literature emerged that disclosed a new British interest in the land and a full-blown Romantic perception of the sublime in nature. For over twenty years thereafter, the *Asiatick Researches* published article after article describing travelers' attempts to trace the course of India's fabled rivers to their sources or to ascend its mountain ranges to survey vistas previously unattained by a European. These narratives are the colonial administration's answer to the Romantic landscapes rendered by such British artists as J.M.W. Turner and Joseph Wright.[144] On a literary level, they consistently proclaimed the power of the landscape to elicit particular emotional reactions, its alluring danger, and its encouragement to the attainment of a religious vision.[145] These pieces were not, however, intended merely to ponder the spiritual power of the land, but to provide cartographic and strategic information to the colonial government about the more remote parts of the Indian subcontinent. The *Researches* effortlessly wedded Romantic contemplation to colonial consolidation. The journal celebrated both the personal heroic quest and the national triumph embodied in the soldier or surveyor who braved extremes of temperature, near-starvation, and innumerable other physical dangers and emerged as the bard whose spiritual meditations on the affective impact of the landscape couched the cold data of latitude, longitude, and altitude.

The chief geographical object of conquest at the turn of the nineteenth century was the source of the river Ganges. Myth told of the river descending from the heavens and falling upon the gracious head of Shiva, who caught its destructive force and allowed it to flow harmlessly through his hair and bless India with its unmatched powers of purification. Such myths persisted, in part, because the actual source of the Ganges was so remote that few human beings had probably ever set eyes on it. Renowned as the site of its terrestrial descent was Gangotri, high in the Himalayas, where a small shrine stood, attended by a few priests and visited seasonally by a few hardy pilgrims. It was known, however, that the river stretched further back beyond this point, where it wound around a rock formation to come into view. No recorded traveler had succeeded in getting past this difficult point to view its actual source.

The first British attempt to chart the course of the Ganges and locate its source was undertaken by army surveyor Lt. W. S. Webb who followed the Ganges northward from Haridwar in 1808, taking with him several Indian assistants who viewed the journey as a religious quest. His account is replete with descriptions of pilgrims and yogis striving to subsist in the remotest parts of India.[146] Webb never succeeded in getting even as far as Gangotri. Intimidated by the already grueling climb and treacherous paths, he deputed one of the assistants traveling with him to ascertain whether the place appeared as described in various Hindu reports. James Baillie Fraser successfully reached

Gangotri in 1815, and in 1820 the *Researches* published his journal from the tour (see figure 4.4).[147]

It was Captain J. A. Hodgson who finally located Gaumukh, the source of the Ganges, in 1817 in a massive glacier that he described only as a puzzling, rocky bank of snow.[148] Having reached Gangotri, where others had been forced to turn back, Hodgson managed to ford the narrow but violent river and continue on for a few days. Embodying the Victorian determination "to behave toward the countryside as if it was a testing ground for muscular endurance," he ascended further.[149] Earthquakes repeatedly brought boulders tumbling toward his party, and they slept every night fearful that one might strike them. Having ventured beyond all sources of food, they were in danger of being stranded without provisions. Pressing well beyond the point any recorded European travelers had achieved, they beheld the magnificent scenery: "The noble three-peaked mountain shines in our front and is the grandest and most splendid object the eye of man ever beheld."[150] They spent hours wading through the slushy snow that often drew them in up to their necks. After some days, they reached Gaumukh, the spur of a glacier from which the river poured. They scaled it and tried to press further, but finally, perceiving that the snow and ice would bear their weight no longer, they turned back, never fully certain that they had, in fact, discovered the source of this branch of the Ganges.

FIGURE 4.4. Gangotri as it appeared to James Baillie Fraser, the first British traveler to reach it, 1815. By permission of the British Library, P48

Reports such as these pushed the borders of the British frontier further back while they expanded Britain's knowledge of its territory. In the interior, a parallel campaign was underway in which the *Researches* played a similar role. Increasingly, officials published in the journal their censuses and surveys of cities, regions, or states that the British already possessed. These reports differed substantially from earlier issues' accounts of tribal peoples occupying the more remote areas controlled by the British. Where earlier descriptions were narrative in form and offered lively, if sometimes fanciful, accounts of the natives, these later articles were largely statistical, often containing extensive tables and charts, with relatively little anecdotal material. They bore titles such as "Statistical View of the Population of Burdwan" and "An Account, Geographical, Statistical, and Historical of Orissa Proper, or Cuttack."[151] Not all cold figures and dry geographical data, they nonetheless were clearly geared to the purposes of administering a growing colonial possession. Indicating the decline of the gentlemanly component of amateur science and the rise of academic professionalization, they were concerned with population data, agricultural production, the availability of building materials, the height of hills, and other details, the command of which was necessary for efficient administration and defense of a region.[152]

James Prinsep's "Census of the Population of the City of Benares" was not atypical of this genre, although, reflecting the discipline and energy he would bring to the Asiatick Society, it is perhaps more thorough than many others.[153] A tightly controlled study employing a rigorous method, the census counted the city's residents, neighborhood by neighborhood, and grouped them according to caste or other relevant family association. Prinsep was able to correct earlier surveys and produce such useful data as a record of the primary staples of the Benarasi people and a twenty-year record of the prices of a dozen different grains.[154] Like other similar studies, Prinsep's census differed from earlier regional surveys in its manifest intent to assist the administration of governmental projects. He was concerned with religion, but his interests lay in such information as the relative number of Hindus and Muslims and the population of resident ascetics living on charity, rather than in beliefs and practices. He considered religious ideas about food, but for the purposes of ascertaining the quantity and price of goods consumed rather than for describing Hindu dietary practices. This report and others like it had an obvious stake in the business of governing people and administering civic institutions, and they are far less captivated by the exotic native culture than earlier reporters. In the early years of the nineteenth century, marked by the East India Company's acquisition of vast tracts of land, the desire for knowledge of India took on a different character. "Knowing the country" implied, as C. A. Bayly has made clear, having access to systems of information that would allow firm control of economic, legal, and military power.[155] The overt assistance the *Asiatick Researches* provided to this effort marks a new age in British discourse about India: "the arcane knowledge of India, purely mysterious to an earlier age, is now reduced to scientific information."[156]

The Differentiation of Scientific and Cultural Discourses

In the late 1700s, William Jones could move freely from translating the *Gītā Govinda* to constructing new branches for the Linnean system of biological classification. He embodied the goals of the infant society whose members were not professional scholars but soldiers and bureaucrats studying in their spare time to crack open the secrets of Asia by interrogating "Man and Nature." In its infant years, during a time in Britain when natural history was more of a national passion than a scientific discipline, a period marked by an "almost total absence of a separate world of professional science," the journal relied as much on the intuition and industry of its contributors as it did on their specialized knowledge.[157] Only as the nineteenth century advanced along with the consolidation of the British hold on India did the journal reflect a professionalized authorship. This progress is evident in the careers of the prominent Sanskritists of the Society—Wilkins, Jones, Wilford, Colebrooke and Wilson—who became increasingly specialized scholars and less full-time administrators with a passionate hobby. The tendency of early Society members to range between scientific and ethnological studies folded the natural and cultural productions of the subcontinent into the same interpretive project. With the expansion of East India Company bureaucracy and the increase in Asiatic Society membership ("Asiatic" was spelled without the "k" beginning in 1825), natural sciences developed a distinctive, quantitatively focused set of descriptive and classificatory concerns. Orientalist essentialism was dismantled in the service of specialization. Two separate audiences for the same journal also developed, one interested in studies in cultural, linguistic, and religious history, the other in the natural sciences.

The diverging needs and practices of the two types of studies led eventually to the publication of a separate journal for science, and finally to the termination of the *Asiatic Researches* altogether. What's more, as Calcutta's monopoly over the production of knowledge eroded, the Asiatic Society lost its own privileged status as other bodies, especially now-retired H. T. Colebrooke's Royal Asiatic Society in London, developed alternative discourses and publications.[158] Whereas cultural studies involving the analysis of texts or descriptions of particular societies required extended labor and resulted in lengthy essays, those Society members devoted to the sciences wanted a journal format that could accommodate shorter articles and preliminary findings. They pushed as well for an accelerated publication schedule in order to foster cooperation between scientists and a sense of a mutual, ongoing undertaking.[159] The Society had published the *Researches* only every two or three years since its inception, and thus clearly catered to the needs and desires of those who were interested in more extended investigations. The pace of scientific discovery easily outstripped the pace of publication. As the differences between these two groups mounted, the Society introduced a new journal devoted strictly to the natural world of Asia, *Gleanings in Science*, in 1829, which became the *Journal of the Asiatic Society of Bengal* under James Prinsep in 1832. The Society also revived its Physical Committee to deal with the flood of scientific questions and papers coming in. The eighteenth volume of *Asiatic Researches* (1833) came out in two parts, all of it scientific and most of it the product of surveying work. In 1836, volume nineteen also presented only scientific findings.

One cost that this increasingly quantitative and technical approach to the study of Indian flora and fauna exacted was the excision of wonder in the accounts of the natural world of India. Gone was the era when someone like Jones meditated in the pages of the *Researches* about the amusing and moody pets he had fawned over. As in contemporaneous accounts of previously un-documented tribal peoples, reports on plants and animals in this era lacked any expression of awe or surprise. Strict classification and dry description re-placed enthusiastic curiosity, if not in the investigators themselves, at least in the literature they produced.

Although not about India, no single article spells this new mood out more graphically than "Some Account of an Orang Outang of Remarkable Height Found on the Island of Sumatra."[160] In a predatory act perhaps appalling to twenty-first-century sensibilities, the author and his team located the seven-foot-tall primate in a forest and pursued him from the ground as he moved from treetop to treetop. As they chased him, they cut down the trees he left behind in his flight until they had cornered him at the edge of a now decimated grove. They then expended all their ammunition, shooting him five times but, failing to kill him, brought him to the ground by chopping down the tree to which he clung. The hunters then repeatedly stabbed the beast with spears and pummeled him with stones until he eventually expired. The author remarked on the reaction of the hunters to their brutal task: "the human-like expression of his countenance, and piteous manner of placing his hands over his wounds, distressed their feelings and almost made them question the nature of the act they were committing."[161] Accompanying this account were engravings of his dissected body which had been skinned and dismembered before transport, a cold reminder of the magnificent animal and a fitting indication of the calcu-lation and violence increasingly at the heart of British colonialism.

5

Constructing Colonial
Dharma in Calcutta

It has become an academic commonplace to observe that Hinduism,
both the term and what it signifies, appeared only in the nineteenth
century, as Europe consolidated its knowledge of Indian religions
and Indians adopted European categories and representational habits.[1] The European contribution to this process has received a great
deal of historiographic scrutiny, and a complex but coherent understanding of Europe's "orientalism" and "construction of the other"
has begun to emerge.[2] On the Indian side, the picture is not as
clear. As of yet, we have no detailed impression of the emergence of
what we might now describe as modern, popular Hinduism—still
an assortment of beliefs and practices, but one possessed of common ideas and idioms described by Wendy Doniger as the "religious
scuttlebutt" of all Hindus.[3] I use "popular" here not in its more
technical sense to indicate religion outside the control of institutions
and reflective of the common religiosity of "the people," but to suggest the simpler idea of religion with appeal to a wide segment of
Hindus and recognized by them as their common property, a religion still under development and most noticeable in Hindu nationalist politics in India today. This Hinduism began to coalesce in the
colonial period as a response to rationalist Hindu reformers, evangelical Christians, and British colonialism. This chapter[4] turns to an
early nineteenth-century Hindu newspaper to point to the emergence of an enduring modern and popular Hinduism that rejected
the rationalist monotheism of nineteenth-century Hindu reformers
and embraced instead a program carried forward to this day by the
slow ascendancy of Hindu nationalism.[5]

Academic usage has come to employ the idea of the "construction of Hinduism" to indicate the West's representation of Hindu-

ism as a unified tradition on the basis of its fragmentary comprehension of a fragmented set of multiple Indian religious traditions. For the indigenous source this chapter examines–the early nineteenth-century Bengali newspaper *Samācār Candrikā*—the phrase has broader implications, describing not only representational practices but also the manipulations of ritual, belief, and their rationale that helped produce a cohesive Hinduism in tune with its multiethnic, multireligious colonial environment. Like "construction," another English word derived from Latin, "manufacture," also aptly describes the work of this newspaper, its root sense suggesting a hands-on approach to the creation of a modern Hindu tradition. Manufacturing this Hinduism proved to be an act less of promoting particular items of doctrine or sites of authority—a strategy pursued especially by the Hindu reformer Rammohan Roy and his religious organization the Brahmo Samaj—and more of patterning a general structure for Hindu action, social and ritual. Of the possibilities available to these traditionally minded Hindus, their ideas for the shape of a modern Hinduism are remarkable for what they did *not* promote: particular deities, texts, or sectarian traditions. While Roy would insist on a rational monotheism rooted in the most ancient Hindu texts, the Vedas, the early nineteenth-century architects of modern Hinduism this chapter examines were strikingly silent on issues of doctrine and deity, and more concerned with promoting a set of norms for Hindu practice than particular items of belief.

The contours of this Hinduism are evident in the Bengali language newspaper *Samācār Candrikā* (*Moonlight of the News*), which first appeared on 5 March 1822 in the colonial city of Calcutta (see figure 5.1). It was only the fourth newspaper ever to appear in Bengali and among the very earliest native newspapers in India. An indigenous voice seeking to shape and deploy popular native opinion in a city recently penetrated by Christian missionaries, this small newspaper was a pioneer in Bengali literature, a spearhead in the "Bengal Renaissance," and a persistent champion of the poor. Allied, however, to its many progressive aspirations was an overarching desire to garrison traditional religious ideas and practices and protect them from the corrosive effects of a pervasive reformism—both western and indigenous. Among the many developments it opposed were feverish proselytizing by Christian missionaries, the reforming zeal of Rammohan Roy and his Brahmo Samaj, the youthful affronts of a growing student population enamored of such western radicals as Thomas Paine, and the intrusive tendencies of a government learning the domestic fruits of utilitarian politics.

Yet the colonial milieu and spread of print technologies called for the construction of a religion capable of both preserving the essentials of tradition and harnessing the now unleashed forces of modernity. Discovering an effective mode of transition meant appealing to the rural village and swelling metropolis alike and addressing directly such urgent questions as, Can Sanskrit retain its privileged position, or should religious expression yield further to vernacular tongues? Is caste a viable social ideology for the modern age? What transformations must ritual and image worship undergo in an age of scientific inquiry? Roy's vision of a monotheistic, de-ritualized Hinduism spoke to the experience

সমাচারচন্দ্রিকা

সদাসমাচারভূষা॰ফলাপিকা॰পদার্থচেষ্টাপরমার্থদায়িকা
বিজৃম্ভতেসর্ব্বমনোনুরঞ্জিকা॰ শ্রিয়াভবানীচরণসাচন্দ্রিকা

৪৮৫ সংখ্যা বৃহস্পতিবার ১ জ্যৈষ্ঠ ১২৩৭ সাল ই॰ ১৮৩০ সাল ১৩ মে

ধর্ম্মসভাধ্যক্ষদিগের প্রতি।

নিবেদনমিদ॰।

ধর্ম্মসভার বিশেষ কর্ম্মের বিবেচনার নিমিত্ত
অধ্যক্ষেরদিগের একত্র হওনের আবশ্যকতা
আছে অতএব আগামি ৪ জ্যৈষ্ঠ রবিবার বেলা
দুইপ্রহর ৩ তিন ঘণ্টার সময় বটতলার গলি
তে ৪১ নম্বরের বাটীতে বৈঠক হইবেক মহা
শয়েরা ঐ নির্ণীত স্থানে ও সময়ে উপস্থিত
হইয়া বিহিত করিবেন জ্ঞাপনমিতি শকাব্দাঃ
১৭৫২ জ্যৈষ্ঠস্য প্রথম দিবসীয়া।

ধর্ম্মসভা সম্পাদক
শ্রীভবানীচরণ বন্দ্যোপাধ্যায়স্য।

ধর্ম্মসভায় ধনদান।

হিন্দু বিশিষ্ট শিষ্ট মহাশয়দিগকে জ্ঞাত করা
যাইতেছে যে বর্ত্তমান শকের পত ৫ মাঘে ধর্ম্ম
সভানামে যে সমাজ স্থাপন হইয়াছে তাহার
কারণ প্রায় অনেকেই জ্ঞাত হইয়াছেন কোন
ব্যক্তি ঐ সভার অংশী হইতে মানস করেন

তিনি চাঁদার বহিতে স্বাক্ষরাঙ্কিত করিবেন
যদ্যপি কাহার নিকট বহি না যায় তেঁহ যাহা
দান করিবেন আপন নাম নিবাস লিখিয়া
চন্দ্রিকায় জ্বালয়ে পত্র পাঠাইলে তাঁহার নাম
ধনদাতার শ্রেণিতে লিখিয়া ল ওয়া যাইবেক।
শ্রীভবানীচরণ বন্দ্যোপাধ্যায়
ধর্ম্মসভা সম্পাদক।

ব্যাঙ্কনোট খোয়াগিয়াছে।

সকলকে জ্ঞাত করাযাইতেছে যে এক
কেতা বাঙ্গাল ব্যাঙ্ক নোট নং ১৫৯৩১ শিক্কা
১০০ এক শত টাকা মোকাম লাল বাজারের
পোলীসের সম্মুখে ৬ মে বৃহস্পতিবার বেলা
দুইপ্রহর ছয়ঘণ্টার সময় খোয়াগিয়াছে যদ্যপি
কেহ পাইয়া থাকহ তবে বাঙ্গাল কোলরে
মে পাইন সাহেবের নিকট পর্হুঁছিয়াদিলে
তাঁহাকে ১০ দশ টাকা পারিতোষিক দেওয়া
যাইবেক ইতি ২৮ বৈশাখ ১২৩৭ সাল।
শ্রী কাশীনাথ চক্রবর্ত্তী।
(২)

FIGURE 5.1.   Cover of the *Samācār Candrikā*, 13 May 1830. By permission of the British Library, 14133.g.6

of an educated, cosmopolitan elite alone; to the *Candrikā* it seemed narrow and dangerously innovative. At the same time, Protestant Christianity, however aggressive, never posed a serious threat to Hindu practice as a popular religious ideal. The *Candrikā*'s editor and the host of anonymous correspondents each calling him or herself only "a certain *Candrikā* reader" aimed to fortify Hindu practice by forging a religious ideology of transition with appeal to a broad constituency that could tap both the energies of popular, traditional religious devotion and broad interest in modern ideas. They celebrated rational government but abhorred its interference with Hindu religious practices, promoted the publication of vernacular schoolbooks but insisted on caste segregation in the schools for which they were intended, and argued over the desirability of female education.[6] Their efforts to imagine a truly popular Hinduism would prove to involve a series of negotiations over the widespread and competing desires aroused by colonialism.

The *Candrikā* is quite unlike the other periodical literature we have examined for clues about colonial-era representations of Hinduism, as much for reasons having to do with the aims of newspaper literature as with the pace and vitality of urban life. Bengalis today say Calcutta is a city of *hujug*, a word implying a quick and passionate embrace of current issues, and one can certainly see this ardor for the controversy of the contemporary moment in the first newspapers of Calcutta. Issues burnt quickly and brightly. But as an enterprise struggling for financial viability and driven by a set of religious principles, it attracted readers not only with its ability to exploit passing trends, but also with its commitment to the welfare of Indian religion and society. Appearing twice a week, it moved quickly to present and interpret contemporary happenings. Although it had a clear set of long-term goals, it deployed these in the everyday life of Calcutta by working them upon the news of the day. When, for example, a new school was announced, it questioned the school's curriculum, the aims and prejudices of its teachers, and the makeup of the student body, and it passed its approval or condemnation on the spot. The *Candrikā* aimed to mobilize public opinion rapidly and efficiently. The *Missionary Papers* and the *Asiatick Researches*, by contrast worked much more slowly and deliberately.

Crisis and Transition

The *Samācār Candrikā* survives only in fragments. Aside from isolated short passages quoted in other newspapers,[7] the National Library in Calcutta holds parts of the paper for the years 1843–1846, and the British Library has a complete set for the Bengali year 1237, corresponding to the western calendar year 15 April 1830 to 14 April 1831.[8] In assessing the appearance of a popular Hinduism to combat the attacks of the colonial government, Christian missionaries, and Indian reformers in Bengal, the earlier surviving editions from 1830 to 1831 are the most useful, for this particular calendar year was a benchmark in the history of colonial India. At the end of the previous year, in December 1829, Governor-General William Bentinck had outlawed the practice known to Indians as *sahamaraṇa* ("dying along with") but called by most British observers "satī."[9] By intervening to prohibit women from burning themselves on the pyres that consumed their husbands' corpses, Bentinck had rejected a promise in place since 1793 that the colonial government would not attempt to regulate religious practice.[10] Long urged by evangelical Christians in Britain and India, this move was also long feared by the orthodox Hindu community. The crisis brought to a head the conflicts brewing among colonial-era religious ideologies in India, for the satī (virtuous wife) had assumed an iconographic status for Christians and Hindus of all stripes. Her erasure by the colonial government in December 1829 led a month later to the establishment of the Dharma Sabhā (Society for Religion), which organized resistance to aspects of British rule in Bengal and to missionary proselytization of Hindus. Although it would espouse a host of causes, in its first year, the Dharma Sabhā was consumed with collecting signatures calling for a repeal of the abolition to be presented to the governor general and to the king in London. Its success in raising funds for these purposes allowed it to hire a British solicitor in Calcutta to take its case to Parliament. With its editor Bhabānīcaraṇ Bandyopādhyāya also serving as the organization's secretary, the *Samācār Candrikā* came to act as the mouthpiece of the Dharma Sabhā, and much of the paper's news focused on the activity of the society and issues that concerned it. At the time, Hindus regarded the foundation of the Dharma Sabhā as "something entirely new,"[11] and historians have tended to agree. If the British had launched a new era by intervening directly in the practice of established Hindu custom for the first time in 1829, some Hindus self-consciously helped shape the new era by forming associations, publishing newspapers, presenting issues from their own perspective, and generally exerting whatever pressure they could marshal on the government.

The *Candrikā* and the Dharma Sabhā were organs of men determined not to resurrect the past but to construct a bridge between the past and the modern age, offering an ideology of transition that would permit Hindus to prosper in the new social and economic context and still consider themselves traditional Hindus. Their concerns were not primarily political or economic but religious, founded in sacred text, mythology, and received ritual tradition, sources to which they repeatedly turned as they encountered competing Hindu and Christian ideologies. The paper greeted the new age in which it found itself with both anxiety and anticipation and saw itself as a guide through the pitfalls of the age to its potential blessings. It once cited a Bengali proverb as a mandate for its leadership. Declaring the golden age of just rulers and overflowing charity past, it reminded its readers that "today, there is no Rama, and there is no Ayodhya," invoking the paradigmatic king and his kingdom.[12] This new age required vigilance, strong leadership, and a sense of communal responsibility for the survival of Hindu dharma.

If evangelical and Orientalist Britons were engaging in a construction of Hinduism as currency for the negotiation of colonial power, the *Candrikā* was engaged in a project with more immediate and concrete effects. Its "construction of Hinduism" was an undertaking far closer to the literal meaning of the phrase, a manipulative as well as an imaginative construction. The *Candrikā* sought not just to craft a public image of Indian religion but also to promote openly Hindu unity and identity by patterning religious activity for Hindus while decentering potentially divisive issues of belief and Hindu sectarianism. It targeted the actual morphology of ritual, caste, and gender relations to foster a unified and normative Hindu practice. This construction surely involved authors and editors in the political theater of representation and counter-representation, but it also pressed them to exert their authority in the temple, in people's homes, before the wedding fire, and in all places where Hindus acted religiously and interpreted those actions for themselves and others. The *Candrikā* dictated the form of specific ritual and social practices, and it suggested the idioms through which Hindus should describe them.

It was obvious to many Bengalis that the British had far greater power than they to publicly characterize and represent Hindus in both India and Britain and that in many cases Britain had co-opted native knowledge and reproduced it, in different forms, as its own. Sisir Kumar Das has called the native pandit a "mere tool" in the consolidation of colonial knowledge of India, and the *Candrikā* regularly cried out against the "parcel of lies" told about Hindus.[13] It was objecting, however, to more than plain untruths, for it well knew that what plagued Hinduism were men with the money and means to imagine publicly a particular brand of Hinduism that advanced their particular interests. On the subject of sahamaraṇa, for instance, one Benaras pandit observed that many shastras had been translated into English, but "they have been translated to serve the interests of the king." The British interpretive method led them to select passages relevant to the practice, but such a method ignored the thrust of the tradition more generally, for the English had "mastery of a partial shastra, which does not embrace the whole of our learning," and this context would be necessary for fathoming the reasons a woman became satī.

Among Bengali language papers, the *Candrikā* had been preceded by the *Samācār Darpan* (*Mirror of the News*) of the Serampore Christian mission, a very short-lived, Indian-owned paper called the *Bengal Gazette*, and Rammohan Roy's own *Saṃbād Kaumudī* (also meaning "Moonlight of the News"), all founded within a very few years of one another (the last two do not survive). Edited by John Clark Marshman, son of Joshua, one of the famous trio at Serampore that included William Carey and William Ward, *Samācār Darpan* had consistently promoted a reformist line of thinking and attempted, at the same time, to avoid outright offense to Hinduism. The *Kaumudī*, on the other hand, promoted Roy's political ideas. These two remained the *Candrikā*'s primary interlocutors in the 1820s and early 1830s. Since its earliest days, and on into modern postcolonial histories, its critics have cast the *Candrikā* as the voice of unyielding religious conservatism. To select certain phrases, its contemporaries and historians have painted the *Candrikā* as the "organ of the ultra-idolatrous party," a "blind champion of social conservatism," the "fanatical champion of orthodox Hinduism," a "consistent advocate of thoroughgoing Hindu orthodoxy," and simply "rigid."[14] Better known for his later satires of Hindu reformers and the Bengali upper class, its editor, Bhabanicaran Bandyopadhyaya, began his journalistic career under his soon-to-be archrival, the renowned Hindu reformer Raja Rammohan Roy, as an associate editor of the *Kaumudī* when Roy first published it on 4 December 1821. But just three months later, he put out the first number of the *Candrikā*, defecting from the *Kaumudī* when Roy's opposition to sahamaraṇa became clear to him.

The *Candrikā* was remarkably long-lived for native newspapers of the period, remaining in publication until 1855. It was not only a pioneer in Bengali journalism; it also worked a significant effect on the development of Bengali prose, for which there were virtually no models in the language before William Carey of Serampore commissioned materials for classroom instruction at the turn of the nineteenth century.[15] Bengali's literary tradition, although long and venerated, was one exclusively of verse. By the time *Kaumudī* and *Candrikā* appeared, at least twenty books had been printed in the language,[16] but it was clearly still in its infancy as a vehicle for prosaic expression. The *Candrikā*'s editor had achieved some command over Bengali prose, but certain letters are almost unintelligible today. By their refinement of modes of expression, the editors of native papers, including the *Candrikā*, were certainly among the foremost architects of modern Bengali.[17]

Bhabanicaran spent the remainder of his life a bitingly satiric antagonist to Roy and his followers.[18] A celebrity in both India and Britain even in his day, Roy was a prolific author.[19] Both he and the reform movement he spearheaded in Bengal have since been the subject of numerous historical works.[20] His influence is primarily seen today in the Brahmo Samaj, a Hindu religious society he formed that preached monotheism, rational religious worship and reform, and the primacy of the Vedas.[21] One of this chapter's underlying suggestions is that Roy has received more than his share of attention relative to other native figures of the period, largely because his program of religious reform and his dialogue with English Christians and Unitarians have endeared him to liberal western scholarship. Certainly, history has rewarded his more orthodox antagonists over his disciples and their strictly monotheist, rationalized faith. His influence, nevertheless, was great, and his figure achieved near mythological status among his opponents as the traitor to religion who had lied to the rulers and threatened to destroy dharma for his own gain. We cannot fully grasp the *Candrikā*'s agenda without knowing something of Roy. He helped shape much of the discourse of the period, but certainly it is far too much to claim him as "the father of modern India," as three different books this century have.[22]

Rammohan Roy came from a wealthy, religiously conservative brahman household and first settled in Calcutta in 1797, where he established a money-lending business and began his association with the British. He very early in his life expressed disapproval of polytheism and image worship, first attaining public notice with a Persian work, *Tuhfat-al-Muwahhidīn*, known in English as "A Gift to the Monotheists," or, more commonly, "Against the Idolatry of All Religions."[23] Heavily influenced by Islamic monotheism, he published translations of Hindu scriptures that emphasized rationalist and monotheistic themes. He considered polytheism and image worship to be irrational religious practices and believed them contrary to the spirit of the Vedas, the oldest and most authoritative Hindu scriptures. His program of reform promoted a rational monotheism, and he found early favor with Christian missionaries and Unitarians, but he would split with the former group in 1820 over the Christian doctrine of the Trinity and the divinity of Jesus Christ, which he found to be polytheistic trappings.[24] He published several books and tracts, and he edited or funded newspapers in three languages (English, Bengali, and Persian). His earliest foray into periodical literature was his publication of the *Brahmunical*

Magazine (1821–1823), which aimed to counter the criticisms and misrepresentations of Hindus that missionaries were generating.[25] The success of Serampore's *Samācār Darpan* prompted him to found the *Saṃbād Kaumudī* as an organ for his own social and theological ideas. Significantly, he opposed the immolation of Hindu widows as an anti-scriptural aberration and warmly argued its abolition to the government, traveling even to England in 1830 when the Dharma Sabha petition went before Parliament. He died in Bristol a celebrity in England and remains to this day a hero to modernizing Indians.

Bhabanicaran came to Calcutta at an early age with his father, an employee of the Calcutta mint. Bhabanicaran received an education in Sanskrit, Persian, and English at the same time as he imbibed elite native culture.[26] An employee of J. Duckett, one of Calcutta's largest shipping companies, and later secretary to Bishops Middleton and Heber and to two Supreme Court Justices, Bhabanicaran could claim familiarity with the English and Indian politics of Calcutta and the acquaintance of many eminent people in both cultures.[27] One of the more prolific native writers of the era, he is remembered today particularly for the window he provided onto the life of the native Calcutta elite. His satires and his *Kalikātā Kamalālaya* spelled out in detail the character and ambitions of the *bhadralok*, a common term of the period meaning "the good people," or "gentlemen," and referring to an emerging commercial class in Bengal not determined by caste.[28]

Bhabanicaran's quick parting with Roy had broad implications for the future of political, religious, and social questions in Bengal. Although individuals like Mṛtyuñjaya Vidyālaṅkār had published individual defenses of strains of Hinduism they called "orthodox," the *Candrikā* was the first sustained effort to counter the constructions of Hindu religion advanced by British and Indian reformers.[29] As the first systematic refutation of these popular programs of reform, it was viewed as an important political voice, and from the date of its first publication, it functioned for the British and Indian communities as the representative of the wealthy Hindu traditionalist. In 1830–1831 the *Candrikā* claimed a circulation of around five hundred; others have offered estimates closer to four hundred.[30] Subscribers were few in a city whose population was likely approaching three hundred thousand,[31] but, however small, these numbers compared favorably with those of other contemporary newspapers, including the *Darpan*, and completely belie the attention it received from British residents of Calcutta and Indians of many classes.[32] Consistently promoting the right of Hindu authorities to decide matters of special interest to them, this paper is one of the earliest printed manifestations of Indian nationalist sentiment, which, by the 1860s, would be a firmly established political force.

Although Bhabanicaran ruled with a firm editorial hand, the *Candrikā* provided a site where competing interests could make themselves heard. The broad appeal it sought and realized for its brand of Hinduism is evident in the scope of its pieces and the composition of its correspondents. It gave voice to Indians of very different classes with very different interests. Government clerks, priests to Kali, reforming educators, and low-caste beggars found their way into the *Candrikā* alongside pandits and businessmen. The *Candrikā* presented, in addition, a mix of scholarly and popular opinion. Pandits spent weeks debating the shastric connotations of the word *vidyā* (wisdom),[33] while other contributors reported possession by *bhūts* (ghosts).[34] Alongside debate about the value of Sanskrit education were grisly reports of peasants torn apart by tigers. Its editor regarded the paper as one venue for showcasing often discrepant public opinion regarding Hindu practice and shaping a cohesive transitional discourse centered on ritual and social structure from it.

Ambivalence in the Kālīyuga

A self-conscious and energetic construction of a cohesive Hindu tradition might have seemed at odds with the negative verdict Hindu thought delivers on the ability of the human will to alter the course of history. In fact, the *Candrikā*'s editor and contributors displayed a deeply equivocal assessment of their historical moment, which had brought together peoples and religious traditions almost wholly unfamiliar to one another. Traditional, fundamentally pessimistic Hindu conceptions of time proved at odds with the recent experiences of the educated and wealthy elite of Calcutta, but the optimism of enlightenment rationalism failed to give an account of the spiritual danger that economic prosperity seemed to pose. The *Candrikā* therefore exhibited both anxiety and hope for the future of colonial Hinduism. It gazed wistfully at a (fanciful) past in which brahmans received proper veneration and enlightened kings took the shastras as their guide, but at the same time it sought to situate castes in a new ordering of power and to lend support to emerging ritual practices. Many of its readers and supporters had profited from the growing economy of Calcutta, and this prosperity, in turn, had fueled new religious endeavors, even at a time when Hindus faced increasing public scrutiny of their religious practices by Indians and foreigners alike.

This tension about the value of the future sprang in some measure from the Hindu belief that the present historical era, the Kālīyuga, marks the fourth and final stage of devolution in which moral and social degradation is rampant. The *Kūrma Purāṇa* describes the difference this way: In the Kṛtayuga people "had equal longevity and pleasure as well as beauty. They were free from grief. Adherence to truth and remaining in solitude was mainly practised. People were engrossed in meditation and penance. They were devoted to Mahādeva (Shiva)" (1.29.16–17). On the other hand, in the Kālīyuga, "[people] commit delusion, malice, and destruction of saintly men and ascetics. Epidemics of fatal disease, perpetual fear of hunger and starvation, fear of droughts and destruction of countries prevail in Kālī Age. Utterly bad subjects born in Kālīyuga are impious, deficient in food and highly furious but lacking in brilliance, liars and greedy" (1.30.1–3).

The conviction that such assaults on tradition as the abolition of satī and the insolence of youths toward brahmans were due to the degradation of the Kālīyuga was a prominent lament in the *Candrikā*. Responding to the *Darpan*'s criticism that lavish Hindu funerals contributed to the spread of poverty and superstition, one writer expressed this anxiety in verse: "Praising truth and affecting religious ways, / you pursue irreligion [*adharma*]. / Why do you commit this sin? Under the influence of Kali, you seek the alluring trappings of her age."[35] The same writer appeared shortly thereafter to describe the inversions typical of the Kālīyuga, when the divine order was subverted and evil provisionally conquered the good: "In the testicle of a rat there are elephants, / and in the belly of the king himself is a pregnant princess. / The brahman eats cow, and people sing his praises, but he has never touched the water of the Ganga [Ganges]."[36]

Alongside this dour assessment of the contemporary situation, however, one hears a more hopeful and optimistic note. If missionaries and Hindu reformers were injecting a strain of venomous critique into contemporary religious discussion, related forces were introducing economic and social opportunities previously unavailable. It was not that *Candrikā*'s angst was soothed by worldly success or that money overcame its principles. The issue was far more tangled. Invigorated economic life offered new possibilities for religious life as well. Those families who had become wealthy through taking advantage of the opportunities opened up by colonial expansion could, in turn, become patrons of pandits, artists, temples, and festivals, shaping a modern Hinduism according to their vision for a more highly organized and cohesive Hindu community. In Calcutta of the 1830s, competition was keen among prominent citizens to stage ever more magnificent celebrations of such festivals as Durgā Pūjā and Kālī Pūjā. The paper advertised books on Hindu subjects translated, published, and printed by the missionaries at Serampore, whose other, primary vocation was not the spread of "pagan" knowledge but the undermining of it. The success of British presses, in turn, had inspired native publication ventures. The activity of the missionaries and foreign economic influence cut both ways: at some levels they appeared to threaten Hindu devotion, at others, to nurture it.

It was similar with the Company's government in Bengal. There were moments of deep disaffection, as in December 1829 when Governor-General Bentinck, after soliciting opinion from members of both the British and Indian communities, abolished the practice of sahamaraṇa, the rite of self-immolation by a widow on the funeral pyre of her husband and the act by which she manifested herself as satī, a virtuous wife. The *Candrikā*'s response is preserved in translation in an English newspaper reporting the ban and Indian reactions. Bhabanicaran thundered,

> At this awful intelligence, we have trembled from head to foot, and are distressed, terrified, and astonished, for even under the Moosoolmans our law shastras were left untouched. It is reported that they sorely vexed the Hindoos, but knowing the Hindoo laws regarding the holy rite of burning up widows and other acts, they never ventured to touch them. Even under those unappeased and wicked sovereigns that sacred rite was preserved. If then it be abol-

ished under a just government, what greater cause of affliction can arise? On hearing this intelligence we have been seized with such alarm, that we believe the Hindoo religion is now on its last legs.[37]

This act by the government marked for *Candrikā* readers one of the darkest events of the colonial era—the sure sign that the Kālīyuga was marching on.

There stood, however, a very broad consensus among *Candrikā*'s contributors that the spread of British power brought great benefits as well. As the Company became involved in the government of India, it took on the administration of civil and criminal justice. A common sentiment among readers was satisfaction that "the Company has enforced many laws which have been to our benefit."[38] *Candrikā*'s readers were almost universal in their praise for the British system of justice—for its impartiality and its willingness to render punishments fit to the evil of a crime. There was appreciation for British attempts to stamp out the corruption of native police constables and officers. Correspondents admired the way English society provided for the poor.[39] Roads were improved and sewers installed. Although unmistakable signs of the Kālīyuga abounded, many devout people delighted in its trappings.

What this ambivalence signals is not an indulgence in the material benefits of the age accompanied by a hypocritical, pious horror at the accompanying religious degradation but a struggle to comprehend the current era according to Hindu temporal categories. The voluntarism modeled by British charitable groups in Calcutta suggested an alternative to pious resignation before the Kālīyuga. A modern organizational spirit called forth, rather, collective efforts for the preservation of dharma and aggressive attacks on the forces of unrighteousness, because, however ominous its presence, British rule contained the possibility of an invigorated collective religious life. One analyst has described this tension as an "emulation-solidarity conflict,"[40] whereas S. N. Mukherjee speaks of two idioms, the traditional and the modern, in which the Calcutta elite framed their discourse.[41] Still others resort to the simple claim that the religious impulses of this class anchored them to the past, whereas their political aims pushed them to consider the present and future.[42] Such easy alignments of "religion" with the "past," especially a venerated, ancient past, however, tend to construct this religious discourse as inherently conservative. We find in the *Candrikā*, however, an urgency to shape a modern, popular Hinduism through emergent discourses promoting a centralization of authority and a common, socially cohesive Hindu identity. This identity would be marked and achieved by the acceptance of normative models for ritual action and the modification of traditional caste hierarchies. The *Candrikā* offers no indications of the superstitious fatalism so prominent in contemporary Orientalist analysis, which charged the Hindu theory of karma with discouraging concern for cultural reform and social welfare. To the contrary, the very clear evidence of religious decline seemed to inspire a widespread effort to rejuvenate Bengali piety and imagine a Hinduism with the organizational and ideological capacity for growth and prosperity in colonial Bengal.

Ritual Query, Ritual Practice

One strategy the *Samācār Candrikā* pursued in this regard was to construct for itself the authority to standardize ritual forms. Ritual would have an essential role in its version of modern Hinduism, and a uniform ritual code would promote a unified and coherent Hinduism. In the first place, the *Candrikā* defended and promoted ritual generally against the rationalist critiques of Rammohan Roy and his followers, Christian missionaries, and student radicals, who found such activity to be absurd, superstitious, or superfluous. In addition, among like-minded Hindus, the newspaper decided questions of authority and performance in ritual matters.

Some of that authority derived from its own involvement with large-scale ritual. The *Candrikā* often promoted elaborate festivals staged by Dharma Sabha members as a show of their wealth and piety. These events could include a custom particularly galling to Christian missionaries, the hook-swinging ceremony, which they erroneously called "carak pūjā," in which large metal hooks were inserted in the flesh of participants, who then swung suspended from a tall pole.[43] As a mark of prestige, wealthy sponsors would erect a pole on which others could swing, often for pay, with the merit accruing to the sponsor of the event. On 15 April 1830, *Candrikā* reported just such a festival at the palace of the Dharma Sabha president Rādhakanta Deb as "the most spectacular" in the area, notable not just for its large crowd, the presence of British and Indian dignitaries, and its overall grandeur, but also for its strict adherence to traditional rules regarding the rite. As Geoffrey A. Oddie maintains with respect to the Bengali rite in general during this period, all these aspects worked together to demonstrate Deb's social and religious standing among different peoples in a multiethnic society.[44]

At other times, the paper's editor or correspondents consulted appropriate sections of the shastras in answer to a question about ritual. When one man wished to know whether he could perform his parents' annual funeral rite, even though he had missed the proper position of the moon, Bhabanicaran cited the text that forbade him to proceed.[45] Another man, the eldest of three brothers, asked how he was to marry off his youngest brother, since the middle sibling had run away with a low-caste woman and defied the tradition that brothers should wed in birth order.[46] Another asked the sticky question about shudras who had acquired an education, a circumstance only imaginable since the English had taken up low-caste education as a concern. If, the writer wondered, they had learned Sanskrit, but were not able to effect the correct pronunciation because they did not have the native ability of brahmans, would their rituals work?[47]

Some of these questions, then, voiced the perennial problems associated with the clash between textual ideal and practical reality. Serving as pandit, the *Candrikā*'s editor mediated between the two, applying the appropriate texts to the difficult issue at hand. Others, like the inquiry regarding shudras speaking Sanskrit, represented problems raised by the conditions of this historical moment. The presence of the Company's government and a widespread concern among both natives and Britons for social and religious reform had given rise to new problems as the social order changed. There was a certain incommensurability to the very terms of the question—a shudra knowing Sanskrit? The circumstance never imagined by the shastras demanded an answer.

The *Candrikā* assumed, therefore, a hermeneutical role. It bridged the gap opening up between the sacred past when the texts were compiled and the declining present. This project offered the kind of opportunity for creative constructions of tradition open to ritualists and religious specialists of all ages. If the medium—the newspaper—was an innovation, the general task was ancient: to adapt historical actions to a timeless ideal. In an earlier age, local authorities or caste tribunals would have resolved these ritual questions. In the 1830s, as Calcutta swelled with people from different communities in the countryside, the *Candrikā* offered itself as a new central authority to mediate ritual questions for all Bengal, aiming to counteract the anti-ritualism of Rammohan Roy by underscoring the centrality of ritual to Hindu, even modern Hindu, identity. In this regard, even in the context of ritual itself, the *Candrikā*'s efforts were no less reformist than Roy's. Social and economic relations were undergoing substantial change, and each party sought ways to make religion relevant to the new context. It is only an ahistorical model for religious belief and practice that could interpret the *Candrikā*'s agenda as "rigid" or "reactionary."

Candrikā, Christians, and Caste

While it contributed to the revisioning of ritual in a new historical context, the *Candrikā* also mediated the potentially more divisive issue of caste. Pradip Sinha and S. N. Mukherjee have described how the means for determining caste status and deciding caste questions were already undergoing significant change in the early nineteenth century. Associations known as *ekjai*, which had traditionally governed such issues, were giving way to new, competing sources of authority on caste.[48] With the influx of new families into Calcutta, village orderings were becoming meaningless to the urban context. Furthermore, the great wealth that was being generated in the city among many native families meant that markers other than simple caste rank were fixing power in new places. Those who had recently acquired economic status in the city were seeking a similar recognition in terms of caste. Consequently, new associations known as *dals* were emerging, headed by often non-brahman members of the new economic elite, including prominent members of the Dharma Sabha. People looked to their head (or *dalpati*) not only for some decision regarding their status relative to other castes, but also for their role in particular rituals, for permission to attend certain ceremonies, and even for approval of marriage partners. Dals were a developing response to the problem of adjusting the ancient institution of caste to the particular circumstances of an urban, mercantile environment.[49]

One writer caused a stir when he sent a letter from far outside Calcutta looking for an authoritative answer to a peculiar question. The shastras had dictated the rites that a student was to perform for his guru when the latter died, but they did not specifically address his situation. A member of the medical vaidya caste, he, along with other vaidyas and brahmans, had lost their guru and were seeking out the correct ritual formula for his funerary cycle. The problem was that their guru was a *satgop*, a low-caste shudra, and to the disciple's knowledge, the shastras did not address how brahman and vaidya students were supposed to conduct a funeral for their shudra guru. Bhabanicaran's reaction to this unusual relationship was brief and understated: "We are publishing this letter as it is, but we have serious doubts about a shudra with brahman and vaidya disciples."[50] Others, however, were more expressive of their outrage and disbelief, one respondent insisting the letter must be a hoax, for such a situation was entirely unimaginable.[51]

Such letters describing unconventional or surprising practices may, in fact, point to the variety of social orderings and ritual traditions that confronted those who were trying to centralize ritual and caste authority. Difficult questions that sparked disbelief in Calcutta may indicate rural or sectarian Hinduisms that departed significantly from what these urban, educated elite would accept as orthodox. The advent of the newspaper in Bengal permitted the collection of information from outlying areas and the development of responses to it. As Partha Chatterjee observes, "print creates its own field of circulation, with new rules of exclusion, new sites of authority, new hierarchies."[52] Publishing these letters provided an opportunity for the *Candrikā* to achieve recognition as an authority on caste questions and to craft a centralized and rationalized Hinduism that still retained caste orderings and a strong ritual focus.

Whereas it positioned itself among Bengali Hindus as arbiter of caste, in exchanges with British officials and Christian missionaries, the *Candrikā* displayed its passionate resistance to any insinuation that caste was incommensurable with a modern religious identity. Beginning in December 1830, a vigorous debate erupted between *Darpan* and *Candrikā* over the character of kulin brahmans and their marriage practices. Kulins were the purest families of the brahman caste, the brahmans of the brahmans. Historically, it seems twelfth-century King Ballal Sen had inaugurated the practice of kulinism as part of his reorganization of caste in Bengal. One of the privileges that accrued to this station was license for multiple marriages outside one's caste, allowing a kulin man to wed women of lower brahman castes and making male kulins desirable marriage partners for young brahman women. On 4 December, the *Darpan* had printed a letter from "an unmarried brahman" complaining that he, a lower caste brahman, and many like him were unable to find eligible spouses because kulins were marrying too many women, leaving a shortage of potential brides for other brahmans. The high demand for marriageable wives also encouraged fathers to sell their daughters to the highest bidder. This brahman's letter produced many angry responses and the extended editorial wrath of Bhabanicaran. Missionaries regularly impugned the character of kulin brahmans, likening their marital institutions to legalized prostitution, but they generally reserved public airing of these charges for English-speaking, Christian audiences.[53] Whereas evangelicals tended to view the kulin priesthood as a thin disguise for exploitation and treachery, those Hindus who wrote to *Candrikā*, none of them apparently kulin, saw them as mediators between humanity and divinity. Slandering kulins was character assassination of Bengali Hindus' purest figures, and these protestors felt the slight redounded upon Hindu people as a whole.[54]

So apparently unthinkable was the idea that such criticism of kulins could come from Hindus, Bhabanicaran from the beginning never entertained the possibility that its author was genuinely the "unmarried brahman" he claimed to be. The editor's initial response was to refrain from debate because he didn't know whether the author was "Unitarian, Christian, or even Muslim." If the critic turned out to be any of these, he was "not qualified to judge the dharma shastras and our peoples." Only if the writer were a Hindu and would prove it by revealing his identity would the *Candrikā* editor take him on. Bhabanicaran did not, however, let the issue rest. He took *Darpan* to task for publishing a letter that he felt irresponsibly misrepresented the history and character of kulins.[55] He bristled particularly at the arrogance of Christians meddling with customs they could not, by virtue of their status as outsiders, understand. Still stewing two weeks later, Bhabanicaran traced the kulin family line back to Brahma the creator himself, a lineage, he said, any Bengali matchmaker would establish.[56]

One important letter that appeared in the debate over kulinism is worthy of mention for its preservation of a voice of one with great stakes in the practice of kulinism: a woman's. The author's prose is stilted and awkward, and some is unintelligible, indicating not only the early stages of the evolution of Bengali writing, but perhaps also her limited education. This woman was responding to a *Darpan* letter (26 February) from the wife of a kulin brahman who suffered loneliness and isolation in a polygamous household. Writing in partial defense of the high status kulin men enjoyed, she was "very saddened" by the *Darpan* letter "because women are [usually] embarrassed to complain about separation from their husbands even to their best friends," and this woman had expressed her pain to the whole city. Nevertheless, the author endorsed the idea that a wife's duty was service to her husband and in-laws, and insisted that such servitude produced great rewards, citing her own lucrative piece of property recently given to her by her son. The opportunity to marry a kulin brahman was a blessing for a woman. Turning to the subject of polygamy, however, she expressed deep suspicion of its practice and the motives of those who supported it. "Some people," she chided, "think they are very learned and they know the shastras better than others, and they endorse multiple marriages for kulin brahmans, which ruins life for many women." She concluded, "It is better not to get married than to marry a man with many wives." While she defended the notion that marrying a kulin was an opportunity afforded by divine grace, she saw that exploitation and misery for women often resulted from misuse.[57]

As often was the case in the paper's clash with government or missionary characterizations of Hindu religion, and as the kulin wife's challenge to the

Candrikā's unqualified praise of kulin polygamy underscores, one of the central issues in debates over caste was the locus of the authority to represent contentious religious matters. The point of fundamental disagreement between the two newspapers was the construction of caste, both conceptually and in terms of actual social ordering. Whose interpretation and whose norms ultimately counted? Christians presented the same set of facts in a light very different from Bhabanicaran and his readers. The kulin wife's letter points to the fact that the issue was subject to various renderings even among high-caste Bengali Hindus. For the *Candrikā*, it was Christians' failure to perceive caste issues as Hindus might, to accept that Hindu interpretations might be worthy of consideration, and finally to allow Hindus the authority to judge these matters on the basis of indigenous categories and traditions that angered them. A generation earlier, Orientalists in the Asiatick Society under Sir William Jones had claimed the authority to craft a representation of Hinduism in light of other British concerns. Since the governor-generalship of Cornwallis (1786–1793), however, native pandits had been ceded the exclusive privilege of constructing actual Hindu practices. If interpretations other than those of the native pandits were possible, the authority to dictate the shape of ritual and religious hierarchy had been left with them, at least in principle. With the abolition of sahamaraṇa, Governor-General Bentinck and the British government implicitly laid claim to this other kind of power—the power to construct not just a representation of Hinduism but also Hindu practice itself.

Bhabanicaran was well aware that the issues of power and knowledge were closely linked in the British assessment of Hindu religion. This awareness is one of the themes that echoes loudly in *Candrikā*. With regard to these two discordant descriptions of kulins—that they were either the holiest of figures or the most treacherous—the crux of the disagreement for Bhabanicaran was epistemological. He maintained that by virtue of their historical and social location, the British were not equipped to perceive the nature and character of kulins or the significance of their marriage customs, and he worried that the dissemination of this decontextualized perspective could lead to the abolition of the institution. What the British portrayed as sexual and economic exploitation, Bhabanicaran and his readers regarded as the grace that overflowed from the well of kulin purity: kulin brahmans offered those who united with them both spiritual and material benefits. Ignorant of the shastras that described this relationship and the lives of the women who wed kulins, British critics could never perceive the true nature of these marriages. If they had had access to the sources that sanctioned and described these institutions, the British "would not have found fault with marriage among kulin brahmans."[58]

Her Lord, Her Life

Bhabanicaran had split with Rammohan Roy in 1822 and founded *Candrikā* when Roy's intention to oppose widow immolation publicly became clear to him. Mounting criticism of the practice and the role it played in British discourse about the responsibilities of British rulers in India continued to give the rite a prominent place in both the British and the Indian imagination through the 1820s. Bentinck's 10 November 1828 survey of his officials on the feasibility of its abolition gave native leaders cause for alarm,[59] and by the dawn of 1830, sahamaraṇa had become the issue to which all who had an interest in describing a certain kind of Hinduism resorted. No one image galvanized English public opinion more than the reluctant and grief-stricken young widow forcibly cremated with the corpse of her husband; no one policy drew Indians into political debate more urgently than the British determination to set legal limits to a wife's ritual expression of her virtue.[60]

In 1830, at the initial news of the impending ban, leaders of Hindu society had "trembled from head to foot" and quickly formed the Dharma Sabha to organize formal protest measures. In 1832, the Dharma Sabha would receive word that it had lost its final appeal to the Crown and that sahamaraṇa was permanently forbidden. The British government would have successfully asserted its right to dictate the forms of expression that Hindu devotion might take. But during the interim, as all interested parties awaited the king's decision and the practice remained under prohibition, the *Candrikā* and its readers began to gather testimony that these sacrifices had the sanction of both the gods and the sorrowful widows. In response to British policy, a new phenomenon appeared. As village constables and relatives began forcibly removing wives from burning grounds, women found new ways of expressing their inseparability from their spouses. Week after week, beginning in July 1830, *Candrikā* reported numerous instances of widows meeting swift death after their husbands' demise, thus proving their devotion. While the government might prevent sahamaraṇa, the act, these events suggested it could in no way interfere with a woman's manifestation of herself as satī, for, it seemed, her virtue was irrepressible. Brief notices began appearing in the paper under the heading "Patiprāṇa Satī," which means "the virtuous wife whose husband (or lord, master; *pati*) is her very life's breath (*prāṇa*)." The phrase implied that husband and wife were indissolubly linked, "ontologically bonded," in Paul B. Courtright's words, such that "even death offers no unbreachable obstacle to their union."[61] A woman's husband and her life were but the same; to lose the first entailed the necessary loss of the second.

Sometimes the paper described the maintenance of this union as an act of will on the wife's part—prevented from entering the flames, she assumed a meditative posture, focused her mind on her husband, and within days or hours was dead.[62] This was the case with a low-caste Teli woman whose son wrote to tell of the misery his mother suffered as a result of being prevented from committing sahamaraṇa. Fearing British authorities, local village officials would not permit her sacrifice and, to thwart her, ordered the son to cremate his father secretly. Upon news of this act, his mother sat and fasted for eighteen days, starving herself to death. Bhabanicaran expressed his outrage at the constable's interference with her plans and consoled the young man, assuring him that his mother's self-willed death still brought her and his father the merit she intended.[63] A different woman in August, again forcibly removed by rela-

tives who feared reprisal, took to bed and asked her sons to carry her to the
Ganges River at 2:30 P.M. on a later day, where she expired at that precise
moment.[64]

Another theme soon emerged in these tales. Correspondents began describing the deaths of widows that were not so much wilful acts of devotion,
as virtue itself—the fiery *sat* or truth that resided in them—achieving its necessary expression. The wife's devotion to her husband had so constituted her
person that his expiration already entailed her own death. Without her husband, she was without her very life's breath, and so upon his demise she fell
herself. In one village, the constable arrived at the cremation of a Ganga Na-
rayan Mitra on hearing reports that the widow was preparing to enter the fire.
He doused the flames while the corpse was burning, an act of astonishing
sacrilege. The distraught wife lay on the extinguished coals and then went
home to her own bed, where, "in true friendship for Mitra, Sir Death himself
came to visit her, and in five days sent the satī to her husband."[65] As the genre
developed into stock tales, the deaths became more mechanical. The widow of
a Kashinath Majumdar declared to the police, "You are an obstacle to the fulfillment of my obligations (*svadharma*), but since my life has already left my
body, when it falls, please burn it with the body of my husband." Instantly, she
fell dead at their feet. Her corpse, as she wished, was burned with her husband's.[66] The editor commented on this rash of similar deaths, "even though
commanded by the shastras, it is obvious that the satī's going with her husband
is God's will [and not solely her own]."[67] His rendering of these events reinforced the notion that the wife's death was the inevitable effect of her devotion
to her mate. The rite did not itself make a woman satī; rather, the rite was
simply the expression of her prior constitution.

The emergence of this virtuous figure whose life was so intertwined with
that of her husband points to the efforts of the *Candrikā* and its correspondents
to mold both religious acts and their interpretations in light of a new ritual
context. Forcibly imposed, a ritual context in which a practice believed sancti-
fied by antiquity and sacred text was suddenly forbidden called for new forms
of expression to signify the older meanings. If a satī could no longer express
her status by dying with her husband, then the possibility had to arise elsewhere. What remained unaltered was the nature of the wife's union with her
husband. Underway in the crystallization of a stock model for the post-
sahamaraṇa satī was the construction of a new paradigm for the rite—a revised
practice altered to conform to new circumstances but exemplifying all the
moral characteristics of the old practice.

The Other's Other

Addressing the debate raging between *Darpan* and *Candrikā* on the issue of
kulin brahman polygamy, a satirist sympathetic to *Candrikā*'s neo-orthodoxy
penned this couplet comparing luminous and ancient Hindu wisdom to the
pale light of missionary preaching:

> When the sun and the moon have gone down,
> There is only the light in the firefly's ass.[68]

The verse mocked the missionaries' pretension that they were carrying the light of rational religion to the dark subcontinent. This response to evangelical Christians in Bengal and many others of the same spirit preserve indications of how intensified contact with Christians promoted emerging discourses of popular Hinduism. The *Candrikā*'s resistance to this aggressive, evangelical Christianity was passionate and resilient, and the counter-constructions of Hinduism this resistance generated display an organized, zealous production of images and themes for a reinvigorated Hinduism. Whereas Serampore's images of Hindus drew from centuries-old stereotypes of heathens and papists, the *Candrikā*'s responses looked to the future, aiming at the formation of a vigorous, coherent Hindu religious tradition that could demonstrate its moral and social relevance to its colonial context. Under attack from missionaries as a monstrous "system," Hinduism was beginning to recognize itself as an entity with a systematic, pan-Indian character.

It was Bhabanicaran's policy not to engage in criticism of other religions or to respond to others' attacks on Hinduism, and, in fact, he claimed religious polemic to be at odds with basic Hindu principles. He refused, however, to endure silently the unrelenting critique that seemed to flow from Christian missionary presses. His rival paper, the *Darpan*, had labeled as "murder" the practice of bearing those near death to the bank of the Ganges to lend their dying moment the highest possible merit; it called lavish funeral rites wasteful and foolish. In this context of escalating religious hostility, the *Candrikā* discovered the rhetorical utility of developing the theme of "tolerance" as a hallmark of the Hindu ethos. Bhabanicaran and his correspondents regularly described the Hindu religious tradition's discourses as entirely self-referential, unconcerned with the religious occupations of others far or near, and Radhakanta Deb himself pleaded that in contrast to Christians, "Hindus have not hurt any other culture or religion."[69] It was in the nature of the Hindu, the authors often said, to leave others to their own ways, and in this respect their faith was different from the aggressive Christianity of proselytizing missionaries. It was not Hindus' ambition to fit other religions into the rubric of their own cosmological frame. Hindus did not try to understand other traditions in terms of their own or to employ foreign customs in the explication of their own. The *Candrikā* characterized its stance toward evangelization primarily in terms of Hindu tolerance in the face of Christian antagonism. In this regard, it carefully distinguished the Christianity of Calcutta's respected rulers from that of proselytizing missionaries, refusing to take up the former out of the mutual respect subsisting between them, while characterizing evangelical Christians as aggressors bent on conversion at any cost, eager to take advantage of the patience and tolerance Hindus encouraged in each other.

Relations between these groups, however, were not wholly antagonistic. To the contrary, all those with a stake in the construction of Hinduism—Company bureaucrats, evangelical Christians, rationalist Hindu reformers, and conser-

vative Hindus—cooperated on issues of social justice and praised each other
for their dedication. English and Bengali newspapers of the day reveal a vigorous public conversation not just on religious but also social reform, especially
with respect to education and poverty. Editors saw themselves as brokers shaping public opinion and directing public debate for the good of society. Newspapers sought to contribute to the character and quality of public discourse
and thereby to improve the lives of the community. The vitality of conversation
between and among many papers of different languages and faiths and their
commonality of purpose no doubt stemmed from what Brian A. Hatcher has
described as the intersection of two cultural idioms in colonial Bengal: the
English concern for "improvement" and the Indian interest in *yatna* or "effort."
Hatcher credits the process he calls "vernacularization," the means by which
"alien discourse and practice become affiliated to indigenous tradition," for
both improving and spreading education.[70] Christians, Hindu reformers, and
the *Candrikā* all regarded the improvement of society through the alleviation
of poverty and the spread of education as a necessary modern reform. Although
Candrikā might see other proposed innovations as the deleria of those Mrtyun-
jaya Vidyalankar labeled "intoxicated moderns,"[71] it held social justice to be a
concern with an ancient Hindu pedigree that commanded, therefore, immediate and coordinated attention.

The terms of the *Candrikā*'s debate with its Hindu and Christian antagonists, then, were not over whether to alter social relations for the better, but
how. As I have been arguing, the *Candrikā* favored a range of reconfigurations
in India's social and religious institutions. The *Candrikā*, like the Brahmo Samaj, which has received more credit for its reformist program, imagined a
popular, invigorated, ritualized, and hierarchical, but also socially conscien-
tious, Hinduism for a new era. Although this construction emerged in the
context of energies and ideas released by the forces of colonial encounter, the
Hindu elite represented by *Candrikā* maintained for themselves the authority
to direct and shape these innovations in Hindu India. The editor and his readers evinced a deep suspicion of missionaries and their activities among Hindus, even those activities with apparently general humanitarian motivation,
such as their work in education, for which many Hindus had long praised
them. Although missionaries insisted they pursued education as a social good
in itself and as a necessary first step for economic and social improvement,
the *Candrikā* warned readers that the education missionaries provided their
children may have been the disguised foundation for conversion.

Two lengthy letters from someone purporting to be a student at Hindu
College seemed to confirm fears about the true motives of missionary educators. The writer reported that he, along with other promising students, was
invited one evening to a "special class" arranged by some English teachers "as
a trick." When they arrived, they immediately perceived that their teachers'
demeanor toward them was warmer than usual. After reading from the Bible
and praying, the teachers began "weeping, shedding tears of devotion" in an
attempt to move the students as well. On this night, their efforts failed. The
student wrote:

We heard that senseless carrying-on and we were amazed. They are always kind and quiet and polite and learned and discrete. When this happened we lost all respect for them, because we wanted to have that [composed] image of the missionaries in our hearts. It is very unfortunate that they tried to convert us, thinking that because we were training with them they could turn the sons of Hindus into Christians. Since we were innocent babies, our parents have taught us about the gods, brahmans, daily worship, and the concepts of karma and dharma. Don't these people know that we are already formed in our own culture from birth? They think that they can spend a few days with us or a few months or a few years and then take us to a special room and tell us to convert to Christianity and we will do it? How could they think this? We would be moved by their tears? Never. On the contrary—we know these were fake tears and they were just trying to arouse us.

The student wrote to warn others that the missionaries' intentions were not pure, regardless of their assurances about avoiding religious topics. He defied his teachers: "I am telling the missionaries . . . that they are not going to convert us." Students, he chided, who were patient with their teachers' enticements to Christianity bore these affronts to their own religion out of self-interest: they wanted an English education that would help them make a prosperous living. The student offered this folktale as an analogy: "A man had a goat who was about to give birth, but its labor was not progressing. The owner offered a pūjā to the goddess and vowed, 'if this birth goes smoothly, I will offer you a buffalo.' The people heard this and said to him, 'are you crazy? A buffalo is much more expensive than a goat.' The man replied, 'Do not think I am a fool. I am tricking the goddess into helping me through this trouble. I am not going to do this thing.' " The student concluded, "That man is just like us," protecting his own interests by flattering his superior.[72]

A fortnight later the same student wrote again to reassure the public that Hindu College students were not covert Christians and to raise further suspicion about missionary tactics and motives. He criticized Christians for their complete lack of appreciation for categories of purity and impurity. Even Islam acknowledged ritual taboos, he observed, but Christians had none at all: "they eat whatever they like, they have no ritual order, and they show no discretion about purity and pollution." Their attention to purity was merely cosmetic, substituting clean, white shirts for ritual baths. Consonant with their superficial purity practices were the false hopes they held out to potential lower-caste converts for achieving a measure of status and respectability in a Christian community. Hindus would lose their families and friends by converting, only to find that among Christians "they are at the very bottom."[73]

Many other writers accused Christians of systematic deceit, trickery, and hypocrisy. Most who made reference to Christians found them to be fundamentally underhanded in their dealings with Hindus and willing to stoop to basic dishonesty if it would serve to make a convert. A regular correspondent to many newspapers in the city who called himself "an ancient subject" cautioned parents against sending their children to missionaries for training, for they had "meticulously planned" a curriculum that could subtly influence innocent children. He predicted, however, that their "tricks will be futile" because true Hindu children would not abandon their dharma, and the missionaries, moreover, would fail to acquire any merit for providing education for the needy because "their project has the underlying motive of destroying other religions.[74]

It was the violence that seemed inherent to Christianity, an apparent drive to dominate and annihilate all rival faiths, that troubled many writers. Missionary Christianity seemed willing to violate basic principles of integrity and its own dictums in order to advance the cause of its hegemony. The widely rumored practice of luring students into a church to attempt some surreptitious conversion was only the most blatant form of missionary deceit.[75] Many believed that the reforms that the missionaries insisted were merely social in nature had the destruction of Hinduism as their hidden end. To underscore the duplicity of Christians, one correspondent attempted an Indian ethnography of Christian ritual, translating a clip from an English newspaper describing the Holy Week celebrations in Rome, complete with footnotes for such "indigenous" European terms as "passion week" and "apostle." The letter is instructive for the ways the translator presented Roman Catholic practices in terms of Hindu categories. He called the hymn singing in St. Peters square *kīrtan*, a form of Vaishnava devotional music in which the more orthodox readers of *Candrikā* would have heard echoes of indecorous emotional displays. He told of people worshiping a wooden relic (the cross) wrapped in violet. Many of them dressed as Christ's apostles and others carried lamps. As described by this reader, all of these items paralleled elements found in Hindu ritual, which could feature the veneration of images, dramas enacting events from sacred literature, and camphor lamps. When conducted by Hindus, of course, Christians labeled these ritual forms idolatry, but here, the reader urged, Christians did very similar things. The reader concluded from this newspaper account that "in their own country, [these] people do not neglect the observation of their own religion, but in a foreign land, they trick the poor people (*chota lok*) into becoming disciples of Jesus."[76] While it is true that evangelical missionaries would have criticized these Catholic practices as idolatrous as well, it was precisely this sort of error with regard to Hindu religion against which the *Candrikā* repeatedly protested: the construction of a monolithic tradition then subjected to a foreign critique lacking the necessary contextual information.

Constructing and Manufacturing Hinduism

What was most deeply unnerving to these Hindus, however, were not the assaults their timeless dharma suffered from English antagonists but the clear social fact that Indians themselves, the children of respectable families, were beginning to show contempt for traditional beliefs and practices. If the abolition of sahamarana was a defining moment in the emergence of modern Hinduism, this was only because it drew Hindus into debate with one another about what alterations tradition must undergo to prosper in the new era. It would be blindly Eurocentric to regard, as many scholars have, the development of Hinduism in the nineteenth century as principally a response to the West, whether to Christianity, western education, or colonial rule. Although contact with the West provided important influences, these developments were undertaken by Hindus for their own benefit. Utilitarian governors and Serampore missionaries were significant irritants, but the reform campaigns launched by Rammohan Roy and his followers seemed actual threats and provoked large-scale responses from Hindus of the same privileged social classes who fought to preserve traditions and ideas under Christian scrutiny. These were all Indians of considerable standing who recognized the political capital that representations of Hinduism provided, but some chose (in Bhabanicaran's mind) to disparage tradition in order to curry favor with the British. Without the support of these apostates, the *Candrikā* believed the British would have left Hindu rites entirely alone. Even at their moments of greatest disappointment, the *Candrikā*'s readers and editor could display almost uncanny respect for British officers and British institutions, none of it sounding insincere. Complaining of the abolition of satī, the paper once shared a sentiment it regularly expressed: "[N]one of our countrymen feel a pleasure in hearing anything to the disadvantage of the honourable Company; they always pray for the welfare of the Government. . . . We have been subject to no distress under the government of the Company; it is only the abolition of Suttees which has given us disquietude."[77] Roy and those Indians who had internalized British criticisms, in contrast, were subjected to withering satire and venomous hostility.[78]

The complexity of these interreligious relations and attitudes in colonial Calcutta are not readily disclosed by an unreflective application of what Ivan Strenski has recently called "first Foucault." Inspired by Foucault's "frank and unapologetic declaration of an extreme form of the conflict model as the basic story line of the human condition,"[79] historiography known sometimes as "postcolonial" has conditioned us to think of intercultural contact in terms of dominance and resistance, of colonial scholarship in terms of power and knowledge, and of the native role in colonial conquest in terms of accommodation, assimilation, and translation. These categories have proven their usefulness for uncovering hidden social practices, but there are a couple of reasons such an approach is not fully adequate for addressing these particular colonial-era relations. First, such a method subsumes religious beliefs and practices under other social phenomena and political currents, such that religion becomes just one more means by which various forms of power are legitimated and deployed. Postcolonial histories often represent religion as epiphenomenal and secondary to other factors, eclipsing its causal or motivational role in human history. It seems clear, however, that the editors and authors of the *Samācār Candrikā* possessed a sophisticated understanding of the subtle workings of colonial domination, and yet they insisted that their concerns were first and foremost religious, not political. It is wise and helpful in this instance to accept the indigenous assessment of the situation. The *Candrikā* writers grasped the complex connections among religion, knowledge, and power, but they could and did distinguish among these categories with respect to the religious beliefs and practices of both Hindus and Christians.

Second, it would be a mistake to overlay ideas about colonial strategies and native resistance onto this particular religious encounter. The Hindu elite, both reformers and orthodox, were widely respected by British officials, whereas evangelical Christians were themselves an embattled group in both Britain and India. Much of the missionaries' polemical engagements with Hindus had something to do with their own fight for legitimacy. Banned from India until 1813, they had long endured the suspicious gaze of the Company government, and many in the government still worried that their religious rhetoric could endanger Company rule.

It is in an awareness of this many-layered public conversation about religion in India and the future of Indian society that we properly grasp the significance of the representational practices of this one multivocal text and of those surviving fragmentary indigenous sources like it. Historians have consistently cast the *Candrikā* as the social force most visibly and vocally challenging reformers who followed Rammohan Roy and largely accepted the editorial analysis of the *Samācār Darpan*. Although substantially correct, the cost of reconstructing the indigenous debate about the shape of Hinduism in this binary way has been to create the impression that those who represented themselves as the guardians of tradition—the Dharma Sabha, the *Candrikā*, Bhabanicaran, and Radhakanta Deb—were unreflective conservative reactionaries bent on the preservation of outmoded religious practices. The observations of David Kopf thirty years ago and, more recently, of S. N. Mukherjee still seem more appropriate in that they find the Dharma Sabha and those sympathetic to it "deeply interested in modernizing" Indian society[80] and that opposing liberals to conservatives or modernists to traditionalists can fundamentally misrepresent the character of these disputes about Indian religion and society.[81]

The *Candrikā*'s appeals to tradition, its veneration of history, and its concern for ancient authority function, in fact, as charters for new ritual formations and new arrangements of power characteristic of modern Hinduism. These constructions represent only another instance of what, after Eric Hobsbawm, we can recognize as the "invention of tradition," and this paper and the reactions it has inspired demonstrate how readily scholars and others conceive religion as an inherently conservative force. The *Candrikā* displays, rather, how progressive, regressive, and oppressive forces can establish complex alliances that facile or monophonic historiography cannot readily exhibit. The *Candrikā*'s active imagining of modern Hindu forms appears not as a defensive reaction to changing external circumstances but as a set of creative and forward-looking accommodations to colonial circumstances.

It is crucial, therefore, to sketch carefully the extent that Hindu contact with Christianity inspired the changes undertaken by the architects of modern Hinduism, neither exaggerating nor underestimating it. Experienced as both an urgent crisis and a source of insight, contact with Christianity was indeed one important catalyst for this energetic pursuit of new religious and social forms. The significance of this contact lies, however, not in the fact that the religion of the indigenous elite had to face the faith of the colonizer on unequal ground. If the character of the relationship between Christianity and Hinduism in colonial Calcutta was one of domination and resistance, on the tenor of the exchanges alone, one would be hard-pressed to discern which was the oppressor and which the oppressed. The *Candrikā*'s tone toward evangelical Christians in Bengal was generally quite defiant. If, in Catherine Bell's words, the *Candrikā*'s bid for the authority to fashion social order and ritual were "strategic, manipulative, and expedient,"[82] its resistance to Christian interventions in and representations of its religion was passionate, spontaneous, and expressive. The *Candrikā*'s spirited defense of tradition against Christian attacks secured for it a measure of power to alter ritual and social order and the Hindu public's understanding of them. If there was little in the content of Christian critique that the *Candrikā* found compelling, its vigor inspired Hindu self-confidence; the recovery of Hindu teachings on poverty, caste, and ritual; and the organizational sensibilities to institutionalize and centralize Hindu practice.

The *Candrikā*'s orchestrations, for example, with respect to ritual, including sahamaraṇa, were clearly more than the distressed reaction of the oppressed Hindu to the exercise of raw power. They were creative, sometimes disturbing, responses to changing political, ritual, and hermeneutical circumstances. The appeal for the legitimacy of these expressions of devotion was to the force of tradition and the authority of ancient texts, but the trajectory of the emerging interpretations was forward, not backward, set in motion by the prestige and foresight of an economic elite who saw a coherent and unified Hindu practice as a more modern, and hence more vital, religious tradition in the context of colonial religious pluralism and competition. The form and rationale for ancient ritual would remain normative for emerging Hinduism, even as accommodations to modernity developed and tolerance for diversity in belief persisted. The very fact of ongoing satī deaths demonstrated both the legitimacy of the old practice and the possibility of new vehicles for the expression of the same message. *Candrikā*'s authors portrayed these deaths as the spontaneous welling up of the inextinguishable forces and energies that before had been manifested in the old rite. If indeed this was Kālīyuga, and dharma was under assault from the forces of adharma, a new paradigm for sahamaraṇa emphasized how an eternal righteousness nevertheless achieved its necessary expression through the bodies of women, and it provided guidelines for those who would display it.

Similarly, although caste would continue to come under increasing scrutiny from westerners and reforming Hindus, and the constitution of independent India would in theory undermine its most oppressive elements, much of modern popular Hinduism still sees it as reflective of larger cosmological structures and forces. Influenced by ancient Hindu tradition, evangelical social work, and utilitarian politics, early modern Hinduism would develop organized networks devoted to the alleviation of social and economic deprivation while retaining an ideological commitment to caste as the work of divine, not human,

actors. Today the reconstruction of tradition by intricately structured organizations permeating all levels of society in an effort to claim a unifying Hindu
tradition for India remains an important factor in national politics, with the
Saṅgh Parivār organizations only the most visible.

For the *Candrikā*, the past continued to possess great authority, but it had
great authority especially for and in the present moment. The meaning of this
critical moment when the forces of unrighteousness seemed to be dismantling
dharma was one of "sacred brokenness," as Jan Heesterman describes such
experiences of ritual crisis,[83] but through the cracks of the broken ritual structure, the sacredness of received authority still manifested itself. The legitimation at work here ran in both directions. Not only did the authority of tradition
justify the present, but also the present itself, even this tragic present, legitimated the ancient authority and proved its superiority to the rational religion
of Hindu reformers. If Bhabanicaran and his correspondents were the kind of
"ritualists" Heesterman imagines, that is, if they aimed to give form and fixity
to a set of actions deriving from contingent circumstances, then their goal was
not just to plug the dike and halt the erosion of traditional religion. Instead,
they offered new paradigms for caste, ritual, and the satī, as well as a heightened compassion for the downtrodden, not just to adapt traditional meaning
to changing situations but also to demonstrate that ancient traditional understandings could find wholly appropriate expression through the new formulations that modernity suggested. With the same moves, moreover, it renego-
tiated the relations of power with missionaries, governors, and reforming
Hindus who had tried, by their assaults on Hindu practice, to undermine
particular centers of religious authority. The Dharma Sabha and the *Candrikā*
sought to vindicate their tradition and reestablish their authority not by the
rigid maintenance of usages but by exploiting the inherent malleability of these
usages. Their actions suggest that what was timeless in their view was precisely
not particular acts but the character of human relationships to which these acts
had given expression.

"Strategic, manipulative, and expedient"—the invention of these new paradigms for modern Hinduism in Bengal was a "construction" and a "manufacture" in senses very close to the root Latin meanings of the terms. It was a
"building along with" the alterations in the contextual fabric that remained
outside the control of the constructors; it was a "hands-on making" of possibilities for modern Hindu religious expression. The creation of these new religious forms was a compromise between the ideal and the real by a group
with a measure of power caught between other groups with their own partial
command over the structure and character of social relations: the colonial government, reforming Hindus, village authorities, and Hindu women, to name
a few. It was a complex act in a complex setting—but one demonstrating conscious Hindu agency in the emergence of modern Hinduism by commercially
successful classes of Indians proposing a mode of religious transition to modern colonial society. In an age no longer governed by the wisdom of Rama,
when the golden city of Ayodhya was only a distant memory, the *Samācār
Candrikā* saw the need and opportunity for the exercise of Hindu self-

determination in religious matters. In this setting the lines of domination/ resistance, oppressed/oppressor, and center/margin are far too crossed to permit any simple bipolar analysis, suggesting, perhaps, the unavoidably human and contingent character of interreligious relations and their easy defiance of theory.

6

Colonial Legacies

Some Concluding Thoughts

Previous chapters in this book have identified specific sites for the production of religion and Hinduism in the context of colonial India. I have tried to extrapolate from the encounters that characterized those sites to suggest how both religion and thinking about religion changed in this period. In the printed word and in visual image, through the transmission of artifact and anecdote, across the desk of colonial functionaries and across the shrinking oceanic divide, Britain and India came more and more to craft a shared religious world of their own making. This process gave birth to the modern formations we know as their respective religions. In this final chapter, I take a step back from early nineteenth-century British India and consider broader questions with methodological and historiographic import for the study of religion. This period has been the object of intense academic scrutiny since the early 1980s. Many scholars from distinct fields have recognized colonial India as critical for the genesis or crystallization of concepts and institutions that reflect and inform the postmodern, postcolonial, globalized world we now inhabit. In the foregoing account of Indians and Britons in the colonial era, I have touched only lightly on four larger issues often raised in the comparative study of religion or the study of interreligious encounter, issues I shall now take up in some slightly more extended fashion. These are: 1) the legitimacy of the category "Hinduism"; 2) the genealogy and cross-cultural applicability of the concept "religion"; 3) the status of discourses that might essentialize religion; and 4) the lingering effects of colonial power relations on current Hindu-Christian relations. My overarching aim in this last chapter is to argue for the retention of the received categories that could function as constructive resources toward alleviating interreligious and intercultural conflict. Specifically, I take up the issues raised by several recent critiques that argue that terms such as "Hinduism" and "religion" cannot find meaningful correspondence in Indian traditions and that scholars ought therefore to dispense with them.

Are We Manufacturing, Inventing, Constructing, or Fabricating Hinduism?

A vigorous debate has churned for at least a decade over the status of the label "Hinduism," but the question at the heart of these debates—Is there any set of pan-Indian practices and identities that one can meaningfully gather under a single label?—has been around for much longer. These disputes generally spring from the ambiguity and multivalency of the adjective "Hindu." At least since the sixth-century B.C.E. reign of Darius of Persia, the word "Hindu" has, by turns, signified regional, religious, or cultural identifications, and from the early twentieth century, in some contexts it has also been charged with nationalist connotations.[1]

On one side of the debate over the appropriateness or utility of the term "Hinduism" are the constructionists,[2] those who claim that in scholarly practice the category Hinduism vacuums up a miscellany of Indic traditions, ideas, and communities that, at their core, have so little in common that their collective identification under this umbrella is at best misleading and at worst an exercise in ideological subterfuge. Stated succinctly, this line of reasoning asserts that "there is hardly a single important teaching in 'Hinduism' which can be shown to be valid for all Hindus, much less a comprehensive set of teachings."[3] Some of the strongest statements of these positions are well-known but worth repeating here. Robert Frykenberg has put the matter this way:

> [T]here has never been any such thing as a single "Hinduism" or
> any single "Hindu community" for all of India. Nor, for that matter,
> can one find any such thing as a single "Hinduism" or "Hindu com-
> munity" even for any one socio-cultural region of the continent. Fur-
> thermore, there has never been any one religion—nor even one sys-
> tem of religions—to which the term "Hindu" can accurately be
> applied. No one so-called religion, moreover, can lay exclusive claim
> to or be defined by the term "Hinduism." The very notion of the
> existence of any single religious community by this name . . . has
> been falsely conceived.[4]

More bluntly still, Frits Staal has insisted, "Hinduism does not merely fail to be a religion; it is not even a meaningful unit of discourse. There is no way to abstract a meaningful unitary notion of Hinduism from the Indian phenomena."[5]

Many postcolonial critiques of the same spirit finger some antagonist whose interests the construction and deployment of the concept "Hinduism" have served. The earlier chapters of this book pursue just such an argument with regard to Christian polity in Britain, the colonial state, and Hindu elites. Christian missionaries are often high on the list of those who charge that western interests misperceived or falsified data for their own ends[6] and produced a systematized representation of disparate regional and caste practices to different ends in both Britain and India in order to counter that constructed tradition with the rational and moral character of Christianity. The expansion of the colonial administration of India in the nineteenth century also demanded a coherent and stable catalog of Hindu laws, sects, ritual practices, and so forth, an end that an essentialized Hinduism certainly furthered.[7] Again, although it is clear from my earlier arguments that I think there is more to the story, the bureaucratization of the colonial state abetted the reification of Hinduism. In the twentieth century, Hindu nationalists, it has been regularly observed, awoke to the political fruits that the concept of a nationally and historically cohesive tradition could yield.[8] Nationalist groups have pieced together a "syndicated Hinduism" in recent historical memory to suggest a monolithic, ancient religion and have thereby sought to manufacture a certain historical integrity and communal unity for all of India. Some observers find that this nationalist revision of contemporary and historical religious pluralism represents a problematic but politically effective assemblage of practices and ideas intended to remake Indic traditions in the image of Christianity and Islam.[9] Others have recently argued, in a general way about religion and also specifically about Hinduism, that the categories serve today to justify university religion departments and to legitimize the religious publishing industry by rationalizing the trade in an entity of dubious ontological status.[10]

On the other side of the issues echo a variety of voices that insist that, however diffuse, variegated, multivalent, and internally contested, "Hinduism" as an analytic category and descriptive label is both meaningful and reasonably true to observed social and historical realities. Among scholars advocating a version of this position are those such as David Lorenzen and Will Sweetman, who argue that the scholar's employment of "Hindu" and "Hinduism" derive from attention to the fact that precolonial and colonial-era Hindus often could espouse a common religious identity long before European bureaucracy and scholarship imposed one on them. "Hinduism" therefore not only possesses some legitimacy with respect to the current era, but aptly corresponds to historically attested indigenous self-understandings.[11]

Others defending the Hinduism category take a slightly different tack. Wendy Doniger tries to liberate it from the expectation that it will correspond to a fixed set of consistent, noncontradictory beliefs and rituals. She suggests the term be used to invoke the idea of a common Hindu conversation on caste, karma, asceticism, and a divine pantheon. Hindus, she holds, share distinctive concepts among themselves but also vigorously debate their meaning. Hinduism is therefore best imagined not as a closed circle of beliefs and practices with a clear boundary, but by means of a Venn diagram of partially overlapping circles to indicate those shared but contested categories.[12] Doniger concludes, "it has proved convenient for us to call this corpus of concepts Hinduism;

naming is always a matter of convenience of the namers, and *all* categories are constructed."[13] Gabriella Eichinger Ferro-Luzzi's defense of the term is similar. She describes Hinduism as a polythetic concept, one for which we can easily identify prototypical features such as worship of major Hindu gods, pilgrimage, and the invocation of certain concepts like dharma, that crisscross and overlap in different combinations in any particular variant of Hinduism.[14]

On balance, I find these defenses persuasive and reflective of the evidence provided by the Indian testimony on the matter found in places such as the *Samācār Candrikā*. It must be said, however, that this book's analysis of specific colonial-era sites on which the modern notion of Hinduism was erected—in nineteenth-century Anglican polity, among Christian missionaries working in India, and in an infant print media among Indian elites—has shown clearly that the constructionists, for all their disregard of such testimony and their often intractable attributions of immeasurable power and creativity to colonialism, have one thing right: colonial modernity decisively altered the character and evolutionary course of Hindu religion. The early nineteenth century displayed an accelerating drive to codify what, by the last quarter of that century, was commonly known among English speakers as "Hinduism." The question cannot simply be put to rest by demonstrating the ways that Hindus conceived their common identity before the arrival of European powers, an important qualification recently offered by Lorenzen and Sweetman. New religious institutions, new forms of religious subjectivity, and new markers of religious identity, all definitely emerged in some manner from the creative agency of Hindus in the context of early nineteenth-century developments, especially the consolidation of the colonial state and the introduction of Protestant missionaries to British India. These social and religious transformations are so significant and so widespread that it seems unnecessarily fussy to insist that Hinduism—in the sense of a cohesive and reasonably uniform religion comparable to contemporary Abrahamic or Semitic traditions—was not the offspring of nineteenth-century colonialism.

This is, however, not the remarkable claim it might seem at first blush. Something similar could be said of all modern religious forms. A bit too much, it seems to me, has been made over the ruptures and discontinuities of the early nineteenth century. Hinduism as we conceive it today is indeed the creation of the nineteenth century, but so are a host of modern religions and modern social institutions. Constructionists are only making a more specific claim about the effects of modernity that have impacted many social formations and relations the globe over. Continuity and the triumph of historical memory over sustained, deliberate, and widely dispersed interventions are also parts of the story we must not overlook. There is, first of all, the matter of what we might regard as the sheer mass and inertia of embodied and embedded tradition. It defies common sense to maintain that a relatively small band of scholars and other observers could virtually invent a religious tradition from fragments of insight and re-present it to its presumed practitioners without inviting an incredulity that is absent from the historical record. Robert Frykenberg, in a move that seems to undercut his major thesis about the constructedness of Hinduism, points out in a footnote that the ratio of Europeans to Indians in the civil services was over 1:1,000.[15] He maintains that

> [d]enigrators of Orientalism give too much credit to Europeans and too little to hosts of Native Indians (mainly Brahmans and others imbued with Brahmanical world views; but also Muslims imbued with Islamic world views) for the cultural constructions (and reconstructions) of India. These Indian elites did as much to inculcate their own views into the administrative machinery and into the cultural framework of the Indian Empire as anything done by the Europeans whom they so outnumbered and with whom they worked so closely.[16]

Western historiography itself has also intervened to deny Hindus their history. The habit of casting competing groups as either "reformers" (e.g., the Brahmo Samaj) or "orthodox" (e.g., the Dharma Sabha) has for too long obscured the modern character of emerging Hindu organizations; their mutually shared goals, interests, and strategies; and their common passion for preserving and embodying the ancient past.[17] Constructionist arguments work also to bolster the weight given to missionary or imperial formulations of Hinduism and to undermine an appreciation of prior indigenous awarenesses of a pan-Indian Hindu identity.[18] I agree, in this context, that too much blame or credit has been assigned to colonialism and share the exasperation of those who cannot accept that "everything was invented in the nineteenth century."[19] Such purportedly anticolonial arguments inevitably end up undermining themselves by assigning all things modern and Indian to foreign influences and nurturing a neo-nostalgia for a pristine, precolonial India that scholarship more sensitive to both western and Indian political exercises in purism would guard against.[20]

There are, I am arguing, powerful historical and political reasons for resisting the most sweeping claims of constructionists. The utter discontinuity with the past, both European and Indian, that a strict constructionist reading of the historical record entails is unwarranted. The body of evidence of precolonial iterations of a Hindu identity is growing. More telling, I believe, is the absence of contemporaneous Hindu contestation of the clearly developing category "Hinduism." Reforming and orthodox groups did not unreflexively borrow or strategically recast a half-cooked British idea.[21] The very articulation of the colonial-era concept "Hindu" was already a collaborative undertaking; discursive interactions between Britons and Indians contributed to the dialogic and heteroglot production known as "Hinduism."[22] The largely unacknowledged pandits who interpreted text and rite for British travelers, traders, and rulers were themselves promoting specific ideas about Hinduism's unifying principles, historical trends, soteriology, and so forth. A spokesperson such as Bhabanicaran Bandyopadhyaya might have located its core in caste and rite; a reformer such as Rammohan Roy might locate it in a Vedic monotheism. What the contested nature of the category among these indigenous theologians indicates is not (or not merely) a rearrangement of power under a colonial administration but, more fundamentally, the clear fact that the category made sense; the emergent concept Hinduism resonated with some prior self-understanding. There would have been no basis for an intercultural debate (i.e., between British rulers and Indian subjects) or an intracultural one (between opposing Indian groups) on issues related to Hindu teaching without some implicit acceptance of the very category already in place. There were loud and vociferous debates in both registers in the early nineteenth century over what properly constituted Hindu society and rite. To my knowledge, however, there was no corresponding debate either among Indians or between Indians and Britons about the appropriateness of the category itself. One would expect to find Hindus raising some objections to the privileging of an imputed unity over a diversity that was manifest to Hindus and Europeans alike in popular newspapers of the day, in the reproduction of Indian public opinion included in virtually every English-language newspaper in India, or in Hindu tracts that answered specific Christian charges about Hindu belief and practice, but I have come across no such discussion, nor has any scholar to whom I have posed the issue. As we have seen, as the idea of Hinduism slowly took shape, Hindus themselves could resist western proposals about the content and character of the ideas and practices that would define such an entity, and they could also debate one another about specific Hindu matters, but they did not argue for the incommensurability of what were coming to be understood as Hinduism's variants. Hindus themselves informed and countered missionary and Orientalist constructions of Hinduism, but they did not call the project itself into question. The deafening silence among indigenous elites on this issue, an issue which, it is critical to remember, had occupied Europeans for centuries at this point, cannot be accounted for by attributing only the basest political opportunism to those elites who did mobilize around the idea. A gaping absence of indigenous critique of the category "Hindu" itself must suggest, at the very least, a ready acceptance of the label among many Hindus and that the concept itself corresponded to some elements of Indian self-understanding. It seems even more likely that the idea, if not the label, was already common Indian currency. The British did not mint this coin; they traded in it because Hindus handed it to them. The historical role of the colonizer was not to invent Hinduism either by blunder or by design, but to introduce an economy of concepts and power relations that dramatically enhanced the value of such identity markers.

Essentially Speaking

Behind some constructionists' antipathy to the term "Hinduism" is a conviction that any essentializing of Indic traditions functions in a hegemonic manner. Many have voiced an opposition to essentialism on the basis of its capacity to deny Indians historical or social agency and to augment the West's sense of its own superiority. These were the two major concerns of Inden's important 1990 book *Imagining India*. In deconstructing the multiple ways that the West has essentialized India, Inden was attacking "the idea that humans and human institutions . . . are governed by determinate natures."[23] The academic practice of representing India by imputing essential natures to it obscures the activity of "relatively complex and shifting human agents" who "make and remake one another through a dialectical process in changing situations."[24] Any characterization of a human institution by reference to its essences must, Inden argues, describe a static, ossified entity.[25] His challenge to western representations of India has reflected a much wider movement. From the postmodern celebration of difference to subaltern studies' resurrection of non-elite knowledges, the scramble to denounce the identification and deployment of essences freighted with ideological weight has been a very noticeable feature in the recent study of Hinduism and religion as a whole. From many corners there has risen an effort to deconstruct and undermine such essences in the interests of restoring agency and giving voice to subaltern formulations of religious identity that may be lost in the imposition of homogenizing wholes.

The attack on essentialized representations of Hinduism, whether those of a brahmanical elite or of western academic discourses, has led to important advances in the field of religious studies and also trained our gaze on religious minorities and communities that might embrace understandings of a tradition that do not reflect dominant interests. What I suggest, however, is that essentialism in and of itself is neither the gravest of descriptive sins nor the loyal servant of hegemony. To paraphrase Talal Asad, some things really are constitutive and essential to a social formation, but they are nonetheless potential targets of subversion and the certain future victims of historical change.[26] The rush to condemn all essentializing discourses also threatens the historian's responsibility to name a social phenomenon's constitutive and characteristic elements. The essential, like its cousin, the definition, plays a critical role in the life of any historical analysis or social theory—not necessarily, however, because it is truly of a thing's *essence*, but precisely because of its imposture. As hypothesis, preliminary proposal, guiding idea, or provisional conclusion, the naming of a set of qualities, characteristics, or principles that constitute or identify a thing is always part of the historian's and theorist's art, as is the meticulous critique of prevailing historiography and theory. Essentialism and the deconstruction of imputed essences is the heart and soul of social and historical inquiry, the means by which it attains greater clarity and further insight.

It might be useful here to make a distinction between two variants of essentializing representations. There is the kind of "hard essentialism" that determines a social formation, such as a religion or culture, to be the passive product of an inherent principle that generates that formation's beliefs, practices, and identities. Inden's analysis of western ideas about Hinduism as a tangled jungle or as the product of imagination unbridled by reason finds fault with just this sort of representational strategy. Hard essentialism posits timeless core essences that travel through history taking on and shedding accretions such that their external forms are ultimately identical and impervious to substantial transformation or innovation. This is a fundamentally antihistorical method, and one that the study of religion has largely outgrown, a fact that its

most vocal detractors steadfastly ignore. Such a hard essentialism may be polemical, as we see in many evangelical representations of Hinduism, like the
claim examined in chapter 3 that Hinduism is fundamentally centered on the
logic of idol worship. In other instances, hard essentialism may evince nostal-
gic or romantic themes, as in some Christian appropriations of eastern spirituality and New Age syncretisms. The harshest critics of the study of religion
paint the discipline with the broad brush of hard essentialism, imagining it a
uniform, monophonic discourse still deeply invested in the homogenizing
methods of the mid-twentieth century for which Mircea Eliade has become the
most prominent effigy.[27]

There is a less egregious form of essentialism, a kinder and gentler version, what we might think of as "soft essentialism," which makes the simple
claim that a social formation—religion as such, a religion, a gender, and so
forth—possesses key identifying properties and characteristics. I have in mind
here the colloquial use of the term "essential," as in the phrase, "Essentially,
what I am saying is x." In this sense, "essentially" means only "more or less,"
"basically," "in sum," or "chiefly." A soft essentialism is provisional and fully
amenable to critique and revision, and we ought not confuse it with the ossi-
fying, hegemonic uses of hard essentialism. Neither, moreover, should scholars
in religious studies departments quietly accept the gross distortions of our
discipline that suggest it is solely in the business of reifying and essentializing
dynamic, variable, and multiform personal and social experiences.

There is no serious doubt about the proposition that colonial and proto-
nationalist discourses in India functioned, and functioned effectively, by means
of the articulation of a cohesive Hinduism oriented around some historical,
textual, or social core essence. From the very moment of their pronouncement,
however, such core essences have been challenged. Indeed, however dominant
the early nineteenth-century discourses that identified Hinduism as a social
and religious system generated from a text (e.g., the Vedas or the Gita), a ritual
logic (that of sacrifice or idol worship), a mythical imagination (the fecund
"spirit of polytheism"), or a system of social ordering (caste as defined by
brahmanical or merchant elites), such essentialist claims have quickly met with
two critical responses. On the one side, there have always arisen the competing
claims that Hinduism coheres in one or another of these essences. On the
other, there have sounded the frustrated British protestations that there was
no one thing that distinguished Hindu practice or identity; namely, that there
was no Hinduism at all. Given the claims about the ubiquity of western essentialism, it is important to note that this second response has always been present in western representations of Hinduism and in intercultural dialogue
throughout the history of European and Indian contact. It is, in fact, a mark
of careful and fruitful scholarship that one attempts both to identify the essence
of some perceived social reality and also carefully to articulate how and why
such an essentialism may be misleading in the messy world of actual human
institutions and relations. We must both theorize and question theory; demonstrate its critical relevance to organic and shifting constellations, and remind
ourselves of its always provisional and homogenizing character. Theories, con-

cepts, and constructions simultaneously falsify and clarify; that is their nature and the nature of all language. The work of the historian of religion lies precisely along the borderland between that falsification and clarification, the territory where our grander and more ambitious proposals shed light on observable human experience and are, at the same time, humbled by its ineffability.

Articulating Religion

The question of the nature and appropriateness of "Hinduism" is also an aspect of the larger question about the genealogy of the concept of religion. Many hold it to possess a strictly modern and western lineage and regard its application to traditions that do not emphasize text, faith, and belief, that is, religious formations that are not Jewish, Christian, or Muslim, to represent an arrogant and wholly misleading imposition of a nonindigenous category on Indian social reality. Given what he takes to be the narrow range of its signification and the suggestions of an exclusive identity the word religion conveys in the West, S. N. Balagangadhara, for one, insists that "there simply could be no 'religion' in India."[28]

Two distinct claims are heard among those who argue against the use of the category. The first asserts that "religion" as a concept that describes a set of universal or near-universal human institutions centered on distinctive beliefs and practices that might invite a cross-cultural comparison of one set to another is a historical latecomer, dating only from the European Enlightenment.[29] A broader application beyond the post-Enlightenment West, therefore, would normalize modern, western, and especially Christian experience. To classify other traditions as religions distorts them and renders them deviant from an ideal type, because they would fall short in some key respects. The second asserts that to employ "religion" as a term of social analysis lends credence to the unverifiable claims and untenable categories of religious practitioners themselves by reproducing the grammar and vocabulary of religious belief. Religions turn on an acceptance of a supersensible reality that the scientific method must exclude. The end of studying religion, this line of reasoning goes, should be to explain *why* people express and embody such beliefs at all and what they achieve socially by doing so, rather than to reinscribe religious ideas and social formations in the academy as if they demanded no interrogation themselves.

Religion as a Strictly Modern and Christian Concept

On the first score, it seems easily demonstrable, however, that a category encompassing a variety of cross-cultural beliefs and practices has been a part of western discourses for centuries longer than many believe, and if they only came to be called religions later, the belief that humans possessed distinct, mutually exclusive traditions of belief and rite has remained fairly consistent. When Augustine wrote *On True Religion* (*De Vera Religione*), he was contrasting

the superstitious rites of Roman pagans with the spiritualized piety of Christians; both qualified as species of the generic category "religion" in his mind,
but one was illumined by reason and revelation, the other pocked with vulgar
error. Had his opening remarks appeared in the *Missionary Papers*, they would
not have sounded the least incongruous:

> The way of the good and blessed life is to be found entirely in the
> true religion wherein one God is worshiped and acknowledged with
> purest piety to be the beginning of all existing things, originating,
> perfecting and containing the universe. Thus it becomes easy to de-
> tect the error of the peoples who have preferred to worship many
> gods rather than the true God and Lord of all things.[30]

When Augustine used the term "religion," he meant the one, true religion,
Catholic Christianity, not chiefly as an institution but as a standard of piety.
He nevertheless posited the ubiquity of two general elements of human culture: belief and rite. He remarked that pagans differed passionately on matters
of belief but participated in common rites at common temples.[31] By contrast,
Christians excluded from their rites those who made competing metaphysical
claims, however similar in nature those claims were.[32] Here, in Augustine's
early work, we find several components of what we commonly take religion to
be today: 1) a very widespread, if not universal, form of human expression of
supernatural reality, 2) a plurality of competing such systems, and 3) their
amenability to mutual comparison.[33] To leap ahead some centuries to illustrate
further,[34] the French reformer John Calvin acknowledged the core of genuine
pious insight that lay at the heart of other faiths when he made the natural
world a primary resource for knowledge about God and declared that Christianity held some characteristic habits in common with pagans. He insisted that
"from the beginning of the world there has been no region, no city, in short,
no household that could do without religion."[35] For Calvin, all human knowledge had suffered the corruption of sin, but what distinguished Christian faith
and piety from pagan belief and practice was the former's possession of a
revealed truth superseding natural knowledge, available through the scriptural
text only to those pre-elected to salvation.[36]

   In short, the case holding that the concept of religion, in terms of a (nearly)
universal human artifact subsisting in mutually exclusive systems of belief and
practice, possesses a strictly modern genealogy has been overstated. It is clear
that the Christian West has always regarded its traditions as one subset among
others of the generic concept "religion" and seen religion as a cross-cultural
element of human thought and behavior.[37] And it is certainly true that, in this
respect, the early church was altering the received meaning of the term somewhat from an older Roman conception of religion as the unassailable traditions
of one's ancestors and manipulating the idea to its own purposes in order to
contrast "true" belief to paganism and heresy.[38] That is to say, the modern
concept of religion indeed has its roots in Christian, specifically Latin Christian,
triumphalism.

   It is equally true, however, that just as the term evolved with changed usage to indicate closed systems of competing and mutually exclusive beliefs, it has, since the initiation of colonial contact, continued to evolve beyond its narrow Christian range of meaning.[39] Current debate over the term marks one more moment in that evolution. With the Enlightenment and the broadening of European contact with other civilizations, it became possible to speak of religion outside this restricted context—not, to be sure, without a significant distortion that we continue to try to temper. Discourses we call "naturalistic," "rationalistic," "humanistic," "academic," "religious studies," and more began their slow evolution and institutionalization in the university.[40] With these developments has come an expanded self-consciousness about the comparative project and the terms by which comparison is conducted and entities compared. The academic usage of "religion" has changed substantially, and under continuing scrutiny, it remains elastic. Its semantic range continues to evolve and expand as scholars critique and examine their own categories and as they apply new data from non-western traditions to the category. Religious studies departments are not, by and large, simply factories for the maintenance of Christian hegemony but do, in very many instances, work assiduously to overcome their own histories and discover truly meaningful and instructive ways to characterize human difference as well as a shared humanity across cultures.

Religion as a Constructed Concept

This last point brings me to a second important aspect of the argument that "religion" is a misleading term for describing systems of belief outside the Abrahamic faiths, one distinctly postcolonial in its concerns and intent. There is a great deal of hand-wringing in the field of religious studies and among scholars who study religion from positions in departments of history and sociology not only over the term's hegemonic potential, but also for religious studies' sloppy demarcation of what counts as its data. A glance at one recent program of the annual meeting of the American Academy of Religion might bear some of these charges out. It suggests that such disparate phenomena as transgender activism, the television serial *The Sopranos,* the sarin gas attacks on Tokyo's subways in 1995, the Harry Potter phenomenon, zazen, family planning, Kierkegaard's ethical thought, the Ku Klux Klan, the camp meeting, and, I cannot resist including him, Hanako the toilet ghost all have a share in some nebulous undertaking named "religion." The alleged ubiquity and centrality of this imagined entity to human societies serves to justify the existence of this professional association and provides its raison d'etre.[41] Whereas one might maintain that its ability to theorize such divergent human expressions and experiences is precisely the strongest argument for the relevance and institutional legitimacy of religious studies,[42] others might perceive an ill-defined object of study. The more serious corollary to this charge, however, is that the study of religion as such is tantamount to an uncritical acceptance, even promotion, of discourses that invoke beings whose presence and existence are not at all in evidence. To take the statements of religious practitioners at face value and to seek to interpret their meaning for those practitioners is—the argument goes—merely to describe what the insider believes and experiences and not to engage in any second-order, explanatory method.

These objections to the practice of religious studies, namely, that its founding concept is simultaneously empty and hegemonic, and that the discipline gives voice to and advances insider approaches to religion (i.e., mythological, theological) over outsider accounts of religious behavior (i.e., social scientific, biological, etc.), implicitly raise questions about the historical processes by which Hinduism came to be understood as one species in a genus of universal human behaviors and hence comparable to others. S. N. Balagangadhara and Richard King have both cast suspicion on the application of the concept religion to Hindu traditions in India, especially because, in each of their views, "religion" refracts its content through a prism of Christian categories. It thereby suggests orderly social realities or closed systems of thought about the origins of the cosmos that are easily distinguishable from their political and social surroundings—things not characteristic of Indian traditions.[43] In response, Will Sweetman notes that religion was not an ossified, static concept into which Hinduism was forced in the eighteenth century but rather an elastic category that continued to stretch and develop as a result of the encounter with Indian religions.[44] I argue that religion is not and has not been the monothetic concept awkwardly applied to Hindu and other data that so many critics would claim. It has proven, in fact, a very useful, if constructed, category for framing colonial contact and highlighting certain features of intercultural encounter. This book has pursued a religious studies approach to the encounter between Hindus and their (largely Christian) British rulers in the early nineteenth century by demonstrating the indispensability of understanding and foregrounding religious categories, rituals, communities, and beliefs in these interactions. It has shown that to reduce religion to mere social practice or political power would be to fundamentally misrepresent and misunderstand the relations between Britons and Indians. More to the point, it has drawn attention to ways in which Hindus and Christians compared themselves to one another and invoked their mutually shared concepts. These groups themselves articulated their similarities and differences, both in terms of specific beliefs and in their more general nature as socially located entities. Christians and Hindus were already doing, albeit in an unselfconscious way, what all good comparativists do—they enumerated contrasts and likenesses, but also examined to what extent the entities in question were comparable. The degree to which one or another set of cultural expressions is a religion is precisely a matter for comparative analysis, not an issue that the comparative method precludes. To propose that Hinduism is not a religion because only Christianity and related faiths are religions is to imply that Hindus and Christians have nothing to say to one another qua Hindus and Christians and that, in a conceptually clearheaded universe, they shouldn't.

Of graver and more immediate import, however, for early twenty-first-century global politics, are the allegiances the vitiation of the concept of religion subtly declares. The marginalization of religion as a concept also entails the marginalization of religious communities and identities from centers of power and knowledge production. The nullification of religion aims to severely restrict access to the critical analysis of religion at the very historical moment when peoples formerly only represented *by* religious studies discourses are achieving a measure of self-representation in the academy and when "religion," whatever the concept's genealogy, has, in fact, evolved as a category of cross-cultural comparison invoked by insiders to non-Christian religious traditions. This comparative undertaking now cuts a number of ways, in the negative evaluation of Christian (and Jewish) conduct and intentions toward others that might prompt some to terrorist violence, in the peaceful resistance to western hegemonies on the basis of religious convictions, and as the proud assertion of a distinctive history and identity vis-à-vis the Christian West. Whatever their intent, the reification of religion and the comparative study of religion are now rampant global exercises, often undertaken by those who would contest a history of western essentialism, alterization, and distortion of colonized religious ideologies.

To narrow the focus and put the matter somewhat bluntly for clarity's sake, if religion is not a real thing, then likewise it is not meaningful to speak of Hinduism or any other "religious" faith as if it were a real thing. This claim in turn denies and devalues the lived experience of, in this case, Hindus and hits at the very heart of what many regard with the greatest reverence as the core of their received identity. Moreover, this claim excludes their voices from the centers of knowledge production about their defining experiences and emotions on that very basis. The arguments that religion is a meaningless category and Hinduism a bungled western construct best dispensed with effectively undercut the geopolitical aims of some Hindus to be taken seriously after centuries of stereotyping, misrepresentation, and demonization at the hands of the Christian West. To seek to deny, moreover, entrance to a conversation about the social and political character and effect of religion to those who espouse religious points of view on the argument that such voices represent not the scholarship of religion but data for scholars of religion, and to claim this at the same time that one claims that religion is a misleading category for cross-cultural comparison, signals an attempt to trump the self-representation card that some non-Christians might now play. It conceals a basic contradiction in the critique of religious studies as nonempirical doublespeak between faulting the discipline for a legacy of imperialism and undermining the authority and agency claimed by those whom imperialism has most directly and negatively affected.

Perhaps the most vociferous recent attack the field that allegedly takes religion as a sui generis, self-evident datum of human cultural life is Timothy Fitzgerald's *The Ideology of Religious Studies*. Briefly, Fitzgerald's major claims, as I read him, are as follows. First, he contends that the category "religion" itself is empty, precisely for the fact that academic and vernacular usage employs the term to identify an enormously varied set of cross-cultural phenomena such that it comes to have no concrete referent at all. Fitzgerald writes, "Religion cannot reasonably be taken to be a valid analytical category since it does not pick out any distinctive cross-cultural aspect of human life."[45] Second,

Fitzgerald argues that all usage of the term "religion" imports an implicitly theological framework into what should remain a strictly anthropological or sociological undertaking.[46] He locates this theological core of religious studies in the work of the founding members of the discipline who conceived religion as a variable but universal and innate human response to universally felt experiences of transcendence. F. Max Müller, Mircea Eliade, and Rudolph Otto are among the seminal comparativists and phenomenologists Fitzgerald accuses of mystifying textual and ethnographic data to construct such an instinctive human faculty. Their approaches presume the very thing they must, instead, demonstrate, namely that there is something distinctive about a set of human behaviors that could legitimately be grouped under the concept "religion." Finally, Fitzgerald identifies the form and character of the ideology of religious studies as a "liberal ecumenical" theology guided by the acceptance of the existence of "a transcendent intelligent Being who gives meaning and purpose to human history."[47] The aim of this discourse is to foster fruitful dialogue, peaceful coexistence, and perhaps even, Fitzgerald seems to fear, a mutual recognition of the validity of distinct religious communities.

Others have taken Fitzgerald to task for a series of shortcomings in his book.[48] He has been criticized for not tapping fields outside religious studies to see how others address the problems of category formation and taxonomy,[49] for recommending a shift to the category "culture," one at least as problematic as "religion,"[50] for his reified concept of the West,[51] and for failing to appreciate the complexity of the question of disciplinary boundaries.[52] In addition, and most relevant to this book's major approach, however, is Fitzgerald's stereotyped and ill-informed representation of the field of religious studies, which he depicts as a dinosaur lumbering among complex and subtle data, clumsily addressing them with theories and ideas generations out of date and crippled by theological commitments. He confidently makes such wide-ranging and damning statements as this: "All the notable theorists of religious studies have placed their usually outstanding scholarship firmly and explicitly in a theological framework, heavily loaded with western Christian assumptions about God and salvation, even if not Christian in an exact confessional sense."[53] In praising Louis Dumont's *Homo Hierarchicus*, a book that thoroughly reifies caste, Fitzgerald says that "religious studies as religious studies has nothing to offer" about questions of power and its mystification.[54] When he surveys the field of religious studies, Fitzgerald sees only the likes of Frazer, Tylor, Müller, and Eliade. His selective vision produces a gross misrepresentation of a discipline. Whether it is attributable to genuine ignorance or simple mischief I cannot say. In the fifty years since Wilfred Cantwell Smith first raised the question about the broad application of the term in his *The Meaning and End of Religion*, religious studies has been vibrantly self-critical and has eagerly interrogated its own founding concept. Smith's own charge that "the term 'religion' is confusing, unnecessary, and distorting"[55] and Jonathan Z. Smith's judgment that religion is solely the creation of the scholar's study have become virtual mantras in the field, regular reminders that, like "culture" and "society," the thing we study does not exist in nature but serves descriptive ends. Fitzgerald, for all his frequent caveats to the effect that there are many excellent scholars in religious studies departments, displays no sense that religious studies or the study of religion could include any but naive, monotheistic, textually oriented phenomenologists. He locates those who actually critique the phenomenologist tradition in religious studies outside the field, a move that allows him to construct the very thing he attacks while he completely ignores significant advances in the study of religion made in the last twenty-five years by, for example, the contributions of feminism, post-modernism, and ethnography.[56]

I find Russell T. McCutcheon's body of theory and criticism altogether different from Fitzgerald's. Although both aim toward similar ends, namely to challenge the assumptions and execution of religious studies, McCutcheon's work is far better informed about the field and his critique is both less polemical and harder hitting than Fitzgerald's. Although I will proceed to disagree with many of his major claims, I believe the quality of current debate among scholars who study something they or others identify as "religion" would be much impoverished without McCutcheon's carefully honed and often pointedly satirical characterization of the field.

McCutcheon's work presents a mixture of important insights, significant overstatements, and rhetorically effective misrepresentations of the field of religious studies, and many of its contributions and shortcomings I cannot address here. One strand of his overall critique of religious studies, however, is especially relevant to this book's characterization of religion in nineteenth-century British India. Some wider summary of McCutcheon's larger project is necessary to get me to that one point. In his first book, *Manufacturing Religion: The Discourse on Sui Generis Religion and the Politics of Nostalgia*, taking Jonathan Z. Smith's famous dictum that religion is solely the creation of the scholar's imagination as his point of departure, McCutcheon maintains that there is no sui generis, self-evident phenomenon that corresponds to our word "religion." We have taken this term in the singular, specific sense to mean a set of beliefs and practices that together constitute a people's distinctive way of constructing and communicating with some other realm that we religious studies scholars, buying into the categories of religious practitioners, have called "the sacred." These constructs, McCutcheon urges, are convenient fictions, and he warns that "rather than simply imagining [religion], we have actively manufactured it."[57] Academic representations, McCutcheon finds, reproduce and authorize religious identities and categories and thereby are implicated in the maintenance of larger geopolitical and sociopolitical realities. Perpetuation of discourse about sui generis religion is more than an act of fancy for McCutcheon: it colludes in the sustenance of these larger networks of political and social relations. He claims that to protect themselves against this awareness, western scholars of religion have tended to think of religion in terms of decontextualized phenomena, a flawed approach that has favored the study of narrative and essentialist symbolism over concern for local and historical backdrops, formalized ritual over ritual process, and religion as a private and privileged discourse over religion as a nexus of many other social discourses.[58]

In his most recent book, *Critics Not Caretakers: Redescribing the Public Study of Religion*, McCutcheon urges that we think of religion as simply "an all too ordinary effect of events in the historical and social world,"[59] a "thoroughly human activity with no mysterious distillate left over"[60] that must be explained by theory and not simply described by means of the very vocabulary ("sacred," "holy," "worship," etc.) employed by practitioners. The scholar's role as scholar is—and McCutcheon is very prescriptive about this—solely to demystify religious assertions and practices and expose them as one of a society's means for authorizing power.[61] In no circumstance should the scholar give voice to or regard religious claims and actions, *or the people making them*, including theologians in the academy, as anything other than his or her data that unveils the authorizing function of religion.[62] Because religion is an everyday affair firmly rooted in its particular linguistic, cultural, social, and political worlds, interreligious understanding is an illusion and a quest best abandoned because such an illusory goal is a part of the European tradition of scholarship not shared by all other traditions and amounts to plundering another's tradition to serve "our" ends.[63] McCutcheon rejects the notion of cross-cultural understanding because, among other reasons, he doubts both that "our" categories can be sufficiently mapped over onto those of "the other" and that this other would be at all interested in attempting to understand us.[64]

There is a fatal blindness in McCutcheon's reasoning on this point, and one that displays either his naiveté or his disregard for the political—a realm about which he claims to care so much. McCutcheon imagines this "other" to be completely uninterested in comprehending "our" ways, but he fails to take account of the contemporary reality in the academy and among many religious communities, namely that what these "others" want is not so much a clearer apprehension of European and American cultural logic (in a globalized economy, this logic is almost everywhere all-too-apparent), but to be understood, on their own terms, according to their own categories, and by means of their own self-representation. In the academic study of Hinduism, powerful and angry Hindu voices have criticized the academic representation of Hinduism and exposed the divergent aims and contexts that motivate religious practitioners and students in the secular study.[65] I remain in complete agreement with Brian K. Smith's demand that scholarship not abrogate its responsibility to contradict false historical, social, or political claims made by religious practitioners,[66] but I maintain that responsible scholarship on religion must seek productive engagement with practitioners that does not scoffingly dismiss their faith. In discounting all religious claims and demanding that only the theorist versed in sophisticated theory—theory forged almost exclusively in academic institutions in or modeled on those in Europe and the United States—be recognized McCutcheon and those similarly disposed reveal their own neocolonialist and elitist agenda. To behave as if the concerns of religious communities do not and should not matter to the scholar of religion, a creature that McCutcheon has thoroughly documented as having great effect on and influence over the practice and understanding of religion, seems arrogant, misguided, and decidedly dangerous. To proceed in such a way, moreover, at this highly charged historical moment when religion and religious identity are invoked by actors in many regional and global dramas as motives for escalating violence, severely undercuts McCutcheon's claim to be fundamentally concerned about the public role of the scholar of religion. To assume that role for McCutcheon means only one thing: to call into question—using the power of the classroom, the microphone, and western critical discourses—the most cherished beliefs, values, and identities of those who may already resent the power of western discourses to characterize them and shape their destinies. In the years immediately following the period this book covers, as some Indian groups began to master the technologies and institutionalizing strategies that would allow them a measure of self-representation, Thomas Babbington Macaulay issued, as a statement of government policy, the famous opinion that "a single shelf of a good European library was worth the whole native literature of India and Arabia."[67] McCutcheon's casual dismissal of religious identity and his exclusion of religious practitioners from the study of religion is tantamount to the same condemnation.

Christians and Hindus

If this book has largely confined itself to a distant half a century of interactions between discrete communities among Hindus and Christians, it has nevertheless done so with the conviction that they are a part of today's conflicts and recriminations. I have tried to proceed as well with an awareness that those persons, Christian and Hindu, our forebears or contemporaries, who have pursued policies and strategies to which I might vehemently object, were themselves political agents plotting specific ends but also bearers of social and historical processes beyond their control or cognizance. It seems fitting to close with a set of thoughts about this longer history that has given rise to a chronic tension afflicting relations between Hindus and Christians.

Two events of 1999 marked a crisis in global Hindu-Christian relations. They cannot in any way be said to represent these relations as a whole, but their wide dissemination through mass media in Europe, Australia, the United States, and India have galvanized opposition of certain segments of each group to one another and communicated to the world that intractability is a hallmark of Hindu-Christian relations at the dawn of the new millennium. That year opened with the horrific murder by right-wing Hindu nationalists of the Australian medical missionary Graham Staines and his two young boys while the family slept in their car outside a hospital Staines had founded. Staines had worked with lepers in India for forty years. Many Indian Christians responded with fear and retreat, and Christians outside India expressed shock and alarm. The second event was the publication of the International Mission Board of the Southern Baptist Convention's pamphlet highlighting the Hindu holiday Divali and urging Christians to pray that Hindus would find the "true" light of Jesus Christ.[68] Fiercely evangelical in tone and crafted to appeal to the lurid fascination with the erotic and bizarre evident in CMS publications nearly two hundred years before, the pamphlet provoked outrage from Hindus and non-Hindus across the globe by rehearsing for its Christian audience the well-worn yarn that "more than 900 million people are lost in the hopeless darkness of Hinduism."[69] In both cases, members of the offended communities reacted with a polemic about the other that projected a monolithic, unified enemy and suggested that Hindus or Christians were uniformly in broad support of these acts. Hindus, especially nationalists with access to microphones and Web sites, suggested that all Christians were ardent evangelicals with no appreciation or understanding of Hindu traditions, whereas Christians lamented the decline of the tolerance they had once admired in Hinduism and the mobilization of popular opinion against Christians in India.

I am not suggesting a moral equivalence between them, but I mention these two incidents for several reasons. The first is their obvious inheritance from the colonial events and encounters narrated in this book. The ghosts of the colonial past have not seen fit to lurk quietly in the shadows but have brought the force of the troubled past to bear on the present.[70] Robert Frykenberg has called Hindu nationalism the "twin" of British interventions in Hindu traditions,[71] and I would at least agree that the always-vehement and sometimes-violent opposition of Hindu nationalists toward Christianity in India is but a late product of the imperial manipulations of religions and the circumstances of aggressive missionary interrogation of Hinduism beginning with the work of men like Abbé Dubois, William Carey, Claudius Buchanan, and William Ward. Although horror at such violence and despair at the current state of Hindu-Christian relations seems an appropriate and natural response, it is difficult not to ascribe a very significant measure of culpability for this state of affairs to the strategies consciously adopted since the colonial era by Christians hoping for the religious transformation of the subcontinent, strategies that have sown resentment deeply in Indian public opinion. I must stress that this argument speaks only to history and its ghosts—not to the motivations or intentions of any contemporary actors. There can be no excusing or rationalizing senseless violence or grave insult. But if relations between Hindus and Christians are to improve, history demands that Christians, particularly non-Indian Christians, take the lead in healing the breach by confessing their affront to the dignity and honor of Hinduism.

Among foreign missionaries, Staines was, by all reliable accounts, a humanitarian of the most compassionate and engaged stripes. He devoted his life to the alleviation of suffering and seems never to have been involved in the demonization of Hinduism or the arrogant propagation of Christianity that many Hindus, with justification, find deeply offensive.[72] The Staines murders were tragic in themselves and also for their impact on Hindu-Christian relations. The Staines' deaths and the attention the Indian and foreign press gave them called yet again to Hindu minds the idea that Christianity was itself largely a foreign force and presence in India. The rightful fury over these crimes obscured the fact that the great measure of suffering and persecution of Christians in India is of Indians themselves, whose homes and churches were reduced to ashes in large numbers in a frightening series of incidents in the late 1990s.[73] Moreover, to Christians the world over, Hinduism became associated with terror and mob violence.

That the Baptist Divali pamphlet has become emblematic of Christian attitudes toward Hindus is itself deeply troubling because it came to suggest that all Christians alike regard Hinduism with disdain. The tract was profoundly wounding to Hindu sensibilities rubbed raw by hundreds of years of abuse at the hands of a very vocal minority of non-Indian Christians who have possessed neither the courtesy nor the self-control to address alien ideas and practices with honest inquiry. Both instances stand as enormous stains on the reputations of two great faiths whose practitioners, by and large, deserve far better representation.

These events point first and perhaps most importantly to the need for an awareness of how poor the state of information that most Hindus and Christians have about one another is and how easily bad information can be mobilized for violence and insult. Evangelical polemic about Hinduism at times seems to have progressed little beyond the juvenile and lurid representations purveyed by the CMS *Missionary Papers* I described in chapter 2. If the Baptist Divali pamphlet serves to demonstrate this ignorance among Christians, a 1999 Indian publication titled *Christianity and Conversion in India* makes the case about Hindus clearly enough.[74] Its pages are filled with thirdhand rumormongering and simple confusion about the realities of global Christianity, which it then marshals to contend that the failure of Christianity in the West has forced its few remaining zealous practitioners to turn to the developing world to compensate for the empty pews in Europe and the Americas. It devotes almost an entire chapter to a speculative episode that is of minor interest to even rabid western conspiracy theorists: the alleged murder of Pope John Paul I in the Vatican a month after his election as pontiff in 1978. The book names this murder, utterly unsubstantiated and seldom discussed seriously in the West, a major crisis in the Christian world that has so drastically eroded the faith of western Christians that evangelists now turn to India to convert her masses to a dying faith.[75] Most pervasive among the book's flaws is the consistent representation of Christianity as a uniform global system, which it often identifies with Roman Catholicism as when, for example, it cites declining enrollment in Catholic seminaries and claims that "without priests, Christianity cannot survive."[76] In this and other places, the book displays complete ignorance about the vibrant and robust state of many strands of Christianity in the West. It is of paramount importance that both Christians and Hindus come to recognize the enormous diversity of communities who call themselves by those names.[77]

Clearly, there is a role for the academic study of religion in stemming these streams of appalling misinformation, but the question of what role is hardly a simple one. The academic study of religion is itself an heir to western exoticization and demonization of religion, and Hindus, in particular, are suspicious of the motives and representations of scholars.[78] This fact is painfully evident in the successive waves of controversy over the academic study of Hinduism initially set in motion by Jeffrey J. Kripal's *Kali's Child*, a book that many scholars regard as a sensitive portrayal of the Hindu ascetic and teacher Ramakrishna, but many Hindus see as a blasphemous denigration of one of their most revered modern teachers.[79] The origin of the ancient Aryans, the import of archaeological remains at the disputed Babri Masjid, the character of past Muslim rule over areas of the subcontinent, and the validity of psychoanalytic interpretation all have erupted as sites of conflict between Hindus and scholars of Hinduism. The fact that the study of religion is nearly absent from post-Independence institutions of higher education in India and has, therefore, very few Hindu voices representing the discipline to Hindus in India, further contributes to the perception that the academic study of religion is a western enterprise dismissive of Hindu traditions.[80]

Global capitalism, the commodification of religion, and the voraciousness of the mass media are each also responsible in some measure for irritating the sensibilities of religious practitioners and provoking a defensiveness that can hinder progress in interreligious understanding. This contemporary situation impacts all religious groups, but two examples will suffice to make the point about Hindus and Christians. A satirical Web site that actually aims to lampoon the commodification of religion and feigns to sell toy "action figures" of various gods and goddesses, armed with modern assault weaponry, has offended Hindus and Christians alike by offering Jesus Christ (complete with "ninja-messiah throwing nails") and Krishna ("cosmic warrior and lover of many women") for sale.[81] An episode of the popular cartoon *Xena: Warrior Princess* offended Hindus when an episode featured Krishna and Hanuman coming to the aid of its superhero protagonist.[82] The invocation of religious symbols for commercial or satirical purposes has contributed to an atmosphere of mistrust and suspicion in which the offended quickly leap to a wounded reclamation of their revered icons, especially in those from societies less accustomed to a freedom of speech as permissive as that in North America and Europe. Although secular market forces help erode traditional values and symbols, they are encouraging a defensive vigilance that leaves religious communities unwilling or unable to assume the posture of openness necessary for fruitful dialogue.

Hindu-Christian encounter takes place all over the globe, but it is in India where contact between Hindus and Christians is most immediate, public, and of greatest historical duration.[83] Here, religion and politics nowhere display or aspire to the separation they enjoy in the West.[84] The character of Hindu-Christian relations shifts with the changing national and international concerns prevailing in the times and places that give rise to encounter. It is critical, therefore, if we are to cast an eye toward the future of such relations, to remind ourselves that Hindu violence against Christians is of very recent historical provenance. It has stemmed largely from Hindu anger and litigation over the right of Christians to proselytize non-Christians in India.[85] By virtue of Christianity's association with the United States and, to a lesser degree, Europe, Hindu-Christian conflict in India has invited the close scrutiny of the press both in India and elsewhere. The Indian press writes for a public informed by and sensitive to its colonial history and postcolonial struggles with that history, whereas the western media is encouraged by noble as well as base motives to cover "trouble spots," particularly those that affect western interests. Hindu nationalist organizations preaching the notion that India is historically and culturally a Hindu nation foster the conflict that attracts this attention. Those religions that did not originate in India—Christianity and Islam in particular— they declare foreign transplants whose practitioners can find acceptance only by acknowledging their foreignness and thereby accepting a secondary status in the life of the nation. "Hindutva" organizations such as the Vishva Hindu Parishad convey this message in both public speech and public ritual spectacle, celebrating Christians and Muslims who identify themselves culturally and nationally as Hindus at the same time that they depict Islam and Christianity as foreign threats to Indian society and state.[86] However, even when Christians explicitly identify themselves as Indian, there is often deep suspicion among Hindus of Christian duplicity. It is readily believed that Christian communities are footholds for foreign influences and also that Christians will adopt whatever disguise might suit their ultimate and governing end: conversion. The recent introduction of anti-conversion bills in state legislatures has been one expression of this suspicion. The now centuries-old Catholic movement to adopt Hindu symbols, concepts, and lifestyles and thus "Indianize" Catholicism, to take another example, has been intensely controversial, with many Hindus regarding "Catholic" ashrams as fraudulent conduits for foreign capital expended for conversion.[87]

It is important to point out that, for all its sites of conflict, India has also offered numerous models for cooperation and mutual appreciation between Hindus and Christians. No one concerned about the state of relations between these two increasingly global communities should forget the rich store of historical and contemporary resources for imagining peaceful and productive engagement between them. Prior to the arrival of Europeans, Hindus and Christians in South India had developed indigenous strategies and patterns for living together. There is ample contemporary evidence, moreover, of day-to-day cooperation and coexistence of Hindus and Christians. Even in ritual settings, there can be much room for rapprochement. The most successful mutual religious undertakings seem to be those that spontaneously and organically evolve at the grassroots level, whereas contrived institutional settings such as Catholic ashrams often incite Hindu resentment.[88] Even assertions of difference among Hindus and Christians in South India employ the common idioms and grammars of divinity that underscore their shared religious sensibilities and make for a kind of civil theology that publicly stages and debates religious claims.[89] Living together certainly does not mean living without conflict or competition. An intricate web of relationships and attitudes binds Hindus and Christians in the state of Kerala but also pits one community against the other.[90] In short, current circumstances in India give no clear signal about the future of Hindu-Christian relations, offering reason for optimism as well as anxiety.

In the late 1980s, just as the nationalist Bharatiya Janata Party was beginning to experience considerable electoral success and Christianity began to assume a prominent place in Hindu nationalist rhetoric, a collection of essays edited by Harold Coward titled *Hindu-Christian Dialogue* was published. It remains the only work of its kind, although the Society for Hindu-Christian Studies has grown significantly in recent years and publishes a journal annually, *Hindu-Christian Studies Bulletin*, which continues to foster dialogue and provide a forum for exchange between Hindus and Christians. Coward's book offered an assessment of the state of Hindu-Christian dialogue then, and its predictions for the future that may be instructive to our current state. In his essay for that volume, Richard W. Taylor noted a general lack of interest in dialogue and identified a growing suspicion among Hindus that dialogue was a cover for proselytization, especially since such conversations were generally initiated and framed by westerners.[91] As we have seen, these concerns persist. In a companion essay, Klaus Klostermaier also anticipated the continued rise of Hindu nationalism.[92] He issued a call for the greater involvement of scholars of religion who could, he imagined, further Hindu-Christian understanding by helping to imagine new articulations of dialogic possibilities.[93]

On the role of scholars in these efforts, Hindu-Christian studies is all too familiar with the double-edged sword the academic study of religion can wield. The field can indeed promote mutual understanding by clarifying the history and nature of the traditions in question, especially by describing the great internal diversity that characterizes both Hinduism and Christianity. The canons of the discipline, however, often put scholars at odds with practitioners, Hindu and Christian alike, because many academics aim to render the historical and metaphysical claims of religious faith *both* as their partisans experience them and as mythologized reflections of merely human desires. It is exactly this "both" that triggers the offended sentiment. Although some might regard this "bothness" as a mark of careful and sensitive scholarship, one that attends to the norms of historiography, ethnography, and hermeneutics, it can strike the devout practitioner as a profound violation. The scholar's craft consists in carefully sketching the contours of a people's imaginings and institutions, thereby revealing, even if unintentionally, humanity in all its depravity and beauty, all its high-mindedness and pettiness, all its elegance and folly. No social institution captures these poles of a people's moral range more than religion; none, however, is more jealously guarded by those who inhabit it. As a consequence, the scrutiny of religious agents and experiences by the academic study of religion has routinely invited misunderstanding and offense.

Scholarship must find a new voice with which to speak about religion. We must forge a language and set of interpretive practices that remain faithful to the demands of rigorous analysis and historical accuracy by refusing to capitulate to religious sentiment as the ultimate jury for what may be said about it, while at the same time acknowledging and very carefully wielding the power the discipline has to shape discourse within and about religious communities themselves. Our world simply cannot afford the disdain or disregard for religious belief and identity that marginalizes some religious subjectivities from the production of knowledge about them or the feverish resentment and violence such a marginalization invites. This book concludes with a new iteration of Klostermaier's exhortation, one informed by the sobering violence and outraged indignation that have marked the encounter between Hindus and Christians in recent years. As Klostermaier suggested, scholars are certainly in a position to contribute their voices to societies' understanding of religious communities as complex, evolving, and exceedingly polyphonic bodies. If they can speak in a manner that displays an openness to patient and extended engagement with these communities, and if they proceed with transparency and honesty about their disciplines' history of collusion with colonial coercion, the study of religion may also demonstrate some means by which religious communities unequally affected by colonialism and those who engage with them can together fashion new modes of encounter.

Notes

CHAPTER I

1. Brian K. Smith, "Re-envisioning Hinduism and Evaluating the Hindutva Movement," *Religion* 26 (1996): 119.

2. Brian K. Smith, "Who Does, Can, and Should Speak for Hinduism?" *Journal of the American Academy of Religion* 69/4 (Dec. 2000): 747.

3. Joan-Pau Rubiés, *Travel and Ethnology in the Renaissance: South India through European Eyes, 1250–1625* (Cambridge: Cambridge University Press, 2000), 394.

4. Ines G. Županov, *Disputed Mission: Jesuit Experiments and Brahmanical Knowledge in Seventeenth-Century India* (New Delhi: Oxford University Press, 1999).

5. Rubiés, *Travel and Ethnology*, 308–48.

6. As Kate Teltscher argues, *India Inscribed: European and British Writing on India, 1600–1800* (Delhi: Oxford University Press, 1995), 74–105. Likewise, Partha Mitter has traced two western traditions about the demonic in India, the secular and the Christian, to present a continuous development of western reception of India, *Much Maligned Monsters: History of European Reactions to Indian Art* (Oxford: Clarendon Press, 1977), esp. 6–10.

7. Teltscher, *India Inscribed*, 3, 229–55.

8. E.g., Mitter, *Much Maligned Monsters*, 140–88.

9. Thomas R. Trautmann, *Aryans and British India* (Berkeley: University of California Press, 1997).

10. John L. Comaroff and Jean Comaroff, *Ethnography and the Historical Imagination* (Boulder, Colo: Westview Press, 1992), 30.

11. George D. Bearce, *British Attitudes toward India, 1784–1858* (London: Oxford University Press, 1961).

12. David Kopf, *British Orientalism and the Bengal Renaissance: The Dynamics of Indian Modernization, 1773–1835* (Berkeley and Los Angeles: University of California Press, 1969).

13. Wilhelm Halbfass, *India and Europe: An Essay in Understanding* (Al-

bany, N.Y.: SUNY Press, 1988); *Indien und Europa: Perspektiven ihrer Geistigen Begegung* (Basel; Stuttgart: Schwabe, 1981).

14. Halbfass, *India and Europe*, 439.

15. E.g., Reena Sen (nèe Mookerjee), "Some Reflections on *India and Europe: An Essay in Understanding*," in *Beyond Orientalism: The Work of Wilhelm Halbfass and Its Impact on Indian and Cross-Cultural Studies*. Poznań Studies in the Philosophy of the Sciences and Humanities 59, ed. Eli Franco and Karin Preisendanz, 103–16 (Amsterdam: Rodopi, 1997).

16. Francis X. Clooney, "Wilhelm Halbfass and the Openness of the Comparative Project," in Franco and Preisendanz, *Beyond Orientalism*, 29–48.

17. See, for example, the many excellent essays in Kimberly C. Patton and Benjamin C. Ray, eds., *A Magic Still Dwells: Comparative Religion in the Postmodern Age* (Berkeley: University of California Press, 2000).

18. Peter van der Veer, *Imperial Encounters: Religion and Modernity in India and Britain* (Princeton, N.J.: Princeton University Press, 2001), 160.

19. I discuss the issue in more depth in later chapters, but for one summary of the ways in which historians have discerned mutual transformations in colonizer and colonized, see Leela Gandhi, *Postcolonial Theory: A Critical Introduction* (New York: Columbia University Press, 1998), 129–35.

20. Edward Said, *Culture and Imperialism* (New York: Vintage Books, 1994), xxii.

21. See Trautmann, *Aryans and British India*, 19–27 and Halbfass, "Research and Reflection: Responses to My Respondents. I. Beyond Orientalism?" in Franco and Preisendanz, *Beyond Orientalism*, 1–25.

22. Partha Chatterjee, "Agrarian Relations and Communalism in Bengal, 1926–1935," in *Subaltern Studies I: Writings on South Asian History and Society*, ed. Ranajit Guha (Delhi: Oxford University Press, 1982), 9–38.

23. Ranajit Guja, "On Some Aspects of the Historiography of Colonial India," also in Guha, *Subaltern Studies I*, 1–8.

24. Saurabh Dube, *Untouchable Pasts: Religion, Identity, and Power among a Central India Community, 1780–1950* (Albany, N.Y.: SUNY Press, 1998).

25. David Hardiman, *The Coming of the Devi: Adivasi Assertion in Western India* (Delhi: Oxford University Press, 1987), 9–11.

26. Hugh B. Urban, *Songs of Ecstasy: Tantric and Devotional Songs from Colonial Bengal* (New York: Oxford University Press, 2001), 8.

27. Urban, *Songs of Ecstasy*, 8.

28. Gerald Larson, *India's Agony over Religion* (Albany, N.Y.: SUNY Press, 1995), 43.

CHAPTER 2

1. John L. Comaroff and Jean Comaroff, *Of Revelation and Revolution: Christianity, Colonialism, and Consciousness in South Africa* (Chicago: University of Chicago Press, 1991–1999), 1:114.

2. Henry Mayhew, *London Labour and the London Poor* (London: Griffin, Bohn, and Co., 1861–62; repr., New York: Dover Publications, 1968), 1:43.

3. Susan Thorne, *Congregational Missions and the Making of an Imperial Culture in Nineteenth-Century England* (Stanford, Calif: Stanford University Press, 1999), 82.

4. See Comaroff and Comaroff, *Ethnography and the Historical Imagination*, 285–94.

5. Comaroff and Comaroff, *Ethnography and the Historical Imagination*, 288.

6. Comaroff and Comaroff, *Ethnography and the Historical Imagination*, 289.

7. Comaroff and Comaroff, *Ethnography and the Historical Imagination*, 290.

8. Bernard Cohn, *Colonialism and Its Forms of Knowledge: The British in India* (Princeton, N.J.: Princeton University Press, 1996), 4.

9. Antoinette Burton, *At the Heart of the Empire: Indians and the Colonial Encounter in Late-Victorian Britain* (Berkeley: University of California Press, 1998), 7.

10. Burton, *At the Heart of the Empire*, 3.

11. *London Quarterly Review* 7 (1856), 239. Quoted in Cecil Peter Williams, "The Recruitment and Training of Overseas Missionaries in England between 1850 and 1900" (M. L. diss., Univ. of Bristol, 1976), chapter 1, note 25.

12. Burton, *At the Heart of the Empire*, 8.

13. Comaroff and Comaroff, *Ethnography and the Historical Imagination*, 293.

14. David Scott, *Refashioning Futures: Criticism after Postcoloniality* (Princeton, N.J.: Princeton University Press, 1999), 65–69.

15. Nicholas Dirks, ed., Introduction to *Colonialism and Culture* (Ann Arbor: University of Michigan Press, 1992), 6.

16. Ann Laura Stoler, *Race and the Education of Desire: Foucault's* History of Sexuality *and the Colonial Order of Things* (Durham, N.C., and London: Duke University Press, 1995), 128.

17. Thorne, *Congregational Missions*, 56.

18. Thorne, *Congregational Missions*, 82–87.

19. Among the growing literature on gender and colonialism, see Mrinalini Sinha, *Colonial Masculinity: The 'Manly Englishman' and the 'Effeminate Bengali' in the Late Nineteenth Century* (Manchester and New York: Manchester University Press, 1995), and Nancy L. Paxton, *Writing under the Raj: Gender, Race, and Rape in the British Colonial Imagination, 1830–1947* (New Brunswick, N.J.: Rutgers University Press, 1999).

20. David Humphreys, *An Historical Account of the Incorporated Society for the Propagation of the Gospel in Foreign Parts* (London: Joseph Downing, 1730; repr., New York: Arno Press, 1969), xvi.

21. Richard Willis, "SPG Anniversary Sermon, 1702," 18–19, quoted in Edgar Legare Pennington, *The SPG Anniversary Sermons, 1702–1783*, n.p., n.d., 12, emphasis in original.

22. *SPG Journal*, vol. 1, 28 April 1710, quoted in E. Pennington, 13. Humphreys describes the SPG's first attempts to convert the slaves and Indians respectively in the American colonies, *Historical Account of the SPG*, 231–49 and 276–311.

23. A typical argument of this sort can be found in the Bishop of London's "Address to Serious Christians among Ourselves," Humphreys, *Historical Account of the SPG*, 250–56.

24. Eugene Stock, *The History of the Church Missionary Society: Its Environment, Its Men, and Its Work* (London: Church Missionary Society, 1899), 1:23.

25. See Thorne, *Congregational Missions*, 24. William Carey, *An Enquiry into the Obligation of Christians to Use Means for the Conversion of the Heathen* (Leicester: Ann Ireland, 1792); reprinted versions have been made available several times since then, e.g., the same title (London: Carey Kingsgate Press, 1961). Carey's appeal followed Thomas Coke's *Plan of the Society for the Establishment of Missions Among the Heathen* (1783) and Melville Horne's *Letter's on Missions* (1784).

26. Charles Grant, "Observations on the State of Society Among the Asiatic Subjects of Great Britain, Particularly with Respect to Morals; and on the Means of Improving it," British Library, Oriental and India Office Collections, Eur MSS E93. On

Grant and the British Government, see Ainslee Thomas Embree, *Charles Grant and British Rule in India* (New York: Columbia University Press, 1962).

27. Thorne charts the rise of the LMS and its connection to class consciousness, *Congregational Missions*, esp. 54–88.

28. The Wesleyan Methodist Missionary Society (WMMS) was founded in 1813, after long work by Thomas Coke. The Methodists' own denominational history of the WMMS is George G. Findley and W. W. Holdsworth's *The History of the Wesleyan Methodist Missionary Society*. 5 vols. (London: Epworth Press, 1921–24). In Scotland two nondenominational bodies, the Scottish Missionary Society (later the Edinburgh Missionary Society) and the Glasgow Missionary Society came into being in 1796. The Church of Scotland Foreign Missions Committee was appointed in 1825. A narrative history of Scottish missions is given in Elizabeth Glendinning Kirkwood Hewat, *Vision and Achievement, 1796–1956: A History of the Foreign Missions of the Churches United in the Church of Scotland* (London and New York: Nelson, 1960).

29. For an overview of the mission and strategy of the RTS, see *A Brief View of the Plan and Operations of the Religious Tract Society* (London: J. Rider, 1827). A good history of the BFBS is William Canton, *A History of the British and Foreign Bible Society*, 5 vols. (London: John Murray, 1904–10).

30. The Laws of the Society are printed in Canton, *History of the BFBS*, 18. Even so benign a project was fiercely controversial. Many saw the BFBS as an agent for the introduction of Dissenting influence into the Church of England. See Nicholas Vansittart, *Three Letters on the Subject of the British and Foreign Bible Society, Addressed to the Rev. Dr. March and John Coker, Esq., by the Right Hon. Nicholas Vansittart* (London: Printed for J. Hatchard, 1812). A very good recent study of the BFBS is Leslie Howsam, *Cheap Bibles: Nineteenth-Century Publishing and the British and Foreign Bible Society* (Cambridge: Cambridge University Press, 1991).

31. Thorne, *Congregational Missions*, 33.

32. See also Thorne, *Congregational Missions*, 16–17.

33. The relationship of churches and chapels to the laboring classes and the poor in the eighteenth and nineteenth centuries has been the subject of academic concern for some years now. The chief problem in sorting out the role of religion in the life of the lower orders is that few records exist of worship attendance before the Parliamentary census of 1851. The argument in this chapter relies not on numbers, nor on the relevance of such numbers to the actual religiosity of these people, but on the perception that organized religion was doing little to address the needs and concerns of the poor. For some of the main positions in the debate, see K. S. Inglis, *Churches and the Working Classes in Victorian England* (London: Routledge and Kegan Paul, 1963); E. R. Wickham, *Church and People in an Industrial City* (London: Lutterworth Press, 1957) 10–106; Hugh McLeod, *Religion and the Working Class in Nineteenth-Century Britain*, Studies in Economic and Social History (London and Basingstoke: McMillan, 1984); Alan D. Gilbert, *Religion and Society in Industrial England: Church, Chapel, and Social Change, 1740–1914* (New York: Longman, 1976).

34. This, anyway, was the position set forth by Inglis in his introduction to the Victorian period, *Churches and the Working Class*, 1–20. He has been largely supported on this score by McLeod, *Religion and the Working Class*, 17–25. On "cottage religion" and female preaching among the working poor, see Deborah M. Valenze, *Prophetic Sons and Daughters: Female Preaching and Popular Religion in Industrial England* (Princeton, N.J.: Princeton University Press, 1985), 50–73.

35. On the Established Church's agitation for better factory conditions and

shorter hours, see R. A. Soloway, *Prelates and People: Ecclesiastical Social Thought in England, 1783–1852* (London: Routledge and Kegan Paul, 1969), 193–200.

36. Thomas Laquer, *Religion and Respectability: Sunday Schools and Working Class Culture, 1780–1850* (New Haven and London: Yale University Press, 1976), argues that Sunday schools were mainly local organizations, conceived and staffed by the working class, 21–30, and that they "sustained a Christian culture" among the poor, 160. Valenze has described popular working-class religion during the spread of Methodism after the death of Wesley, especially the roles played by women, see, e.g., *Prophetic Sons and Daughters*, 245–73.

37. Soloway, *Prelates and People*, 267–78 discusses contemporary clerical anguish over the issue.

38. McLeod, *Religion and the Working Class*, 17.

39. Edward Miall, *The British Churches in Relation to the British People* (London: Arthur Hall, 1849), quoted in Inglis, *Churches and the Working Classes*, 19.

40. Quoted in McLeod, *Religion and the Working Class*, 20.

41. Mayhew, *London Labour*, 1:21.

42. Mayhew, *London Labour*, 1:43.

43. Inglis, *Churches and the Working Classes*, 20. These innovations likely mimicked the practices of the successful Primitive Methodists and other itinerant preachers.

44. Deryck W. Lovegrove, *Established Church, Sectarian People: Itinerancy and the Transformation of English Dissent, 1780–1830* (Cambridge: Cambridge University Press, 1988), 20.

45. Lovegrove, *Established Church*, 22–23.

46. Anglican debates about the necessity and ends of Sunday schools are presented in Soloway, *Prelates and People*, 349–58.

47. Many schools did teach writing and arithmetic but often drew harsh criticism both from denominational authorities who abhorred using the Sabbath for these secular pursuits and from middle- and upper-class laity who thought educating the poor very dangerous to the stability of society. For a good discussion of the debate, see Laquer's chapter 5, "Detriments of Curriculum," *Religion and Respectability*, 124–46.

48. Linda Colley, *Britons: Forging of the Nation, 1707–1837* (New Haven, Conn., and London: Yale University Press, 1992), 274.

49. Susan Pedersen reads her Cheap Repository Tracts as a "broad evangelical assault on late eighteenth-century popular culture" and all its material and spiritual depredations. "Hannah More Meets Simple Simon: Tracts, Chapbooks, and Popular Culture in Late Eighteenth-Century England," *Journal of British Studies* 25/1 (January 1986): 85.

50. Stuart Piggin, e.g., suggests that a "culture of respectability . . . permeated the [missionary] movement." "Assessing Nineteenth-Century Missionary Motivation: Some Considerations of Theory and Method," *Religious Motivation: Biographical and Sociological Problems for the Church Historian*. Papers read at the Sixteenth Summer Meeting and the Seventeenth Winter Meeting of the Ecclesiastical History Society, ed. Derek Baker (Oxford: Published for the Ecclesiastical History Society by Basil Blackwell, 1978), 333.

51. Comaroff and Comaroff, *Ethnography and the Historical Imagination*, 41–42.

52. In her preoccupation with rules for dress and conduct, one modern critic claims to detect anal-retention and masturbation guilt. John McLeish, *Evangelical Religion and Popular Education: A Modern Interpretation* (London: Methven, 1969), 116.

53. Thorne, *Congregational Missions*, 39.

54. Thorne, *Congregational Missions*, 43; see also 72–87.

55. And so Linda Colley sees her as providing a new model for political activism for women, *Britons: Forging the Nation, 1707–1837* (New Haven, Conn., and London: Yale University Press, 1992), 274–81.

56. Hannah More, "The Hackney Coachman," *The Works of Hannah More*, 2 vols. (Philadelphia: J. J. Woodward, 1830), 1:62.

57. Clare Midgley, *Women Against Slavery: The British Campaigns, 1780–1870* (New York and London: Routledge, 1992), 28.

58. Abstention rhetoric was also often connected back to political motivations. Beginning in 1791, women active in the abolitionist movement spearheaded a drive to boycott products, especially sugar, produced by slave labor. Midgley, *Women Against Slavery*, 35–40.

59. Cf. Pedersen, "Hannah More Meets Simple Simon," 106–108.

60. More, "Betty Brown, the St. Giles Orange Girl," *Works of Hannah More*, 1: 275–79.

61. More, "Practical Piety, or, the Influence of the Religion of the Heart on the Conduct of the Life," *Works of Hannah More*, 1:471.

62. More, "Practical Piety," *Works of Hannah More*, 1:505.

63. Clare Midgley contrasts More's "conservative vision of freedom as the establishment of proper hierarchies" with the more "radical vision of freedom as equality" that activist women like Mary Wollstonecraft and Helen Maria Williams described, *Women Against Slavery*, 29.

64. Some historians, however, see the roots of working-class political activism in charity education, see especially Lacquer, *Religion and Respectability*, 147–86. By contrast, see E. P. Thompson, *Making of the English Working Class* (New York: Vintage Books, 1966), 375–79, which describes Sunday schools as a mechanism of social control.

65. Soloway describes Anglican evangelization of the poor as motivated primarily by fear of revolution, *Prelates and People*, 55–64.

66. Arthur Young, *An Enquiry into the State of the Public Mind amongst the Lower Classes, and on the Means of Turning It to the Welfare of the State* (London: W. J. and J. Richardson, 1798), 25.

67. More, *Works of Hannah More*, 1:63.

68. See, for example, his letter of 29 April 1807 to William Hey cautioning that Roman Catholics would always be inherently enemies to the Protestant state and thus should be targets for conversion themselves, and his diary entry of 5 May 1808, in which he worries about the influence of priests and priestcraft over Catholic members of Parliament, should emancipation pass. Both are preserved in Samuel Wilberforce, *Life of William Wilberforce*, rev. and condensed ed. (London: John Murray, 1868), 284 and 292–93. See also Robin Furneaux, *William Wilberforce* (London: Hamish Hamilton, 1974), 319.

69. William Wiberforce, *A Practical View of the Prevailing Religious System of Professed Christians in the Higher and Middle Classes of Society, Contrasted with Real Christianity* (New York: Robert Carter and Brothers, 1851).

70. John Pollock, *Wilberforce* (London: Constable and Co., 1977), 64.

71. Wilberforce, letter to Dudley Ryder, 27 September 1787, quoted in Pollock, *Wilberforce*, 63–64.

72. Letter to Christopher Wyvill, 25 July 1787, quoted in Pollock, *Wilberforce*, 62.

73. Samuel Wilberforce, *Life of Wilberforce*, 50.

74. *Missionary Papers* XV (Michaelmas 1819). These papers seem to survive exclusively in two unpaginated collections assembled by the CMS on important anniversaries: *The First Fifteen Years' Quarterly Papers of the Church Missionary Society: to Which Is Prefixed a Brief View of the Society for the First Ten Years* (London: Richard Watts, 1833); *The First Ten Years' Quarterly Papers of the Church Missionary Society To Which Is Affixed a Brief View of the Society* (London: Seeley and Son, 1826). A search of the CMS archives in London turned up no record or copy of them. All references to these papers hereafter will cite them only as *Missionary Papers* and provide the date under which they originally appeared.

75. Quoted in Pollack, *Wilberforce*, 61.

76. On the connection of these groups to charitable societies, see Donna T. Andrew, *Philanthropy and Police: London Charity in the Eighteenth Century* (Princeton, N.J.: Princeton University Press), 173–74. On the SSV, see M.J.D. Roberts, "The Society for the Suppression of Vice and its Early Critics," *Historical Journal* 26/1 (March 1983): 159–76.

77. Kristen Drotner points out that among working-class children, leisure was both a primary precondition for religious instruction and one of its obstacles. Children whose long days were filled with factory labor would seldom sit quietly in their few spare hours for lessons without some inducement. The challenge for instructors was to give the leisure they so craved and deserved and also provide some spiritual substance. *English Children and Their Magazines, 1751–1945* (New Haven and London: Yale University Press, 1988), 27, 33–35.

78. The general charge levied against criminal offenders, quoted in Pollack, *Wilberforce*, 59.

79. Sydney Smith, *Selected Writings of Sydney Smith*, ed. W. H. Auden (New York: Farrar, Straus, and Cudahy, 1956), 296. Even an attempt at a sympathetic account of these moments in Wilberforce's career makes him look cruel and unfeeling toward the poor, Ernest Marshall Howse, *Saints in Politics: The "Clapham Sect" and the Growth of Freedom* (Toronto: University of Toronto Press, 1952), 118–22.

80. Howse, *Saints in Politics*, 136–67.

81. Alan Smith, *The Established Church and Popular Religion, 1750–1850*. Seminar Studies in History, ed. Patrick Richardson (London: Longman, 1971), 55–56. This remark echoes E. P. Thompson's characterization of Methodism in the late eighteenth century as a kind of "psychic exploitation," *Making of English Working Classes*, 375.

82. A difficulty to which Stuart Piggin has devoted some concern, "Assessing Nineteenth Century Missionary Motivation," 327–37.

83. Comaroff and Comaroff, *Ethnography*, 200–201.

84. The desire for such conformity appeared in nonreligious discourse as well as an indicator of both the social nature of sexuality in popular discourse and of anxieties about changes in economic arrangements. See Thomas W. Lacquer, "The Social Evil, the Solitary Vice, and Pouring Tea," in *Fragments for a History of the Human Body, Part Three*. Zone 5, ed. Michael Feher (New York: Zone Press, 1989), 335–42.

85. Larson, *India's Agony Over Religion* (Albany, N.Y.: SUNY Press, 1995), 282.

86. Larson, *India's Agony*, 43.

87. Brian K. Smith, "Who Does, Can, and Should Speak for Hinduism," *Journal of the American Academy of Religion* 68/4 (December 2000), 747.

88. See, e.g., Wilberforce's letter to his sister of October 1793 where he argued that the fate of church and state rested on national, public worship "more than any

other single circumstance," William Wilberforce, *The Correspondence of William Wilberforce*, ed. Robert Isaac Wilberforce and Samuel Wilberforce (London: John Murray,
1840), 1:101.

89. On the differences between the evangelism practiced by the Methodist
movement and Dissenters on the one hand, and the Established Church on the other,
see Valenze, *Prophetic Sons and Daughters*, 17–20.

90. Chapter 3 will underscore ways we might distinguish between these two
groups. As the Comaroffs have pointed out, dissenting evangelicals were often only
recent members of the middle classes, a circumstance that put them in an ambivalent
position with respect to the "lower orders" and the heathen: they could simultaneously identify with them and recoil from their habits, *Ethnography and the Historical
Imagination*, 194–96. Drotner makes a similar point with respect to ethics among
British laborers and middle classes, *English Children*, 46–47.

91. See, e.g., Stuart Piggin, "Sectarianism Versus Ecumenism: The Impact on
British Churches of the Missionary Movement to India, c.1800–1860," which traces
the gradual erosion of this cooperation through the course of the nineteenth-century
in Britain. *Journal of Ecclesiastical History* 27/4 (October 1976): 387–402.

92. As Soloway notes through most of his text, providing the poor with church
pews did not solve the problems associated with mixing the rich and poor in church.
See, e.g., *Prelates and People*, 267–78.

93. The piece was privately circulated until its publication was ordered by the
House of Commons in 1813 during the debate about the renewal of the East India
Company's charter and again in 1831. A handwritten original is in the India Office
Library, London. For an overview of the text and a comparative analysis of its various
versions, see Nancy Gardner Cassels, "Some Archival Observations on an Evangelical
Tract," *Indian Archives* 30/1 (1981): 47–57.

94. The title of his fourth chapter, 146.

95. Colley, *Britons*, 367–48.

96. Eugene Stock, *History of the Church Missionary Society: Its Environment, Its
Men, and Its Work*, 3 vols. (London: Church Missionary Society, 1899), 1:63.

97. Josiah Pratt's often quoted circumscription of the CMS's moves to gain the
blessing of the church hierarchy. Stock, *History of the CMS*, 1:64. Piggin notes that in
the succeeding generation, this apparently "irregular" support for dissension was deliberately scuttled as a gesture to win the bishops' backing, "Sectarianism," 393.

98. The historian of the nineteenth-century CMS, Eugene Stock, himself calls
attention to this tension, and weaves the Baptist missionary Carey's efforts into the
narrative as if he were part of the same movement, *History of the CMS*, 1:57–98.

99. That the status of the body was of concern from its earliest days is evident
in Wilberforce's letter to Rev. Thomas Gisborne, 6 December 1799. *Correspondence of
Wilberforce*, 1:189–90.

100. Peter Hinchcliff, "Voluntary Absolutism: British Missionary Societies in the
Nineteenth-Century," in *Voluntary Religion: Papers Read at the 1985 Summer Meeting
and 1986 Winter Meeting of the Ecclesiastical History Society*. Studies in Church History
23 (Oxford: published by Basil Blackwell for the Ecclesiastical History Society, 1986),
367.

101. See, e.g., D. G. Paz, *Popular Anti-Catholicism in Mid-Victorian England* (Stanford, Calif.: Stanford University Press, 1992), 23–33.

102. Daniel Wilson, *A Defense of the Church Missionary Society Against the Objections of the Rev. Josiah Thomas, M.A., Archdeacon of Bath*, 12th ed. (London: G. Wilson,
1818), 18. The fact that this tract ran to twelve editions in a year may itself be an indi-

cation of the interest the controversy attracted, or, perhaps, only the CMS's wide distribution of it as favorable propaganda.

103. Thorne describes the LMS's organization and execution of these meetings well, *Congregational Missions*, 62–65.

104. His response to the invitation is included in Wilson, *A Defense of the CMS*, 40.

105. My account follows closely Wilson's report in *A Defense of the CMS*. Thomas's own tract confirms this outline of the argument and many of the details of the exchange, Rev. Josiah Thomas, *An Address to a Meeting Holden at the Town-Hall, in the city of Bath, the First Day of December, 1817, for the Purpose of Forming a Church Missionary Society in that City* (Bath: Meyler and Son, 1817).

106. Sympathizers of the CMS soon discovered that in spite of his praise, he was not a member of that society either.

107. *Second Protest against the Formation of the Church Missionary Society* (Bath: J. Hatchard, 1818).

108. George Pryme, *Counter-Protest of a Layman*, etc., 3d ed., corrected (Cambridge: W. Metcalfe, 1818).

109. Wilson, *A Defense of the CMS*, 31.

110. A Member of the Church Missionary Society, *Cursory Observations on a Letter Recently Addressed by the Rev. William Baily Whitehead, M.A., to the Rev. Daniel Wilson, M.A.* (Bristol: J. Richardson, 1818).

111. Wilson's *Defense of the CMS* published in London ran into at least twelve editions in the first year, and eight within the first week.

112. *Proceedings of the Church Missionary Society*, 1818–1819 (London: L. B. Seeley, 1819), 61.

113. Josiah Pratt to Daniel Corrie, 21 July, 1818, CMS archives C I/1 E 2/14.

114. George Freer, *A Parochial Sermon: In Aid of the National Society for the Education of the Poor in the Principles of the Established Church* (St. Neots, UK: J. Stanford, 1823), 14, 17.

115. *Proceedings of the CMS*, 1817–1818, 54.

116. John MacDonald, *Statement of Reasons for Accepting a Call to Go to India as a Missionary* (Glasgow, 1839), 19, quoted in Piggin, "Sectarianism," 400.

117. Thorne, *Congregational Missions*, 76.

118. Sometimes suffering and poverty among Britons and foreigners offered as much a motivation for undertaking the missionary life as the conviction that the heathen were daily falling into hell, Piggin, "Assessing Missionary Motivation," 330–31.

119. Rev. Professor [William?] Farish, "A Sermon, etc.," CMS Eighteenth-Anniversary Sermon, in *Proceedings of the CMS*, 1817–1818, 19.

120. This was a common practice for sermons generally. On the CMS, see, e.g., Rev. Josiah Allport, *A Sermon Preached at Coleford, July 18, 1813, in Aid of the Church Missionary Society for Africa and the East* (Monmouth, UK: Charles Heath, 1813), and a longer tract collected from many sermons, *The Spirit of British Missions: Dedicated to the Church Missionary Society* (London: A. M'Intosh, 1815).

121. Andrew, *Philanthropy and Police*, 8.

122. Allport, *Sermon*, 23.

123. Hinchcliff remarks that it is "to the eternal credit of the missionaries that they often protested against exaggerated accounts of their successes." "Voluntary Absolutism," 375.

124. Allport, *Sermon*, 14.

125. Allport, *Sermon*, 25.

126. See, e.g., John Wolffe, *The Protestant Crusade in Great Britain, 1829–60* (Oxford: Clarendon Press, 1991), 113–19.

127. *Proceedings of the CMS, 1820–1821*, 37–40.

128. Hinchcliff notes that this attitude stands in utter opposition to the CMS's oversight of its missionaries in the field, over whom it exercised "strict and direct control," Peter Hinchcliff, "Voluntary Absolutism: British Missionary Societies in the Nineteenth-Century" in *Voluntary Religion: Papers Read at the 1985 Summer Meeting and 1986 Winter Meeting of the Ecclesiastical History Society*, Studies in Church History 23 (Oxford: published by Basil Blackwell for the Ecclesiastical Society, 1986), 370.

129. Andrew, *Philanthropy and Police*, e.g., 98–134.

130. Regulation VII governing Church Missionary Associations, *Proceedings of the Church Missionary Society, 1820–1821*, xii.

131. These survive primarily in bound volumes sold by the society on significant anniversaries. See *The First Ten Years' Quarterly Papers of the Church Missionary Society To Which is Affixed a Brief View of the Society* (London: Seeley and Son, 1826) and *The First Fifteen Years' Quarterly Papers of the Church Missionary Society*, etc. (London: Richard Watts, 1833).

132. Andrew, *Philanthropy and Police*, 135–202.

133. Joel Wiener, *The War of the Unstamped: The Movement to Repeal the British Newspaper Tax, 1830–36* (Ithaca, N.Y., and London: Cornell University Press, 1969), 2–9.

134. *Missionary Papers* V (Lady-Day 1817).

135. *Missionary Papers* VI (Midsummer 1817) and XXX (Midsummer 1823).

136. *Missionary Papers* XXIII (Michaelmas 1821).

137. *Missionary Papers* VIII (Christmas 1817).

138. Maina Chawla Singh, *Gender, Religion, and "Heathen Lands": American Missionary Women in South Asia (1860s–1940s)* (New York: Garland, 2000), 148.

139. "Notice Respecting Collectors," *Proceedings of the CMS, 1817–1818*, xv.

140. *Proceedings of the CMS, 1817–18*, xv.

141. *Missionary Papers* VI (Midsummer 1817).

142. *Missionary Papers* VIII (Christmas 1817).

143. Linda Colley makes a similar argument about the domestication of the British soldiery, *Britons*, 283–319.

144. On working-class sentiment and the radical press, see Wiener, *War of the Unstamped*, 115–36.

145. *Missionary Papers* VII (Michaelmas 1817).

146. *Missionary Papers* II (Midsummer 1816).

147. See, e.g., *The Evils of a Late Attendance on Divine Worship*, no. 60 (London: Religious Tract Society, n.d. but probably 1800).

148. This participation of this chief turned out to be no more than a very clever ruse. The CMS brought him to England to show what promise these enlightened natives held forth. The Society took him on a tour of the country, where excited Christians showered him with money and supplies. He brought these back to New Zealand with him, and on his return used them to launch a vicious war against his enemies and to repress missionary activity, displaying contempt for their gods, their religion, and the liberal educational programs they had begun to implement among his people, Cyril Davey, *The March of Methodism: The Story of Methodist Missionary Work Overseas* (London: Epworth Press, 1951), 47.

149. *Missionary Papers* III (Michaelmas 1816).

150. *Missionary Papers* VIII (Christmas 1817).

151. *Missionary Papers* VIII (Christmas 1817).

152. *Missionary Papers* VI (Midsummer 1817). The theme of the simple child converting the sinful or jaded adult was widespread in Sunday school literature. See Laquer, *Religion and Respectability*, 7.

153. *Missionary* Papers XL (Christmas 1825).

154. *Missionary Papers* II (Midsummer 1816).

155. See, e.g., *Missionary Papers* II (Midsummer 1816); VI (Midsummer 1817); VII (Michaelmas 1817); and XVII (Lady-Day 1820).

156. All these figures have been taken from the printing costs listed in the Society's annual budget in *The Proceedings of the Church Missionary Society* for the years 1817–22, 1823–24, and 1831–32.

157. *War of the Unstamped*, 184.

158. *Missionary Papers* XXII (Midsummer 1821).

159. Drotner cites a variety of figures and sources for comparable literature, *English Children and Their Magazines*, 25–27.

160. Laquer, *Religion and Respectability*, 117–18.

CHAPTER 3

1. On the strategy and activity of itinerant missionary preachers, see Antony Copley, *Religions in Conflict: Ideology, Cultural Contact and Conversion in Late Colonial India* (New Delhi: Oxford University Press, 1997), 14–17.

2. According to the *Oxford English Dictionary*, the first use was in 1829. For more detail, see John Stratton Hawley, "Naming Hinduism," *Wilson Quarterly* 15/3 (Summer 1991): 30–34. Dermot Killingley is given credit for discovering Roy's use, *Rammohun Roy in Hindu and Christian Tradition: The Teape Lectures, 1990* (Newcastle upon Tyne: Grevatt and Grevatt, 1993), 60. See also Richard King, *Orientalism and Religion: Postcolonial Theory, India, and 'The Mystic East'* (New York: Routledge, 1999), 100. David N. Lorenzen cites several British usages prior to 1829 but after Roy's, "Who Invented Hinduism," *Comparative Studies in Society and History* 41/4 (Oct. 1999): 629.

3. Richard H. Davis, *Lives of Indian Images* (Princeton, N.J.: Princeton University Press, 1997), 9.

4. Davis, *Lives of Indian Images*, 10.

5. Davis, *Lives of Indian Images*, 21.

6. On the importance of the anthropologizing of distinct colonizing communities in colonized lands, see Ann Laura Stoler, "Rethinking Colonial Categories: European Communities and the Boundaries of Rule," in Nicholas B. Dirks, ed., *Colonialism and Culture* (Ann Arbor: University of Michigan Press, 1992): 319–52.

7. See Davis, *Lives of Indian Images*, 26–49.

8. Diana L. Eck, *Darśan: Seeing the Divine Image in India*, 2d ed. (Chambersburg, Pa.: Anima Books, 1985), 32–44.

9. *Vedāntacandrikā*, in *Rāmmohan Racanābalī*, ed. Ajitkumar Ghosh (Calcutta: Abdul Ajij al Aman, 1973), 615–33. A somewhat loose translation is available as *An Apology for the Present System of Hindoo Worship* (Calcutta: Printed by G. G. Balfour at the Government Gazette Press, 1817).

10. Moshe Halbertal and Avishai Margalit, *Idolatry* (Cambridge, Mass., and London: Harvard University Press, 1992), 45–48.

11. Halbertal and Margalit, *Idolatry*, 108–12.

12. See, e.g., *Missionary Papers* LIII (Lady-Day 1829).

13. Comaroff and Comaroff, *Of Revelation and Revolution*, 2:64.

14. Comaroff and Comaroff, *Of Revelation and Revolution*, 2:66.

15. Van der Veer, *Imperial Encounters*, 36.

16. Sam Smiles, *The Image of Antiquity: Ancient Britain and the Romantic Imagination* (New Haven, Conn., and London: Yale University Press, 1994), 8.

17. Smiles, *Image of Antiquity*, 24.

18. See, e.g., Colley, *Britons*, 117–32.

19. Stukeley's works are reprinted in an unnumbered single volume in the series Myth and Romanticism: A Collection of the Major Mythographic Sources used by the English Romantic Poets, ed. Burton Feldman and Robert D. Richardson, Jr. (New York: Garland, 1984). See also Smiles, *Image of Antiquity*, 84–86.

20. Henry Rowlands, *Mona Antiqua Restaurata* (1723; repr., Myth and Romanticism 21, New York: Garland, 1979), 69–70.

21. Peter F. Fischer, "Blake and the Druids," *Journal of English and German Philology* 58: (1959): 589–612.

22. See e.g., Edward Ledwich's "Dissertation on the Religion of the Druids," *Archaeologia* VII (1785): 303–22; Smiles, *Image of Antiquity*, 88–112.

23. For a postmodern reassertion of this image, see Bruce Lincoln, "The Druids and Human Sacrifice," in *Death, War and Sacrifice: Studies in Ideology and Practice* (Chicago and London: University of Chicago Press, 1991), 176–87.

24. See Smiles, *Image of Antiquity*, 94–25.

25. *Missionary Papers* LIII, Christmas, 1829.

26. See, e.g., Colin Hayden, *Anti-Catholicism in Eighteenth-Century England, c. 1714–1780: A Political and Cultural Study* (Manchester: Manchester University Press, 1993), and on the seventeenth century, see Caroline M. Hibbard, *Charles I and the Popish Plot* (Chapel Hill: University of North Carolina Press, 1983), esp. 168–226.

27. See, e.g., Claudius Buchanan, *Christian Researches in Asia, with Notices of the Translation of the Scriptures into the Oriental Languages* (London: T. Cadell and W. Davies, 1819), 123–24.

28. For a brief summary of political, theological, and popular manifestations of post-Reformation anti-Catholicism, see Hayden, *Anti-Catholicism*, 5–7.

29. Paz, *Popular Anti-Catholicism*, 4. Very good histories of the political battle for emancipation may be found in G.I.T. Machin, *The Catholic Question in English Politics, 1820–1830* (Oxford: Clarendon Press, 1964); and Wendy Hinde *Catholic Emancipation: A Shake to Men's Minds* (Oxford and Cambridge, Mass.: Blackwell, 1992). The act itself is reprinted in E. R. Norman's *Anti-Catholicism in Victorian England* (New York: Barnes and Noble, 1968), 13–22.

30. On the last two points, see Colley, *Britons*, 324–34.

31. Gauri Viswanathan, *Outside the Fold: Conversion, Modernity, and Belief* (Princeton, N.J.: Princeton University Press, 1998), 4–11.

32. *Hansard's Parliamentary Debates*. 3d Ser., CXV (1851) 266. Quoted in Paz, *Popular Anti-Catholicism*, 17.

33. Machin, *Catholic Question*, 16.

34. Charles Lloyd, Bishop of Oxford, to Peel, 14 August 1827. British Museum Mss. 40343.f.63. Quoted by Machin, *Catholic Question*, 1.

35. As Paz argues, one factor in the escalation of vituperative exchanges between Catholics and Protestants was the development of stronger, well-managed Catholic organizations that were themselves more aggressive (see his chapter 3, "Militant Roman Catholicism" in *Popular Anti-Catholicism*, 81–102). It would not be quite accurate to portray Catholics as the weak victims of Protestant bullies. As I am interested only to

pursue the relationship of rhetoric about Catholics to the rhetoric about Hindus, I cannot pursue these other aspects of the Catholic question here.

36. *Weekly Observator* 16 June 1716; quoted in Hayden, *Anti-Catholicism*, 22.

37. On the roll of public opinion and the press in the development of anti-Catholicism in the nineteenth century, see Frank H. Wallis, *Popular Anti-Catholicism in Mid-Victorian Britain*, Texts and Studies in Religion 60 (Lewiston, N.Y.: Edwin Mellen, 1993).

38. Teltscher, *India Inscribed*, 90–98.

39. James Howe, *A Reply to the Letters of the Abbé Dubois on the State of Christianity in India* (London: L. B. Seeley and Son, 1824), 83.

40. John Poynder, *Human Sacrifices in India* (London: J. Hatchard and Son, 1827).

41. John Poynder, *Popery the Religion of Heathenism* (London: printed for George Wilson, successor to Mr. Bickerstaff, 1818); 1835 edition published in London by J. Hatchard and Son and by Seeley and Sons. See also his *History of the Jesuits, In Answer to Mr. Dallas's Defense of That Order* 2 vols. (London: Baldwin, Cradock, and Joy, 1816).

42. Poynder *Popery the Religion of Heathenism*, viii.

43. Colley, *Britons*, 18–30.

44. See, e.g., Hayden, who argues that simple popular hatred of Catholics, and not working-class anxiety, was the cause of this uprising, *Anti-Catholicism*, 204–44.

45. For an overview of Dubois's perceptions of Hinduism, see Copley, *Religions in Conflict*, 43–45.

46. Now readily available in a later form as J. A. Dubois, *Hindu Manners, Customs and Ceremonies*, ed. and trans. Henry K. Beauchamp, 3d ed. (London: Oxford University Press, 1928).

47. Sylvia Murr, "Nicolas Desvaulx (1745–1823) Véritable Auteur de Moeurs, Institutions et Cérémonies des Peuples de l'Inde, de l'Abbé Dubois?" *Puruṣārtha* 3 (1977): 245–67.

48. Dubois, *Hindu Manners, Customs, and Ceremonies*, 9.

49. Dubois, *Hindu Manners and Customs*, 4–5.

50. J. A. Dubois, *Letters on the State of Christianity in India; In which the Conversion of the Hindoos Is Considered Impracticable* (London: Longman, Hurst, Rees, Orme, Brown, and Green, 1823), 69.

51. On Protestant missions' use of scriptural translations, see Teltscher, *India Inscribed*, 101–103.

52. Dubois, *Letters*, 12.

53. Dubois, *Letters*, 29.

54. Dubois, *Letters*, 32, 34.

55. Dubois, *Letters*, 35–41.

56. Dubois, *Letters*, 69.

57. Dubois, *Letters*, 145.

58. Dubois, *Letters*, 149.

59. Dubois, *Letters*, 151.

60. Dubois, *Letters*, 148. See also Ward's letter to Miss Hope of Liverpool in *Farewell Letters to a Few Friends in Britain and America, on Returning to Bengal, in 1821* (New York: E. Bliss and E. White, 1821), 60–77.

61. Henry Townley, *An Answer to the Abbé Dubois* (London: Printed by R. Clay, 1824), 80. See also Teltscher, *India Inscribed*, on Jesuit "accommodation," 74–76.

62. Hough, *Reply*, 83.

63. Hough, *Reply*, 108–9.

64. Hough, *Reply*, 122.

65. John Clark Marshman, *The Life and Times of Carey, Marshman, and Ward, Embracing the History of the Serampore Mission*, 2 vols. (London: Longman, Brown, Green, Longmans, and Roberts, 1859), 1:137.

66. Marshman, *Life of Carey, Marshman, and Ward*, 1:138.

67. Marshman, *Life of Carey, Marshman, and Ward*, 1:69.

68. Marshman, *Life of Carey, Marshman, and Ward*, 1:139. This scene was entirely expunged, except for the administration of the rite itself, in the popular, one-volume abridged edition of 1864, *The Story of Carey, Marshman, and Ward, the Serampore Missionaries* (London: J. Heaton and Son), 57.

69. Comaroff and Comaroff, *Of Revelation and Revolution*, 1:81.

70. Thorne, *Congregational Missions*, 67–72.

71. Copley, *Religions in Conflict*, 10.

72. Comaroff and Comaroff, *Ethnography and the Historical Imagination*, 184.

73. Thorne, *Congregational Missions*, 68.

74. William Ward, "William Ward's Missionary Journal" (Serampore College Archives), entry dated 25 Sept., 1807. Permission to use material from Ward's journal has been generously granted by its transcriber, E. Daniel Potts.

75. Copley, *Religions in Conflict*, 13.

76. Both printed at the Serampore Press. Ward has caused great difficulty to generations of librarians by slightly altering the title of his piece at different printings and using different titles on the title pages of separate volumes of the same edition. The second volume of this edition, to which I will refer throughout this study, is actually titled *A View of the History, Literature, and Religion of the Hindoos*. The first British edition was printed by Black, Parbury, and Allen in London, 1817, now in an India reprint edition (Delhi: Low Price Publications, 1990). Most historians date the publication of Ward's first volume to 1806, but his journal of 1 June 1807 reports, "My first volume is finished and at press. I now see that it will make 3 vols. to 4."

77. See Ward's journal, 3 Sept.–10 Oct., 1807. In the end, the government required only that the press submit works for official approval before publishing, an arrangement that may have expired with a change in government staffing and allowed for the more critical second edition.

78. E. Daniel Potts, *British Baptist Missionaries in India, 1793–1837: The History of Serampore and Its Missions* (Cambridge: Cambridge University Press, 1967), 92.

79. Although it completely whitewashes Ward's attack on Hinduism, a useful basic biography of Ward is available in Bengali, Sunil Chatterjee, "Reverend William Ward, 1769–1823," *Serampore College Students' Magazine* (1972): 86–97.

80. On the journal, see E. Daniel Potts, "William Ward's Missionary Journal," *The Baptist Quarterly* 25/3 (July 1973): 111–114. The journal itself is available in the Baptist Missionary Society Archives and the Serampore College archives.

81. Stuart Piggin, "Assessing Missionary Motivation," 334–35.

82. A. Christopher Smith, "Mythology and Missiology: A Methodological Approach to the Pre-Victorian Mission of the Serampore Trio," *International Review of Mission* 83 (July 1994): 451–75.

83. Potts, *British Baptist Missionaries*, 94.

84. In James Mill, *The History of British India* 5th ed. Notes by Horace Hayman Wilson. Introduction by John Kenneth Galbraith (London, 1858; reprint, New York: Chelsea House, 1968), 301n.

85. A contemporary evaluation of Ward's work can be found in Stephen Neill, *A History of Christianity in India, 1707–1858* (Cambridge: Cambridge University Press, 1985), 449. On Ward's reliance on anecdotal evidence, see Brian K. Pennington, "Reverend William Ward and His Legacy for Christian (Mis)perception of Hinduism," *Hindu-Christian Studies Bulletin* 13 (2000): 5–11.

86. For a brief summary of the shift from philological to anthropological models in the study of religion, see Bruce Lincoln, *Theorizing Myth: Narrative, Ideology, and Scholarship* (Chicago: University of Chicago Press, 1999), 68–73.

87. Edwin J. McAllister, " 'Our Glory and Joy': Stephen Riggs and the Politics of Nineteenth-Century Missionary Ethnography among the Sioux," in *Christian Encounters with the Other*, ed. John C. Hawley (New York: New York University Press, 1998), 153–154.

88. Ward, *View of the Hindoos*, 1:34.

89. Ward, *View of the Hindoos*, 1:ix.

90. Copley, *Religions in Conflict*, 11.

91. Ward, *View of the Hindoos*, 1:106.

92. Ward, *View of the Hindoos*, 1:135.

93. Ward, *View of the Hindoos*, 1:203.

94. See Dubois's *Letters*, 145–75.

95. Ward, *View of the Hindoos*, 1:161–83.

96. Ward, *View of the Hindoos*, 1:139.

97. Mrinalini Sinha, *Colonial Masculinity*.

98. Ward, *View of the Hindoos*, 1:139.

99. Ward, *View of the Hindoos*, 2:312.

100. Ward, *View of the Hindoos*, 2:317.

101. Ward, *View of the Hindoos*, 2:318–21.

102. Ward, *View of the Hindoos*, 1:215.

103. Ward, *View of the Hindoos*, 1:215.

104. Ward, *View of the Hindoos*, 1:209.

105. Ward, *View of the Hindoos*, 2:252.

106. Ward, *View of the Hindoos*, 2:252.

107. Ward, *View of the Hindoos*, 1:216.

108. Ward, *View of the Hindoos*, 1:214, 1:216.

109. Ward, *View of the Hindoos*, 1:216.

110. Ward, *View of the Hindoos*, 2:348.

111. In a note, Ward cited Buchanan's account of the wretched state of pilgrims to Jagannātha and used his estimate of the number of corpses he encountered along the way from which to extrapolate his own estimate of pilgrims who died annually. Ward, *View of the Hindoos*, 2:322; Buchanan, *Christian Researches in Asia*, 18–38.

112. Ward, *View of the Hindoos*, 2:xiv.

113. Ward, *View of the Hindoos*, 2:16.

114. Ward, *View of the Hindoos*, 2:322

115. Ward, *View of the Hindoos*, 2:458.

116. Ward, *View of the Hindoos*, 2:458.

117. Jörg Fisch, "A Pamphlet War on Christian Missions in India 1807–1809," *Journal of Asian History* 19 (1985): 26–28.

118. Letter to Wilberforce, 30 August 1808, Wilberforce, *Correspondence of Wilberforce*, 2:140.

119. Letter of 4 October 1814, CMS archives C/IE 66.

120. Hugh Pearson, *Memoirs of the Life and Writings of the Rev. Claudius Buchanan, D.D., Late Vice-Provost of the College of Fort William in Bengal*, 2 vols. (London: T. Cadell and W. Davies, 1819), 1:35.

121. Pearson, *Memoirs of Buchanan*, 1:111.

122. Pearson, *Memoirs of Buchanan*, 1:177.

123. Pearson, *Memoirs of Buchanan*, 1:177.

124. For a history of the College of Fort William, see Kopf, *British Orientalism*, 65–126 and 215–36. A brief chapter in Samita Sinha's *Pandits in a Changing Environment: Centres of Sanskrit Learning in Nineteenth Century Bengal* (Calcutta: Salat Book House, 1993) also provides a good history of the college, 82–106.

125. Kopf, *British Orientalism*, 133–34.

126. Kopf, *British Orientalism*, 221–33.

127. Marshman's *Life of Carey, Marshman, and Ward* offers a missionary perspective on the formation and curtailment of the Fort William, 1:286–87. A short history of Haileybury and a guide to its records may be found in Anthony Farrington, ed., *The Records of the East India College Haileybury and Other Institutions*, India Office Records, Guides to Archive Groups (London: Her Majesty's Stationery Office, 1976).

128. Pearson, *Memoirs of Buchanan*, 1:308. For a bibliography of some of the essays written in competition for these prizes, see Jörg Fisch, "A Solitary Vindicator of the Hindus: The Life and Writings of General Charles Stuart, 1757/58–1828," *Journal of the Royal Asiatic Society of Great Britain and Ireland* (1984): 65–70.

129. Jörg Fisch, "A Solitary Vindicator of the Hindus: The Life and Writings of General Charles Stuart, 1757/58–1828," *Journal of the Royal Asiatic Society of Great Britain and Ireland* (1984): 35.

130. Claudius Buchanan, *Memoir of the Expediency of an Ecclesiastical Establishment for British India* (London: T. Cadell and W. Davies, 1805), xi.

131. Buchanan, *Memoir of the Expediency of an Ecclesiastical Establishment*, 3.

132. Buchanan, *Christian Researches*, 18.

133. Buchanan, *Christian Researches*, 19.

134. Buchanan, *Christian Researches*, 22–23, n.

135. Buchanan, *Christian Researches*, 30.

136. Buchanan, *Christian Researches*, 28.

137. Buchanan, *Christian Researches*, 29.

138. Buchanan, *Christian Researches*, 71.

139. A brief overview of the various Christian groups in South India is available in Corrine G. Dempsey, *Kerala Christian Sainthood: Collisions of Culture and Worldview in South India* (New York: Oxford University Press, 2001), 5–8. Stephen Neill's two volume *History of Christianity in India: The Beginnings to AD 1707* (New York: Cambridge University Press, 1984) summarizes in more detail the history of Christianity in the south, passim.

140. On the means and effects of the Latinization of some of the Malabar churches, see Joseph Perumthottam, *A Period of Decline of the Mar Thoma Christians (1712–1752)* (Vadavathoor, Kerala State: Oriental Institute of Religious Studies, India, 1994). A more comprehensive survey of the Syrian church in South India absorbs great portions of James Hough's *The History of Christianity in India from the Commencement of the Christian Era*, 5 vols. (London: Seeley and Burnside, 1850); on the conflict with Roman authorities, see esp. 1:238–463. See again Neill's two volume *History of Christianity in India*, passim.

141. Buchanan *Christian Researches*, 126, n.

142. Many of the CMS's annual reports detail enthusiastically the state of their relationship to the Syrian Church and its progress. See *Proceedings of the CMS, Nineteenth Year, 1818–1819,* 315–27, *Twentieth Year, 1819–1820,* 341–48. A history of their relationship may be found in P. Cheriyan, *The Malabar Syrians and the Church Missionary Society, 1816–1840* (Kottayam: The CMS Press and Book Depot, 1935).

143. Quoted in Cheriyan, *Malabar Syrians and the CMS,* 73.

144. Neill, *History of Christianity in India, 1707–1858,* 238; see also 236–54.

145. Buchanan, *Christian Researches,* 151–52.

146. The popularity of Inquisitional literature was undiminished even in the nineteenth century. Edward Peters, *Inquisition* (Berkeley: University of California Press, 1988), 204–22, 231–62.

147. Quoted in Pearson, *Memoirs of Buchanan,* 158.

148. Buchanan, *Christian Researches,* 176.

149. Quoted in Pearson, *Memoirs of Buchanan,* 2:162.

150. Buchanan, *Christian Researches,* 178.

151. King, *Orientalism and Religion,* 26.

152. Pearson, *Memoirs of Buchanan,* 2:188.

153. Josiah Pratt to Schnarre and Rhenius, 10 March 1815, CMS Archives C I/E.

154. Quoted in Howse, *Saints in Politics,* 91.

155. Van der Veer, *Imperial Encounters,* 22.

156. On the British debate over the colonial government's support and patronage of Hindu temples, see Nancy Gardner Cassels, *Religion and the Pilgrim Tax under the Company Raj.* South Asian Studies 17 (New Delhi: Manohar, 1988).

157. Actually, of the first twenty-four missionaries commissioned by the CMS, seventeen were German Lutherans, because bishops were reluctant to ordain clergy for missionary work. In its first fifteen years, the CMS could send out only seven English missionaries, and only three of them were ordained, Stock, *History of the CMS,* 1:91.

158. *The First Ten Years' Quarterly Papers,* 10, 17–18.

159. I treat this text and its representation of Hindu idolatry in much greater detail in my Ph.D. dissertation, "The Firefly and the Moon: Representing and Constructing Religion in the context of Colonial Bengal" (Emory University, 1998), 145–59.

160. H. L. Machow, *Gothic Images of Race in Nineteenth-Century Britain* (Stanford, Calif.: Stanford University Press, 1996), 2–3.

161. *Missionary Papers* V (Lady-Day 1817).

162. *Missionary Papers* VI (Midsummer 1817).

163. *Missionary Papers* XIV (Midsummer 1819) and XXIII (Michaelmas 1821).

164. *Missionary Papers* XX (Christmas 1820).

165. See also "Deplorable Effects of Heathen Superstition, as Manifested by the Natives of Hindoostan," Cheap Tract 13 (Dunfermline, Scotland: John Miller, 1828).

166. See also Paul B. Courtright, *Satī: The Goddess and the Dreadful Practice* (New York: Oxford University Press, forthcoming).

167. This work went into multiple editions. 2d ed. (London: Seely and Son, 1830).

168. Teltscher *India Inscribed,* 51–68.

169. *Missionary Papers* XXVI (Midsummer 1822).

170. On British representations of the rite, see Paul Courtright, "The Iconographies of Satī," in *Satī, the Blessing and the Curse: The Burning of Wives in India,* ed. John Stratton Hawley (New York and Oxford: Oxford University Press, 1994), 41–47,

and Catherine Weinberger-Thomas, *Ashes of Immortality: Widow-Burning in India*, transl. Jeffrey Mehlman and David Gordon White (Chicago: University of Chicago Press, 1999), 196–210.

171. *Missionary Papers* XXXIII (Lady Day 1824).

172. Teltscher, *India Inscribed*, 53.

173. Teltscher, *India Inscribed*, 46.

174. Teltscher, *India Inscribed*, 16.

75. *Missionary Papers* XXIII (Michaelmas 1821).

176. *Missionary Papers* XXXIX (Michaelmas 1825). Quoted from Ward's *View of the Hindoos*, 2:157.

177. Ronald Inden, *Imagining India* (Oxford: Basil Blackwell, 1990), 2.

178. Inden, *Imagining India*, 3.

179. Van der Veer *Imperial Encounters*, 159.

180. Inden *Imagining India*, 3; emphasis in original.

CHAPTER 4

1. Sir William Jones, "A Discourse on the Institution of a Society for Inquiring into the History, Civil and Natural, the Antiquaries, Arts, Sciences, and Literature of Asia," in *The Works of Sir William Jones, With the Life of the Author by Lord Teignmouth*, ed. Garland Cannon (London: John Stockdale and John Walker, 1807; repr., New York: Curzon Press, 1993), 3:2. Quoted by Duff in *India and Indian Missions* (Edinburgh: J. Johnstone, 1839), 196. I will cite Jones's writings as they appear in his *Works* because it is relatively easy to find, but all other pieces from the *Asiatick Reseaches* I will cite as they originally appeared.

2. Duff, *India and Indian Missions*, 197–78.

3. Trautmann, *Aryans and British India*, 52–61.

4. The claim is David Kopf's, "European Enlightenment, Hindu Renaissance and the Enrichment of the Human Spirit: A History of Historical Writings on British Orientalism," *Orientalism, Evangelicalism and the Military Cantonment in Early Nineteenth-Century India: A Historiographical Overview*, ed. Nancy Gardner Cassels (Lewiston, N.Y.: Edwin Mellen Press, 1991), 21. Garland Cannon is another who trumpets Jones's disinterested scholarship. See *The Life and Mind of Oriental Jones: Sir William Jones, the Father of Modern Linguistics* (Cambridge: Cambridge University Press, 1993), xv. John Drew dismisses political categories in his treatment of Jones, *India and the Romantic Imagination* (Delhi: Oxford University Press, 1987), 43–82. Teltscher, *India Inscribed* 192–224, Cohn, *Colonialism and Its Forms of Knowledge* 68–72, Trautmann, *Aryans and British India*, 29–61, and Lincoln, *Theorizing Myth* 76–100 are among recent voices outlining the numerous ways Jones and the British Orientalism he largely inspired were implicated in colonial hegemonies. In many ways, these recent critiques are careful elaborations of Said's important but now fairly dated and much-critiqued *Orientalism*, which also views Jones as helping to construct discourses that furthered colonial conquest, although, as Kopf points out, there is little evidence that Said had read Jones, Edward Said, *Orientalism* (New York: Vintage Books, 1978), 77–79, and Kopf, "European Enlightenment," 21–22. For one developed critique of Said's analysis, see Trautmann, *Aryans and British India*, 19–27.

5. King, *Orientalism and Religion*, 131.

6. Teltscher, *India Inscribed*, 223.

7. Inden, *Imagining India*, 88.

8. Inden, *Imagining India*, 87.

9. Inden, *Imagining India*, 128.

10. The spelling was modernized to *Asiatic Researches* with volume 15 in 1825. The volumes were printed between 1788 and 1839 at the Company's Press in Calcutta and elsewhere under the full title (which occasionally varied) *Asiatick Researches: Transactions of the Society Instituted in Bengal for Inquiring into the History and Antiquities, the Arts, Sciences, and Literature of Asia.*

11. Trautmann, *Aryans and British India*, 37–52.

12. Trautmann, *Aryans and British India*, 138.

13. *Asiatic Journal* 12 (Sept.–Dec., 1833), 1.

14. *Histoire de Nader Chah* (London: P. Elmsly, 1770); *The History of the Life of Nader Shah, King of Persia* (London: J. Richardson, 1773), reprinted in Jones's *Works*, vols. 11 and 12. *A Grammar of the Persian Language* (London: W. W. Richardson 1771), *Works* 5:165–446.

15. For a general discussion of Jones's politics, see S. N. Mukherjee, *Sir William Jones: A Study in Eighteenth-Century British Attitudes to India.* Cambridge South Asian Studies (Cambridge: Cambridge University Press, 1968), 49–72.

16. Mukherjee, *Jones*, 40.

17. For insight into this early attitude, see, for example, his list of academic goals composed on his passage to Bengal, which include wide-ranging histories of Asia and the composition of proofs of the historical accuracy of the Christian scriptures, O. P. Kejariwal, *The Asiatic Society of Bengal and the Discovery of India's Past, 1784–1838* (Delhi: Oxford University Press, 1988), 29.

18. Jones, "Discourse on the Institution of a Society," *Works*, 3:5.

19. For a brief history and overview of the journal, see Michael John Franklin's introduction in the reprint of volume 1 in *Representing India: Indian Culture and Imperial Control in Eighteenth-Century British Orientalist Discourse*, vol. 7 (London: Routledge, 2000), v–xv.

20. Kejariwal, *Asiatic Society of Bengal*, 54.

21. Kejariwal, *Asiatic Society of Bengal*, 54.

22. Kejariwal, *Asiastic Society of Bengal*, 54, Mukherjee, *Jones*, 88 n. See also Garland Cannon's *Sir William Jones: A Bibliography of Primary and Secondary Sources.* Amsterdam Studies in the Theory and History of Linguistic Science 5; Library and Information Sources in Linguistics, vol. 7 (Amsterdam: John Benjamins B.V., 1979).

23. *Asiatick Researches*, 1:iii.

24. David Elliston Allen, *The Naturalist in Britain: A Social History* (London: Allen Lane, 1976), 27–51.

25. Lorraine Datson and Katharine Park, *Wonders and the Order of Nature 1150–1750* (New York: Zone Books, 1998), 329.

26. Datson and Park, *Wonders*, 137, 160.

27. Nathan Reingold, *Science, American Style* (New Brunswick, N.J., and London: Rutgers University Press, 1991), 31–44.

28. Harriet Ritvo, *The Platypus and the Mermaid and Other Figments of the Classifying Imagination* (Cambridge, Mass.: Harvard University Press, 1997), 21.

29. Datson and Park, *Wonders*, 360.

30. See also Datson and Park, *Wonders*, 137–46.

31. *Asiatick Researches*, 1:300–308.

32. *Asiatick Researches*, 1:306.

33. John MacDonald, "By Mr. MacDonald, with a Specimen of Gold," *Asiatick Researches*, 1:336–69. See also "On Three Natural Productions of Sumatra," 4:19–33, in which he discusses the island's copper, coral, and camphor resources.

34. Jones, "On the Loris, or Slowpaced Lemur," *Works*, 4:360–66; Athar Ali Khan, "On the Baya, or Indian Gross-Beak," transl. William Jones, *Works*, 4:353–55; Matthew Leslie, "On the Pangolin of Bahar," *Asiatick Researches*, 1:376–68.

35. Adam Burt, "On the Dissection of the Pangolin," *Asiatick Researches*, 2: 353–38.

36. See William Roxburgh, "A Discourse on the Plant Butea," *Asiatick Researches*, 3:469–74, which instituted the new format.

37. Ritvo, *The Platypus and the Mermaid*, 18, 51–68. On the encounter between Indian and European science in the colonial era, see Deepak Kumar, "The 'Culture' of Science and Colonial Culture, India 1820–1920," *British Journal for the History of Science* 29/2 (June 1996): 195–209.

38. Mitter, *Much Maligned Monsters*, 2–30, and Ritvo, *The Platypus and the Mermaid*, 1–50.

39. John Williams, "On the Cure of Persons Bitten by Snakes," *Asiatick Researches*, 2:323–39.

40. John Corse, *Asiatick Researches*, 3:229–48.

41. Captain Hardwicke, "Description of a Species of Meloe," *Asiatick Researches*, 5:213–14.

42. Ali Ibrahim Khan, "On the Trial by Ordeal, Among the Hindus," 1:389–401, and John Shore, "On Some Extraordinary Facts, Customs, and Practices of the Hindus," *Asiatick Researches*, 4:331–50.

43. "The Rudhiradhyaya, or Sanguinary Chapter; Translated from the Calica Puran," trans. W. C. Blaquiere, *Asiatick Researches*, 5:371–91.

44. Londa Schiebinger, *Nature's Body: Gender in the Making of Modern Science* (Boston: Beacon Press, 1993), 27.

45. Volumes 18 (1833) and 19 (1836) were all or mostly scientific in content, and the *Journal of the Asiatic Society of Bengal* became the Society's preferred vehicle for publishing scientific findings. Kejariwal, *Asiatic Society of Bengal*, 149, 151.

46. Jones, "Remarks on the Two Preceding Papers," *Asiatick Researches*, 1:142; M. Joinville, "On the Religion and Manners of the People of Ceylon," 7:400–402.

47. Charles Wilkins, "Seeks and Their College," *Asiatick Researches*, 1:288. Unfortunately, what could have been an important document in the development of a British consciousness of the Sikhs has apparently been lost. William Ward of Serampore presented a paper to the Society titled, "An Account of the Sikhs" on April 4, 1810. Kejariwal, *Asiatic Society of Bengal*, 111.

48. John Malcolm, "Sketch of the Sikhs," *Asiatick Researches*, 11:197–292.

49. Wilkins, "Seeks," *Asiatick Researches*, 1:292.

50. Wilkins, "Seeks," *Asiatick Researches*, 1:293–34.

51. On prototypicality in the definition of Hinduism, see Gavin Flood, *An Introduction to Hinduism* (Cambridge and New York: Cambridge University Press, 1996), 6–9.

52. Wilkins, "A Royal Grant of Land, Engraved on a Copper Plate, Bearing Date Twenty-Three Years before Christ; and Discovered among the Ruins at Mongueer," *Asiatick Researches*, 1:123–30. The charge is contained in note 1 on page 129.

53. Jones, "Remarks on the Two Preceding Papers," *Asiatick Researches*, 1:142–24.

54. Samuel Turner, "Copy of an Account Given by Mr. Turner of his Interview with Teeshoo Lama at the Monastery of Terpaling," *Asiatick Researches*, 1:199–205.

55. Samuel Turner, "An Account of a Journey to Tibet," *Asiatick Researches*, 1: 207–20.

56. H. T. Colebrooke, "Particular Tenets of Certain Muhammedan Sects," *Asia-*

tick Researches 7:338–44. In the tenth volume J. H. Howington offered "Remarks upon the Authorities of Mosulman Law," 475–512, and John Malcom contributed "Translations of Two Letters of Nadir Shah," 526–47. These are the only two other articles that were directly related to Islamic issues and neither treated religion explicitly. Similarly, J. Leyden's "On the Rosheniah Sect and its Founder Bayzid Ansari" dealt with Islam only by way of its detractors, 11:363–428.

57. *Index to the First Eighteen Volumes of the Asiatick Researches* (Calcutta: G. H. Huttman at the Bengal Military Orphan Press, 1835).

58. In addition to Vansittart, see William Jones, *Histoire de Nader Chah*, and "A Conversation with Abram, an Abyssinian, Concerning the City of Gwendor and the Sources of the Nile," which Jones recorded as reliable because he found Abram's "whole demeanor so remote from any suspicion of falsehood," *Works*, 4:314–19. W. Franklin's "An Account of the Present State of Delhi" relies in part on Muslim historian Firishtah, *Asiatick Researches*, 4:419–32.

59. Cohn, *Colonialism and Its Forms of Knowledge*, esp. 45–56, 76–105.

60. One history written by a Hindu and regarded as reliable was included, but its author, Casi Raja Pandit, recorded it as part of his office as servant to the Muslim government's vizier, hence it still emerged from the context of Muslim rule. See "An Account of the Battle of Paniput," trans. James Browne, *Asiatick Researches*, 3:88–139.

61. He also mentioned favorably a history of the Afghans composed by one of their chiefs, Hafiz Rahmat Khan, from whom "the curious reader may derive much information," "On the Descent of the Afghans from the Jews," *Asiatick Researches*, 2:67–75.

62. Vansittart, "Letter from Henry Vansittart to the President," *Asiatick Researches*, 2:67–78.

63. Jones, "Fourth Anniversary Discourse," *Works*, 3:47–70.

64. James T. Blunt, "A Description of the Cuttub Minar," *Asiatick Researches*, 4:313–16. See also William Dunkin, "Extract of a Diary," 4:401–404 and William Franklin, "An Account of the Present State of Delhi," 4:419–32.

65. "Some Account of the Cave in the Island of Elephanta," *Asiatick Researches*, 4:409–17.

66. John Carnac, "Introduction," *Asiatick Researches*, 4:407. On Bengalis as effeminate, see Mrinalini Sinha, *Colonial Masculinity*.

67. W. Francklin, "An Account of the Present State of Delhi," *Asiatick Researches*, 4:420–21.

68. Francklin, "Present State of Delhi," *Asiatick Researches*, 4:422–23.

69. Parts IX and X of the constitution and their related schedules identify some of these groups and the procedures for naming others. Technically speaking, "tribal" applies only to certain peoples and territories in Assam. Others are referred to as "scheduled tribes" or "scheduled areas." A fuller explanation of the terse constitutional statements is available in Anil Chandra Banerjee and Krishna Lal Chatterji's *A Survey of the Indian Constitution* (Calcutta: A. Mukherjee, 1957), 243–54.

70. George Stocking, *Victorian Anthropology* (New York: Free Press, 1987), 30–36.

71. Stocking, *Victorian Anthropology*, 41–45.

72. G. Hamilton, "A Short Description of Carnicobar," *Asiatick Researches*, 2:337–44.

73. R. H. Colebrooke, "On the Islands of Nancowry and Comarty," *Asiatick Researches*, 4:133.

74. Thomas Shaw, "On the Inhabitants of the Hills near Rajamahal," *Asiatick Researches*, 4:45–107.

75. John Rawling, "On the Manners, Religion, and Laws of the Cucis, or Mountaineers of Tipra," *Asiatick Researches*, 2:187–93.

76. John Eliot, "Observations on the Inhabitants of the Garrow Hills," *Asiatick Researches*, 3:17–37. For a more exhaustive analysis of the cultural naturalism attributed to non-Hindus, see Pennington, "The Firefly and the Moon," 189–93.

77. Hamilton, "Carnicobar," *Asiatick Researches*, 2:337–44.

78. These figures are not exact. The *Researches* did not always divide articles neatly; often several contributions on the same subject appeared alongside one another, and at other times lengthy introductions or commentary by someone other than the author of the main article accompanied it. In general, I have treated these cases as a single article, except where the authors voiced significant differences.

79. Jones, *Works*, 3:24–46.

80. Jones, "Third Anniversary Discourse," *Works*, 3:29.

81. Arvind Sharma, "Of Hindu, Hindustān, Hinduism and Hindutva," *Numen* 49/1 (2002): 5

82. Jones, "Discourse on the Institution of a Society," *Works*, 3:2.

83. Jones, "Discourse on the Institution of a Society," *Works*, 3:5.

84. Cohn, *Colonialism and Its Forms of Knowledge*, 55. See also Teltscher, *India Inscribed*, 208.

85. See especially Jones, "On the Origin and Families of Nations," *Works*, 3:185–204.

86. Kejariwal, *Asiatic Society of Bengal*, 28; Kopf, *British Orientalism*, 5.

87. See, for example, David Haberman, "On Trial: The Love of Sixteen Thousand Gopis," *History of Religions* 33/1 (August 1993): 44–70.

88. Jones, "On the Gods of Greece, Italy, and India," *Works*, 3:319–97.

89. Jones, "On the Gods of Greece, Italy, and India," *Works*, 3:320.

90. See Lincoln, *Theorizing Myth*, 85–95 for a detailed summary of Jones's reconstruction of human history.

91. Trautmann, *Aryans and British India*, 8–9.

92. Lincoln *Theorizing Myth*, 80.

93. A. J. Arberry, *Oriental Essays* (London: George Allen and Unwin, 1963), 83.

94. Jones, "On the Gods of Greece, Italy, and India," *Works*, 3:319.

95. Jones, "On the Gods of Greece, Italy, and India," *Works*, 3:321–22.

96. Trautmann, *Aryans and British India*, 45–52.

97. See, for example, some of his hymns to Hindu deities, *Works*, 13:242–331, and John Drew's analysis of his poetry, *India and the Romantic Imagination* (Delhi: Oxford University Press, 1987), 43–82.

98. Jones, "On the Musical Modes of the Hindus," *Works*, 4:193.

99. Jones, "Sixth Anniversary Discourse," *Works*, 3:126–67.

100. Jones, "Third Anniversary Discourse," *Works*, 3:33.

101. Jones, "On the Chronology of the Hindus," *Works*, 4:1–48.

102. Jones, "Tenth Anniversary Discourse," *Works*, 3:217.

103. As in "The Lunar Year of the Hindus," *Works*, 4:126–31, and "On the Musical Modes of the Hindus," 4:192–23.

104. Jones, "On the Musical Modes of the Hindus," *Works*, 4:184.

105. See, for example, Halbfass, *India and Europe* 62–63; Drew, *India and the Romantic Imagination*, 43–82; and S. Mukherjee, *Jones*, 42–24.

106. Jones, "Second Anniversary Discourse," *Works*, 3:13.

107. Jones, *Works*, 3:32.

108. Ranajit Guha, *An Indian Historiography of India: A Nineteenth-Century Agenda and Its Implications*, S. G. Deuskar Lectures on Indian History, Center for Studies in Social Sciences (Calcutta: K. P. Bagchi, 1988), 11–13.

109. William Chambers, "Some Account of the Sculptures and Ruins at Mavalipuram, a Place a Few Miles North of Madras, and Known to Seamen by the Name of the Seven Pagodas," *Asiatick Researches*, 1:157.

110. Reuben Burrow, "A Method of Calculating the Moon's Parallaxes in Latitude and Longitude," *Asiatick Researches*, 1:320–25, and "A Demonstration of One of the Hindoo Rules of Arithmetick," 3:145–57.

111. Burrow, "A Proof that the Hindoos Had the Binomial Theorem," *Asiatick Researches*, 2:487–92.

112. John Playfair, "Questions and Remarks on the Astronomy of the Hindus," *Asiatick Researches*, 4:159–63.

113. Samuel Davis, "On the Astronomical Computations of the Hindus," *Asiatick Researches*, 2:225–66.

114. On the personal and academic relationship between Jones and Bryant, see Trautmann, *Aryans and British India*, 44–47.

115. Kejariwal, *Asiatic Society of Bengal*, 68.

116. Trautmann, *Aryans and British India*, 89–93.

117. Jones, "Remarks on the Preceding Essay," *Asiatick Researches*, 3:463, 467.

118. Francis Wilford, "Remarks on the City of Tagara," *Asiatick Researches*, 1: 369–75.

119. Wilford, Letter "To the President," June 10, 1787, *Asiatick Researches*, 1:368.

120. Wilford, "On Egypt and Other Countries adjacent to the Cali River, or Nile of Ethiopia, from the Ancient Books of the Hindus," *Asiatick Researches*, 3:296–67.

121. Wilford, "On Egypt and Other Countries," *Asiatick Researches*, 3:295–462.

122. Wilford, "On the Chronology of the Hindus," *Asiatick Researches*, 5:241–95, see especially 2:243–56.

123. Wilford, *Asiatick Researches*, 5:270.

124. Wilford, *Asiatick Researches*, 5:241.

125. Cohn, *Colonialism and Its Forms of Knowledge*, 78.

126. Kejariwal, *Asiatic Society of Bengal*, 102. Wilford's "Sacred Isles of the West" appeared in three parts (*Asiatick Researches*, 8:245–368; 9:32–243; 11:11–152). His painful confession is found on 8:246–62.

127. Sir John Shore, "On Some Extraordinary Facts, Customs, and Practices of the Hindus," *Asiatick Researches*, 4:331–50.

128. Kejariwal, *Asiatic Society of Bengal*, 93–95; Kopf, *British Orientalism*, 67–68.

129. On the differences between his and Jones's approach to formulating a law code for India, for example, see Cohn, *Colonialism and Its Forms of Knowledge*, 68–75.

130. H. T. Colebrooke, "On the Duties of a Faithful Hindu Widow," *Asiatick Researches*, 4:209–19.

131. See Kopf, *British Orientalism*, 17–21. P. J. Marshall sees the development of the Permanent Settlement of 1793 as a series of moves to wed inherited forms of Bengali government and administration to the East India Company's need for expanding revenue. He finds British law in India "wholly alien" to the people it attempted to accommodate, *Bengal—The British Bridgehead: Eastern India, 1740–1828*, New Cambridge History of India 2.2 (Cambridge: Cambridge University Press, 1987), 116–29.

132. Cohn, *Colonialism and Its Forms of Knowledge*, 74.

133. In "Enumeration of Indian Classes," Colebrooke provided an exegesis of the "Jātimāla" and other texts to account for and describe the caste system, *Asiatick Researches*, 5:53–67. Colebrooke's "On the Religious Ceremonies of the Hindus, and of the Brahmens Especially," *Asiatick Researches*, 5:345–68, and *Asiatick Researches*, 7:232–311 described daily baths, service to guests, puja, funeral rites, and more.

134. John Duncan, "Account of Two Fakeers," *Asiatick Researches*, 5:37–52.

135. *Missionary Papers* II (Midsummer 1816).

136. Horace Hayman Wilson, "An Essay on the Hindu History of Cashmir," *Asiatick Researches*, 15:1.

137. Wilson, "Sketch of the Religious Sects of the Hindus," *Asiatick Researches*, 16:1–136; 17:169–313.

138. Wilson, "Sketch of Sects," *Asiatick Researches*, 16:7.

139. Cohn, *Colonialism and Its Forms of Knowledge*, 53–54.

140. Wilson, "Sketch of the Religious Sects of the Hindus," *Asiatick Researches* 17:193–202.

141. Cohn, *Colonialism and Its Forms of Knowledge*, 46; see also 54–55.

142. See, for example, Wilson's introductions to both the "Sketch of Sects," *Asiatick Researches* 16:1–2 and "Notice of Three Tracts Received from Nepal," 16:450–51.

143. See William Hunter, "Narrative of a Journey from Agra to Oujein," *Asiatick Researches* 6:7–78; Mahony, "On the Course of the Ganges, through Bengal," 7:1–31; J. T. Blunt, "Narrative of a Route from Chunarghur, to Yertnagoodum, in the Ellore Circar," 7:57–169; William Lambton, "An Account of a Method for Extending a Geographical Survey Across the Peninsula of India," 7:312–37.

144. Wright's work is probably the most apt comparison, for he painted landscapes as well as portraits depicting scholars poring over their data, probing nature's secrets, or seeking philosophical enlightenment. See James B. Twitchell, *Romantic Horizons: Aspects of the Sublime in English Poetry and Painting, 1770–1850* (Columbia: University of Missouri Press, 1983), 60–108.

145. Allen, *Naturalist in Britain*, 54.

146. F. V. Raper, "Narrative of a Survey for the Purpose of Discovering the Sources of the Ganges," *Asiatick Researches* 11:446–563.

147. James Baillie Fraser, "An Account of a Journey to the Sources of the Jumna and Bhagirathi Rivers," *Asiatick Researches* 13:171–249; Fraser, *Journal of a Tour Through Part of the Snowy Range of the Himala Mountains, and to the Sources of the Rivers Jumna and Ganges* (London: Rodwell and Martin, 1820); *Views of the Himala Mountains* (London: Rodwell and Martin, 1820).

148. J. A. Hodgson, "Journal of a Survey to the Heads of the Rivers, Ganges and Jumna," *Asiatick Researches* 14:60–152.

149. Allen, *Naturalist in Britain*, 77.

150. Hodgson, "Journal of a Survey to the Heads of the Rivers, Ganges and Jumna," *Asiatick Researches* 14:109.

151. By W. B. Bayley, *Asiatick Researches* 12.547–65, and A. Stirling, 15:163–338, respectively.

152. Roy Porter, "Gentlemen and Geology: The Emergence of a Scientific Career," *Historical Journal* 21/4 (December 1978): 809–36.

153. On Prinsep's contribution to the Asiatic Society and the assistance he lent to further clarifying its aims, see Kejariwal, *Asiatick Society of Bengal*, 162–220.

154. *Asiatick Researches* 17:470–98.

155. C. A. Bayly, "Knowing the Country: Empire and Information in India," *Modern Asian Studies* 27/1 (1993): 3–43.

156. Bayly, "Knowing the Country," 35.

157. Allen, *Naturalist in Britain*, 83.

158. Trautmann, *Aryans and British India*, 138.

159. See the introduction to volume eighteen, which addressed the concerns of scientists and the previous inability of the journal to meet their needs, 18:i–iv.

160. By Clark Abel, *Asiatick Researches* 15:189–98.

161. Captain Cornfoot, "Some Account of an Orang Outang," *Asiatick Researches* 15:491.

CHAPTER 5

1. E.g., Robert Eric Frykenberg, "The Emergence of Modern 'Hinduism' as a Concept and as an Institution: A Reappraisal with Special Reference to South India," in *Hinduism Reconsidered*, ed. G. D. Sonthheimer and H. Kulke (New Delhi: Manohar, 1989), 29–49.

2. Edward Said initiated this discussion with his *Orientalism* in 1978. Recent important contributions include those of Cohn, *Colonialism and Its Forms of Knowledge*, and King, *Orientalism and Religion*.

3. Wendy Doniger, "Hinduism by Any Other Name," *Wilson Quarterly* 15/3 (Summer 1991): 41.

4. An earlier version of this chapter first appeared as Brian K. Pennington, "Constructing Colonial Dharma: A Chronicle of Emergent Hinduism, 1830–1831," *Journal of the American Academy of Religion* 69/3 (Sept. 2001): 577–603. Used by permission of Oxford University Press.

5. See, for example, Partha Chatterjee, "History and the Nationalization of Hinduism," in *Representing Hinduism: The Construction of Religious Traditions and National Identity*, ed. Vasudha Dalmia and Heinrich von Stietencron (New Delhi and Thousand Oaks, Calif.: Sage Publications, 1995), 103–28.

6. Smarajit Chakraborti, *The Bengali Press (1818–1868): A Study in the Growth of Public Opinion* (Calcutta: Firma KLM Private, Ltd., 1976), 35.

7. See Brajendranath Bandyopādhyāya, *Sambād Patre Sekāler Kathā*, 2 vols., 4th ed. (Calcutta: Bangīya Sāhitya Parisat, 1971), and Benoy Ghose, ed., *Selections from English Periodicals of Nineteenth-Century Bengal* (Calcutta: Papyrus, 1978).

8. For his assistance in reading and translating this paper, I am indebted to Sunanda Sanyal of Lesley University. His advice and insight have been invaluable to me; all errors remain my own.

9. In recent scholarship, both western and Indian, the use of different terms to refer to this practice and those women who undertook it has replicated an inconsistency that grew out of English usage of this period. See John Stratton Hawley's introduction to *Sati, the Blessing and the Curse: The Burning of Wives in India* (New York and Oxford: Oxford University Press, 1994), 11–15. In this chapter, I will use "sahamarana" to refer to the practice and "satī" to refer to the woman who undertakes the practice because such usage is consistent with Bengali usage of the time.

10. On the history of this policy and its waning influence in the early to mid-1800s, see Cassels' *Religion and Pilgrim Tax*, esp. 1–7 and 147–54.

11. *Samācār Candrikā*, 22 Apr. 1830.

12. *Samācār Candrikā*, 15 Nov. 1830.

13. Sisir Kumar Das, *Sahebs and Munshis: An Account of the College of Fort William* (Calcutta: Orion, 1978), 107; *Candrikā* quoted in the *Bengal Hurkaru and Chronicle*, 1 Dec. 1829.

14. Duff, *India and Indian Missions*, 617; A. F. Salahuddin Ahmed, *Social Ideas and Social Change in Bengal, 1818–1835* (Calcutta: Rddhi, 1976), 33, 101; P. N. Bose and H.W.B. Moreno, *A Hundred Years of the Bengali Press* (Calcutta: Moreno, 1920), 16; C. A. Bayly, *Indian Society and the Making of the British Empire*, New Cambridge History of India 2.1 (Cambridge: Cambridge University Press, 1988), 73.

15. Sisir Kumar Das, *Early Bengali Prose: Carey to Vidyasagar* (Calcutta: Bookland Private, Ltd., 1966), 4. The early history of journalism and printing in Calcutta is still being written. Two valuable works on the years up to 1800 are Graham Shaw, *Printing in Calcutta to 1800: A Description and Checklist of Printing in the Late Eighteenth Century* (London: The Bibliographic Society, 1981), and P. Thankappan Nair, *A History of the Calcutta Press: The Beginnings*, A Tercentenary History of Calcutta Series (Calcutta: Firma KLM Private, Ltd., 1987).

16. Das, *Early Bengali Prose*, 23. Following James Long's 1855 report, S. N. Mukherjee puts the number at thirty-seven, *Calcutta: Essays in Urban History* (Calcutta: Subarnareka, 1993), 70.

17. S. K. Das calls the Bengali of early newspapers the "second phase" in the development of the modern language following the initial cultivation of it in textbooks associated with the Serampore mission's educational program, *Early Bengali Prose*, 169.

18. Although it deals almost entirely with his satires, the most extensive consideration of Bhabanicaran's literary contribution is Abu Hena Mustafa Kamal, *The Bengali Press and Literary Writing, 1818–1831* (Dhaka, Bangladesh: University Press, 1977), esp. chapters 3 and 4, 47–108.

19. The standard English version of his works is *The English Works of Raja Rammohun Roy*, 4 vols., ed. Jogendra Chander Ghose (Allahabad, India: Bahadurganj, 1906; repr. New Delhi: Cosmo Publishers, 1982); Bengali and English writings of his are available in *Rāmmohan-Samīkṣā*, 2d ed., ed. Dilīpkumar Visvās (Calcutta: Sārasvata Library, 1994).

20. The classic biography is S. D. Collet's *The Life and Letters of Raja Rammohun Roy* (London: Collet, 1900). Recent studies of Rammohan include S. Cromwell Crawford, *Ram Mohan Roy: Social, Political, and Religious Reform in Nineteenth-Century India* (New York: Paragon House, 1987); Bruce Carlisle Robertson, *Raja Rammohan Ray: The Father of Modern India* (Delhi: Oxford University Press, 1995).

21. For studies of the Brahmo Samaj in the context of other regional political and religious movements, see Aparna Bhattacharya, *Religious Reform Movements of Bengal and Their Socio-Economic Ideas, 1800–1850* (Patna, India: Aparna Bhattacarya, 1981), 172–209; Kenneth W. Jones, *Socio-Religious Reform Movements in British India*, New Cambridge History of India 3.1 (Cambridge: Cambridge University Press, 1989), 30–41; David Kopf, *The Brahma Samaj and the Shaping of the Modern Indian Mind* (Princeton, N.J.: Princeton University Press, 1979). A good overview of Brahmo theology is J. N. Pankratz, "The Response of the Brahmo Samaj," in *Modern Indian Responses to Religious Pluralism*, ed. Harold G. Coward (Albany, N.Y.: SUNY Press, 1987), 19–38.

22. Robertson, *Raja Rammohan Ray: The Father of Modern India*; Satis Chandra Chakravorti, *Father of Modern India: Commemoration Volume of the Rammohun Roy Centenary Celebrations, 1933* (Calcutta: Rammohun Roy Centenary Committee, 1935); Marie-A Reynaud-Beauveri, *Ram Mohan Roy, Le Pere de l'Indi Moderne a Paris en 1837* (Lyon, France: E. Bellier 1987).

23. An English translation is reprinted in Roy, *English Works*, 4:941–58.

24. See his *Precepts of Jesus* and the three *Appeals to the Christian Public* that fol-

lowed it and constituted his rehouses to missionary attacks on his representation of Christ, Roy, *English Works*, 3:481–4.874.

25. Only four numbers of the magazine appeared. The are reprinted in Roy, *English Works*, 1:143–98.

26. On his life, see Brajendranāth Bandyopādhyāya, *Bhabānīcaraṇ Bandyopādhyāya* (Calcutta: Baṅgīya Sāhitya Pariṣat), 1982.

27. Bandyopādhyāya, *Bhabānīcaraṇ Bandyopādhyāya*, 8–11.

28. Bandyopādhyāya, Bhabānīcaraṇ *Kalikātā Kamalālaya*, ed. and transl. by Satyabrata Dutta (Calcutta: Firma KLM, 1990). See also his *Rasaracanāsamagra*, ed. by Sanatkumar Gupta (Calcutta: Nabapatra Prakāśan, 1987). On the history of the term *bhadralok* and this class, see S. N. Mukherjee, *Calcutta in Urban History* (Calcutta: Subarnareka, 1993), 70–81 and Sumanta Banerjee, *The Parlour and the Streets* (Calcutta: Seagull Books, 1989), 54, 147–98.

29. Mṛtyuñjaya Vidyālaṅkār, *Vedāntacandrikā*. Although it considers only Sanskrit sources, a very important study of later orthodox polemics against British commentators is Richard Fox Young's *Resistant Hinduism: Sanskrit Sources on Anti-Christian Apologetics in Early Nineteenth-Century India*, Publications of the De Nobili Research Library 8, ed. Gerhard Oberhammer (Vienna: Institut für Indologie der Universität Wien, 1981).

30. The *Candrikā*'s figure appeared in an advertisement that reappeared regularly in the paper in 1830. Ahmed's estimate is 500; *Social Ideas*, 102.

31. Ahmed, *Social Ideas*, 12.

32. In the same period, some of the most widely read English-language papers had the following circulations: *Bengal Hurkaru and Chronicle*—750 (1829), *India Gazette*—522 (1833), *John Bull*—281 (1833); Mrinal Kanti Chanda, *History of the English Press in Bengal* (Calcutta and New Delhi: K. B. Baggchi and Co., 1987), 33.

33. *Samācār Candrikā*, 2–26 Sept. 1830.

34. *Samācār Candrikā*, 15 and 22 Apr. 1830.

35. *Samācār Candrikā*, 3 Feb. 1831.

36. *Samācār Candrikā*, 7 Feb. 1831.

37. *Bengal Hurkaru and Chronicle*, 1 Dec. 1829.

38. *Samācār Candrikā*, 27 May 1830.

39. *Samācār Candrikā*, 3 June 1830.

40. John N. Gray, "Bengal and Britain: Culture Contact and the Reinterpretation of Hinduism in the Nineteenth Century," in *Aspects of Bengali History and Society*, Asian Studies at Hawaii 12, ed. Rachel Van M. Baumer (Honolulu: University Press of Hawaii, 1976), 102.

41. Mukherjee, *Calcutta*, 115.

42. Abu Hena Mustafa Kamal, *The Bengali Press and Literary Writing, 1818–1831* (Dacca, Bangladesh: University Press, Ltd., 1987), 125.

43. Carak Pūjā ("carak" means "circle" or "wheel") was, in fact, a festival in honor of Shiva, one part of which could be hook-swinging, but this swinging often took place independent of the festival. On the different theological interpretations of this practice and its history under British rule, see Geoffrey A. Oddie, *Popular Religion, Elites, and Reform: Hook-Swinging and Its Prohibition in Colonial India, 1800–1894* (New Delhi: Manohar, 1995).

44. Oddie, *Popular Religion*, 72–73.

45. *Samācār Candrikā*, 20 May 1830.

46. *Samācār Candrikā*, 5 July 1830.

47. *Samācār Candrikā*, 6 Dec. 1830.

48. Mukherjee, *Calcutta*, 86–91.

49. Mukherjee, *Calcutta*, 168–86.

50. *Samācār Candrikā*, 20 Sept. 1830.

51. *Samācār Candrikā*, 23 Sept. 1830.

52. Chatterjee, "The Disciplines in Colonial Bengal," in *Texts of Power: Emerging Disciplines in Colonial Bengal*, ed. Partha Chatterjee. Perspectives in Social Sciences Series (Minneapolis and London: University of Minnesota Press and Centre for Studies in Social Sciences, 1995), 25.

53. See, e.g., William Ward's letter to a Miss Hope of Liverpool, where he had made a well-publicized presentation on the status of women in India, *Farewell Letters*, 60–77.

54. *Samācār Candrikā*, 16 Dec. 1830.

55. *Samācār Candrikā*, 9 Dec. 1830.

56. *Samācār Candrikā*, 16 and 27 Dec. 1830.

57. *Samācār Candrikā*, 7 March 1831.

58. *Samācār Candrikā*, 27 Dec. 1830.

59. William Cavendish Bentinck, et al, *The Correspondence of Lord William Cavendish Bentinck, Governor-General of India, 1828–1835*, ed. C. H. Philips (Oxford: Oxford University Press, 1977), 90–92.

60. On the various perspectives on the practice, see Paul B. Courtright, *Satī: The Goddess and the Dreadful Practice* (New York: Oxford University Press), forthcoming.

61. Courtright, "Iconographies of Satī," 28.

62. The wife's immediate decision to follow her husband in death is, in Indian constructions of sahamaraṇa, an important piece of evidence that her motives are pure and she is not acting under any compulsion. This purity of motive proves her to be truly devoted to her husband and her sacrifice then renders her satī. See Lindsey Harlan, "Perfection and Devotion: Sati Tradition in Rajasthan," in Hawley, *Sati*, 82–83.

63. *Samācār Candrikā*, 15 July 1830.

64. *Samācār Candrikā*, 19 Aug. 1830.

65. *Samācār Candrikā*, 23 Sept. 1830.

66. *Samācār Candrikā*, 11 Oct. 1830.

67. *Samācār Candrikā*, 16 Dec. 1830.

68. *Samācār Candrikā*, 3 Feb. 1831.

69. *Samācār Candrikā*, 9 Dec. 1830.

70. Brian A. Hatcher, *Idioms of Improvement: Vidyāsāgar and Cultural Encounter in Bengal* (Calcutta: Oxford University Press, 1996), 7.

71. Quoted in Kopf, *British Orientalism*, 206.

72. *Samācār Candrikā*, 20 Sept. 1830.

73. *Samācār Candrikā*, 4 Oct. 1830.

74. *Samācār Candrikā*, 16 Aug. 1830.

75. *Samācār Candrikā*, 18 Oct. 1830.

76. *Samācār Candrikā*, 30 Sept. 1830.

77. S. Cromwell Crawford, *Ram Mohan Roy*, 145.

78. See Mustafa Kamal, *The Bengali Press*, 47–108.

79. Ivan Strenski, "Religion, Power, and Final Foucault," *Journal of the American Academy of Religion* 66/2 (Summer 1998): 346.

80. Mukherjee, *Calcutta*, 146.

81. Kopf, *British Orientalism*, 192, 204–13.

82. Catherine Bell, *Ritual Theory, Ritual Practice* (New York: Oxford University Press, 1992), 82.

83. Jan Heesterman, *The Broken World of Sacrifice: An Essay in Ancient Indian Ritual* (Chicago and London: University of Chicago Press, 1993), 6.

CHAPTER 6

1. Sharma, "Of Hindu, Hindustān, Hinduism and Hindutva."

2. I take the term from Lorenzen, "Who Invented Hinduism," 630.

3. Heinrich von Stietencron, "Hinduism: On the Proper Use of a Deceptive Term," in *Hinduism Reconsidered*, South Asian Studies 24, ed. Günther-Dietz Sontheimer and Hermann Kulke (New Delhi: Manohar, 1997), 36.

4. Frykenberg, "The Emergence of Modern 'Hinduism,' " 82.

5. Frits Staal, *Ritual and Mantras: Rules without Meaning* (Delhi: Motilal Banarsidass, 1996), 397.

6. E.g., Heinrich von Stietencron, "Religious Configurations in Pre-Muslim India and the Modern Concept of Hinduism," in *Representing Hinduism: The Construction of Religious Traditions and National Identity*, ed. Vasudha Dalmia and Heinrich von Stietencron (New Delhi: Sage Publications, 1995), 73–77.

7. On various ways the colonial state mined and catalogued Indian practices, see Cohn, *Colonialism and Its Forms of Knowledge*, 57–75; Bayly, "Knowing the Country"; Rosane Rocher, "British Orientalism in the Eighteenth Century: The Dialects of Knowledge and Government," in *Orientalism and the Postcolonial Predicament: Perspectives on South Asia*, South Asia Seminar Series, ed. Carol A. Breckenridge and Peter van der Veer (Philadelphia: University of Pennsylvania Press, 1993), 220–25.

8. See the recent formulations of this argument in, for example, Mary Searle-Chatterjee, " 'World Religions' and 'Ethnic Groups': Do These Paradigms Lend Themselves to the Cause of Hindu Nationalism?," *Ethnic and Racial Studies* 23/3 (May 2000): 497–515, and John Zavos, "Defending Hindu Tradition: Sanatana Dharma as a Symbol of Orthodoxy in Colonial India," *Religion* 31 (2001): 109–23. See also Brian K. Smith's rejoinder that in fact it is a diffuse, not a unified, tradition that Hindu nationalists invoke, "Questioning Authority: Constructions and Deconstructions of Hinduism," *International Journal of Hindu Studies* 2, 3 (Dec. 1998): 313–39.

9. Romila Thapar, "Syndicated Hinduism," in *Hinduism Reconsidered*, South Asian Studies XXIV, ed. Günther-Dietz Sontheimer and Hermann Kulke (New Delhi: Manohar, 1997), 54–81.

10. Timothy Fitzgerald, *The Ideology of Religious Studies* (New York: Oxford University Press, 2000), 10–15 and chapter 7, "Hinduism," 134–55.

11. Lorenzen, "Who Invented Hinduism?," 630–59; Will Sweetman, "Unity and Plurality: Hinduism and the Religions of India in Early European Scholarship," *Religion* 31 (2001): 209–24.

12. Doniger, "Hinduism by Any Other Name," 41.

13. Doniger, "Hinduism by Any Other Name," 36.

14. Gabriella Eichinger Ferro-Luzzi, "The Polythetic-Prototype Approach to Hinduism," in *Hinduism Reconsidered*, ed. Sontheimer and Kulke, 294–304.

15. Robert Frykenberg, citing Peter Schmitlhenwer, "Constructions of Hinduism at the Nexus of History and Religion," *Journal of Interdisciplinary History* 23/3 (Winter 1993): 535, note 11.

16. Frykenberg, "Constructions of Hinduism," 534.

17. Zavos, "Defending Hindu Tradition."

18. This claim corresponds roughly to Thomas Trautmann's own view, *Aryans and British India*, 67–68.

19. Paul Brass, quoted in Lorenzen, "Who Invented Hinduism," 646.

20. Rocher, "British Orientalism in the Eighteenth Century," 243.

21. As Heinrich von Stietencron comes very close to alleging, "Religious Configurations in Pre-Muslim India," 73.

22. See Eugene F. Irschick, *Dialogue and History: Constructing South India, 1795–1895* (Berkeley: University of California Press, 1994).

23. Inden, *Imagining India*, 2.

24. Inden, *Imagining India*, 2.

25. Inden, *Imagining India*, e.g., 17–18.

26. *Genealogies of Religion: Discipline and Reasons of Power in Christianity and Islam* (Baltimore, Md.: Johns Hopkins University Press, 1993), 18.

27. E.g. King, *Orientalism and Religion*, 68–70, Russell T. McCutcheon, *Manufacturing Religion: The Discourse on Sui Generis Religion and the Politics of Nostalgia* (New York: Oxford University Press, 1997), and Timothy Fitzgerald, whose polemical diatribe against the field of comparative religious studies is informed only by entirely outdated and outmoded scholarship, *Ideology of Religious Studies*, 33–53.

28. S. N. Balagangadhara, *"The Heathen in his Blindness . . .": Asia, the West and the Dynamic of Religion*, Studies in the History of Religions LXIV (Leiden, the Netherlands: E. J. Brill, 1994), 394.

29. Peter Harrison, *"Religion" and the Religions in the English Enlightenment* (Cambridge: Cambridge University Press, 1990), the direct claim is made on 1; also, Wilfred Cantwell Smith, *The Meaning and End of Religion* (San Francisco: Harper and Row, 1978), 37–41.

30. Augustine, *De Vera Religione*. In *Augustine: Earlier Writings*, Library of Christian Classics, Ichthus Edition, trans. John H. S. Burleigh (Philadelphia: Westminster Press, 1953), 218–83, 1.1.

31. Augustine, *De Vera Religione* 5.8.

32. Augustine, *De Vera Religione* 5.9.

33. On this issue, I am expressing some difference of opinion from Harrison, who argues that the term "religion" emerged as a generic category including distinct, identifiable systems, only after the Middle Ages, especially among reformers, Christian Platonists, and Renaissance thinkers. See *'Religion' and the Religions*, esp. 5–18. W. C. Smith also claimed that *De Vera Religione* did not portray systems of "observances or beliefs," a reading I clearly do not accept, *The Meaning and End of Religion*, 29.

34. W. C. Smith believed the terms "religion" and "religious" were seldom used in the Middle Ages except as designating monastic offices, but Peter Biller has found the term regularly employed in senses rather similar to our contemporary usage. Smith, *The Meaning and End of Religion*, 31–32; Peter Biller, "Words and the Medieval Notion of 'Religion,' " *Journal of Ecclesiastical History* 36/3 (July 1985): 351–69.

35. John Calvin, *Institutes of the Christian Religion*, ed. John T. McNeill, transl. Ford Lewis Battles, Library of Christian Classics 20 (Philadelphia: Westminster Press, 1960), 1.3.1.

36. Harrison, *'Religion' and the Religions*, 8, 19–28. See Calvin, *Institutes* 1.6–7.

37. See also Biller, "Words and the Medieval Notion of 'Religion.' "

38. King, *Orientalism and Religion*, 36–38.

39. Will Sweetman, " 'Hinduism' and the History of 'Religion': Protestant Presuppositions in the Critique of the Concept of Hinduism," *Method and Theory in the Study of Religion* 15/4 (2003): 341.

40. J. Samuel Preus, *Explaining Religion: Criticism and Theory from Bodin to Freud* (New Haven, Conn.: Yale University Press, 1987).

41. The annual meeting of the American Academy of Religion has over eight thousand scholars of religion in attendance annually. These themes were culled from the program book of the Nov. 17–20, 2001 meeting held in Denver, Colorado.

42. Walter H. Capps, *Religious Studies: The Making of a Discipline* (Minneapolis, Minn.: Fortress Press, 1995.

43. King, *Orientalism and Religion*, 35–61; Balagangadhara, *The Heathen in His Blindness*, e.g., 384–45.

44. Sweetman, "Unity and Plurality," 218–19.

45. Fitzgerald, *The Ideology of Religious Studies*, 4.

46. Fitzgerald, as in *The Ideology of Religious Studies*, 19–24.

47. Fitzgerald, *The Ideology of Religious Studies*, 7.

48. For a fuller critique of Fitzgerald's book, see the series of reviews published together in *Religious Studies Review* 27/4 (Apr. 2001). They include Benson Saler, "Some Reflections on Fitzgerald's Thesis," 103–5; Gustavo Benavides, "Religious Studies Between Science and Ideology," 105–8; and Frank Korom, "(H)ideology: The Hidden Agenda of Religious Studies," 108–10. Fitzgerald's reply follows these as "A Response to Saler, Benavides, and Korom," 110–15.

49. Saler, "Some Reflections," 104.

50. Saler, "Some Reflections," 103–4.

51. Benavides, "Religious Studies."

52. Korom, "(H)ideology."

53. Fitzgerald, *The Ideology of Religious Studies*, 33–34.

54. Fitzgerald, *The Ideology of Religious Studies*, 52.

55. W. C. Smith, *The Meaning and End of Religion*, 50.

56. The data is incompletely reported, but an indication of the increasingly interdisciplinary approaches of many departments of religious studies may be found in the preliminary report of the American Academy of Religion's 2001 survey of religion and theology programs. "Religion and Theology Programs Census: 'The Study of Religion Counts,' " *Religious Studies News* 16/4 (Fall 2001): i–iii.

57. McCutcheon, *Manufacturing Religion*, 26.

58. In the same vein, George Alfred James has identified three characteristics of this trend in academic thought about religion—that its practices are ahistorical, atheoretical, and antireductive, *Interpreting Religion: The Phenomenological Approaches of Pierre Daniël de la Saussaye, W. Brede Kristensen, and Gerardus van der Leeuw* (Washington, DC: Catholic University of America Press, 1995), 47–50.

59. Russell T. McCutcheon, *Critics Not Caretakers: Redescribing the Public Study of Religion* (Albany, N.Y.: SUNY Press, 2001), 5.

60. McCutcheon, *Critics Not Caretakers*, xi.

61. E.g., McCutcheon, *Critics Not Caretakers*, 138–89.

62. McCutcheon, *Critics Not Caretakers*, xiv, 17.

63. McCutcheon, *Critics Not Caretakers*, 81.

64. McCutcheon, *Critics Not Caretakers*, 80.

65. E.g., "Protest Letters for *Kali's Child*." Sword of Truth, June 3, 2001, http://www.swordoftruth.com/swordoftruth/news/betweenthelines/Kalischildletters.html.

See also the exchange between Michael Witzel and David Frawley in the English, language Indian daily *The Hindu*, 5 Mar., 25 June, 16 July, 6 Aug., 13 Aug., and 20 Aug., 2002, available online at http://www.hinduonnet.com.

66. Brian K. Smith, "Re-envisioning Hinduism."

67. Thomas Babbington Macauley, "Mr. Lord Macaulay's Great Minute," in W.F.B. Laurie, *Sketches of Some Distinguished Anglo-Indians* (London: W. H. Allen, 1888; repr. New Delhi: Asian Educational Services, 1999), 174.

68. "Divali: Festival of Lights. Prayer for Hindus," (n.p.: International Mission Board, Southern Baptist Convention, 1999).

69. "Divali," 1.

70. See Brian K. Pennington, "Renaissance or Retrenchment? Hindu-Christian Dialogue at a Crossroads," *Indian Journal of Theology* 42/1 (2000): 74–87.

71. Robert Eric Frykenberg, "The Construction of Hinduism as a 'Public' Religion: Looking Again at the Religious Roots of Company Raj in South India," in *Religion and Public Culture: Encounters and Identities in Modern South India*, ed. Keith E. Yandell and John J. Paul (Richmond: Curzon Press, 2000), 3–4.

72. Sumit Sarkar, "Hindutva and the Question of Conversions," in *The Concerned Indian's Guide to Communalism*, ed. K. N. Panikkar (New Delhi: Viking, 1999), 77.

73. Sarkar, "Hindutva and Conversions," 72–75.

74. Indian Bibliographic Centre (Research Wing), *Christianity and Conversion in India* (Varanasi: Rishi Publications, 1999).

75. Indian Bibliographic Centre, *Christianity and Conversion*, 54–59.

76. Indian Bibliographic Centre, *Christianity and Conversion*, 95.

77. A need that one theologian, John Brockington, recognizes, *Hinduism and Christianity* (New York: St. Martin's Press, 1992), ix–x. See also Brian K. Pennington, "Reverend William Ward," 5–6.

78. See John Stratton Hawley, "Who Speaks for Hinduism—And Who Against?" *Journal of the American Academy of Religion* 68/4 (Dec. 2000): 711–20.

79. Jeffrey J. Kripal, *Kali's Child: The Mystical and the Erotic in the Life and Teachings of Ramakrishna* (Chicago: University of Chicago Press, 1995); the response by Swami Tyagananda of the Ramakrishna Mission, is "Kali's Child Revisited or Didn't Anyone Check the Documentation?" *Evam: Forum on Indian Representations* 1/1–2 (2002): 173–90, to which Kripal has responded in turn in the same volume, "Textuality, Sexuality, and the Future of the Past: A Response to Swami Tyagananda," 191–205.

80. Hawley, "Who Speaks for Hinduism," 714–15.

81. From the Jesus Christ Superstore, http://www.Jesuschristsuperstore.net.

82. Rashmi Luthra, "The Formation of Interpretive Communities in the Hindu Diaspora," in *Religion and Popular Culture: Studies on the Interaction of Worldviews*, ed. David A. Stout and Judith M. Buddenbaum (Ames: Iowa State University Press, 2001), 125–39.

83. For a summary of some discrete sites of this contact between Hindus and Christians, see Sita Ram Goel, *History of Hindu-Christian Encounters* (New Delhi: Voice of India, 1989).

84. E.g., William S. Sax, "Conquering the Quarters: Religion and Politics in Hinduism," *International Journal of Hindu Studies* 4/1 (April, 2000): 39–60.

85. On the legal status of the right to convert, see Ronald Neufeldt, "Conversion and the Courts," *Hindu-Christian Studies Bulletin* 13 (2000): 12–18.

86. See, e.g., Lise McKean, *Divine Enterprise: Gurus and the Hindu Nationalist*

Movement (Chicago: University of Chicago Press, 1996), 115–22; Richard H. Davis, "The Iconography of Rama's Chariot," in David Ludden, ed., *Making India Hindu: Religion, Community, and the Politics of Democracy in India* (Delhi: Oxford University Press, 1997), 27–54.

87. On the contemporary movement itself, see Selva J. Raj, "Adapting Hindu Imagery: A Critical Look at Ritual Experiments in an Indian Catholic Ashram," *Journal of Ecclesiastical Studies* 37/3–4 (Summer-Fall 2000): 333–53. For a Hindu attack on them as fraudulent, see Sita Ram Goel, *Catholic Ashrams: Sannyasins or Swindlers?* (New Delhi: Voice of India, 1989).

88. Raj, "Adapting Hindu Imagery," 350–52.

89. Joanne Punzo Waghorne, "Chariots of the God/s: Riding the Line between Hindu and Christian," *History of Religions* 39/2 (Nov. 1999): 95–116. For a study of Christian practices that are more strategically and less organically Hindu, see in the same volume Eliza F. Kent, "Tamil Bible Women and the Zenana Missions of Colonial South India," 117–49.

90. *Kerala Christian Sainthood*, 52–87.

91. Richard W. Taylor, "Current Hindu-Christian Dialogue in India," in *Hindu-Christian Dialogue: Perspectives and Encounters*, ed. Harold Coward (Maryknoll, N.Y.: Orbis Books, 1989), 122–24, 126.

92. Klaus Klostermaier, "The Future of Hindu-Christian Dialogue," in *Hindu-Christian Dialogue*, ed. Harold Coward (Maryknoll, N.Y.: Orbis Books, 1989), 263.

93. Klostermaier, "The Future of Hindu-Christian Dialogue," 265–56.

Works Cited

NEWSPAPERS, TRACTS, AND UNPUBLISHED SOURCES

Newspapers and Collected Selections from Newspapers

Bandyopadhyay, Brajendranath. *Sambād Patre Sekāler Kathā*. 2 vol. 4th ed. Calcutta: Bangīya Sāhitya Pariṣat, 1971.
Bengal Hurkaru and Chronicle, 1829.
Ghose, Benoy, ed. *Selections from English Periodicals of Nineteenth-Century Bengal*. Calcutta: Papyrus, 1978.
Samācār Candrikā, 1830–31, British Library 14133.g.6.

Tracts and Unpublished Sources

Allport, Rev. Josiah. *A Sermon Preached at Coleford, July 18, 1813, in Aid of the Church Missionary Society for Africa and the East*. Monmouth, Eng.: Charles Heath, 1813.
A Brief View of the Plan and Operations of the Religious Tract Society. London: J. Rider, 1827.
Carey, William. *An Enquiry into the Obligation of Christians to Use Means for the Conversion of the Heathen*. Leicester, UK: Ann Ireland, 1792; reprint, London: Carey Kingsgate Press, 1961.
Deplorable Effects of Heathen Superstition, as Manifested by the Natives of Hindoostan. Cheap Tract 13. Dunfermline, Scotland: John Miller, 1828.
"Divali: Festival of Lights. Prayer for Hindus." N.p.: International Mission Board, Southern Baptist Convention, 1999.
Dubois, J. A. *Letters on the State of Christianity in India; In Which the Conversion of the Hindoos Is Considered Impracticable*. London: Longman, Hurst, Rees, Orme, Brown, and Green, 1823.
The Evils of a Late Attendance on Divine Worship. No. 60. London: Religious Tract Society, n.d. but probably 1800.

The First Fifteen Years' Quarterly Papers of the Church Missionary Society; to Which Is Prefixed a Brief View of the Society for the First Ten Years. London: Richard Watts, 1833.

The First Ten Years' Quarterly Papers of the Church Missionary Society to Which Is Affixed a Brief View of the Society. London: Seeley and Son, 1826.

Freer, George. *A Parochial Sermon: In Aid of the National Society for the Education of the Poor in the Principles of the Established Church.* St. Neots, UK: J. Stanford, 1823.

Grant, Charles. "Observations on the State of Society Among the Asiatic Subjects of Great Britain, Particularly with Resepct to Morals; and on the Means of Improving It." British Library, Oriental and India Office Collections, Eur MSS E93.

Hough, James. *A Reply to the Letters of the Abbé Dubois on the State of Christianity in India.* London: L. B. Seeley and Son, 1824.

A Member of the Church Missionary Society. *Cursory Observations on a Letter Recently Addressed by the Rev. William Baily Whitehead, M.A., to the Rev. Daniel Wilson, M.A.* Bristol: J. Richardson, 1818.

Peggs, James. *India's Cries to British Humanity Relative to the Suttee, Infanticide, British Connection with Idolatry, Ghaut Murders, and Slavery in India.* 2d ed. London: Seely and Son, 1830.

Poynder, John. *History of the Jesuits in Answer to Mr. Dallas's Defense of That Order.* 2 vols. London: Baldwin, Cradock, and Joy, 1816.

———. *Human Sacrifices in India.* London: J. Hatchard and Son, 1827.

———. *Popery the Religion of Heathenism.* London: George Wilson: 1818. Reissued as *Popery in Alliance with Heathenism.* London: J. Hatchard and Son, 1835.

Pryme, George. *Counter-Protest of a Layman, In Reply To the Protest of Archdeacon Thomas Against the Formation of an Association at Bath in Aid of the Church Missionary Society.* 3d ed., corrected. Cambridge: W. Metcalfe, 1818.

Second Protest Against the Formation of the Church Missionary Society. Bath: J. Hatchard, 1818.

The Spirit of British Missions: Dedicated to the Church Missionary Society. London: A. M'Intosh, 1815.

Thomas, Rev. Josiah. *An Address to a Meeting Holden at the Town-Hall, in the City of Bath, the First Day of December, 1817, for the Purpose of Forming a Church Missionary Society in That City.* Bath: Meyler and Son, 1817.

Townley, Henry. *An Answer to the Abbé Dubois.* London: R. Clay, 1824.

Vansittart, Nicholas. *Three Letters on the Subject of the British and Foreign Bible Society, Addressed to the Rev. Dr. March and John Coker, Esq., by the Right Hon. Nicholas Vansittart.* London: J. Hatchard, 1812.

Ward, William. *Farewell Letters to a Few Friends in Britain and America, on Returning to Bengal, in 1821.* New York: E. Bliss and E. White, 1821.

———. "William Ward's Missionary Journal, 1799–1811." Transcribed by E. Daniel Potts. Serampore College Archives.

Wilson, Daniel. *A Defense of the Church Missionary Society Against the Objections of the Rev. Josiah Thomas, M.A., Archceacon of Bath.* 12th ed. London: G. Wilson, 1818.

Young, Arthur. *An Enquiry into the State of the Public Mind amongst the Lower Classes, and on the Means of Turning It to the Welfare of the State.* London: W. J. and J. Richardson, 1798.

OTHER PUBLISHED SOURCES

Aberry, A. J. *Oriental Essays*. London: George Allen and Unwin, 1963.

Allen, David Elliston. *The Naturalist in Britain: A Social History*. London: Allen Lane, 1976.

Andrew, Donna T. *Philanthropy and Police: London Charity in the Eighteenth Century*. Princeton, N.J.: Princeton University Press, 1989.

Asad, Talal. *Genealogies of Religion: Discipline and Reasons of Power in Christianity and Islam*. Baltimore, Md.: John Hopkins Press, 1993.

Asiatick Researches: Transactions of the Society Instituted in Bengal for Inquiring into the History and Antiquities, the Arts, Sciences, and Literature of Asia. 20 vols. Calcutta and London, 1799–1839.

Augustine. *De Vera Religione*. In *Augustine: Earlier Writings*. Library of Christian Classics, Ichthus Edition. Translated by John H. S. Burleigh, 218–83. Philadelphia: Westminster Press, 1953.

Balagangadhara, S. N. *"The Heathen in his Blindness . . .": Asia, the West and the Dynamic of Religion*. Studies in the History of Religions LXIV. Leiden, the Netherlands: E. J. Brill, 1994.

Bandyopādhyāya, Brajendranāth. *Bhabānācaraṇ Bandyopādhyāya*. Calcutta: Baṅgīya Sāhitya Pariṣat. 1982.

———. *Sambād Patre Sekāler Kathā*. 2 vols. 4th ed. Calcutta: Baṅgīya Sāhitya Pariṣat. 1971.

Banerjee, Anil Chandra, and Krishna Lal Chatterji. *A Survey of the Indian Constitution*. Calcutta: A. Mukherjee, 1957.

Banerjee, Sumanta. *The Parlour and the Streets*. Calcutta: Seagull Books, 1989.

Bayly, C. A. *Indian Society and the Making of the British Empire*. New Cambridge History of India 2.1. Cambridge: Cambridge University Press, 1988.

———. "Knowing the Country: Empire and Information in India." *Modern Asian Studies* 27/1 (1993): 3–43.

Bearce, George D. *British Attitudes toward India, 1784–1858*. London: Oxford University Press, 1961.

Bell, Catherine. *Ritual Theory, Ritual Practice*. New York and Oxford: Oxford University Press, 1992.

Benavides, Gustavo. "Religious Studies Between Science and Ideology." *Religious Studies Review* 27/4 (Apr. 2001): 105–8.

Bentinck, William Cavendish. *The Correspondence of Lord William Cavendish Bentinck, Governor-General of India, 1828–1835*. Edited by C. H. Philips. Oxford: Oxford University Press, 1977.

———. *Rasaracanāsamagra*. Edited by Sanatkumar Gupta. Calcutta: Nabapatra Prakāśan, 1987.

Bhabānīcaraṇ, Bandyopādhāyaya. *Kalikātā Kamalālaya*. Edited and translated by Satyabrata Dutta. Calcutta: Firma KLM, 1990.

Bhattacharya, Aparna. *Religious Reform Movements of Bengal and Their Socio-Economic Ideas, 1800–1850*. Patna, India: Aparna Bhattacarya, 1981.

Biller, Peter. "Words and the Medieval Notion of 'Religion.' " *Journal of Ecclesiastical History* 36/3 (July 1985): 351–69.

Bose, P. N., and H.W.B. Moreno. *A Hundred Years of the Bengali Press*. Calcutta: Moreno, 1920.

Brockington, John. *Hinduism and Christianity*. New York: St. Martin's Press, 1992.

Buchanan, Claudius. *Christian Researches in Asia, with Notices of the Translation of the Scriptures into the Oriental Languages*. London: T. Cadell and W. Davies, 1819.

—————. *Memoir of the Expediency of an Ecclesiastical Establishment for British India: Both as the Means of Perpetuating the Christian Religion among Our Own Countrymen, and as a Foundation for the Ultimate Civilization of the Natives*. London: T. Cadell and W. Davies, 1805.

Burton, Antoinette. *At the Heart of the Empire: Indians and the Colonial Encounter in Late-Victorian Britain*. Berkeley: University of California Press, 1998.

Calvin, John. *Institutes of the Christian Religion*. Library of Christian Classics 20. Edited by John T. MacNeill. Translated by Ford Lewis Battles. Philadelphia: Westminster Press, 1960.

Cannon, Garland. *The Life and Mind of Oriental Jones: Sir William Jones, the Father of Modern Linguistics*. Cambridge: Cambridge University Press, 1993.

—————. *Sir William Jones: A Bibliography of Primary and Secondary Sources*. Amsterdam Studies in the Theory and History of Linguistic Science 5. Library and Information Sources in Linguistics, vol. 7. Amsterdam: John Benjamins B.V., 1979.

Canton, William. *A History of the British and Foreign Bible Society*. 5 vols. London: John Murray, 1904–10.

Capps, Walter H. *Religious Studies: The Making of a Discipline*. Minneapolis, Minn.: Fortress Press, 1995.

Cassels, Nancy Gardner, *Religion and Pilgrim Tax under the Company Raj*. South Asian Studies 17. New Delhi: Manohar, 1988.

—————. "Some Archival Observations on an Evangelical Tract." *Indian Archives* 30/1 (1981): 47–57.

Chakraborti, Smarajit. *The Bengali Press (1818–1868): A Study in the Growth of Public Opinion*. Calcutta: Firma KLM Private, Ltd., 1976.

Chakravorti, Satis Chandra. *Father of Modern India: Commemoration Volume of the Rammohun Roy Centenary Celebrations, 1933*. Calcutta: Rammohun Roy Centenary Committee, 1935.

Chanda, Mrinal Kanti. *History of the English Press in Bengal*. Calcutta and New Delhi: K. B. Baggchi and Co., 1987.

Chatterjee, Partha. "Agrarian Relations and Communalism in Bengal, 1926–1935." In *Subaltern Studies I: Writings on South Asian History and Society*. Edited by Ranajit Guha, 9–38. Delhi: Oxford University Press, 1982.

—————. "The Disciplines in Colonial Bengal." In *Texts of Power: Emerging Disciplines in Colonial Bengal*. Edited by Partha Chatterjee. Published in conjunction with the Centre for Studies in Social Sciences, as part of its Perspectives in Social Sciences Series. Minneapolis and London: University of Minnesota Press, 1995: 1–29.

—————. "History and the Nationalization of Hinduism." *Representing Hinduism: The Construction of Religious Traditions and National Identity*. Edited by Vasudha Dalmia and Heinrich von Stietencron. New Delhi and Thousand Oaks, Calif.: Sage Publications, 1995: 103–28.

Chatterjee, Sunil. "Reverend William Ward, 1769–1823." *Serampore College Students' Magazine* (1972): 86–97.

Cheriyan, P. *The Malabar Syrians and the Church Missionary Society, 1816–1840*. Kottayam: The CMS Press and Book Depot, 1935.

Cohn, Bernard. *Colonialism and Its Forms of Knowledge: The British in India*. Princeton, N.J.: Princeton University Press, 1996.

Collet, S. D. *The Life and Letters of Raja Rammohun Roy*. London: Collet, 1900.

Colley, Linda. *Britons: Forging the Nation, 1707–1837*. New Haven, Conn. and London: Yale University Press, 1992.

Comaroff, John L., and Jean Comaroff. *Ethnography and the Historical Imagination*. Boulder, San Francisco, and Oxford: Westview Press, 1992.

———. *Of Revelation and Revolution: Christianity, Colonialism, and Consciousness in South Africa*. 2 vols. Chicago: University of Chicago Press, 1991–1999.

Copley, Antony. *Religions in Conflict: Ideology, Cultural Contact and Conversion in Late Colonial India*. New Delhi: Oxford University Press, 1997.

Courtright, Paul B. "Iconographies of Satī." *Satī, the Blessing and the Curse: The Burning of Wives in India*. Edited by John Stratton Hawley. New York and Oxford: Oxford University Press, 1994: 27–49.

———. *Satī: The Goddess and the Dreadful Practice*. New York: Oxford University Press, forthcoming.

Crawford, S. Cromwell. *Ram Mohan Roy: Social, Political, and Religious Reform in Nineteenth-Century India*. New York: Paragon House, 1987.

Das, Sisir Kumar. *Early Bengali Prose: Carey to Vidyasagar*. Calcutta: Bookland Private, Ltd., 1966.

———. *Sahebs and Munshis: An Account of the College of Fort William*. Calcutta: Orion, 1978.

Datson, Lorraine, and Katharine Park. *Wonders and the Order of Nature 1150–1750*. New York: Zone Books, 1998.

Davey, Cyril. *The March of Methodism: The Story of Methodist Missionary Work Overseas*. London: Epworth Press, 1951.

Davis, Richard H. "The Iconography of Rama's Chariot." In *Making India Hindu: Religion, Community, and the Politics of Democracy in India*. Edited by David Ludden, 27–54. Delhi: Oxford University Press, 1997.

———. *Lives of Indian Images*. Princeton, N.J.: Princeton University Press, 1997.

Dempsey, Corrine G. *Kerala Christian Sainthood: Collisions of Culture and Worldview in South India*. New York: Oxford University Press, 2001.

Dirks, Nicholas, ed. *Colonialism and Culture*. Ann Arbor: University of Michigan Press, 1992.

Doniger, Wendy. "Hinduism by Any Other Name." *Wilson Quarterly* 15/3 (Summer 1991): 35–41.

Drew, John. *India and the Romantic Imagination*. Delhi: Oxford University Press, 1987.

Drotner, Kristen. *English Children and Their Magazines, 1751–1945*. New Haven, Conn., and London: Yale University Press, 1988.

Dube, Saurabh. *Untouchable Pasts: Religion, Identity, and Power among a Central India Community, 1780–1950*. Albany, N.Y.: SUNY Press, 1998.

Dubois, J. A. *Hindu Manners, Customs and Ceremonies*. Edited and translated by Henry K. Beauchamp. 3d ed. London: Oxford University Press, 1928.

Duff, Alexander. *India and Indian Missions*. Edinburgh: J. Johnstone, 1839.

Durkheim, Emile. *The Elementary Forms of the Religious Life*. Translated by Joseph Ward Swain. New York: The Free Press, 1965.

Eck, Diana L. *Darśan: Seeing the Divine Image in India*. 2d ed. Chambersburg, Pa.: Anima Books, 1985.

Embree, Ainslee Thomas. *Charles Grant and British Rule in India*. New York: Columbia University Press, 1962.

Farrington, Anthony, ed. *The Records of the East India College Haileybury and Other Institutions.* India Office Records, Guides to Archive Groups. London: Her Majesty's Stationery Office, 1976.

Feher, Michael, Ramona Naddaff, and Nadia Tazi, eds. *Fragments for a History of the Human Body.* Zone 3–5. New York: Zone, 1989.

Ferro-Luzzi, Gabriella Eichinger. "The Polythetic-Prototype Approach to Hinduism." In *Hinduism Reconsidered.* Edited by Günther Dietz Sontheimer and Hermann Kulke, 294–304. New Delhi: Manohar, 1997.

Findley, George G., and W. W. Holdsworth. *The History of the Wesleyan Methodist Missionary Society.* 5 vols. London: Epworth Press, 1921–24.

Fisch, Jörg. "A Pamphlet War on Christian Missions in India 1807–1809." *Journal of Asian History* 19 (1985): 22–70.

———. "A Solitary Vindicator of the Hindus: The Life and Writings of General Charles Stuart, 1757/58–1828." *Journal of the Royal Asiatic Society of Great Britain and Ireland* (1984): 35–57.

Fischer, Peter F. "Blake and the Druids." *Journal of English and German Philology* 58 (1959): 589–612.

Fitzgerald, Timothy. *The Ideology of Religious Studies.* New York: Oxford University Press, 2000.

———. "A Response to Saler, Benavides, and Korom." *Religious Studies Review* 27/4 (Apr. 2001): 110–15.

Flood, Gavin. *An Introduction to Hinduism.* Cambridge and New York: Cambridge University Press, 1996.

Franklin, Michael John, ed. *Representing India: Indian Culture and Imperial Control in Eighteenth-Century British Orientalist Discourse.* Vol. 7 *Asiatick Researches, or, Transactions of the Society Instituted in Bengal for Inquiring into the History and Antiquities, the Arts, Sciences, and Literature of Asia.* Vol. 1. London: Routledge, 2000.

Fraser, James Baillie. *Journal of a Tour through Part of the Snowy Range of the Himala Mountains, and to the Sources of the Rivers Jumna and Ganges.* London: Rodwell and Martin, 1820.

———. *Views of the Himala Mountains.* London: Rodwell and Martin, 1820.

Frykenberg, Robert Eric. "The Construction of Hinduism as a "Public" Religion: Looking Again at the Religious Roots of Company Raj in South India." In *Religion and Public Culture: Encounters and Identities in Modern South India.* Edited by Keith E. Yandell and John J. Paul, 3–26. Richmond, UK: Curzon Press, 2000.

———. "Constructions of Hinduism at the Nexus of History and Religion." *Journal of Interdisciplinary History* 23/3 (Winter 1993): 523–50.

———. "The Emergence of Modern 'Hinduism' as a Concept and as an Institution: A Reappraisal with Special Reference to South India." In *Hinduism Reconsidered.* Edited by G. D. Sonthheimer and H. Kulke, 29–49. New Delhi: Manohar, 1989.

Furneaux, Robin. *William Wilberforce.* London: Hamish Hamilton, 1974.

Gandhi, Leela. *Postcolonial Theory: A Critical Introduction.* New York: Columbia University Press, 1998.

Gilbert, Alan D. *Religion and Society in Industrial England: Church, Chapel, and Social Change, 1740–1914.* New York: Longman, 1976.

Goel, Sita Ram. *Catholic Ashrams: Sannyasins or Swindlers?* New Delhi: Voice of India, 1989.

———. *History of Hindu-Christian Encounters.* New Delhi: Voice of India, 1989.

Gray, John N. "Bengal and Britain: Culture Contact and the Reinterpretation of Hinduism in the Nineteenth Century." In *Aspects of Bengali History and Society*, Asian Studies at Hawaii 12. Edited by Rachel Van M. Baumer, 99–131. Honolulu: University Press of Hawaii, 1976.

Guha, Ranajit. *An Indian Historiography of India: A Nineteenth-Century Agenda and Its Implications*. S. G. Deuskar Lectures on Indian History. Center for Studies in Social Sciences. Calcutta: K. P. Bagchi, 1988.

———. "On Some Aspects of the Historiography of Colonial India." In *Subaltern Studies I: Writings on South Asian History and Society*. Ranajit Guha, 1–8. Delhi: Oxford University Press, 1982.

Haberman, David. "On Trial: The Love of Sixteen-Thousand Gopis." *History of Religions* 33/1 (August 1993): 44–70.

Halbertal, Moshe, and Avishai Margalit. *Idolatry*. Cambridge, Mass., and London: Harvard University Press, 1992.

Halbfass, Wilhelm. *India and Europe: An Essay in Understanding*. Albany, N.Y.: SUNY Press, 1988.

———. "Research and Reflection: Responses to My Respondents. I. Beyond Orientalism?" In *Beyond Orientalism: The Work of Wilhelm Halbfass and Its Impact on Indian and Cross-Cultural Studies*. Poznań Studies in the Philosophy of the Sciences and Humanities 59. Edited by Eli Franco and Karin Preisendanz, 1–25. Amsterdam: Rodopi, 1997.

Hardiman, David. *The Coming of the Devi: Adivasi Assertion in Western India*. Delhi: Oxford University Press, 1987.

Harlan, Lindsey. "Perfection and Devotion: Sati Tradition in Rajasthan." In *Sati, the Blessing and the Curse: The Burning of Wives in India*. Edited by John Stratton Hawley, 79–91. New York and Oxford: Oxford University Press, 1994.

Harrison, Peter. *'Religion' and the Religions in the English Enlightenment*. Cambridge: Cambridge University Press, 1990.

Hatcher, Brian A. *Idioms of Improvement: Vidyāsāgar and Cultural Encounter in Bengal*. Calcutta: Oxford University Press, 1996.

Hawley, John Stratton. "Naming Hinduism." *Wilson Quarterly* 15/3 (Summer 1991): 30–34.

———. ed. *Sati, the Blessing and the Curse: The Burning of Wives in India*. New York and Oxford: Oxford University Press, 1994.

———. "Who Speaks for Hinduism—And Who Against?" *Journal of the American Academy of Religion* 68/4 (Dec. 2000): 711–20.

Hayden, Colin. *Anti-Catholicism in Eighteenth-Century England, c. 1714–1780: A Political and Cultural Study*. Manchester: Manchester University Press, 1993.

Heesterman, Jan. *The Broken World of Sacrifice: An Essay in Ancient Indian Ritual*. Chicago and London: University of Chicago Press, 1993.

Hewat, Elizabeth Glendinning Kirkwood. *Vision and Achievement, 1796–1956: A History of the Foreign Missions of the Churches United in the Church of Scotland*. London and New York: Nelson, 1960.

Hibbard, Caroline M. *Charles I and the Popish Plot*. Chapel Hill: University of North Carolina Press, 1983.

Hinchcliff, Peter. "Voluntary Absolutism: British Missionary Societies in the Nineteenth-Century." *Voluntary Religion: Papers Read at the 1985 Summer Meeting and 1986 Winter Meeting of the Ecclesiastical History Society*. Studies in Church History 23. Oxford: published by Basil Blackwell for the Ecclesiastical History Society, 1986: 363–79.

Hinde, Wendy. *Catholic Emancipation: A Shake to Men's Minds.* Oxford and Cambridge, Mass.: Blackwell, 1992.

Hobsbawm, Eric, and Terence Ranger, eds. *The Invention of Tradition.* Cambridge and New York: Cambridge University Press, 1992.

Hough, James. *The History of Christianity in India from the Commencement of the Christian Era.* 5 vols. London: Seeley and Burnside, 1850.

———. *A Reply to the Letters of the Abbé Dubois on the State of Christianity in India.* London: L. B. Seeley and Son, 1824.

Howsam, Leslie. *Cheap Bibles: Nineteenth-Century Publishing and the British and Foreign Bible Society.* Cambridge: Cambridge University Press, 1991.

Howse, Ernest Marshall. *Saints in Politics: The "Clapham Sect" and the Growth of Freedom.* Toronto: University of Toronto Press, 1952.

Humphreys, David. *An Historical Account of the Incorporated Society for the Propagation of the Gospel in Foreign Parts.* London: Joseph Downing, 1730. Reprint, New York: Arno Press, 1969.

Inden, Ronald. *Imagining India.* Oxford: Basil Blackwell, 1990.

Index to the First Eighteen Volumes of the Asiatick Researches. Calcutta: G. H. Huttman at the Bengal Military Orphan Press, 1835.

Indian Bibliographic Centre. Research Wing. *Christianity and Conversion in India.* Varanasi: Rishi Publications, 1999.

Inglis, K. S. *Churches and the Working Classes in Victorian England.* London: Routledge and Kegan Paul, 1963.

Irschick, Eugene F. *Dialogue and History: Constructing South India, 1795–1895.* Berkeley: University of California Press, 1994.

James, George Alfred. *Interpreting Religion: The Phenomenological Approaches of Pierre Daniël de la Saussaye, W. Brede Kristensen, and Gerardus van der Leeuw.* Washington, D.C.: Catholic University of America Press, 1995.

Jones, Kenneth W. *Socio-Religious Reform Movements in British India.* New Cambridge History of India 3.1. Cambridge: Cambridge University Press, 1989.

Jones, Sir William. *Histoire de Nader Chah.* London: P. Elmsly, 1770.

———. *The Works of Sir William Jones, With the Life of the Author by Lord Teignmouth.* London: John Stockdale and John Walker, 1839; reprint, edited by Garland Cannon, New York: Curzon Press, 1993.

Kejariwal, O. P. *The Asiatic Society of Bengal and the Discovery of India's Past, 1784–1838.* Delhi: Oxford University Press, 1988.

Kent, Eliza F. "Tamil Bible Women and the Zenana Missions of Colonial South India." *History of Religions* 39/2 (Nov. 1999): 117–49.

Killingley, Dermot. *Rammohun Roy in Hindu and Christian Tradition: The Teape Lectures, 1990.* Newcastle upon Tyne: Grevatt and Grevatt, 1993.

King, Richard. *Orientalism and Religion: Postcolonial Theory, India, and 'The Mystic East.'* New York: Routledge, 1999.

Klostermaier, Klaus. "The Future of Hindu-Christian Dialogue." In *Hindu-Christian Dialogue: Perspectives and Encounters.* Edited by Harold Coward, 262–74. Maryknoll, N.Y.: Orbis Books, 1989.

Kopf, David. *The Brahmo Samaj and the Shaping of the Modern Indian Mind.* Princeton, N.J.: Princeton University Press, 1979.

———. *British Orientalism and the Bengal Renaissance: The Dynamics of Indian Modernization, 1773–1835.* Berkeley and Los Angeles: University of California Press, 1969.

———. "European Enlightenment, Hindu Renaissance and the Enrichment of the

Human Spirit: A History of Historical Writings on British Orientalism." In *Orientalism, Evangelicalism and the Military Cantonment in Early Nineteenth-Century India: A Historiographical Overview*. Edited by Nancy Gardner Cassels, 19–53. Lewiston, N.Y.: Edwin Mellen Press, 1991.

Korom, Frank. "(H)ideology: The Hidden Agenda of Religious Studies." *Religious Studies Review* 27/4 (Apr. 2001): 108–110.

Kripal, Jeffrey J. *Kali's Child: The Mystical and the Erotic in the Life and Teachings of Ramakrishna*. Chicago: University of Chicago Press, 1995.

————. "Textuality, Sexuality, and the Future of the Past: A Response to Swami Tyagananda." *Evam: Forum on Indian Representations* 1/1–2 (2002): 191–205.

Kumar, Deepak. "The 'Culture' of Science and Colonial Culture, India 1820–1920." *British Journal for the History of Science* 29/2 (June 1996): 195–209.

————. "Textuality, Sexuality, and the Future of the Past: A Response to Swami Tyagananda." *Evam: Forum on Indian Representations* 1/1–2 (2002): 191–205.

The Kūrma Purāṇa. Translated by Ganesh Vasudeo Tagare. Delhi: Motilal, 1981.

Laquer, Thomas, *Religion and Respectability: Sunday Schools and Working Class Culture, 1780–1850*. New Haven, Conn., and London: Yale University Press, 1976.

————. "The Social Evil, the Solitary Vice, and Pouring Tea." *Fragments for a History of the Human Body, Part Three*. Zone 5. Edited by Michael Feher. New York: Zone Press, 1989: 334–42.

Larson, Gerald James. *India's Agony over Religion*. Albany, N.Y.: SUNY Press, 1995.

Ledwich, Edward. "Dissertation on the Religion of the Druids." *Archaeologia* VII (1785): 303–22.

Lincoln, Bruce. *Death, War and Sacrifice: Studies in Ideology and Practice*. Chicago and London: University of Chicago Press, 1991.

————. *Theorizing Myth: Narrative, Ideology, and Scholarship*. Chicago: University of Chicago Press, 1999.

Lorenzen, David N. "Who Invented Hinduism?" *Comparative Studies in Society and History* 41/4 (Oct. 1999): 630–59.

Lovegrove, Deryck W. *Established Church, Sectarian People: Itinerancy and the Transformation of English Dissent, 1780–1830*. Cambridge: Cambridge University Press, 1988.

Luthra, Rashmi. "The Formation of Interpretive Communities in the Hindu Diaspora." In *Religion and Popular Culture: Studies on the Interaction of Worldviews*. Edited by David A. Stout and Judith M. Buddenbaum, 125–39. Ames: Iowa State University Press, 2001.

Macaulay, Thomas Babbington. "Mr. Lord Macaulay's Great Minute." In W.F.B. Laurie, *Sketches of Some Distinguished Anglo-Indians*, 170–85. London: W. H. Allen, 1888. Reprint, New Delhi: Asian Educational Services, 1999.

Machin, G.I.T. *The Catholic Question in English Politics, 1820–1830*. Oxford: Clarendon Press, 1964.

Machow, H. L. *Gothic Images of Race in Nineteenth-Century Britain*. Stanford, Calif.: Stanford University Press, 1996.

Marshall, P. J. *Bengal—The British Bridgehead: Eastern India, 1740–1828*. New Cambridge History of India 2.2. Cambridge: Cambridge University Press, 1987.

Marshman, John Clark. *The Life and Times of Carey, Marshman, and Ward, Embracing the History of the Serampore Mission*. 2 vols. London: Longman, Brown, Green, Longmans, and Roberts, 1859.

————. *The Story of Carey, Marshman, and Ward, the Serampore Missionaries*. Abridged edition. London: J. Heaton and Son, 1864.

Mayhew, Henry. *London Labour and the London Poor.* 4 vols. London: Griffin, Bohn, and Co., 1861–62; reprint, New York: Dover Publications, 1968.

McAllister, Edwin J. " 'Our Glory and Joy': Stephen Riggs and the Politics of Nineteenth-Century Missionary Ethnography among the Sioux." In *Christian Encounters with the Other.* Edited by John C. Hawley, 150–66. New York: New York University Press, 1998.

McCutcheon, Russell T. *Critics Not Caretakers: Redescribing the Public Study of Religion.* Albany, N.Y.: SUNY Press, 2001.

———. *Manufacturing Religion: The Discourse on Sui Generis Religion and the Politics of Nostalgia.* New York: Oxford University Press, 1997.

McKean, Lise. *Divine Enterprise: Gurus and the Hindu Nationalist Movement.* Chicago: University of Chicago Press, 1996.

McLeish, John. *Evangelical Religion and Popular Education: A Modern Interpretation.* London: Methven, 1969.

McLeod, Hugh. *Religion and the Working Class in Nineteenth-Century Britain.* Studies in Economic and Social History. London and Basingstoke: McMillan, 1984.

Miall, Edward. *The British Churches in Relation to the British People.* London: Arthur Hall, 1849.

Midgley, Clare. *Women Against Slavery: The British Campaigns, 1780–1870.* New York and London: Routledge, 1992.

Mill, James. *The History of British India.* 5th ed. Notes by Horace Hayman Wilson. Introduction by John Kenneth Galbraith. London, 1858. Reprint, New York: Chelsea House, 1968.

Mitter, Partha. *Much Maligned Monsters: History of European Reactions to Indian Art.* Oxford: Clarendon Press, 1977.

More, Hannah. *The Works of Hannah More.* 2 vols. Philadelphia: J. J. Woodward, 1830.

Mukherjee, S. N. *Calcutta: Essays in Urban History.* Calcutta: Subarnareka, 1993.

———. *Sir William Jones: A Study in Eighteenth-Century British Attitudes to India.* Cambridge South Asian Studies. Cambridge: Cambridge University Press, 1968.

Murr, Sylvia. "Nicolas Desvaulx (1745–1823) Véritable Auteur de Moeurs, Institutions et Cérémonies des Peuples de l'Inde, de l'Abbé Dubois?" *Puruṣārtha* 3 (1977): 245–67.

Mustafa Kamal, Abu Hena. *The Bengali Press and Literary Writing, 1818–1831.* Dhaka Bangladesh: University Press, Ltd., 1977.

Nair, P. Thankappan. *A History of the Calcutta Press: The Beginnings.* A Tercentenary History of Calcutta Series. Calcutta: Firma KLM Private, Ltd., 1987.

Neill, Stephen. *A History of Christianity in India: The Beginnings to AD 1707.* New York: Cambridge University Press, 1984.

———. *A History of Christianity in India, 1707–1858.* Cambridge: Cambridge University Press, 1985.

Neufeldt, Ronald. "Conversion and the Courts." *Hindu-Christian Studies Bulletin* 13 (2000): 12–18.

Norman, E. R. *Anti-Catholicism in Victorian England.* New York: Barnes and Noble, 1968.

Oddie, Geoffrey A. *Popular Religion, Elites, and Reform: Hook-Swinging and Its Prohibition in Colonial India, 1800–1894.* New Delhi: Manohar, 1995.

Pankratz, J. N. "The Response of the Brahmo Samaj." *Modern Indian Responses to Religious Pluralism.* Edited by Harold G. Coward. Albany, N.Y.: SUNY Press, 1987: 19–38.

Patton, Kimberly, and Benjamin C. Ray, eds. *A Magic Still Dwells: Comparative Religion in the Postmodern Age*. Berkeley: University of California Press, 2000.

Paxton, Nancy L. *Writing Under the Raj: Gender, Race, and Rape in the British Colonial Imagination, 1830–1947*. New Brunswick, N.J.: Rutgers University Press, 1999.

Paz, D. G. *Popular Anti-Catholicism in Mid-Victorian England*. Stanford, Calif.: Stanford University Press, 1992.

Pearson, Hugh. *Memoirs of the Life and Writings of the Rev. Claudius Buchanan, D. D., Late Vice-Provost of the College of Fort William in Bengal*. 2 vols. London: T. Cadell and W. Davies, 1819.

Pedersen, Susan. "Hannah More Meets Simple Simon: Tracts, Chapbooks, and Popular Culture in Late Eighteenth-Century England." *Journal of British Studies* 25/1 (Jan. 1986): 84–113.

Pennington, Brian K. "Constructing Colonial Dharma: A Chronicle of Emergent Hinduism, 1830–1831." *Journal of the American Academy of Religion* 69/3 (Sept. 2001): 577–603.

———. "The Firefly and the Moon: Representing and Constructing Religion in the Context of Colonial Bengal." Ph.D. diss., Emory University, 1998.

———. "Renaissance or Retrenchment? Hindu-Christian Dialogue at a Crossroads." *Indian Journal of Theology* 42/1 (2000): 74–87.

———. "Reverend William Ward and His Legacy for Christian (Mis)perception of Hinduism." *Hindu-Christian Studies Bulletin* 13 (2000): 5–11.

Pennington, Edgar Legare. *The SPG Anniversary Sermons, 1702–1783*. N.p., n.d.

Perumthottam, Joseph. *A Period of Decline of the Mar Thoma Christians (1712–1752)*. Vadavathoor, Kerala State: Oriental Institute of Religious Studies, India, 1994.

Peters, Edward. *Inquisition*. Berkeley: University of California Press, 1988.

Piggin, Stuart. "Assessing Nineteenth Century Missionary Motivation: Some Considerations of Theory and Method." *Religious Motivation: Biographical and Sociological Problems for the Church Historian*. Papers read at the Sixteenth Summer Meeting and the Seventeenth Winter Meeting of the Ecclesiastical History Society. Edited by Derek Baker. Oxford: Published for the Ecclesiastical History Society by Basil Blackwell, 1978: 327–37.

———. "Sectarianism Versus Ecumenism: The Impact on British Churches of the Missionary Movement to India, c.1800–1860." *Journal of Ecclesiastical History* 27/4 (October 1976): 387–402.

Pollock, John. *Wilberforce*. London: Constable and Co., 1977.

Porter, Roy. "Gentlemen and Geology: The Emergence of a Scientific Career." *Historical Journal* 21/4 (Dec. 1978): 809–36.

Potts, E. Daniel. *British Baptist Missionaries in India, 1793–1837: The History of Serampore and Its Missions*. Cambridge: Cambridge University Press, 1967.

———. "William Ward's Missionary Journal." *The Baptist Quarterly* 25/3 (July 1973): 111–14.

Preus, J. Samuel. *Explaining Religion: Criticism and Theory from Bodin to Freud*. New Haven: Yale University Press, 1987.

Proceedings of the Church Missionary Society, 1817–1824, 1831–1833. London: L. B. Seeley, 1819–1833.

"Protest Letters for *Kali's Child*." Sword of Truth, June 3, 2001, http://www.swordoftruth.com/swordoftruth/news/betweenthelines/Kali'schildletters.html.

Raj, Selva J. "Adapting Hindu Imagery: A Critical Look at Ritual Experiments in an Indian Catholic Ashram." *Journal of Ecclesiastical Studies* 37/3–4 (Summer–Fall 2000): 333–53.

Reingold, Nathan. *Science, American Style*. New Brunswick, N.J., and London: Rutgers University Press, 1991.

"Religion and Theology Programs Census: 'The Study of Religion Counts.' " *Religious Studies News* 16/4 (Fall 2001): i–iii.

Reynaud-Beauveri, Marie-A. *Ram Mohan Roy, le Pere de l'Indi Moderne a Paris en 1837*. Lyon, France: E. Bellier, 1987.

Ritvo, Harriet. *The Platypus and the Mermaid and Other Figments of the Classifying Imagination*. Cambridge, Mass.: Harvard University Press, 1997.

Roberts, M.J.D. "The Society for the Suppression of Vice and its Early Critics." *Historical Journal* 26/1 (March 1983): 159–76.

Robertson, Bruce Carlisle. *Raja Rammohan Ray: The Father of Modern India*. Delhi: Oxford University Press, 1995.

Rocher, Rosane. "British Orientalism in the Eighteenth Century: The Dialects of Knowledge and Government." In *Orientalism and the Postcolonial Predicament: Perspectives on South Asia*, South Asia Seminar Series. Edited by Carol A. Breckenridge and Peter van der Veer, 219–45. Philadelphia: University of Pennsylvania Press, 1993.

Rowlands, Henry. *Mona Antiqua Restaurata*. 1723. Reprint, Myth and Romanticism 21. New York: Garland, 1979.

Roy, Rammohan. *The English Works of Raja Rammohun Roy*. 4 vols. Edited by Jogendra Chander Ghose. Allahabad, India: Bahadurganj, 1906. Reprint. New Delhi: Cosmo Publishers, 1982.

———. *Rāmmohan-Samīkiṣā*. 2d ed. Edited by Dilīpkumar Visvās. Calcutta: Sārasvata Library, 1994.

Rubieś, Joan-Pau. *Travel and Ethnology in the Renaissance: South India through European Eyes 1250–1625*. Cambridge: Cambridge University Press, 2000.

Said, Edward. *Culture and Imperialism*. New York: Vintage Books, 1994.

———. *Orientalism*. New York: Vintage Books, 1978.

Salahuddin Ahmed, A. F. *Social Ideas and Social Change in Bengal, 1818–1835*. Calcutta: Rddhi, 1976.

Saler, Benson. "Some Reflections on Fitzgerald's Thesis." *Religious Studies Review* 27/4 (Apr. 2001): 103–5.

Sarkar, Sumit. "Hindutva and the Question of Conversions." In *The Concerned Indian's Guide to Communalism*. Edited by K. N. Panikkar, 73–106. New Delhi: Viking, 1999.

Sax, William S. "Conquering the Quarters: Religion and Politics in Hinduism." *International Journal of Hindu Studies* 4/1 (Apr. 2000): 39–60.

Schiebinger, Londa. *Nature's Body: Gender in the Making of Modern Science*. Boston: Beacon Press, 1993.

Scott, David. *Refashioning Futures: Criticism after Postcoloniality*. Princeton, N.J.: Princeton University Press, 1999.

Sen, Reena (née Mookerjee). "Some Reflections on *India and Europe: An Essay in Understanding*." In *Beyond Orientalism: The Work of Wilhelm Halbfass and Its Impact on Indian and Cross-Cultural Studies*. Poznań Studies in the Philosophy of the Sciences and Humanities 59, ed. Eli Franco and Karin Preisendanz (Amsterdam: Rodopi, 1997).

Searle-Chatterjee, Mary. " 'World Religions' and 'Ethnic Groups': Do these Paradigms Lend Themselves to the Cause of Hindu Nationalism?" *Ethnic and Racial Studies* 23/3 (May 2000): 497–515.

Sharma, Arvind. "Of Hindu, Hindustān, Hinduism and Hindutva." *Numen* 49/1 (2002): 1–35.

Shaw, Graham. *Printing in Calcutta to 1800: A Description and Checklist of Printing in the Late Eighteenth Century.* London: The Bibliographic Society, 1981.

Singh, Maina Chawla. *Gender, Religion, and "Heathen Lands": American Missionary Women in South Asia (1860s–1940s).* New York: Garland, 2000.

Sinha, Mrinalini. *Colonial Masculinity: The 'Manly Englishman' and the 'Effeminate Bengali' in the Late Nineteenth Century.* Manchester and New York: Manchester University Press, 1995.

Sinha, Pradip. *Calcutta in Urban History.* Calcutta: Firma KLM, 1978.

Sinha, Samita. *Pandits in a Changing Environment: Centres of Sanskrit Learning in Nineteenth Century Bengal.* Calcutta: Sarat Book House, 1993.

Smiles, Sam. *The Image of Antiquity: Ancient Britain and the Romantic Imagination.* New Haven, Conn., and London: Yale University Press, 1994.

Smith, A. Christopher. "Mythology and Missiology: A Methodological Approach to the Pre-Victorian Mission of the Serampore Trio." *International Review of Mission* 83 (July 1994): 451–75.

Smith, Alan. *The Established Church and Popular Religion, 1750–1850.* Seminar Studies in History. Edited by Patrick Richardson. London: Longman, 1971.

Smith, Brian K. "Questioning Authority: Constructions and Deconstructions of Hinduism." *International Journal of Hindu Studies* 2, 3 (Dec. 1998): 313–39.

———. "Re-envisioning Hinduism and Evaluating the Hindutva Movement." *Religion* 26 (1996): 119–28.

———. "Who Does, Can, and Should Speak for Hinduism?" *Journal of the American Academy of Religion* 68/4 (Dec. 2000): 741–49.

Smith, Sydney. *Selected Writings of Sydney Smith.* Edited by W. H. Auden. New York: Farrar, Straus, and Cudahy, 1956.

Smith, Wilfred Cantwell. *The Meaning and End of Religion.* San Francisco: Harper and Row, 1978.

Soloway, R. A. *Prelates and People: Ecclesiastical Social Thought in England, 1783–1852.* London: Routledge and Kegan Paul, 1969.

Staal, Frits. *Ritual and Mantras: Rules without Meaning.* Delhi: Motilal Banarsidass, 1996.

Stietencron, Heinrich von. "Hinduism: On the Proper Use of a Deceptive Term." In *Hinduism Reconsidered.* South Asian Studies 24. Edited by Günther-Dietz Sontheimer and Hermann Kulke, 32–53. New Delhi: Manohar, 1997.

———. "Religious Configurations in Pre-Muslim India and the Modern Concept of Hinduism." In *Representing Hinduism: The Construction of Religious Traditions and National Identity.* Edited by Vasudha Dalmia and Heinrich von Stietencron, 51–81. New Delhi: Sage Publications, 1995.

Stock, Eugene. *The History of the Church Missionary Society: Its Environment, Its Men, and Its Work.* 3 vols. London: Church Missionary Society, 1899.

Stocking, George. *Victorian Anthropology.* New York: Free Press, 1987.

Stoler, Ann Laura. *Race and the Education of Desire: Foucault's History of Sexuality and the Colonial Order of Things.* Durham, N.C., and London: Duke University Press, 1995.

———. "Rethinking Colonial Categories: European Communities and the Boundaries of Rule." In *Colonialism and Culture.* Edited by Nicholas B. Dirks, 319–52. Ann Arbor: University of Michigan Press, 1992.

Strenski, Ivan. "Religion, Power, and Final Foucault." *Journal of the American Academy of Religion* 66/2 (Summer 1998): 345–67.

Stukeley, William. *Stonehenge: A Temple Restor'd to the British Druids.* London: W. Innis and R. Manby, 1740; *Abury: A Temple of the British Druids.* London: W. Innys, R. Manby, B. Tod, and J. Brindley, 1743; both reprinted in a single volume under their joint title in the series, Myth and Romanticism: A Collection of the Major Mythographic Sources used by the English Romantic Poets. Edited by Burton Feldman and Robert D. Richardson, Jr. New York and London: Garland, 1984.

Sullivan, Lawrence E. *Introduction to Religious Regimes in Contact: Christian Missions, Global Transformations, and Comparative Research: Bibliography.* Cambridge, Mass.: Harvard Center for the Study of World Religions, 1993.

Sweetman, Will. " 'Hinduism' and the History of 'Religion': Protestant Presuppositions in the Critique of the Concept of Hinduism." *Method and Theory in the Study of Religion* 15/4 (2003): 329–53.

––––––. "Unity and Plurality: Hinduism and the Religions of India in Early European Scholarship." *Religion* 31 (2001): 209–24.

Taylor, Richard W. "Current Hindu-Christian Dialogue in India." In *Hindu-Christian Dialogue: Perspectives and Encounters.* Edited by Harold Coward, 119–28. Maryknoll, N.Y.: Orbis Books, 1989.

Teltscher, Kate. *India Inscribed: European and British Writing on India, 1600–1800.* Delhi: Oxford University Press, 1995.

Thapar, Romila. "Syndicated Hinduism." In *Hinduism Reconsidered.* South Asian Studies XXIV. Edited by Günther-Dietz Sontheimer and Hermann Kulke, 54–81. New Delhi: Manohar, 1997.

Thompson, E. P. *Making of the English Working Class.* London: Victor Gollancz, 1964.

Thorne, Susan. *Congregational Missions and the Making of an Imperial Culture in Nineteenth-Century England.* Stanford: Stanford University Press, 1999.

Trautmann, Thomas R. *Aryans and British India.* Berkeley: University of California Press, 1997.

Twitchell, James B. *Romantic Horizons: Aspects of the Sublime in English Poetry and Painting, 1770–1850.* Columbia: University of Missouri Press, 1983.

Tyagananda, Swami. *"Kali's Child* Revisited or Didn't Anyone Check the Documentation?" *Evam: Forum on Indian Representations* 1/1–2 (2002): 173–90.

Urban, Hugh B. *Songs of Ecstasy: Tantric and Devotional Songs from Colonial Bengal.* New York: Oxford University Press, 2001.

Valenze, Deborah M. *Prophetic Sons and Daughters: Female Preaching and Popular Religion in Industrial England.* Princeton, N.J.: Princeton University Press, 1985.

Van der Veer, Peter. "Hindu Nationalism and the Discourse of Modernity." In *Accounting for Fundamentalisms: The Dynamic Character of Movements.* The Fundamentalism Project, vol. 4. Edited by Martin E. Marty and R. Scott Appleby, 653–67. Chicago and London: University of Chicago Press, 1994.

––––––. *Imperial Encounters: Religion and Modernity in India and Britain.* Princeton, N.J.: Princeton University Press, 2001.

Vidyālaṅkār, Mṛtyuñjaya. *Vedāntacandrikā.* In *Rāmmohan Racanābali.* Edited by Ajitkumar Ghosh, 615–33. Calcutta: Abdul Ajij al Aman, 1973.

––––––. *An Apology for the Present System of Hindoo Worship.* Calcutta: Printed by G. G. Balfour at the Government Gazette Press, 1817.

Viswanathan, Gauri. *Outside the Fold: Conversion, Modernity, and Belief.* Princeton, N.J.: Princeton University Press, 1998.

Waghorne, Joanne Punzo. "Chariots of the God/s: Riding the Line between Hindu and Christian." *History of Religions* 39/2 (Nov. 1999): 95–116.

———. *The Raja's Magic Clothes: Revisioning Kinship and Divinity in England's India.* University Park, PA: Pennsylvania State University Press, 1994.

Wallis, Frank H. *Popular Anti-Catholicism in Mid-Victorian Britain.* Texts and Studies in Religion 60. Lewiston, N.Y.: Edwin Mellen, 1993.

Ward, William. *Account of the Writings, Religion, and Manners of the Hindoos.* 4 vols. Serampore: Mission Press, 1806–11.

———. *Farewell Letters to a Few Friends in Britain and America, on Returning to Bengal, in 1821.* New York: E. Bliss and E. White, 1821.

———. *History, Literature, and Religion of the Hindoos.* Serampore: Mission Press, 1817. Reprint. Delhi: Low Price Publications, 1990.

———. *A View of the History, Literature and Mythology of the Hindoos: Including a Minute Description of Their Manners and Customs, and Translations from Their Principal Works.* 2d ed. Serampore: Mission Press, 1815.

Weinberger-Thomas, Catherine. *Ashes of Immortality: Widow-Burning in India.* Translated by Jeffrey Mehlman and David Gordon White. Chicago: University of Chicago Press, 1999.

Wickham, E. R. *Church and People in an Industrial City.* London: Lutterworth Press, 1957.

Wiener, Joel. *The War of the Unstamped: The Movement to Repeal the British Newspaper Tax, 1830–36.* Ithaca, N.Y. and London: Cornell University Press, 1969.

Wilberforce, Samuel. *Life of William Wilberforce.* Revised and condensed from the original edition. London: John Murray, 1868.

Wilberforce, William. *The Correspondence of William Wilberforce.* 2 vols. Edited by Robert Isaac Wilberforce and Samuel Wilberforce. London: John Murray, 1840.

———. *A Practical View of the Prevailing Religious System of Professed Christians in the Higher and Middle Classes of Society, Contrasted with Real Christianity.* New York, Robert Carter and Brothers, 1851.

Williams, Cecil Peter. "The Recruitment and Training of Overseas Missionaries In England between 1850 and 1900." M. L. diss., Univ. of Bristol, 1976.

Wolffe, John. *The Protestant Crusade in Great Britain, 1829–60.* Oxford, Clarendon Press, 1991.

Young, Richard Fox. *Resistant Hinduism: Sanskrit Sources on Anti-Christian Apologetics in Early Nineteenth-Century India.* Publications of the De Nobili Research Library 8. Edited by Gerhard Oberhammer. Vienna: Institut für Indologie der Universität Wien, 1981.

Zavos, John. "Defending Hindu Tradition: Sanatana Dharma as a Symbol of Orthodoxy in Colonial India." *Religion* 31 (2001): 109–23.

Županov's, Ines G. *Disputed Mission: Jesuit Experiments and Brahmanical Knowledge in Seventeenth-Century India.* New Delhi: Oxford University Press, 1999.

Index